Regards from the

Hersir Sigurg----

Palgrave Macmillan Studies in Banking and Financial Institutions

Series Editor

Professor Philip Molyneux
Bangor University
UK

The Palgrave Macmillan Studies in Banking and Financial Institutions series is international in orientation and includes studies of banking systems in particular countries or regions as well as contemporary themes such as Islamic Banking, Financial Exclusion, Mergers and Acquisitions, Risk Management, and IT in Banking. The books focus on research and practice and include up to date and innovative studies that cover issues which impact banking systems globally.

More information about this series at
http://www.springer.com/series/14678

Ásgeir Jónsson • Hersir Sigurgeirsson

The Icelandic Financial Crisis

A Study into the World's Smallest Currency Area
and its Recovery from Total Banking Collapse

palgrave
macmillan

Ásgeir Jónsson
University of Iceland
Reykjavik, Iceland

Hersir Sigurgeirsson
University of Iceland
Reykjavik, Iceland

Palgrave Macmillan Studies in Banking and Financial Institutions
ISBN 978-1-137-39454-5   ISBN 978-1-137-39455-2   (eBook)
DOI 10.1057/978-1-137-39455-2

Library of Congress Control Number: 2016955815

Cover illustration: Cover image © Bjarki Reyr EYJ / Alamy Stock Photo

Printed on acid-free paper

This Palgrave Macmillan imprint is published by Springer Nature
The registered company is Macmillan Publishers Ltd.
The registered company address is: The Campus, 4 Crinan Street, London, N19XW, United Kingdom

The economic, political and moral fallout of the collapse of Iceland's banks was enormous. This fascinating book gives a full and comprehensive account and analysis of the Icelandic banking crisis, its aftermath and the struggles and policies that led to Iceland's remarkable recovery after it was hit by the "perfect storm". It will be required reading by scholars, regulators and policy makers interested in financial crises, their consequences and how to respond to them.

—**Friðrik Már Baldursson,** Professor of Economics,
School of Business, Reykjavik University

Iceland's 2008 financial crisis and subsequent recovery is a rich story, and the debate on the causes and lessons to be learned will doubtless go on for years to come. Ásgeir Jónsson's Why Iceland was an important early contribution to the history of the prelude to the crisis and became considered a "must read". Now Ásgeir Jónsson and Hersir Sigurgeirsson have written a sequel on the financial sector recovery that has the promise to fall into the same category.

—**Már Guðmundsson,** Governor, Central Bank of Iceland

Contents

List of Figures

List of Tables

1

Introduction

1.1 Gala at Harpa

At 8 a.m. on October 27, 2011, the brand new Reykjavík Concert Hall
and Conference Centre, Harpa, received a steady stream of formally
attired dignitaries, both national and foreign. They were attending a
conference presented jointly by the Icelandic government and the International Monetary Fund (IMF): "Iceland's Recovery – Lessons and
Challenges."[1] An impressive panel of speakers had assembled, including
Nobel laureates Paul Krugman and Joseph Stiglitz, Willem Buiter, chief
economist of Citigroup, and various ministers representing Iceland's
government. As often had been the case in Iceland over the past several
years, the event also attracted a throng of protesters, who waved picket
signs denouncing the IMF, the local government, or the general conclusion that three years after an epic collapse, Iceland was now an example of

---

[1] International Monetary Fund (2011, October 27). *Iceland's Recovery – Lessons and Challenges.*
http://www.imf.org/external/np/seminars/eng/2011/isl/index.htm

© The Author(s) 2016   **1**
Á. Jónsson, H. Sigurgeirsson, *The Icelandic Financial Crisis,*
DOI 10.1057/978-1-137-39455-2_1

successful economic rehabilitation. As this was an international conference, the crowd had written out their slogans in English.

Harpa was the ideal location for such a meeting. What better symbolized Iceland's pre-crisis *folie de grandeur* and its Icarus-style downfall? Set against the backdrop of Faxa Bay and the Esja mountain range to the north, Harpa sits on the east side of Reykjavík's old harbor like a giant iceberg washed onto shore, directly facing the Central Bank to the south. According to tradition, this is precisely where it all started. In 874, the legends say, the Norwegian chieftain Ingólfur Arnarson became an outlaw in Norway and fled the country. He set his sights on a new, uncolonized island in the North Atlantic Ocean. When land was in sight, he threw his high seat pillars into the sea and swore to the gods that he would build his farm wherever they directed the pillars. After three years of searching along the coastline, his slaves found the pillars on the east side of a small bay on the southwest coast – what would become Reykjavík's harbor. Although his slaves thought it a remote headland, Ingólfur nonetheless made good on his oath and founded the first organized settlement in the new country at that very place.

Whether divine guidance played a role in Harpa's construction is left to speculation. But accomplished hands certainly guided its planning and design. Henning Larsen Architects designed the building in cooperation with Ólafur Elíasson, a Danish-Icelandic artist. The building's steel framework is clad in geometrically shaped glass panels of different colors and mirrored finishes. Fitted together, the panels create the effect of a crystallized rock wall, reminiscent of Iceland's crystalline basalt columns, which glitters magnificently in the dark. The winner of various architectural awards, Harpa has been cited as an example of how "architects are only now gaining the courage to crawl out from the under their (functionalist) rocks and begin to explore, once more, the frivolous joys of ornament,"[2] and received the Mies van der Rohe prize for modern architecture in 2013.[3]

---

[2] Gibberd, Matt and Hill, Albert. (2013, August 20). The return of ornamentation. *The Telegraph.* http://www.telegraph.co.uk/luxury/property-and-architecture/7279/the-return-of-ornamentation.html
[3] Mies van der Rohe Prize. (2013). *Harpa – Reykjavik Concert Hall and Conference Centre.* http://www.miesarch.com/work/535

Decades in the making, Harpa was the dream-home to the Iceland Symphony Orchestra, a source of great pride since the foundation of the republic in 1944. Nearly 70 years after independence, Iceland's population had almost tripled to 330,000,[4] but it still had fewer residents than at least 50 American cities.[5] Nevertheless, Icelanders wanted world-class accommodation for their orchestra as a matter of principle. This is a nation that expects its sporting teams – football, handball, chess or any other – to compete on equal footing with the best, and win. To this end, the nation offers its champions total devotion. Icelanders are driven by the almost incessant urge to show the world they deserve a seat alongside more populous nations. Quite often, their implacable will can triumph against long odds, even in popular sports such as football. In the European Championship of 2016, Iceland progressed to the quarter-final stage after an unbeaten three-match streak in the group stage, and captured a historic win against England in the first knockout round before losing to hosts France at their national stadium. Quite remarkably, these games were attended by almost 10 % of the island's entire population.

Back home, the best performers deserved the best buildings. In the early 1990s, the football scene in Iceland had been revolutionized with large-scale investments in thermally heated indoor football stadiums, which allowed the Icelandic youth to play through the long winters. Soon, Iceland was rewarded with a trove of world-class players. In 2005, the nation's newfound wealth funded the construction of a new Reykjavík landmark: Harpa.

The first genuine, purpose-built musical hall in Reykjavík, Harpa was only one part of the ambitious "World Trade Center Reykjavík" redevelopment plan that would transform the east harbor district. The plan also included a 400-room five star hotel, luxury apartments, retail units, restaurants, a car park, and the new headquarters of Landsbanki, one of the three Icelandic banking giants. All these projects were to be funded and built by private enterprises – without state assistance – when construction began in 2007, at the apex of the financial bubble.

---

[4] Iceland's population in 1944 was 126,000 (Statistics Iceland, hagstofa.is).
[5] United States Census Bureau. American FactFinder. http://factfinder.census.gov/faces/tableservices/jsf/pages/productview.xhtml?src=bkmk

About a year later, in October 2008, the financial crisis engulfed the economy and the whole project went bankrupt. Like most other building projects on the island, Harpa stood half-built, awkward, in stasis, and its incomplete, ghostly cement walls testified both to aspiration and failure, in equally grand proportions. It was a true testament to Iceland's most recent saga of boom and bust.

In March 2009, the World Trade Center project was "bailed out" and nationalized, and acquired at scrap value by a company jointly owned by the treasury and the municipality of Reykjavík.[6] Construction resumed on Harpa, and the nationalization effort was subject to hot debate. Some believed that Harpa should remain unfinished: its bare walls a memorial to – and a warning of – the financial follies and blind ambition that had nearly bankrupted the nation. Others called it a white elephant whose development was totally unacceptable at a time of downsized state budgets and IMF oversight. Any money earmarked for Harpa would be better spent on the struggling national health system.[7] Various bloggers and commentators swore they would never set foot inside such a wasteful, outrageous monument to snobbery.

Despite the criticism, work continued. The Icelandic Symphony Orchestra held its first concert in Harpa on May 4, 2011. The total cost of the building turned out to be €164 million (ISK 27 billion) or about 1–2 % of Iceland's GDP at the time. This more than doubled the initial cost assessment of €73 million (ISK 12 billion). But much of the cost was borne by foreign creditors – Deutsche Bank in particular – since the first year of construction was basically written off prior to the nationalization.[8]

At about the same time Harpa opened, the Icelandic economy turned a corner and embarked on a new growth path, which did not go unnoticed abroad. It was not only that Iceland had become better: other European countries had grown a lot worse as the international financial crisis

---

[6] Reykjavík Mayor. (2013, February 5). Tillaga að fjármögnun Hörpu. (A proposal for Harpa's financing.) (Letter no. R13010037), http://reykjavik.is/sites/default/files/Frettir_skjol/tillaga_greinargerd_harpa.pdf.

[7] For example, this was the position of MP Þór Saari when debating the national budget in 2011, http://www.althingi.is/altext/raeda/140/rad20111110T160252.html

[8] Minister of Finance. (2016, May 31). Svar fjármála- og efnahagsráðherra við fyrirspurn frá Haraldi Einarssyni um byggingarkostnað Hörpu. (The Minister of Finance's answer to Haraldur Einarsson's inquiry on the cost of construction of Harpa.) http://www.althingi.is/altext/145/s/1388.html

morphed into the Eurozone crisis. Initially seen as a warning, Iceland was increasingly hailed as an example. In 2008, Iceland had been the first advanced country to seek the assistance of the IMF since the UK in 1977. To the surprise of many, the nation had sought and received leeway to deviate from the Washington consensus of free market liberalism by imposing capital controls, thus creating a firewall against the punishing forces of international financial markets. Furthermore, the IMF's insistence on austerity and fiscal adjustment had been much less strident than had been the case in previous programs in Asia or South America. The IMF had also provided a seal of approval for a wide range of *force majeure* measures implemented by the Icelandic authorities just before the collapse of the nation's three main banks. These, most notably, included emergency legislation that rewrote the bankruptcy code for financial institutions and gave priority to deposits. The legislation also gave the Icelandic Financial Supervisory Authorities (FSA) the power to seize these guaranteed deposits and Icelandic assets from the collapsing banks at "fair value," which then were used to found new domestic banks.[9]

Just two months before the October Iceland-IMF conference, Iceland graduated from the IMF program with flying colors. "Iceland's Fund-supported program has been a success, and program objectives have been met," declared a press release that accompanied the sixth and final review from the IMF.[10]

The Icelandic government was keen on showcasing its success and refurbished international reputation. The first center-left government in Iceland's post-war history had been elected in the spring of 2009 and was led by Jóhanna Sigurðardóttir, the chairman of the Social Democrats and the first female prime minister of Iceland. The minister of finance was the chairman of the Left-Green Party, Steingrímur J. Sigfússon. A long-time radical, Sigfússon had on numerous occasions denounced the IMF as the

[9] Ministry of Finance. (2011, March). *Skýrsla fjármálaráðherra um endurreisn viðskiptabankanna. (Minister of finance report on the restoration of the commercial banks).*
[10] International Monetary Fund. (2011, August). *Iceland: Sixth Review Under the Stand-By Arrangement and Proposal for Post-Program Monitoring.* IMF Country Report No. 11/263. https://www.imf.org/external/pubs/ft/scr/2011/cr11263.pdf

watchdog of international capital. He originally protested the IMF plan as an MP, but found himself having to work directly with the IMF once in office.

This pair – Sigurðardóttir and Sigfússon – had an agenda, and declared they were going create a "new Iceland" through enactment of many controversial moves: applying for European Union (EU) membership; initiating a nationwide vote on a special assembly to rewrite the constitution; and imposing new taxes on the wealthy and big businesses, which in Iceland meant fishing companies and aluminum smelters. Political forces from both left and right lodged criticism of this vision. On one hand, the ruling coalition was accused of anti-business bias; on the other they were taunted as IMF sell-outs. There were also calls for household debt relief from across the political spectrum, which grew louder by the day. Indeed, many protesters outside Harpa on October 27 were advocates of debt relief. In a letter sent to the media and all speakers of the conference, the main advocates of the protests pointed out that the general price level had risen about 40 %, and household purchasing power subsequently decreased by 27 % since 2007.[11] Since about 80 % of all household loans in the country were inflation-indexed, the principal of the loans had also increased by 40 %. Thus, the protesters maintained, the burden of the crisis was borne by the public while the banks were being restored under the auspices of the IMF.

So, after three years of extreme hardship, Iceland was mending fences with the IMF and Europe. And while its citizens objected – loudly and openly – to the new status quo, few could deny the nation had made remarkable progress after its spectacular financial wreck. But what exactly was the lesson to be gleaned from the nation's crisis and recovery?

1.2   One Letter and Six Months?

In the autumn of 2008, London traders popularized this joke: "What's the difference between Iceland and Ireland? Answer: One letter and about six months."[12] Both countries were staggering under the weight of a financial sector bloated to eight to ten times the national GDP. The

---

[11] Statistics Iceland. www.hagstofa.is
[12] Krugman, Paul. (2010, November 25). Eating the Irish. *The New York Times*.

banks began to look like dead weight after the Lehman Brothers default on September 15, 2008, which eroded market confidence.

Ireland's response was a blanket guarantee of its domestic banks on Monday, September 29. It was successful in the sense that it was credible and the bank run stopped. Ireland was a part of the euro area and was able to supply its banks with a reserve currency. With the guarantee in place, harsh austerity measures were hammered through the Irish parliament. It was tough economic medicine, but there stood Iceland as an imminent warning of what might happen should Ireland refuse it.

In Iceland, also on September 29, the government had attempted to nationalize Glitnir, one of the three massive, now failing, banks. The consequences were disastrous. Carnage ensued with a severe ratings downgrade: Moody's took Glitnir down three notches, from A2 to Baa2 on September 30.[13] This triggered covenants in loans and credit lines, which were contingent on the maintenance of certain ratings. Glitnir, which originally needed €600 million in liquid funds, suddenly faced a hole €2 billion deep.[14] The other two large banks, Kaupthing and Landsbanki, also suffered downgrades and liquidity evaporation. (See a more detailed discussion in Sect. 2.2.) As the smallest currency area in the world (no other nation with less than 2 million citizens has its own currency), Iceland could only respond to the crisis by printing illiquid krónur (ISK). Lacking a lender of last resort, all three banks collapsed by the end of the following week. Within months, almost all financial institutions in Iceland – except for some small rural savings banks and investment management boutiques – would go under.

But much had changed in both Ireland and Iceland in the aftermath of these shocks. The comparison between the countries was no longer a joke. As early as 2010 there arose healthy debate over which response to the crisis had worked out better.

---

[13] Moody's Investors Service. (2008, September 30). *Rating Action: Moody's downgrades Glitnir to Baa2/Prime-2/D from A2/Prime-1/C-.*
[14] Baldursson, F. M., & Portes, R. (2013, September). Gambling for resurrection in Iceland: the rise and fall of the banks. *Available at SSRN 2361098.*

In the third review by the IMF on the progress of the economic program, made public on October 4, 2010, the IMF's economists would write the following conclusion:

> *Under the recovery program, Iceland's recession has been shallower than expected, and no worse than in less hard-hit countries. At the same time, the krona has stabilized at a competitive level, inflation has come down from 18 to under 5 percent, and CDS spreads have dropped from around 1000 to about 300 basis points. Current account deficits have unwound, and international reserves have been built up, while private sector bankruptcies have led to a marked decline in external debt, to around 300 percent of GDP. The outlook is for an investment-led recovery to begin during the second half of 2010, and for growth of about 3 percent in 2011.*[15]

This would prompt Paul Krugman to write, in a November 24, 2010 blog post:

> *What's going on here? In a nutshell, Ireland has been orthodox and responsible – guaranteeing all debts, engaging in savage austerity to try to pay for the cost of those guarantees, and, of course, staying on the euro. Iceland has been heterodox: capital controls, large devaluation, and a lot of debt restructuring – notice that wonderful line from the IMF, above, about how "private sector bankruptcies have led to a marked decline in external debt". Bankrupting yourself to recovery! Seriously.*[16]

Earlier, in June the same year, Krugman had written in a blog post:

> *The moral of the story seems to be that if you're going to have a crisis, it's better to have a really, really bad one. Otherwise, you'll end up taking the advice of people who assure you that even more suffering will cure what ails you.*[17]

---

[15] International Monetary Fund. (2010, October). *Iceland: 2010 Article IV Consultation and Third Review under Stand-By Arrangement and Request for Modification of Performance Criteria.* IMF Country Report No. 10/305. https://www.imf.org/external/pubs/ft/scr/2010/cr10305.pdf

[16] Krugman, Paul. (2010, November 24). Lands of Ice and Ire. *The New York Times.* http://krugman.blogs.nytimes.com/2010/11/24/lands-of-ice-and-ire/?_r=0.

[17] Krugman, Paul. (2010, June 30). The Icelandic Post-crisis Miracle. *The New York Times.* http://krugman.blogs.nytimes.com/2010/06/30/the-icelandic-post-crisis-miracle/?scp=1&sq=+Iceland%

Krugman reiterated this view nearly a year later when he addressed the assembled group at Harpa. He praised the heterodox policies implemented in Iceland, whose success, he argued, validated his conviction that fiscal austerity was a draining, misguided policy response to this particular crisis.[18]

He concluded by issuing a stark warning to the Icelanders not to let go of their currency and adopt the euro.

Citigroup's chief economist, Willem Buiter, a former Professor at London School of Economics, drew the exact opposite lesson from the Icelandic experience (although he was just as brash in his conclusions and rhetoric as Krugman). He began by using phrases such as "collective madness," "near universal suspension of common sense," and "collective stupidity that I have not seen in any advanced countries" to characterize the precursors to the Icelandic crisis.[19] In his view, the collapse showed that countries without the ability to print a reserve currency could not sustain an international banking system. Furthermore, this collapse displayed the importance of scale: Iceland was just too small to sustain its own currency and conduct independent monetary policy. There simply was not enough brainpower to staff the necessary institutions for an independent currency area (even without the collective madness). It was important to think beyond the present stabilization policies, Buiter said. In his view, the capital controls could never be fully abolished on portfolio financial flows in and out of Iceland. Only foreign direct investment (FDI) should be given free passage. Small countries such as Iceland needed to "join larger clubs." This prompted the following policy advice: "Pray that the EU survives, pray that the euro survives."

To conclude the sermon, Buiter suggested that Iceland should have "a jubilee in the biblical sense." Literally speaking, this meant a total debt write-off every 50 years. Buiter, however, thought writing mortgage debt down to about 70 % of the value of the underlying collateral was sufficient – the rest should be turned into equity and handed over to the banks.

---

[18] "Iceland's Recovery – Lessons and Challenges", IMF, Reykjavik, October 27, 2011. http://www.imf.org/external/np/seminars/eng/2011/isl/
[19] "Iceland's Recovery – Lessons and Challenges", IMF, Reykjavik, October 27, 2011. http://www.imf.org/external/np/seminars/eng/2011/isl/

There was no clear agreement at the conference over what had been done correctly in Iceland and what corrective measures had failed. Altogether, it seemed somewhat of a mixed bag. Some thought that capital controls had been a mistake. Others argued that the domestic/foreign division of the banks was the problem – a good bank–bad bank division was the optimal categorization. And then there were those that thought Iceland was not really a success case at all.

For one sitting in the newly completed Harpa on that bright day of October 27, it nonetheless seemed that Iceland had been vindicated after its utter humiliation just three years earlier. At least the nation was back in the international spotlight – and mostly for positive reasons. However, the ultimate lesson, the one that made sense of so much crisis and correction, proved elusive, and Iceland's way forward was no clearer than any other recovering nation's. In fact, few Icelanders would have described their conditions as ideal in 2011. In 2012, the IMF estimated both the gross debt incurred during the crash and its aftermath in 2008–2011, and the net cost to the treasury, accounting for the value of assets acquired against that debt.[20] This analysis found that the direct fiscal cost of the Icelandic collapse amounted to 43.1 % of GDP; the net fiscal cost, adjusted for appropriated assets, totaled 19.2 % of GDP. The biggest single item was the recapitalization of the Central Bank of Iceland (CBI) owing to losses from repurchase agreements (repo lending), or about 6.8 % of GDP. By comparison, the recapitalization of the commercial banks amounted to only 2.3 % of GDP. (See a more detailed discussion in Chap. 9.)

All in all, Icelandic public debt had increased by a staggering 72 % of the GDP between 2007 and 2012 (jumping from 41 to 113 % of GDP in those years). This is comparable to Ireland's increase in public debt – amounting to 82 % of GDP – during the same period. To be sure, Ireland was spared the collateral damage caused by the currency crisis, double-digit inflation, banking collapse, and the social upheaval that engulfed Iceland. In addition, Ireland was not effectively locked out from the rest of the world by capital controls and denied access to foreign capital investment. The protesters outside Harpa had abundant evidence on their side.

---

[20] International Monetary Fund. (2012. April). *Iceland: Ex Post Evaluation of Exceptional Access Under the 2008 Stand-by Arrangement.*

The ideals stated in the emergency legislation, which cut the links between the sovereign and the banks, may have appealed to economists. But everyday lives and business still felt the pain of radical choices.

1.3   The Unfinished Business of 2011

In 2011 there was little sense of how policies enacted in the crisis would turn out when the recovery finally came, which probably explains why views at the Harpa conference diverged to such an extent. The domestic/foreign partition of the failing banks at the heat of the crisis had created a new banking system with a lot of non-performing loans, and at the start about 70 % of the new banks' loan portfolios was in arrears – not exactly trustworthy status. All in all, about 20 % of households went under with negative equity, and 15 % of mortgages went into arrears. The numbers were much more severe for corporations, 70–80 % of which went into negative equity territory.

In 2011, after numerous debates between the banks, creditors, and the government (and much handwringing), universal debt restructuring measures were implemented, which effectively transposed the write-downs that had been made at the founding of the new banks to actual debt reduction for the banks' clients. Small to medium-sized businesses (with total outstanding debt below 1 billion ISK, or €7 million) would go onto a fast track and could apply for debt relief if they could credibly document positive cash flow (EBITDA) from future activities. About a third of the restructuring involved a convertible loan with a deferred repayment after three years, which the company could buy from the bank at a discount prior to maturity. These led to corporate debt write-offs that amounted to about 60–70 % of Iceland's GDP. (See a more detailed discussion in Sect. 4.4.)

The households would also get their debt reduction. Household mortgage debt in excess of 110 % of the fair value of each property was written off. Furthermore, specific relief measures (administered by a bank or a new debtors' ombudsman) were put in place for those that could not service a reduced loan. Low-income, asset-poor households with high-interest mortgage payments got a temporary subsidy from the government. In addition, the government attempted to bolster the bargaining power of individuals against the banks by making bankruptcy an easier process, and by allowing claims, as a general rule, to expire only two years after a formal default.

This, however, was not enough for the public. In the spring of 2013, the left-wing government suffered a crushing defeat. The combined electoral strength of the two coalition parties went from 51.5 % down to 23.8 % – a record loss in Iceland for any government since independence. A new right-wing government ascended while promising general household debt relief, which it delivered in 2014 to the benefit of 100,000 households (out of about 180,000). The relief was funded with a special tax on the old banks' estates, with the motto "culprits should pay." (See a more detailed discussion in Sect. 5.6.)

In 2011, the currency reserves of the CBI – net of foreign debt – were still close to zero. The bank had been unable to replenish the foreign currency reserves by open market purchases. On the contrary, the bank had to be a net seller in the market while tightening the currency controls to support the ISK. Even though the 50 % devaluation of the ISK had led to a sharp reduction in imports, thereby engineering a turnaround of the balance of trade, the export sector was stationary. This was unsurprising, since fishing and aluminum smelting, the main export industries, both faced quantity restrictions.

Government-issued quotas, based on the estimated size of fishing stocks, determine how much fishing firms are allowed to catch. The marine output of the country is thus determined by biology, not the export prices.

Aluminum smelters always run on full and stable capacity, regardless of currency movements. And given that domestic investment levels had collapsed to historical lows – and there was no FDI coming from abroad – there were no new export sectors in the making. Indeed, when the new banks were criticized for not lending out, they would simply answer that lending is a two-way street: they were open for business, but there were no new clients asking for new loans – just the old ones asking for debt reduction.

However, in 2010 the glacier-volcano Eyjafjallajökull erupted, which blocked flight traffic over the North Atlantic for weeks and brought the international spotlight back to Iceland. The short-term effects of the eruption on the Icelandic tourist industry were disastrous, but at the same time it was a breath-taking advertisement for the country's geology and landscapes. (It also became a new tongue twister for the linguistically inquisitive!) In the next few years, nature's marketing campaign paid off. In 2011, Iceland received about half a million foreign visitors; by 2016, visitors had almost quadrupled to 1.8 million. The tourist industry subsequently became the leading driver of the economy in terms of export earnings, real estate prices and job creation. There was further benefit from Reykjavík's rapid development as a transatlantic flight hub, thanks to the rapid expansion of Icelandair, the flag carrier. Today 25 airlines use Keflavík International Airport; a decade ago there were only two or three. (See a more detailed discussion in Sect. 5.4.)

The volcanic *deus ex machina* did not draw much attention at the 2011 Harpa conference, but soon afterwards there was abundant new foreign demand that altered all economic fundamentals, for the better. The new growth came in the wake of the extensive debt restructuring, and these two forces restored the equity ratios of both companies and households. The banks' position also changed drastically as the ratio of non-performing assets went south and their profitability went north. The new banks were able to mark up assets they had received from the old banks at "fair" value. The surge in tourism also facilitated a northward shift in the current account, and finally gave the CBI the chance to replenish its foreign reserves. From 2014 onwards, the CBI has purchased about 50–70 % of all currency offered in the interbank market and accumulated €3.3 billion (500bn ISK) in reserves. (See a more detailed discussion in Sect. 5.3.)

In a national referendum in April 2011, voters rejected an extension of a government guarantee on the Icesave online accounts. These had been offered prior to the collapse by Landsbanki in the UK and the Netherlands with an Icelandic deposit guarantee. There had been about 425,000 online accounts (300,000 in the UK and 125,000 in the Netherlands). The total sum the Icelandic population was asked to guarantee was up to €4 billion, or 40–60 % of Iceland's GDP, depending on the valuation of the ISK. It was known in 2011 that the asset recovery of the Landsbanki estate would be sufficient to repay the principal, but nevertheless there were large claims outstanding from both the British and the Dutch concerning interest payments. In 2011 these respective governments resorted to litigation. With a ruling on January 28, 2013, the Court of Justice of the European Free Trade Association (EFTA) States cleared Iceland of all charges – leaving the governments with only "first priority claim" on the Landsbanki receivership. Landsbanki made its last installed payment on January 11, 2016 – thereby closing the claim. (See a more detailed discussion in Sect. 5.2.)

In 2011, offshore ISK assets, the remains from the once blooming carry trade, stood at the equivalent of €3.1 billion, or 30 % of GDP.[21] The principal purpose of capital controls in the wake of the collapse was to prevent large-scale outflows from burdening the general public via an excessively low exchange rate. In 2011, the CBI started efforts to eliminate the accumulated overhang within the scope of the capital account.[22] It created a special auction market where asset swaps could be conducted at a lower exchange rate than the publicly quoted onshore rate. This prevented the reduction from disturbing the real economy by lowering the ISK exchange rate and ensured that the trade surplus was not used to convert offshore ISK to foreign currency. The overhang had been cut in half by year-end 2015. (See a more detailed discussion in Sect. 5.5.)

In 2011, the main challenge associated with the Icelandic recovery was still practically unnoticed: this was the transfer problem resulting from the distribution from the old banks' default estates. The original intention had been to partition the banking system into a domestic part, which would be recapitalized, and a foreign part that would go into liquidation. It did not turn out that way. To start with, owing to FSA controls, some domestic assets were not transferred to the new banks. Examples include derivatives and assets moved to foreign special purpose vehicles (SPVs). Second, and more importantly, the deposits of the domestic branches of the failed banks were considerably less than the value of their domestic assets, owing to large-scale wholesale funding. On a parent company basis, domestic deposits were 18 % of Glitnir's total funding, and 14 % of Landsbanki's and Kaupthing's. Half of the banks' wholesale funding was

---

[21] Central Bank of Iceland. (2011, March 25). *Áætlun um losun gjaldeyrishafta. (A plan for lifting capital controls.)* http://www.cb.is/lisalib/getfile.aspx?itemid=8673
[22] *Ibid.*

foreign, and the banks subsequently reloaned this to Icelandic and foreign corporations (this is reflected by the fact that at the beginning of 2008, around 68 % of total bank lending to Icelandic corporations was in foreign currency, or currency-linked). Even after steep write-offs, the new banks had considerably more assets than deposits, and had to issue bonds to the old banks to cover the difference. (See a more detailed discussion in Sect. 6.2.)

Recapitalizing an entire banking system with a significant amount of non-performing assets of uncertain value entailed a huge risk for the government – if not from loan losses then by litigation by the creditors. Thus, the government was quite happy to be relieved from some of that burden by letting the creditors pick up the tab from the recapitalization by converting the bonds issued by the new banks to the old banks into equity. It retained only 5 % in Íslandsbanki (New Glitnir) and 13 % in Arion (New Kaupthing), but with a shareholder agreement that gave the government-appointed board member veto power regarding these "privatized" banks in certain situations. However, the government kept 80 % of Landsbanki and later acquired the bank almost in full. Furthermore, by allowing the creditors to turn bonds into equity, and thus assume the risk and benefits from a downside or upside for the new banks, the government was able to avoid litigation risk concerning the "fair value" of the asset transferred to the new banks from the estates. Instead, everyone could just agree on a rather low initial valuation of the asset base of the new banks, since the creditors would, as shareholders, reap the benefits from a later mark-up. (See a more detailed discussion in Sect. 6.3.)

Thus, when the tourist boom began to move the economy, the banks churned out profits that would bolster their equity. By 2014, the new banks had equity ratios of about 20–30 % despite having paid out substantial dividends. Thus, the estates held ISK assets to the tune of €5–6 billion, or about 50 % of Iceland's GDP, most of which was equity holdings in the new banks. Since the overwhelming majority of the creditors were foreign, the distribution of these ISK assets had to go through the currency market. Of course, there are limits on how much capital can be transferred from one currency area to another through the capital account without sending the exchange rate to a level inappropriate to foreign trade balance.

In March 2012, the Icelandic parliament withdrew the estates' exemption from the capital controls. This move locked the assets of the estates away from the creditors and empowered the CBI to prevent all payouts to creditors, whether in foreign exchange (FX) or ISK, and greatly enhanced the bargaining power of the Icelandic authorities. Until a deal regarding Iceland's balance of payments was in place, no payments would be allowed from the estates. By that time, the vulture hedge funds had long since taken control of the estates by acquiring a majority of claims. (See a more detailed discussion in Sect. 7.4.)

Indeed, the hedge funds had managed to stake positions about three to six months after the crisis. By spring of 2009, they had created a forum to negotiate the purchase of the new banks from the government. When the first claim registries appeared between November 2009 and January 2010, approximately 23.5 % of claims to Glitnir were owned by the major hedge funds; the figure was 30 % for claims on Kaupthing. The number for Landsbanki was much lower – just 11 % – because at that time it was not anticipated that the estate's assets would cover priority claims (i.e. the Icesave deposits). The hedge funds' total positions would continue to grow in following years, as German banks sold their claims one by one as did small savings banks or Landesbanks. At the time of composition, hedge funds owned approximately 70 % of claims to Glitnir and 50 % of Kaupthing's. For Landsbanki, the figure had risen to 80 %, since the Dutch government had by then sold the remainder of the Icesave claim. (See a more detailed discussion in Sect. 6.4.)

By locking up the estates within the capital controls, the Icelandic authorities would find themselves in direct confrontation with hedge funds. A multiyear standoff ensued. In the end, on June 8, 2015, the authorities issued an ultimatum to the hedge funds. The estates could reach composition agreements with creditors meeting certain stability conditions, which basically implied that they would surrender most of their ISK assets to the government, or they would be subjected to a 39 % stability tax on all of their assets. All the estates – eight in total – took the first option. In other words, they were forced to relinquish their control of domestic assets in order to secure the foreign assets. Their combined contributions totaled €4 billion, or the equivalent to 26.8 % of Iceland's 2015 GDP. Thus, by applying the capital controls as a bargaining tool, the Icelandic authorities forced about 10, 16, and 24 % haircuts on the creditors of Landsbanki, Kaupthing, and Glitnir respectively. (See a more detailed discussion in Sect. 7.5.)

Five years after the Harpa conference, the Icelandic treasury has not only recovered the direct fiscal cost from the crisis; it has actually reaped gains. This is the result of several factors: capital gains from the recapitalization of the commercial banks, taxes on the estates, and the stability contributions from the estates. (See a more detailed discussion in Chap. 9.)

1.4   Lessons Learned?

After the three banks collapsed and the Icelandic authorities responded with "heterodox" policies, the country became a sort of "crisis tourism" destination. When a Eurozone nation got into trouble with fiscal austerity, "internal devaluation," or other disciplinary acts forced upon them by the common currency, Iceland was cited as the counterexample: the country that not only devalued its own currency to gain a new competitive edge but also imposed capital controls to circumvent the laws of international finance. When the debate in the United States or Europe heated up regarding bank bailouts, bankers' greed, arrogance, or special interest, Iceland was often cited as a nation where the banks were allowed to fail, bankers were sent to jail, and bondholders got haircuts. As a rule, "crisis tourists" claimed to find what they had sought: hard evidence to question the approach taken by the authorities at home. But more often than not the verdict was reached with both creative and selective readings of the real facts. Eight years after the crisis, it is time to ask what lessons can be gleaned from Iceland's exceptional heterodoxy. In the authors' view, five main lessons can be drawn from the Icelandic experience; three concern banking and two concern international finance.

1.4.1 Lessons in Banking

Regarding the lender of last resort, the most obvious lesson – as noted by Willem Buiter – is that small countries without a reserve currency cannot sustain an international banking system in the longer term. The Icelandic "financial center" was originally built on the AAA rating of the Icelandic republic – awarded by Moody's in 2002 – which automatically transferred it to the three too-big-to-fail banks also. The good ratings gave access to the private capital market at a good price in fair weather times. But there was no safety net when the storm hit credit markets in 2008; the CBI was unable to serve as a lender of last resort by printing the illiquid ISK for a banking system whose liquidity needs were in foreign currency.

It also turned out that the neighboring issuers of reserve currencies were reluctant to extend liquidity to this tiny currency area. After the Lehman collapse, Iceland became the one western country *not* to receive help from the US Fed, even while it simultaneously faced aggressive demands for cash from the ECB and the Bank of England. (See a detailed discussion in Chap. 2.) The reason can perhaps be read from the minutes of the Bank of England Committee of non-executive directors (NEDCO) from October 15, 2008: "The number of smaller countries that promoted themselves as centres for financial services ought to reduce. Iceland was a very telling example." Importantly, the failure of Iceland posed no systematic risk to other regions or countries save for Britain, where the run on Icesave online savings accounts undermined public confidence in the European deposit guarantee system. The UK authorities dealt with this risk by forcing Icelandic bank subsidiaries into liquidation as well as freezing assets by invoking the terrorist act against not only the respective commercial bank (Landsbanki) but also the Central Bank of Iceland. (See a detailed discussion in Chap. 3.)

There is, however, no evidence that the asset quality of the Icelandic banks – despite some missteps in connected party lending – was any better or worse than for comparable European banks. Most of their foreign subsidiaries are still operating today under new owners and the estimated recoveries of two British subsidiaries forced into liquidation by the UK authorities – Kaupthing Singer & Friedlander and Landsbanki's Heritable Bank – are 86, and 98 pence in the pound, respectively. (See a detailed discussion in Sect. 6.1.)

These three combining factors – an illiquid currency, a large international banking system, and indifference (or even outright hostility) from the world's main central banks – in great part explain why Iceland became the first advanced country to suffer a systematic banking collapse in 2008. Not only were Icelandic banks too-big-to-save at home; Iceland itself was too-small-to-save abroad.

Second, from the general perspective, the Icelandic collapse is a testimony to the failure of the European banking model, which is withering away slowly but painfully on the continent. Western Europe stands out in the world with oversized financial systems, with an average ratio of bank assets to GDP in excess of three. This can be traced to the distinct European banking model – sometimes called relationship banking – by which banks issue senior unsecured bonds in large quantities and lend the proceeds to corporations as part of a close business partnership. This runs opposite to the American model, under which the banks serve as intermediaries that assist corporations in obtaining direct market financing. As a consequence, the banking system is much smaller and more maneuverable in market-based than in bank-based models.

By the European bankruptcy code, these senior bonds are *pari passu* to deposits, which effectively creates a government guarantee, since giving depositors haircuts in a bank failure is politically toxic. In other words, bondholders in European banks hold depositors as human shields! Despite the crisis, and a number of close calls, this guarantee has held up on the European continent so far. Indeed, holders of senior bank bonds have turned out to be safer than holders of sovereign debt; the recurrent Greece crisis is a salient manifestation of this fact. Therefore, Iceland is still the only European country where the senior bondholders suffered a haircut during the financial crisis.[23]

---

[23] In 2014 Portugal's Central Bank (Banco de Portugal) founded a "new" bad bank – Novo Banco – as a destination for toxic assets from the failed Banco Espírito Santo. In December 2015 the PCB transferred five (out of 52) senior bond issues with a book value of €2.2 billion to Novo Banco in a measure "needed to ensure that the losses from Banco Espírito Santo are absorbed firstly by shareholders and creditors and not by the financial system and taxpayers," according to a statement from the bank." https://www.bportugal.pt/en-US/OBancoeoEurosistema/ComunicadoseNotasdeInformacao/Pages/combp20151229-2.aspx. The decision was rejected by a Lisbon court in last April, however, and is still under legal scrutiny.

This public subsidization of wholesale funding is undoubtedly a chief reason for the financial overextension in Europe before the relationship banking model hit a rock in 2007–2008. With the EU's evolution into a single financial market came cross-border financing and loose monetary policy. European banks displayed almost cancerous balance sheet growth, which is proving to be extremely difficult to unwind. If it had not been for the tremendous printing power of the common currency, which has provided life support for oversized banks of the euro area, a significant number of European countries would have been forced to downsize and recapitalize their banking systems. Not only are European banks yet to accept hefty loan losses; their business model has been undone by the crisis, as their current price of funding is simply uncompetitive. A wide range of larger corporations can now fund themselves at a much lower rate than the banks can offer.

In October 2008, Iceland had no other resort than to break the *pari passu* between bonds and deposits with an emergency legislation that rewrote the European bankruptcy code ex post, giving priority to deposits. European regulators have attempted to implement the same change ex ante by introducing various forms of bail-in bonds, such as CoCos (contingent convertible bonds), which are not only perpetual but also allow the issuer to skip coupon payments and even convert into equity in time of distress. Such bonds were at first greeted with enthusiasm by investors, especially when they derived from issuers deemed to be too-big-to-fail. However, in early 2016 fear that options embedded in these instruments might actually be exercised was growing. A very large sell-off ensued, which led CoCos issued by bedrock European banks such as Deutsche Bank, Santander, and UniCredit to trade at 70–85 cents on the euro. Of course, the market turmoil does open up the opportunity for these respective banks to turn liquidity into equity, as they could buy back their own bonds at a discount and pocket the difference as an equity gain. Nevertheless, this clearly displays the difficulty of letting investors of today absorb the losses made yesterday. Bail-in bonds are not the way to finance new lending or recapitalize the European banking system.

It is, however, difficult to promote Icelandic-style bank failure and the imposition of losses on shareholders and bondholders as a winning strategy. Bank failure, or the bankruptcy of a whole banking system, causes significant collateral damage in the real economy, political upheaval, and subsequent unforeseen consequences. Moreover, since the overwhelming majority of bondholders of the Icelandic banks were foreign, the cost of the failure was directed outwards, which also explains the relatively benign effect of the collapse on the Icelandic economy. The same does not hold true for most other countries.

Nevertheless, the alternative route for Europe's oversized banking sector is financial repression. This is the Japanese way, where losses are not acknowledged, banks become ossified, new loans disappear, and economic growth stagnates. Banking failure has high direct upfront cost, whereas financial repression costs output loss and higher costs of a banking system over a long period of time.

The recipe for solving a bank crisis, after emergency liquidity has been provided to avert a collapse, is to accept losses, and then identify those that have to bear them. Through this acceptance, the balance sheet of the banks should be cut down to size. The Icelandic example points to the need – but perhaps not the method – of both accepting and allocating losses from the earlier financial excesses.

Third, the financial reconstruction of Iceland offers a unique perspective on the very nature of banking finance and alternative routes of dealing with systematic financial crisis – though it may be short on ready-made solutions to be applied elsewhere. In our view, each financial crisis has distinct characteristics and thus demands its own unique solution. Iceland received a lot of foreign advice based on other countries' experience – both solicited and otherwise – but in almost all cases it imparted limited value. Nonetheless, one might compile a useful list of dos and don'ts in financial reconstruction based on the Icelandic experience, and even add on a few new options for future countries in crisis.

As mentioned above, the failed banks were divided along a national line; domestic deposits and assets were placed into de novo entities that were recapitalized. This approach was devised and implemented by the Icelandic FSA. The move was smooth in the sense that households never lost access to their accounts and did not experience any disruption in the provision of banking services. But the division itself was a complicated affair, involving protracted negotiations over the "fair value" of the defaulted banks' assets as they were transferred to the new, post-crisis banks. In the end, creditors to the old banks wound up placing capital in the new banks, thus ensuring their stake in any potential upside from an economic recovery. The old and now "foreign" banks, on the other hand, were shielded by a moratorium from enforcement actions of creditors. But they still kept their banking licenses and were able to conduct some regular operations, such as lending and extending new credit. And despite the bruises between the governments of Iceland and the UK, Her Majesty's Treasury would still lend to the estates of the failed Icelandic banks so that their British clients would not be left in the cold. (See a detailed discussion in Chap. 6.)

However, countless observers – such as Willem Buiter – argued for a good bank–bad bank split, which is the customary approach to bank restructuring, despite the fact that such a split had no practical application in Iceland. The failed banks held a lot of good foreign assets; capitalized on the balance sheet of a living bank, they would have exacted huge fiscal outlays. Furthermore, it was doubtful that the Icelandic authorities would have been able to fund these new banks, since they did not have access to foreign capital markets. Lastly, given the almost perfect storm in Icelandic credit markets, the majority of domestic assets would have counted as bad assets, thus rendering a good bank–bad bank separation meaningless when applied to such systematic credit problems.

The exact domestic vs. foreign asset division was also subject to foreign scrutiny. The only foreign experts in the country at the height of the crisis while the split was being carried out were from J.P. Morgan, employed by the CBI. They proposed as an alternative that only deposits should be transferred into the new banks. Subsequently, the government could just issue bonds backed with the asset base in the old banks to cover the asset side. Although this approach would have been less risky for the government, as there was no uncertainty in the real asset value of the banks that were being recapitalized, it was effectively impossible in practice with the three largest banks. However, this method was applied to the fourth largest depository institution, Reykjavík Savings Bank (SPRON), which failed in early 2009. The consequences were disastrous. The provision of banking services requires the simultaneous use of assets and liabilities, and transferring deposits to a new institution while leaving debts in the old failed bank led to a disruption for the clients of SPRON, almost triggering a run on the institution to which the deposits were transferred (New Kaupthing). (See a detailed discussion in Sect. 4.3.)

Furthermore, one of the conditions of the joint IMF economic plan, implemented in November 2008, was that a "well-reputed expert in banking" would be appointed to manage the bank restructuring process.[24] The person appointed was Mats Josefsson, a veteran of the Swedish banking crisis of the early 1990s. He proposed the use of National Asset Management Companies (AMCs) to carry out the needed corporate debt restructuring, much as had been done in Sweden, with shining results. This proposal was met with almost unified opposition by the new banks' management, the creditors, and the Icelandic corporate sector – which were all coming to terms with how the pending restructuring might be applied. A bit later the government was brought to the table, and the four parties in question agreed on universal guidelines, implemented in 2010–2011, whose main objective was to recalibrate the financial fundamentals of Icelandic business. The fact of the matter, however, is that AMCs have only been used efficiently for narrowly defined purposes, such as resolving real estate-related portfolios that only constitute a limited segment of the market aimed for liquidation. This applied to Sweden in 1992 but not in Iceland in 2008. (See a detailed discussion in Sect. 4.3.)

People also tend to overlook the distributional or democratic angle of how debt restructuring can be implemented. In all other Western countries, a 50 % devaluation and up to 20 % inflation would in itself have led to a universal debt reduction by eroding the principal of nominal loan contracts. However, Icelandic lenders are veterans of many currency alignments and inflationary shocks, and practically all long-term lending was either infla-tion- or currency-linked in anticipation of such events. Thus, a currency devaluation and inflation would lead to a ballooning of debt and instant insolvency.

The initial lack of a uniform approach to the debt problem created great consternation in egalitarian Iceland. People wondered why they did not receive the same favorable treatment from their bank as their uncle, neighbor, or coworker enjoyed at their bank. A citizen from a larger

---

[24] International Monetary Fund. (2008, November 15). *Iceland: Letter of Intent and Technical Memorandum of Understanding.* https://www.imf.org/external/np/loi/2008/isl/111508.pdf

nation might find this quaint, but uniformity is crucial to the vitality of the social contract in Iceland, and directly linked to the public's willingness to service debts despite the horrendous equity losses and steep increases in the burden of payment Icelandic debtors suffered almost overnight. Indeed, there were a number of grass-root organizations, or interest groups, which sprang up after the crisis that attempted to organize a "debtors' strike" in various forms. Seen in aggregate, these groups presented the single greatest threat to the new banks. These populist challenges could only be answered with a democratic, or egalitarian, approach to debt relief – which was only comprehended by outsiders post factum. (See a detailed discussion in Sect. 4.4.)

This absolute insistence on equal treatment caused a delay, of course. The debt reduction was implemented in several phases, and did not end until 2014 when a comprehensive household debt relief program, financed with a tax on the old bank estates, was implemented. (See a detailed discussion in Sect. 5.6.)

In sum, the authors believe that the Icelandic experience places many new items on the menu for financial restructuring of both businesses and households, especially when countries are faced with a systematic crisis. It is, however, open to question how much these new items are applicable elsewhere, just as many successfully tested foreign solutions turned out to be inapplicable to Iceland.

1.4.2 Lessons in International Finance

There is no question that the national sovereignty embedded in the ability to not only print your own money but also regulate its convertibility empowered the Icelandic authorities to rebalance the balance of payment after the crisis. In fact, one could easily make the case that the Icelanders were able to turn their minuscule and illiquid currency into an advantage to prevent the "socialization of losses" from the banking collapse.

By applying capital controls, the Icelandic authorities were able to stop the ISK part of the bank run and fund the domestic part of the banking system, which was restored and recapitalized. The Icelandic deposit account holders had nowhere to go once the capital account had been closed. They could convert their deposits into physical ISK banknotes, but to what end? The new banking system was government-owned in the beginning and enjoyed a blanket guarantee of deposits, and thus the same counterparty risk was at play with these non-convertible asset classes. Therefore, the capital controls restored confidence in the financial system and ensured the funding of the new banks, despite their alarming levels of non-performing assets.

The capital controls, of course, prevented large-scale capital outflows, which would have led to an excessive currency depreciation and inflation. The ISK depreciated about 50 % before the controls were imposed, but in the free offshore market it was only trading at 25 % of its pre-crisis value. The controls also allowed the Icelandic authorities to apply both monetary and fiscal policy to stabilize output without consideration to the currency market. Austerity measures were not implemented until 2010, more than a year into the crisis, and thus fiscal automatic stabilizers kept up demand at the crisis impact point. Furthermore, the CBI was able to lower its policy rate despite the high level of short-term foreign holdings in the financial system. Without the controls, the Icelandic economy would undoubtedly have contracted by more than the actual 10 % in 2009–2010. (See a detailed discussion in Sect. 5.4.)

The capital controls also granted bargaining power to the authorities against those stuck behind the controls, and allowed them to impose conditions on them to solve the transfer problem stemming from offshore ISK assets. The CBI was able to create a special auction market, where asset swaps could be concluded at a lower exchange rate than the publicly quoted onshore rate. This not only prevented the reduction from disturbing the real economy, it also ensured that the trade surplus was not used to convert offshore ISK to foreign currency. (See a detailed discussion in Sect. 5.5.) The CBI was also able to prevent all payouts from the old defaulted banks unless the creditors would oblige to "stability conditions" as the estates entered composition. In effect, this meant that they either handed over the domestic part of their asset base as a "stability contribution" or faced a 39 % stability tax on all of their assets. The combined contributions of the estates totaled €4 billion, or the equivalent of 26.8 % of Iceland's 2015 GDP. This ensured a stable balance of payment and a complete direct fiscal cost recovery from the crisis. (See a detailed discussion in Chap. 7.)

It is thus very likely that future textbooks will portray the Icelandic capital controls from 2008 as a success – and perhaps an example for others. We do not fully agree with such an assessment. Imposing capital controls in an advanced country – as was done in Iceland in 2008 – demands heavy use of coercive power and an infringement of personal rights, which can hardly be tolerated in a democratic country. It was only made possible in Iceland by the wholesale bankruptcy of almost every financial institution, which led to an effective cut-off of the Icelandic financial sector from the foreign financial market. Imposing capital controls on live and active international banks is often simply impossible, or freighted with the risk of significant collateral damage. (See a detailed discussion in Sect. 7.2.)

It is also clear that the controls – which are now well into their eighth year – have inflicted a very large cost on the Icelandic economy by isolating the business sector from the outside world. The problem is not only that foreign investment will not come in; domestic investment cannot get out! Although foreign currency is now pouring in from the tourist boom, it is nevertheless a low-skill service sector that cannot be considered a growth leader in the longer term. Like the other Scandinavian countries, Iceland needs to build niche-playing multinationals; companies that have a sharp focus but a wide scope around the world. Indeed, given its minuscule market, Iceland is in dire need of both specialization and scale economics that cannot be achieved merely with a free flow of physical goods across the world. It also needs capital. The controls have not only chased away a lot of the pre-existing multinationals but also aspiring ones, which will now choose to be headquartered outside Iceland once they reach a certain level of development. Even though the controls will be removed – which is now about to happen – their return will always be anticipated. Neither Icelandic investors nor corporates want to be caught up in frozen funds again, locked in the Icelandic financial system as happened in 2008. (See a detailed discussion in Sect. 7.6.)

The latter lesson concerns the question of a monetary union versus monetary independence. Paul Krugman has repeatedly used the Iceland crisis as a manifestation of the fact that nations are better off with their own adjustable currencies rather than in a union. He is not alone – his view is shared by practically every American economist that has voiced an opinion on the matter. However, to most Icelandic economists, this view is naïve or even ironic, coming from the most successful monetary union in history – the United States – whose printed issues have currency all over the world. Initially, the Icelanders sought national independence, but monetary independence was forced upon them. The nation received sovereignty in 1918 as part of the Scandinavian Currency Union, which then fell apart in 1920. Since that time the currency market has been a constant source of disturbance and instability; either too much money was flowing in through the balance of payments or too little. Iceland stands out from all other advanced economies because of high inflation and volatile domestic demand, as would be expected given the high level of imports in consumption and intense pass-through of currency movements into prices. Exchange rate risk furthermore permeates all business operation in the country – regardless of size and sector.

The overwhelming policy concern in Iceland has always been to keep the currency stable. To this end Iceland has participated in every international exchange rate project available: the gold standard, Bretton Woods, and the European Monetary System. However, the deep-rooted suspicion of supra-national power, or dominance by the larger neighboring powers, has prevented the nation from adopting the euro, since a membership to the EU is a precondition. If the euro had been a stand-alone project, the Icelanders would probably be in. The fact of the matter is that in a small open economy like Iceland, exchange rate stability is the only way to achieve economic stability, and the former can only be ensured with capital controls. Indeed, Iceland was forced to abandon full convertibility of its currency in 1920, just two years into sovereignty, and then follow through with full-fledged capital controls in 1931 which were kept in place until 1994. Furthermore, the seven-year span from 2001 to 2008 is the only period in the almost 100-year history of the ISK as an independent currency that it has been floating in a free-trading currency market. (See a detailed discussion in Sect. 7.1.)

The experiment is not likely to be repeated any time soon: current discussion in Reykjavík is not about abolishing the eight-year-old controls, but easing them and making them permanent, with as little collateral damage as possible. This is to some extent in line with changed opinions worldwide of both economists and policymakers in the wake of the financial crisis, as capital controls have been reintroduced under the name "Capital Flow Management Measures" and seem to be gaining a new acceptance. On June 4, 2016, the CBI published new "Rules on special reserve requirements for new foreign currency inflows,"[25] whose main purpose is obtain a new policy instrument to restrict financial inflows. These measures give the bank the authority to control new foreign currency inflows, including the special reserve base, holding period, special reserve ratio, settlement currency, and interest rates on deposit institutions' capital flow accounts. In other words, the controls seem to be here to stay in Iceland.

It is of course true that a flexible currency has its benefits. The currency depreciation in 2008 led to a very sharp adjustment in the economy, a turnaround in the trade balance and a new lease on life for the export sector. What the economy needed was maybe a 25 % depreciation; the free currency market delivered 75 %, though by applying capital controls, the Icelandic authorities settled for 50 %. In other words, if currency depreciation is a policy remedy, then the authorities are unable to control its dosage, and quite often the cure is worse than the disease. In the absence of capital controls, the authorities can only respond to a currency collapse by steep interest rate hikes and fiscal austerity. Thus, the privilege of being able to set your own monetary policy has actually turned against the respective nation, since the need for currency stabilization will lead to policies that will exacerbate output contraction. This is not only the case for Iceland but for countless other small open economies and emerging markets.

However, from the standpoint of financial stability, an independent currency does offer some protection to banks. In fact, no systemically important bank in a small independent currency area will ever have to worry that it will succumb to a bank run in the domestic currency. If the money starts to flee, the only way out of the financial system is through

---

[25] Central Bank of Iceland. (2016, June 4). *Rules on special reserve requirements for new foreign currency inflows*. (Rules no. 490/2016.) http://www.cb.is/library/Skraarsafn---EN/Rules/Rules%20no. %20490%202016.pdf

the currency market. As funds begin to flow out of the country, the currency will depreciate and impose haircuts on those wanting to flee. At some point, perhaps after a 50–70 % devaluation, the flow will stop. On the other hand, systemically important banks operating in small countries, but within a larger currency area, face a different reality. They can be emptied out within a short time frame (as has happened in a number of "Club Med" countries within the euro area). On the flip side, large, deposit-rich banks in a small currency area can be a menace to their currency if they start losing liquidity. They will then cause an instant currency crisis.

To sum up, Iceland's monetary history clearly illustrates that the country has been unable to reap the full benefits from free trade owing to stability concerns in the currency market – the free flow of capital is just beyond reach as long as the ISK is maintained. Given Iceland's small size and need for economies of scale, that is a very steep price to pay. Moreover, the country is also unable to conduct monetary policy without the use of capital controls. Last but not least, the systemic collapse of the banking system in 2008 also displays the helplessness of Icelandic policymakers to preserve financial stability without stringent controls of the capital account. Therefore, in all earnest, Iceland cannot be used as an example to advance the case for national monetary independence – quite the reverse. However, the counterargument can also be made that this is just a question of scale; the economy is just too small to sustain its own independent monetary framework.

1.5 The "Appalling Blank"

In one of the first theoretical attempts to explain business cycles, the London banker John Mills took stock of the six panics he identified in Britain from the beginning of the nineteenth century to his present in a paper titled *On Credit Cycles and the Origin of Commercial Panics,* presented to the Manchester Statistical Society in December 1867. According to Mills, business cycles are essentially cycles of credit expansion; he originated the theory that expectations or "commercial moods" were leading drivers of both booms and panics.[26] In his paper Mills made the following observation about financial panics:

> After the violence of a crisis has subsided, it becomes clear that it is not upon Capital, nor even upon legitimate commerce that the blow has fallen heaviest. As a rule, Panics do not destroy capital; they merely reveal the extent to which it has been destroyed by its betrayal into hopelessly unproductive works. . . . But there is a change. Something has passed away, and left an appalling blank behind it. . . . Broadly defined, then, Panic is the destruction, in the mind, of a bundle of beliefs.[27]

These words have a very strong resonance within the Icelandic experience. Countless foreign journalists visited Iceland after the crisis in search of visible signs of both past excesses and the present misery, to almost no avail. There were several conspicuous structures – such as Harpa and the newly built Kaupthing HQ – that stood as evidence of a boom and bust, but there was little else. Furthermore, there were very few outward signs of the human misery that was supposed to follow the financial crisis. Some journalists were creative in their dispatches, the most notable example being bestselling author Michael Lewis, who in 2009 wrote an article in *Vanity Fair* titled "Wall Street on the Tundra," with this subhead:

> Iceland's de facto bankruptcy – its currency (the krona) is kaput, its debt is 850 percent of G.D.P., its people are hoarding food and cash and blowing up their new Range Rovers for the insurance – resulted from a stunning collective madness.[28]

---

[26] These ideas were further developed by Mills's friend William Stanley Jevons into what is now known as the "sunspot theory" or the idea the arbitrary changes in expectations might influence the economy, even if they bear no relation to fundamentals. See *Business Cycles and Depressions: An Encyclopedia*. Edited by David Glasner. Published by Garland Reference Library of Social Science, 1997.

[27] John Mills. 1867 Article read before the Manchester Statistical Society, December 11, 1867, On Credit Cycles and the Origin of Commercial Panics. Transactions of the Manchester Statistical Society, session 1867–68.

[28] Lewis, Michael. (2009, April). Wall Street on the Tundra. *Vanity Fair.* http://www.vanityfair.com/culture/2009/04/iceland200904

Practically every claim made in that short statement ran counter to the facts on the ground. More fabrications followed in the article itself: there are, for example, no known cases of people blowing up luxury cars – or any car for that matter – in Iceland in the aftermath of the crisis.[29] Lewis republished this article in a bestselling book.[30]

However, the Icelandic boom was in essence an "irrational exuberance" in the stock market borne out by leveraged holding companies buying stakes in foreign companies, with limited effects on the productive capital of the country. One has to keep in mind that in every economy the sum of financial assets is always equal to zero. With the foam blown away, the structure of the economy stood intact. People would bicker about the post-crisis distribution of the financial assets – about debt owed and equity owned – and some would have to face reckoning for their leveraged spending spree during the boom. But for the nation as a whole it was just business as usual, although with purchasing power that had decreased by 25–30 % owing to post-crisis inflation. The real economy stood firm, and so did the much prized welfare system with inflation-linked benefits that provided an efficient safety net. There was also a general consensus of restoring the purchasing power of the lowest wages, and effectively raising the minimum wage, in the aftermath of the crisis to keep working people above the poverty line. Those who bore the brunt of the crisis were mostly young middle-class professionals who had recently got a job at the expanding banks or other upcoming multinationals and were laid off abruptly in the crisis, and the construction industry, which suffered an almost complete collapse. Nevertheless, there was no mass exodus from the country even though the neighboring Norway – spurred by high oil prices – was booming at the time with plenty of vacancies in the construction sector.[31]

---

[29] See a list of false statements made by Michael Lewis in: Moody, Jonas (2009, March 18). Vanity Fair's Fishy Tales From Iceland. *New York Magazine.* http://nymag.com/daily/intelligencer/2009/03/reality_check_vanity_fairs_fis.html#

[30] Vanity Fair and Graydon Carter. (2010). *The Great Hangover: 21 Tales of the New Recession from the Pages of Vanity Fair.* Harper Collins.

[31] Net immgration to Norway from Iceland from 2009 to 2015 was about 9500 people. (Statistics Iceland, www.hagstofa.is.)

In fact, many social indicators improved after the crisis, and people felt a greater sense of equality or togetherness. An old Icelandic proverb states that "a mutual shipwreck is a happy one." The "appalling blank" left behind in the mind of the population was, in effect, diminished expectations of future earnings and consumption. Now, eight years after the crisis, the boom is usually referred to as a certain state of mind; of unfounded optimism, blind ambition, or even moral lapse that was corrected. For some, it was even a liberation.

The truth of the matter is that Mills was right. A financial boom is built on the system of belief, leading to misallocation of capital. In Iceland, the same national urge, or devotion, of a small nation that expects its football team to beat England or its chess team to beat Russia, and uses 1–2 % of its GDP to build a music hall for its symphony orchestra, was also the main factor for the overzealous drive to turn the banks of the island into financial powerhouses on an international scale. This was moreover an endeavor in which the Icelandic "corporate Vikings" succeeded – getting into the big league – but only for a brief time, as the ambition overextended the capabilities of the country. (See a more detailed discussion in Sect. 3.1.) "When clients ask us why the Icelandic banks are considered to have a higher risk profile than their other European peers," explained Richard Thomas, a Merrill Lynch credit analyst in 2006, "one does not have to search hard for answers: rapid expansion, inexperienced yet aggressive management, high dependence on external funding, high gearing to equity markets, connected party opacity. In other words: too fast, too young, too much, too short, too connected, too volatile."[32]

In many ways, the phrase "collective stupidity" is fitting, although the label cannot apply solely to Icelanders. It is also apt for those who rated the economy and the banks, and funded them. There was nothing secret about the whole affair; in the spring of 2006, the country suffered a liquidity run for a couple of months in the so called Geyser Crisis, which fully exposed the weakness of the "canary in the coal mine," as Iceland was frequently referred to at the time. After that, the Icelandic banks would have to pay 30–40 basis points over comparable banks with a similar

---

[32] Thomas, Richard. (2008, March 31). *Resolving Iceland's banking "crisis"*. London: Merrill Lynch.

rating, which were hosted by larger countries. This was the premium for not having a credible lender of last resort. As it turned out, this thin spread constituted a gigantic mispricing of risk on behalf of the international financial community. (See a more detailed discussion in Sect. 2.5.)

Nevertheless, harsh as the remedy may have been and the large "appalling blank" left behind, Icelanders have come to terms with the new reality. The common view in Iceland was that the crisis – commonly referred to as "The Collapse" (*Hrunið*) in national discussion – was more than just a financial meltdown. It was an institutional collapse for the republic as a whole. Although everyone agrees that the crisis should be a catalyst for both reconstruction and change, there is no consensus on the nature and details of that change. The post-crisis Icelandic political debate has been fraught with a certain degree of restlessness and division, which at times has completely paralyzed the parliament and is rather unusual in a historical perspective. Thus, eight years after the crisis, the nation has hosts of unresolved political questions awakened by the collapse but with no clear consensus for resolution.

However, in keeping with Mills's observation that capital is destroyed during booms but not in panics, it is of utmost importance to acknowledge these losses and then allocate them to some relevant party, whether it be shareholders, bondholders, taxpayers, the respective national government, or even some supra-national body such as the EU. The current banking crisis was mistakenly viewed as a liquidity crisis in the beginning, but the view has shifted to that of a more deep-rooted solvency crisis. Thus, the original solution, to give out state guarantees against losses, was both incomplete and costly to Europe, although it might work in the USA where the banking system is smaller and less dependent on wholesale markets. Europe's bailout path risks diverting ever more resources to failing enterprises, thereby postponing and deepening the problem. Thus, the likelihood is that we have not seen the end of Europe's banking woes, and that large recapitalization is imminent in order to restore the health of the financial system on the continent. Iceland's restructuring was both painful and costly for the population, but the government did not throw good money after bad, and the taxpayers were spared a nationalization of private debts. European taxpayers may not be so lucky when the final costs are tallied.

2

The Worst Case Scenario

2.1 Midnight at the Mansion

On Saturday, October 4, 2008, Prime Minister Geir Haarde withdrew from his official residence at Pond Street in Reykjavík, Iceland's capital, an hour before midnight. Located in a serene setting by the pond at the center of the capital's old town, the ministerial mansion had its beginnings in Iceland's mountainous Westfjords. A gift from a Norwegian whaler to Iceland's first prime minister at the start of the twentieth century, the mansion is a tall, wooden structure, ornamented with elaborate carvings on the outside and filled with many rooms. After being transported to Reykjavík, it came to house Iceland's prime ministers until towards the end of World War II. Since then, its rooms have been used intermittently for important meetings and receptions. On this night, every room was occupied, and crowded.

Haarde, who was 57 at the time, was heading for a meeting in the Althing, Iceland's parliament, just a few blocks away. He walked without handlers or bodyguards, as is customary in Iceland – and he was in a hurry. But there was no escaping the mob of journalists gathered at the

© The Author(s) 2016
Á. Jónsson, H. Sigurgeirsson, *The Icelandic Financial Crisis*,
DOI 10.1057/978-1-137-39455-2_2

bottom of the mansion's steps. Like everyone else in Iceland, they expected Haarde to speak.

The media had been camping out in front of the mansion all weekend. There was nowhere else to go for answers. The residence had become a makeshift crisis control center, and most of the government's decisionmakers had holed up inside the house. The press had watched all the major bigwigs in Iceland come and go: labor union representatives, business leaders, bankers, pension fund managers, central bankers, lawyers, economists, and every politician who counted. On their way out, some were discreet while others paused for comment. Nevertheless, the information gathered by journalists did not quite add up to a coherent news story. Iceland's leaders seemed to have widely differing views of what was happening inside the mansion – and of the master plan that would save the Republic from an impending disaster.

Many wondered if the leadership was capable of overcoming the crisis. Haarde was a man with a sound educational background in economics and international relations from American universities, but a rather lackluster political profile. Generally, he was considered indecisive and conflict-averse. Critics maintained that his preferred policy approach was to wait optimistically for change without intervention. Prior to his tenure as prime minister he had chaired the center-right Independence Party and served as Minister of Finance, but the party's identity was still defined by the old chairman, Davíð Oddsson, who served as prime minister from 1991 until 2004.

Oddsson's profile was the opposite of Haarde's: he was decisive, opinionated, controversial, and enjoyed steadfast loyalty from Independence stalwarts. One quote defined his attitude toward his successor. "How can you take a house-trained cat and make it into a lion?" he reputedly quipped when Haarde won the top government post.[1] Comfortable in his perch as Governor of the Central Bank of Iceland (CBI), Oddsson still cast a long shadow over Iceland's business and identity. Meanwhile, as the crisis reached a climax, the nation hoped the house cat had transformed into a lion.

---

[1] Jónsson, Ásgeir. (2009). *Why Iceland?: How One of the World's Smallest Countries Became the Meltdown's Biggest Casualty.* McGraw Hill Professional. p. 146.

A lion was needed, as panic reminiscent of the Great Depression swept across the island. On Friday, October 3, a business professor from the University of Iceland declared on record that the financial system had "defaulted" and the banks would be closed over the weekend.[2] Prime Minister Haarde and Governor Oddsson immediately disputed the claim, but the uproar could not be quelled. People desperate for hard cash spilled into the streets and lined up in front of the banks. On a typical Friday, about 200 million Icelandic krónur (ISK), the equivalent of €1.3 million, could be expected to leave the banks' vaults; on October 3, 5.5 billion in ISK banknotes (€37 million) left the bank branches, representing a 45 % increase in currency circulation in just a day. At the same time, foreign transactions had all but ceased. Small riots had broken out on the eastern edge of the island when Polish workers seeking their wages from a local bank were denied payments in euros. Police and fire brigades were called out to restore order.

Grocery stores were jammed with hoarders who anticipated a shortage of foreign reserves to import necessities. Some residents, desperate to find shelters for their money, bought up rare wines, Cognac, Rolex watches, and even luxury apartments. Not surprisingly, grocery chains welcomed the onrush of business; Bónus, the largest grocery chain, bombed the media with calls for customers to "stock up" that first October weekend. One blogger compared the frenetic scene to "the day before nuclear winter."

Reports from foreign media provided no comfort. "Iceland Is Frozen" and "Iceland Is Bankrupt" were typical headlines in the British weekend editions. Iceland's business journals reported that the credit default swap (CDS) spreads on two of the major banks, Kaupthing and Glitnir, stood near 2500 basis points; the third, Landsbanki, had shot up to 3000. All the banks' bonds were trading on the expectation of default. The rumors were plentiful, and dire: banks would not open on Monday morning; Iceland, the nation, was indeed bankrupt.

---

[2] The comments were made by Gylfi Magnússon, an associate professor of business at the University of Iceland, in a news interview on Friday, October 3, on the Icelandic National Broadcasting Service.

On Sunday, no one yet knew what face Haarde would show. The media were just as impatient as the rest of the country. Despite the promise of news to be heard around the world, disappointment grew as the night progressed. An autumn storm was sweeping through the capital, straight in from the Atlantic. Umbrellas gave no shelter to the furious downpour and wind that blew the rain sideways. Other than the media huddle, Reykjavik's streets were all but abandoned. Prime Minister Haarde felt so sorry for the journalists that he called in a bus to provide a bit of shelter.

Haarde refused all interview requests over the weekend. In fact, there were no forthcoming explanations of the crisis at all. With the weekend drawing to a close, the frustration and tension reached boiling point amid the soggy pack of reporters outside Haarde's residence.

So when they at last cornered the prime minister an hour before midnight, the questions came down harder than the rain. Was it true that Iceland was going to seek shelter by asking for a fast-track membership to the European Union (EU)? Were the foreign assets of the pension funds going to be transferred home to shore up the banks? Had both the Federal Reserve ('the Fed') and the European Central Bank (ECB) refused to lend money to Iceland? Was Iceland going to seek help from Russia, or even the International Monetary Fund (IMF)? Would the banks be able to open in the morning?

Haarde's first response was a shake of the head. Then, bowing at last to the pressure, he made a statement that stunned the nation. "This weekend has delivered such good results that no special action is needed," he said.

The incredulous reporters demanded clarification. Haarde quickly recoiled, and declared that he needed rest. "I haven't really had a decent breakfast yet," he protested, delivering an anticlimax for the ages. For many Icelanders, that tossed-off remark, the most rank of understatements, could never be forgotten or forgiven. The house cat had not transformed into a ferocious defender of the nation. Haarde's reputation was damaged beyond repair.

The astounded journalists retreated; but instinct drew many of them back. Sure enough, a taxi pulled up to the mansion a little past midnight. Out stepped three well-tailored Englishmen, financial experts from J.P. Morgan UK, who had flown in that afternoon at the request of the governor of the CBI – Davíð Oddsson. They had been sequestered at CBI headquarters, and now they hurried up the steps to meet with Iceland's cabinet, although technically that body was in conference until 2 a.m.

Iceland had a coalition government; after parliamentary elections in 2007, the Independence Party partnered with the Social Democratic Alliance. Adding to the confusion and desperation was the fact that Social Democratic Alliance leader and foreign minister, Ingibjörg Sólrún Gísladóttir, was seriously ill with cancer. In addition, there was to some extent institutional rivalry between the CBI and the Financial Supervisory Authority (FSA), which can be sourced in part to interparty tensions. The Independence Party looked to the CBI, which was under the authority of the prime minister's office as well as the governorship of the party's former chairman. The Social Democratic Alliance turned to the FSA, which was under their power via the Ministry of Trade and Commerce.

Yet by October 3, the CBI and the FSA were drawing the same conclusions about the crisis and its resolution. Officials from both institutions spent the weekend trying to coax Haarde into taking decisive action. The three banks on the edge of the precipice had all laid out plans for the government, each of which included some kind of merger between them and a loan from the foreign reserves. But the reserves were hopelessly inadequate to cover even a single bailout, let alone three. The prime minister listened and asked questions, but gave no orders. The financial authorities found his inaction just as bewildering as the media did. By Sunday night, FSA director Jónas Fr. Jónsson had left the mansion in despair over the lack of decisiveness. It was then that Oddsson, who was nothing if not tenacious, summoned the J.P. Morgan experts to see if they could chart a course of action. He knew from long experience that his fellow countrymen would much rather listen to outside advice – especially from reputed foreign experts who could not be accused of bias. The obvious had to be pointed out and accepted.

2.2   The Botched Bailout

The unraveling had begun on September 23, when Bayerische Landesbank (BL) refused to roll over loans to Glitnir amounting to €150 million. The justification was that the CBI had recently borrowed

€300 million from BL and Iceland had reached its credit threshold. The same day, the Scandinavian bank Nordea broke off negotiations with Glitnir in relation to the acquisition of the Icelandic bank's Norwegian subsidiary, which it had been trying to sell for some time. Simultaneously, Deutsche Bank slashed Glitnir's credit line by €500 million.

Suddenly, Glitnir was facing payments of €600 million, which would come due between October 13 and 15, when all funding markets would be closed. The bank's only option was to appeal to the CBI on September 25 for an emergency loan of €600 million. The size of Glitnir's balance sheet was about 2.5 times the Icelandic gross domestic product (GDP), and the significance of its request can be grasped by considering that it represented nearly a quarter of the CBI's €2.6 billion in total foreign reserves.

The CBI rejected Glitnir's loan request, but made a counteroffer. The CBI would take a 75 % equity stake in the bank for the same amount on September 28. Hard though this negotiation was, Glitnir's main shareholders knew that the wall pressed against their backs was even harder. They agreed at the last minute, but formal acceptance was subject to confirmation at an October 11 shareholders' meeting. The actual transaction would have to wait until then.

The takeover backfired dramatically. When the market closed on September 26, Glitnir's total market value was about €1.5 billion. Once the forced sale was negotiated, the bank's shareholders were left with 25 % of the stake, valued at €70 million, which roughly amounted to an 85 % haircut. They were not amused. The largest stake – about 32 % – belonged to a company under the control of retail mogul Jón Ásgeir Jóhannesson. The next day he declared on record that the takeover was "the biggest bank robbery in Iceland's history." It was, furthermore, a political "vendetta" waged by CBI governor Oddsson. Jóhannesson insisted he would vote against the deal at the shareholders' meeting.[3] The two had a long history of conflict. Indeed, Oddsson had once referred to Jóhannesson as a "street hooligan," and sought to curtail his business activities in Iceland, most notably by proposing legislation in March 2004 that would have prohibited any single agent from owning more than 25 %

---

[3] Þjóðnýting óhugnanleg ("Nationalization horrifying"). (2008, September 30). *Fréttablaðið*, front page. http://timarit.is/view_page_init.jsp?issId=278421

of a media company.[4] This proposal was vetoed by the president (and will be discussed in Chap. 5).

The specifics of the deal did not hold up to the scrutiny of international financial markets. It was clear that Glitnir's liquidity needs in foreign currency would soon outstrip CBI's reserves. The takeover deal was contingent on either Glitnir or the Icelandic republic tapping outside funding markets. But these markets would be closed when the deal became official and Glitnir's outstanding debts came due.

Meanwhile, Glitnir's woes wreaked havoc on the credibility of Landsbanki and Kaupthing; did these two giants have similar funding problems lurking beneath their glittering surfaces? It was also known that both banks had loaned Glitnir's main shareholders considerable sums of money on the value of the stock. Thus, the 85 % equity wipe-off all but guaranteed large loan losses.

The currents stirring up global financial unrest also affected the Glitnir situation. The takeover was to an extent a gamble that depended on foreign affairs breaking in Iceland's favor. After Lehman Brothers defaulted on September 15, authorities in the USA reversed policy and pledged to buy bad assets in the banking system to maintain confidence in the credit markets. Once the Emergency Economic Stabilization Act (EESA) was announced, worldwide markets staged a recovery. On Friday, September 19, the Dow Jones newswire published a report headlined "U.S. Plan Lifts Iceland." The report quoted economists at both Danske Bank and Nordea, who opined that small, heavily leveraged economies would most profit from the bill.

No nation was smaller and more heavily leveraged than Iceland. Authorities in Iceland heaved a sigh of relief when the US Senate passed EESA on September 28. However, the House of Representatives voted down the legislation the very next day. The bear was again set free from its cage.

---

[4] Bill on the amendment of the Act on radio no. 53/2000 and the Act on competition no. 8/1993. http://www.althingi.is/altext/130/s/1525.html

Bergmann, E.(2014) *Iceland and the International Financial Crisis: Boom, Bust and Recovery*, Palgrave Macmillan.

That same Monday, the Dow Jones Industrial Index fell 777 points, the largest drop in its history. Markets worldwide toppled back into chaos. Congress voted on EESA a second time on Friday, October 3, and the bill passed into law. But the week between the two votes saw the fate of Icelandic banks all but sealed.[5]

The carnage that ensued began with ratings downgrades. The CBI's botched Glitnir takeover led to a downgrade of Iceland's sovereign debt; ratings agencies noted that the government was now at risk of assuming massive foreign liabilities accumulated by the private banks. Moody's took Glitnir down three notches, from A2 to Baa2, on September 30. This downgrade triggered covenants in loans and credit lines, which were contingent on the maintenance of certain ratings. Glitnir, which originally needed €600 million in liquid funds, watched the hole deepen to more than €2 billion. Kaupthing and Landsbanki also suffered downgrades and liquidity evaporation.

Iceland, for all the wrong reasons, had the world's attention. The downgrades had residual effects abroad. Many British citizens had put savings into online accounts offered by Kaupthing's British subsidiary, Kaupthing Singer & Friedlander (KSF), and Landsbanki's UK branch. Now they began to withdraw their money in fear of more bad news.

On Friday, October 3, the UK Financial Services Authority (FSA) demanded a total of €2.3 billion in transfers from Landsbanki and Kaupthing to the Bank of England. The same day, the ECB placed a €1 billion margin call on the collateralized lending of Glitnir and Landsbanki in Luxembourg. The call was triggered by the rating downgrades; now the ECB threatened to reject all Icelandic assets unless they would deliver cash. Then, over the weekend, the British press published a raft of headlines proclaiming doomsday for Iceland. Before Saturday breakfast was over, customers of Icesave, Landsbanki's online savings account brand operating in the UK and the Netherlands, were logging on to

---

[5] Numerous reports have been written on the situation in the global financial markets – and in Iceland –between the fall of Lehman Brothers and the EESA's passage. For example: pp. 6–7 of the so-called Liikanen report, Erkki Liikanen (2012, October). High-level Expert Group on reforming the structure of the EU banking sector, Final Report; pp. 436–37 of Paulson, Henry (2010). *On the Brink: Inside the Race to Stop the Collapse of the Global Financial System.* New York: Business Plus.; Shockwaves that took Europe by surprise. (2008, October 4). *The Financial Times.*

2 The Worst Case Scenario

withdraw their money. On Sunday night, it was estimated that about €5 billion were needed as an emergency liquidity infusion for the Icelandic banks to keep their doors open in the following week. Iceland's foreign reserves were only €2.6 billion at the time – barely half of the needed amount. Thus, the attempted takeover of Glitnir had triggered a systematic run on the Icelandic financial system.

As if matters were not bad enough, the CBI was also facing unexpected physical limitations on its ability to print the domestic currency and deliver liquidity in physical form to the banks. Withdrawals rates were brisk at Icelandic branches on September 29, in the wake of the botched government takeover of Glitnir, and gathered steam as the week progressed. By Friday, banknotes in circulation had increased by 53 %. In fact, the CBI's note supply was almost exhausted; there were very few 5000 krona notes (the largest denomination at the time) left on the island.[6] Icelandic banknotes are printed in the UK, and new orders usually take two to three months to deliver. Branch managers had little recourse beyond praying that the clocks would jump forward to the 4 p.m. closing hour. Before then, many resorted to rationing their note supplies.

2.3   A Rejection from the US Fed

The predicament faced by Icelandic authorities was far worse than imagined, even by the most pessimistic journalists outside the prime minister's residence that Sunday night. By then, it was apparent that the CBI could not serve as a lender of last resort for an oversized banking system by printing an illiquid currency that served as a legal tender for 330,000 people. What the banks really needed was liquidity support to meet foreign obligations. The only way to secure that liquidity was for the Icelandic government to borrow in international capital markets and relend the funds to the banks. Yet that option was closed off as well – both in private and public markets for foreign funds. Nor could the Icelandic taxpayers

---

[6] Central Bank of Iceland (2009). *Fjármálastöðugleiki (Financial Stability)*. http://www.sedlabanki.is/library/Skraarsafn/Fjármálastöðugleiki/FS_2009.pdf

recapitalize such a large system without the country taking on a crushing debt load.

The nation was considering the most desperate measures to save the financial system. Even the Icelandic pension funds were considered as a source of liquidity. The funds owned about €3.5 billion in foreign assets. There was some discussion of them cashing in their assets and selling the proceeds to the CBI for ISK, which would in turn lend the hard currency to the banks. Yet even with the funds thrown into the ring, there was no guarantee that the rescue could work.

Still there was no help forthcoming from abroad: the ECB and US Federal Reserve had rejected Iceland's official pleas for help. On September 24, the Fed announced $30 billion in swaps with four central banks – Australia, Denmark, Sweden, and Norway – to address "elevated pressures" in their currency markets. Iceland's omission from this list was eye-catching, since it was now the only Western European country without a line from the Fed. What was more, the Fed continued to offer these lines to nations around the globe, but CBI officials knew this only by reading the newspapers. Following the Fed's implicit (and privately explicit) decision to wash its hands of Iceland, the nation's currency market effectively froze; the ISK had no bidders. By October 3, the traffic across the CBI's currency desk dwindled to small, essential trades that facilitated the purchase of food, medical supplies, and gasoline.

The Fed's explanation for the rejection was blunt: "Iceland's financial system was so large in proportion to its economy that a currency swap agreement would have to be larger than the Federal Reserve considered itself able to commit to."[7] By most readings, this is the "too-big-to-save" argument. But it had a dire converse in this case. Was Iceland in fact too small and isolated to save?

The island nation of 330,000 citizens is far away from Europe, both geographically and politically. It is not part of the EU or any regional block that risked contagion during its collapse. Culturally, of course, it is a

---

[7] Central Bank of Iceland. (2008, October 9). *Currency swap agreements and attempts to reinforce the foreign exchange reserves.* http://www.cb.is/publications/news/news/2008/10/10/Currency-swap-agreements-and-attempts-to-reinforce-the-foreign-exchange-reserves-/

2 The Worst Case Scenario   45

Nordic country, but that meant little economically in 2008. In May of that year, the CBI had secured swap lines with three Nordic central banks, at $500 million apiece.[8] However, during the Icesave dispute with Britain, it was revealed that Norway's bank was the only entity to allow – reluctantly – Iceland to draw on this line. Sweden and Denmark refused. Far from having a severe impact on the Scandinavian markets, Iceland's downfall brought about opportunities for bargaining. After the collapse, Nordic banks acquired Icelandic subsidiaries at rock-bottom prices.

Iceland had long assumed that it had a special relationship with the USA. Icelanders belong to the group of nations claiming to have fathered the true discoverer of North America, the early eleventh-century explorer Leif Erikson. Geographically located between continental Europe and North America, Iceland became a strategically important location for US military presence during World War II in barring Nazi Germany from the Western Hemisphere. The USA was the first country to recognize Iceland's independence from Denmark in 1944, and five years later Iceland – a country with no army – became a founding member of the North Atlantic Treaty Organization (NATO). The USA and Iceland signed a bilateral defense agreement in 1951, according to which the USA would obtain basing rights for its forces in Iceland in return for providing for Iceland's defense on behalf of NATO. Iceland held great strategic significance for the USA during the Cold War. Its position at the center of the GIUK gap was critical enough for the Americans to strengthen Naval Air Station Keflavik (NASKEF) after World War II's conclusion, as a means to now restrict – rather than supplement – the power of the Soviet Union. In return for helping to keep Soviet nuclear submarines out of the greater Atlantic, Iceland extracted economic and political aid from post-war America, most notably during the Cold War

---

[8] Central Bank of Iceland (2004, May 16). *The Central Bank of Iceland concludes swap facility arrangements.* http://www.cb.is/publications/news/news/2008/05/16/The-Central-Bank-of-Iceland-concludes-swap-facility-arrangements/

with the British navy in the early 1970s. Iceland also enlisted in the coalition of willing nations during the 2003 invasion of Iraq.[9]

But by 2008, the Cold War was a memory, and NASKEF had closed in 2006. The special relationship had ended. Icelandic authorities even looked towards the east for new friends, approaching Russia at the onset of its financial crisis, albeit without success.

Despite the Fed's rejection, Icelandic bankers always believed the ECB would enact a rescue, as German banks had the most to lose from an Icelandic banking collapse. Germans had effectively underwritten the Icelandic banking expansion. By 2008, Iceland's banks held about $46 billion in wholesale debt, of which $21 billion was owed to German banks.[10] There was, moreover, a very close strategic alliance between Deutsche Bank and Kaupthing. Beyond this, the cultural ties between the two countries remained strong.

Ultimately, the Germans and the ECB also remained hands-off during the crisis. The reasons have never been wholly explained, but the fact remains that the world of European central bankers is extremely close-knit. And by 2008, Iceland's banks had made themselves distinctly unpopular in this insular community.

Iceland's rapid expansion into foreign markets had been built on aggressive investment banking fueled by wholesale funds. When the first clouds of the economic crisis rolled in during the autumn of 2007, Iceland's bankers had shifted their energies into online deposit funding. This tactical move had the feeling of a raid on a quiet seashore town and generated great resentment among domestic banks on the continent. While maintaining branch networks and payment mechanisms, they were now easily outbid by Internet upstarts from a small island. Prior to 2007, Europe's retail deposit market was a sleepy, cozy province, coddled by years of minimal competition. The Dutch bank ING had started branchless Internet banking under the name ING Direct, but when the Icelanders swooped in, they drove up marginal costs of funding and indirectly closed liquidity taps at perhaps the worst possible moment.

---

[9] The White House (2003, March 27). Who are the current coalition members? http://georgewbush-whitehouse.archives.gov/infocus/iraq/news/20030327-10.html

[10] Hay, George (2008, October 27). Frozen assets. *Breaking Views*.

Moreover, regulators were suspicious of any aggressive investment banks funding themselves with government-guaranteed retail deposits (as is the case with Goldman Sachs's recent foray into online deposit funding). Wholesale investors are reputedly sophisticated, being able to invest without state supervision. If they wanted to roll the dice by funding investment activities, it was to be at their own risk without using funds from foreign depositors.

There was more. Since Iceland was a member of the European Economic Area (EEA), its bonds remained eligible as collateral in the Europeans' monetary system. Nevertheless, the ECB had reservations about both the quantity and quality of the assets the Icelandic banks were pledging. The ECB's reservations were not exclusive to Iceland's activity, though; many European banks were also improvising ways to obtain central bank funding. But the Icelanders' style was especially bothersome and unpopular. Their banks behaved like motherless lambs, stealing milk from other ewes and being kicked back. They could not obtain liquidity backup at home, like most other commercial banks, and the CBI could not serve as a lender of last resort. Iceland's currency was the smallest in the world and the CBI was free to print as many ISK as it pleased. But even an ocean filled with ISK was of limited use to the banks, since 70 % of their funding needs derived from foreign currency.[11]

The shift into online retail funding had bolstered the Icelandic banks' stature in the United Kingdom, Iceland's largest single trading partner. The banks had €15 billion outstanding in foreign Internet savings accounts, €8 billion of which were owed to British savers. Now this strength was turning against the banks. In the first days of October the Internet accounts were under a run and hemorrhaging liquidity. The British reaction to the turmoil in Icelandic banks quickly became hostile. Rather than commit any funds to their rescue, they piled on and demanded cash from the Icelanders.

---

[11] The Financial Supervisory Authority. (2007, February). *Reikningsskil í erlendri mynt (Accounting in foreign currency)*. http://www.fme.is/media/utgefid-efni/08_03_2007_Reikningsskil-i-erlendri-mynt_Skyrsla-FME-um-uppgjor-i-erlendri-mynt.pdf

Around supper on Sunday, October 5, a fuming Gordon Brown, then Prime Minister of the UK, phoned Haarde to vent over an alleged money transfer made by Kaupthing out of the UK and into Iceland through the subsidiary Kaupthing Singer & Friedlander (KSF).[12] This accusation proved to be baseless – there was an outstanding loan from KSF to Kaupthing, but no new money was being transferred. Still, it was effective ammunition at the peak of the crisis. Brown pleaded with Haarde to seek IMF assistance. It was the first and last time the two men spoke to each other directly.[13]

So, gathered in the prime minister's residence on October 5 was a group of very bewildered cabinet ministers. It was as if the world had turned against them. Being under a systemic bank run was one thing – the same could be said about almost all other Western countries in the wake of the Lehman default. But to be singled out as the one country to not receive help from the US Fed was another. However, facing very aggressive and simultaneous demands for cash from the ECB and the Bank of England, the sense of abandonment was multidimensional. Not only were the banks about to go under. It was as if the central banking community had conspired against them.

2.4   The WaMu Way?

The Monday morning cabinet meeting was adjourned at 2 a.m. The J.P. Morgan advisors were blunt. Iceland was at a point of no return. The official policy of making Iceland an international financial center had failed. The banks had become too-big-to-save. There was a small glimmer of hope that the largest, Kaupthing, might survive, but Glitnir and Landsbanki were certainly doomed. The task now was not to rescue the banks from default, but rather to rescue the sovereign from the same fate.

---

[12] Bowers, S. (2012, June). "Iceland Banking collapse: Diary of a Death Spiral". *The Guardian.* https://www.theguardian.com/business/2012/jun/26/iceland-banking-collapse-diary-death-spiral
[13] Special Investigation Commission. (2010). Report of the Special Investigation Commission. Volume 7, p. 254.

Haarde's advisory council looked to the USA for a possible solution. Just ten days earlier, J.P. Morgan had purchased Washington Mutual Bank (WaMu) from the Federal Deposit Insurance Corporation (FDIC) in a secret auction for $1.9 billion, and thereby assumed the bank's secured debts and liabilities to depositors.

The FDIC had seized WaMu bank operations from the holding company Washington Mutual Inc., which was about to succumb to a bank run. WaMu Inc. sought bankruptcy protection just the day after. With this action, US regulators were enforcing a deposit guarantee scheme written into US law, which granted priority to the FDIC over other claimants, as well as the authority to directly intervene in order to prevent losses that could ultimately be borne by the taxpayer.

The WaMu takeover had been studied carefully both at the FSA, the CBI, and elsewhere in Iceland. However, now the cabinet ministers would get to know it first hand.

The J.P. Morgan representatives drew out an Icelandic version of the 'WaMu Way' on a chalkboard to get the message across. The Icelandic FSA needed to seize domestic retail branch operations from the failing banks, and thereby enforce a de facto separation of domestic and foreign operations. Domestic operations would be ring-fenced and recapitalized, while the foreign part of the holdings would go into liquidation.

This action could attain two goals: authorities could guarantee domestic deposits and ensure uninterrupted domestic retail banking operations; it would also sever any link between the sovereign and the damaged banks, effectively removing the 'too-big-to-fail' guarantee on the banks' funds that posed the immediate threat of national bankruptcy.

After the presentation finished, Haarde asked the Morgan representatives to leave the room and wait outside. They were called back directly for some questions. Haarde kept the real facts concerning the severity of the crisis solely within his tight circle of advisors until the last hours. Most attendees did not realize the full scale of the troubles until the Morgan advisors set up their chalkboard. Faced with the truth, many experienced shock. Or, perhaps, a moment of clarity.

The three J.P. Morgan advisors left the residence. Having come on short notice, they were the bearers of bad tidings and their primary role in Reykjavík was to lend credibility to the CBI's and FSA's contingency planning. They would work as advisors to the CBI and the FSA for the remainder of the week. They would, however, advocate applying the emergency legislation to partition the banks in a manner that differed from Iceland's ultimate crisis prescription (see Chap. 4).

In any event, on Wednesday, October 8, the British government requested that J.P. Morgan pull their advisors out of the country immediately and cease assistance to the Icelandic government. That was just hours before UK authorities invoked a terrorist legislation to freeze Icelandic assets. However, J.P. Morgan refused to acquiesce to that request.

Meanwhile, Iceland's decision makers realized they could not simply copy the motions of the FDIC in the USA. There were substantial regulatory differences between the WaMu situation and that of the Icelandic banks. Iceland had become a member of the EEA in 1994, which today effectively amounts to backdoor access to the greater EU (Norway, Liechtenstein, and Iceland are the only remaining non-EU member states within the EEA). The flow of goods, services, labor, and capital among member countries was unimpeded, and those countries in turn worked EU directives and regulations into their legal frameworks. Moreover, the EEA agreement entails a "passport" provision for financial institutions, and it was on this basis, combined with excellent credit ratings, that the Icelandic banks had achieved their phenomenal foreign expansion.

However, the EU legal framework did not give priority to deposits over bonds. In fact, a large and vital part of bank funding in Europe had been through the issuance of senior unsecured bonds that held equal status, or *pari passu*, to deposits. These were the instruments the Icelandic banks had used to obtain the wholesale funding needed to grow outside the limited domestic base (Icelandic deposits constituted only about 20–30 % of their total liabilities). However, the *pari passu* clause, written into European law, had never been seriously tested or questioned since the last major European bank default in June 1974, when the German Herstatt Bank went bankrupt.[14]

A concise summary of the European bond market playbook (prior to the Lehman collapse) appeared on March 12, 2008, just days before the

---

[14] Basel Committee on Banking Supervision. (2004, April). *Bank Failures in Mature Economies*. Working Paper No. 13. http://www.bis.org/publ/bcbs_wp13.pdf

Bear Stearns rescue. The report, written by Richard Thomas, a research analyst at Merrill Lynch, was titled "Eschatological. Time to go long."[15]

> ***The simple fact: banks don't default*** *Because the simple fact is: banks rarely default. Northern Rock, IKB, Landesbank Sachsen, Banca Italease – all point to this one fact that is supported by decades of empirical evidence. Yes, banks do fail – they fail more than corporates do, hardly surprising given their high level of gearing and the perverse incentive structure under which they operate (by which we mean banks or rather their managements have relatively little to lose by taking lots of risk and quite a lot to gain). [. . .] Will it be different this time? The evidence in Europe so far is: no. Viewed ex ante, Northern Rock was not a systemically important bank. But it became one when it failed. [. . .] Could we have another run on a European bank? We are skeptical though it is something that we must consider. In the UK, the run on the Northern Rock was the first in 150 years.*
>
> *Banking crises actually follow a well-trodden path and timeline. [. . .] The first thing that a bank will preserve is its liquidity (banks disappear because they go illiquid not because they are insolvent), whilst a plan is made to deal with the bad assets, either by writing them down or by putting them into a (usually) Government sponsored vehicle (a bad bank). If confidence is poor, the Government may step in and start to guarantee deposits explicitly. Some form of recapitalization may be needed too at this point, if there is a chance that the bank can survive on a stand alone basis. Or it can be taken over by a stronger domestic or foreign partner. In serious instances of systemic stress, the Government may have to buy certain banking assets or replace them with Government paper so that the bank can continue to tick over. Nationalization is the very last resort when all other solutions have completely failed.*

In sum, the "well trodden path" of European banking crisis leads to a clear destination, at which senior bonds are fully insured whatever measures are taken against the issuer. This has, in fact, pretty much held up on the European continent so far. Holders of senior bank bonds have turned out to be safer than holders of sovereign debt; the recurrent Greece crisis is a salient manifestation of this fact. Thus, the *pari passu* status of senior bonds and deposits in Europe had extended a de facto government

---

[15] Merrill Lynch (2008, March 12). *Eschatological. Time to go long.*

guarantee to wholesale funding prior to the crisis. That meant that even small banks such as Northern Rock had become too-big-to-fail.

Certainly, the same went for the three Icelandic banks, all of which were rated Aaa by Moody's just 20 months earlier in February 2007. It was the same rating held by the Icelandic republic and many continental European banks at the time. However, as Moody's explained on that occasion:

> ... *financial institutions have historically had similar, if not safer, credit risk profiles than similarly rated corporate issuers. ... Specifically, no systemically important bank in the developed world has defaulted upon its deposits since 1931 (where systemic importance is defined by a large domestic deposit share or an important role in the payments system). Moreover, no rated bank, no matter what its size, has defaulted upon local currency deposits - outside of some sovereign-related crises in the emerging markets.*[16]

By October 2008, Kaupthing, Landsbanki and Glitnir held about 70 % of the Icelandic deposit base, almost the equivalent of 80 % of Iceland's GDP. They also contained about €15 billion worth of foreign deposits, most notably the Icesave Internet savings accounts, which came with an Icelandic deposit guarantee. The nation's total GDP was €10 billion. According to EU regulation – accepted by Iceland via EEA contract – the government could not discriminate between foreign and domestic depositors. Furthermore, the banks had about €46 billion (four to five times of Icelandic GDP) worth of senior bonds that were *pari passu* with deposits. Of course, Iceland had a deposit guarantee scheme, as mandated in the European Common Market, with minimum of €20,880 for each account. The legal responsibility for this guarantee lay, as with all European nations, with the Depositors' and Investors' Guarantee Fund (DIGF). That fund, however, had only €130 million on hand. The paucity of the DIGF fund was in itself not unusual in Europe, and it would not have been problematic except that the fund did not have priority over other claimants to a default bank estate. The credibility of

---

[16] Moody's Investors Service, Global Credit Research. (2007, March). *Incorporation of Joint-Default Analysis into Moody's Bank Ratings: A Refined Methodology.* (Report number 102639).

the protection was thus contingent on the willingness of the government to support the fund against imminent payments.

This was a key hinge in the trap the Icelanders felt closing on that fateful Sunday night. In just hours, not days, Landsbanki would go under. And even while the J.P. Morgan trio considered one bank, Kaupthing, as possible salvage, the banking system as a whole was teetering on collapse. When it failed, almost the entire Icelandic deposit base would be frozen inside defaulted estates where the depositors would wait with the bond-holders for the asset recovery to materialize. Then, the government would be forced to make good on the minimum guarantee by issuing new debt.

An erosion of the domestic deposit base and an increase in government debt was one thing, but it was inconceivable that the economy could function without retail bank services, or a payment system for that matter.

So the rulebook had to be torn apart. That task fell to the Icelanders themselves.

At 8 a.m. on Monday, October 6, Haarde called a new cabinet meeting, which was also attended by the FSA director and the permanent secretary of ministry commerce. The two officials presented what would later be called the "Emergency Legislation." Behind all the chaos, locked away from the madding crowds, FSA director Jónsson and a team from the FSA, Ministry of Commerce, and outside legal counsel had worked around the clock to complete the legislation over the weekend. Actually, this legislation had been in the making since 2006, when the country had suffered through the so-called Geyser Crisis. At last, the Icelandic government was ready to listen and take decisive action.

2.5   The Geyser Warning

In early 2006, Iceland received an advance warning about the risk associated with hosting a large and international banking system and being dependent on foreign capital. This was the so-called "Geyser Crisis," a liquidity squeeze that lasted about three months.

It was a crisis born of a number of factors. For one, there had been a hiccup in the global carry trade, which led to a sharp 20–30 % depreciation of the Icelandic króna. There were also general worries: the economy was overheating, an asset bubble was in the making, and a growing trade deficit made the country too dependent on foreign inflow of capital. And then, of course, there were hedge funds taking advantage of the opportunity to short Iceland.

The Icelandic banks contributed to the crisis with their aggressive foreign expansion in the preceding year. Combined, the three banks issued €15 billion worth of new debt in 2005, an amount considerably larger than the total GDP of Iceland. These funds were drawn almost exclusively from the European MTN (medium-term note) market. General Motors created the market in the early 1970s as an extension of the commercial paper market. It had become the vehicle of choice for large companies and even governments to pay for their medium-term financing needs. MTNs are typically non-callable, unsecured, senior debt securities, with fixed coupon rates and investment-grade credit ratings that are not listed, but rather sold directly to investors.

The Icelandic banks discovered that with their excellent credit ratings they could exploit the country quotas that banks and investment funds kept in their portfolios. The quotas were maintained for assets with risk that ran counter to the international financial market, and thus incrementally decreased the total risk of their portfolio adjusted for return. Since the Icelandic sovereign was debt-free and created no need to issue foreign bonds, the quota spaces were completely empty, waiting for Icelandic banks to fill them.

With the MTN issuing in 2005, the three banks raced to capture these country quotas; ultimately, they oversupplied the European market. It was only a matter of time before investors assessed the banks as representing the same credit risk coming from the same financial system. Once their accumulated debt was totaled and compared with the GDP of Iceland, many began to wonder if the Icelanders had jumped out of their league. On November 23, 2005, the Royal Bank of Scotland issued the first credit report on Kaupthing, and the Icelandic banking system in general. The report noted that "a small number of investors had concerns about Icelandic banks," but "the applicable rating agencies remained convinced by the robustness of the major players to the system." The report highlighted the key concerns investors had about Kaupthing and the other Icelandic banks: the private equity positions, the reliance on wholesale funding, and the apparent mismatch between the maturities of assets and liabilities of the banks. Last, it was noted that Kaupthing, at the time with a balance sheet 2.5 times Iceland's GDP, was simply too large to be rescued by the sovereign.

What made the Geyser Crisis a distinctive event, however, was the intensity with which the entire world focused on a single, tiny dot on the financial map, even if the focus lasted just two months. Iceland was deemed the canary in the coal mine. As the smallest independent currency region in the world, the island had the "smallest lungs," and was expected to faint when liquidity became scarce. Its gasping would provide an early warning for the rest of the world. In this sense, Iceland became almost a natural experiment in global banking. As a result, a steady stream of analysts, prominent bankers, and journalists visited the three major banks all through 2006. News reports with garish headlines – "Iceland Melting," "Icelandic Eruption," "Hot Lava," "Geyser Crisis" – appeared daily. In the UK, the spike in news coverage created so much general interest that in a first, British Airways offered direct flights to Reykjavik to meet increased tourist demand. Such was the hothouse climate of the "Geyser Crisis" (the name was taken from Iceland's famous hot spring, Geysir, which is known for its intermittent, hot, violent eruptions).

Whether the crisis was a harbinger of bad things to come or just a deviation was a question that fueled ongoing debate. Curiously, analysts at the Danish Danske Bank played a key role. They issued a research report aptly titled "Iceland: Geyser Crisis" on March 21.[17] The report's general conclusion was that Iceland, frozen out of the international capital market, was going down in a singular financial crisis with a sharp output contraction. However, since Iceland was so small, its downfall would have little or no impact on the outside world. To demonstrate this point, Danske Bank closed all lines to Iceland, including the CBI, and refused all trading in the Icelandic króna, just prior to the report's release.

There is a strong historical link between Iceland and Denmark (the island had been a part of the Danish kingdom for more than 500 years), and many residents took offense when Danske Bank's commentary hit

---

[17] Danske Bank (2006, March 21). *Iceland: Geyser crisis.* http://www.mbl.is/media/98/398.pdf

the domestic media. The "colonial master" paradigm lingers in Iceland's collective memory, and it informs a sort of sibling rivalry that was piqued when Iceland's population received Danske Bank's analysis. It was seen as belittling, and Iceland took it personally. Public opinion shifted to the banks, which became national champions of a sort. This was an important development; prior to this scuffle, many Icelanders had harbored deep reservations about the blind ambitions of the banks, and suspicion about the motives of their owners.

If the Danske Bank analysts had been correct, it probably would have been the first time a whole country was taken down by hedge funds when waters were relatively calm in international financial markets. Two years later, however, many other nations would be facing precisely the same problems, created by their own oversized banking systems and independent currencies. Denmark, for instance, suffered the collapse of a larger housing bubble than that of Iceland, and in Q2 2008 it also became the first country in Europe to enter into recession. Danske Bank, which had followed the same reckless growth strategy as the Icelandic trio by acquiring banks in Ireland and the Scandinavian countries, had to be bailed out by the Danish government in 2008, with extra funding from the US Fed.

The Icelandic banks saw their CDS spreads rise sharply during the crisis or from 20bp in October 2005 to about 60–70bp in July 2006. But then the dust settled: that summer the Icelandic banks' bond spreads stabilized, but at a level 30–40 basis points higher than banks with a similar rating. This was the risk premium awarded by the financial market, which acknowledged the aggressive business models and the lack of support from their central bank and government (i.e. a credible lender of last resort). As it turned out, there were a lot of takers for their debt issues in the months ahead.

Bankers and policymakers claimed they had taken a lot of lessons from the mini-crisis. However, the critical takeaway – that the banks, too big relative to the country, should slow down or stop expanding their balance sheets – was not recognized. Thus the Geyser Crisis was a warning that went unheeded by Iceland and global financial markets at large. Nonetheless, the "canary in the coal mine" label stuck. Icelandic asset markets – the currency, equities, or bonds – would become the favorite vehicles for hedge funds of all stripes to "express an opinion" on global financial conditions, by either going long or short on Iceland.

The lesson the bankers did take from this episode, however, was that they needed to diversify and draw out the maturity of the funding base. Hence, the *Icelandics*, as the banks were usually referred to in the City – the financial district of London – would stay clear of the European MTN market. Kaupthing issued bonds in Japan, Canada, Mexico, Australia, and the USA. Landsbanki began to offer online savings accounts – Icesave – with great initial success. Thus, when the real crisis hit in 2007, the banks were prepared in the sense that their whole funding was much more diverse and with a longer maturity than was typical of banks on both sides of the Atlantic. That diversification kept them alive for a year into credit crisis, despite being locked out of international capital markets from September 2007 onwards.

Many in the banking community viewed the crisis of 2006 as a necessary evil that would kick-start reforms and make them stronger and better. They inferred that they had faced a test and passed. So as 2006 came to an end, there was undeniable hubris in the banks as they planned further growth abroad. The international financial community seemed to have reached a similar conclusion about Iceland's resilience. By the autumn of 2006, many of the big global players – for example Barclays and Standard Chartered – were willing to lend the main stakeholders of the Icelandic banks huge sums of money on the value of their equity into holding companies. The proceeds would be used to transform these holding companies into multinational investment vehicles with great ambitions, as will be discussed in Chap. 3. In 2006, the Icelandic banks had assets roughly – seven to eight times the domestic economy, but this ratio would rise to about ten times GDP by the depreciation of the krona in 2008, as many of the banks' assets were denominated in foreign currency.

What the Icelandic bankers failed to grasp was that the virtuous cycle of risk diversification through foreign acquisitions had been reversed during the Geyser Crisis, and could not be turned back around. Instead of becoming more "international" by acquiring foreign banking assets, they simply became larger and larger regional banks, since every foreign asset they touched became, instantly, "Icelandic," that is, classified as part of the indigenous financial system.

Ben Ashby, a fixed income analyst at J.P. Morgan, drew the following conclusions on March 24, 2006:[18]

> *Interesting thing statistics. Obviously as the Icelanders have expanded abroad they have bought more overseas assets, in the form of other financial institutions. By definition, financial institutions have leveraged balance sheets. Obviously as purchases by Icelandic-domiciled firms these get aggregated to become "Icelandic" overseas obligations – even though some of these businesses have previously had nothing to do with Iceland.*
>
> *We would imagine that if Scotland ever goes independent then RBS and HBOS would have a rather similar effect on Scotland's GDP. Or perhaps closer to home just the City of Westminster or more specifically Curzon Street and Berkeley Square on a standalone basis relative to the rest of London. What we do see as an issue is that when these firms do buy anything overseas quite often it will get reclassified to Icelandic risk by certain financial institutions' risk departments.*

One of the most tested principles – or stylized facts – in banking is that international banks are only international when alive and well; as soon as they get sick or die, they become a domestic concern.

This was the bitter fact the Icelanders faced on Sunday night, October 5, 2008.

2.6   A Force Majeure Action

In early 2006, the foreign currency reserves of the CBI were around €1 billion; during the hottest days of the Geyser crisis, that amount was equivalent to the total turnover on the Icelandic currency market. In other words, the foreign reserves were sufficient to defend the ISK against hedge fund attacks for a day or two. The CBI did double its reserves with a new bond issue in the autumn of 2006. But that did not fundamentally

---

[18] Ben Ashby (2006, March 24). Icelandic banks. Typical investor Q&A, and our response. *European Credit Research*. J.P. Morgan.

preclude the government's foreign currency holdings from being far below what was needed to ensure the liquidity of its currency area, or even give the appearance that reserves would be sufficient in a time of crisis. This was perhaps not surprising, given that neither rating agencies nor the financial market in general had placed any importance on foreign currency reserves prior to the crisis of 2008. In fact, when Moody's upgraded its rating of the Icelandic republic for long-term debt in foreign currency to Aaa in 2002, the upgrade was, in part, a result of a change in the company's methodology, which assigned equal footing to the ability to pay in foreign currency *and* in domestic currency.[19] The implicit assumption was that Iceland could access the private capital market at any time should the need for foreign currency arise; thus stock-keeping foreign liquidity was unnecessary.

There was also little change in the government's policy towards the banks. In February 2005, Prime Minister Halldór Ásgrímsson, Geir Haarde's predecessor, publicly floated the idea of making the nation into a new global financial center. To achieve this, Ásgrímsson maintained, "we have to have our goals clear and keep on going on the same road and show the same daring that we have shown thus far." The initiative received overwhelming popular support. In November 2005, a special committee was appointed to draft actionable proposals. The 12-person committee included three permanent secretaries (of the finance ministry, prime ministry, and ministry of trade and commerce), one central bank governor (out of three), and the chairman of the board of Kaupthing. Taking Switzerland as a role model, the committee agreed on some general proposals and published them in October 2006. By and large, they recommended further expansion of the financial services sector.[20] When Haarde assumed office as prime minister in May 2007, the policy declaration of his coalition government unequivocally

---

[19] Moody's Investors Service (2002, October 20). *Rating Action: Moody's upgrades foreign currency ratings of Australia, New Zealand and Iceland to Aaa.*

[20] The Prime Minister's Committee on International Financial Operations (2006, October). *Alþjóðleg fjármálastarfsemi á Íslandi. (International Financial Operations in Iceland).* https://www.forsaetisraduneyti.is/media/frettir/Skyrsla.pdf

announced that the financial sector "can continue to grow in Iceland and break new ground in competition with other market areas."[21]

Behind the scenes, there was evidence of lasting impacts at the FSA and CBI. The Geyser Crisis and uncomfortable questions posed by foreign investors and analysts led both institutions to chart possible options should the banks fail. There had been a broad political consensus on augmenting the FSA's powers to intervene and effect change on the operations and financial structure of the banks. In 2004 – at the very start of the banking expansion abroad – a special committee of high-ranking officials was tasked with formulating authoritative responses to "possible difficulties in the financial market." But it wasn't until the advent of the Geyser Crisis that the committee managed to wrap up its protracted review process; its final report was delivered in February 2006. It stressed the need for coordination between various administrative units and strongly recommended legislative amendments that would expand the FSA's power to intervene in the event of a banking crisis. The report was published on the website of the prime minister's office.[22] But as soon as the crisis abated, the political will to push the matter further seemed to evaporate.

However, a new director at the Icelandic FSA, Jónas Fr. Jónsson, who assumed office in July 2005, was very keen to change the legislative framework. Already at the time of the report in February 2006, the FSA had drafted legislation providing emergency powers to the FSA. In April 2008, Jónsson presented to a cooperation committee of the FSA, CBI, and three ministries a list of necessary policies for contingency planning – named "the unappetizing menu." He suggested that a bill on contingency measures should be concluded, referring to the draft of 2006 as a starting point. During the summer of 2008, officials from the institutions of the cooperation committee worked on a second draft, but it was unclear whether or when such a proposal could be submitted for legislation.

---

[21] Prime Minister's Office (2007, May 24). *Policy Statement 2007: Policy Declaration of the Government of the Independence Party and the Social Democratic Alliance 2007.* https://eng.forsaetisraduneyti.is/news-and-articles/nr/2646

[22] Consultation group on preparedness for possible difficulties in financial markets. (2006, February 17). Viðbúnaður stjórnvalda vegna hugsanlegra erfiðleika á fjármálamarkaði. (A contingency plan for possible difficulties in financial markets). https://www.forsaetisraduneyti.is/media/frettir/Skilabref,_greinargerd_og_samkomulag.doc

The Icelandic banks were already under immense pressure, and it was feared that such a drastic change in the legislative framework could damage their credibility. It was not until after the botched takeover of Glitnir and its repercussions that the contingency law proposal took shape. During the weekend of October 3–5, the proposal was finalized.

The output of their work, the aforementioned "emergency legislation," gave the FSA virtually unlimited powers to intervene in financial institutions.[23] The law gave the FSA the ability to take over a shareholders' meeting, transfer assets and liabilities to other financial undertakings, and merge a bank with another financial undertaking. The emergency legislation made deposits priority claims, which enabled the FSA to transfer deposits from the old banks to new operators, together with assets to match their value, and thereby establish new banks.

By adopting this legislation the Icelandic parliament, Althingi, used *force majeure* to effectively rewrite loan contracts concerning the *pari passu* status of bonds and deposits, and thus override the European legal framework. It looked like a desperate, Herculean measure to the ministers and government officials. The Icelandic republic would certainly be hit with litigation from all over world, and even countermeasures from other European states.

But there seemed to be no other plan. The Icelanders felt cornered and isolated: the rulebook rewrite was a matter of necessity to them.

It later seemed counterintuitive, but the government also decided to grant Kaupthing a four-day, €500 million emergency loan. Kaupthing's shares in the Danish bank FIH were put up as collateral. FIH had equity of about €1.3 billion, but the equity was unlisted. Thus, effectively, Kaupthing became the national champion for survival. Separately, the government would issue a blanket guarantee of all deposits in the country, but that declaration was never ratified by the parliament or made into law. Therefore, the guarantee was not, strictly speaking, legally binding, but rather optional.[24]

These measures were introduced under the name "shield wall" after the defense tactics deployed by the Viking armies (which, legend tells, were

---

[23] Act no. 125/2008.

[24] Prime Minister's Office. (2008, October 6). *Yfirlýsing ríkisstjórnarinnar (Declaration by the government).* https://www.forsaetisraduneyti.is/frettir/nr/3032

invented by the wise one-eyed god Odinn himself). Thus, the government wanted to project an image of a total protection for both households and business in Iceland.

2.7   God Bless Iceland

At 4 p.m. on Monday, October 6, Geir Haarde called a press conference that was broadcast live. With most of his constituents glued to the screen, he delivered a stunning message. The speech was intended to inspire confidence in the government's control by erasing all doubt surrounding deposit protection. However, Haarde confessed that the government would not support the banks, because this would entail too much risk for the nation:

> The Government has stated that it will do what is in its power to support the banking system. With this aim in view many important steps have been made over recent weeks and months. But in the perilous situation which exists now in the world's financial markets, providing the banks with a secure lifeline poses a great risk for the Icelandic nation. People must bear this in mind when there is talk about the Icelandic state taking on loans of thousands of billions to defend the banks in the rough waters which they now find themselves in.
> There is a very real danger, fellow citizens, that the Icelandic economy, in the worst case, could be sucked with the banks into the whirlpool and the result could be national bankruptcy. No responsible government takes risks with the future of its people, even when the banking system itself is at stake. The Icelandic nation and its future takes precedence over all other interests.[25]

The speech quickly became the stuff of legend. It ended with the words "God bless Iceland," emulating what has become the expected way for US presidents to end official speeches, by invoking God. Politicians in Iceland do not customarily invoke God in their speeches, and it has not caught on

---

[25] Financial crisis: Full statement by Iceland's prime minister Geir Haarde. (2008, October 6). *The Telegraph*. http://www.telegraph.co.uk/news/worldnews/europe/iceland/3147806/Financial-crisis-Full-statement-by-Icelands-prime-minister-Geir-Haarde.html

as a political expedient. Icelanders are overwhelmingly Lutherans, and by and large members of a single denomination, the state-sponsored National Church. They tend to stay true to the Third Commandment: "Thou shalt not take the name of the Lord thy God in vain." Nonetheless, Haarde's peroration clearly demonstrated to the nation the gravity of the situation.

With years of hindsight, the speech makes perfect sense. However, on that Monday afternoon it clarified nothing. Instead of calming people, it raised alarm and a lot of unanswered questions. It has to be kept in mind that the preparation of the emergency legislation had been kept secret; not even the bankers or the regular MPs knew about it. Various players had gone to the media with assurances that the banks were safe and all kinds of bailout packages were being discussed. And had not Haarde himself told the nation, just 17 hours earlier, "no special action is needed"?

The first response was fear. Withdrawals from the banks had subsided, but they started again with a vengeance on Tuesday morning and would continue for the next three days. Confidence returned by Friday, October 10, at which time the supply of banknotes in circulation had increased by 250 % from October 1.

The second response was anger and distrust, which continued unabated and led to the undoing of Haarde's government in early 2009.

After delivering the "God bless Iceland" speech, Haarde went straight to parliament and proposed the emergency legislation. The deliberations took about six hours, and the proposal passed into law at 11:19 p.m. During the short time it took for the parliament to pass the Emergency Act into law, a number of critical clauses were added to the act concerning how the failed banks (from that moment referred to more commonly as "the old banks") should be operated. These are discussed in more detail in Chap. 6.

On Monday afternoon, as the FSA staff worked feverishly in advance of the legislation being passed, issues of governance came up. Even if the FSA gained power to seize control of the banks, it would be both practical and preferable to keep the regular operations of a seized bank at a remove. Hence, it was necessary for the FSA to be able to appoint some kind of a board, and act more as a controlling shareholder (as well as supervisor). Consequently, a clause was added to the bill that enabled the FSA to appoint a Resolution Committee, which would take on the duties of a board, assume responsibility for asset maintenance, and follow instructions issued by FSA.

After this eventful day, Icelandic depositors were still in the dark, and so were international depositors in Landsbanki. Following Haarde's "God bless Iceland" speech was a run on the Icesave accounts, 40 % of which were sight deposits, callable on demand. These were online accounts, which of course meant that people had access to them 24 hours a day. Daily data for the overall international deposits at Landsbanki, including Icesave deposits in the Netherlands as well as wholesale deposits, are not available. Monthly data indicate, however, that between September 30 and October 6, deposits dropped by €1.4 billion. Judging from the development of the UK Icesave deposits, it is reasonable to assume that a large portion of the drop occurred on Monday, October 6.[26]

That morning, Landsbanki formally requested a loan of £200 million from the CBI, but to no avail. Later that same day, Landsbanki requested permission from the FSA in the UK to halt payments from the Icesave accounts for 60 days, as provided in the terms of the accounts. This also was refused. Finally, in the evening, the London branch of the bank was closed. At around midnight on Monday, after a meeting of Landsbanki's board, two of its CEOs came to the Icelandic FSA and said the bank could no longer meet its obligations. The FSA then seized control of the bank and put it into receivership, acting on its authority granted by the emergency legislation passed a couple of hours earlier.

Quite ironically, the main owners of Glitnir made a U-turn over the weekend of October 3–5. After an earlier declaration that a "bank robbery" was afoot, they now lobbied hard for the government to stand by the proposal of buying a 75 % equity stake. They urged the FSA to move its shareholder meeting to October 6 from the 11th to expedite the proposal's ratification. But the FSA refused, and on Tuesday night it was Glitnir's turn to tumble into receivership.

By the end of Tuesday, Kaupthing was the only bank still standing. However, its outlook was bleak, to say the least. The bank was funded – like Landsbanki – to a large extent by online retail savings deposits called

---

[26] Baldursson, F. M., & Portes, R. (2013, September). Gambling for resurrection in Iceland: the rise and fall of the banks. *Available at SSRN 2361098.*

Kaupthing Edge. The outstanding balance was €3.5 billion (£2.8 billion) as of October 1. These accounts were offered by its British subsidiary, Kaupthing Singer and Friedlander (KSF), and therefore had a British deposit guarantee, unlike the Icesave accounts that had an Icelandic guarantee. The nationality of the deposit guarantee was of crucial importance: An Icelandic deposit guarantee offered from a branch of an Icelandic bank in the UK gave the flexibility to move the proceeds upstream, out of the UK, and into the parent company in Iceland, with relative ease. Under a British deposits guarantee offered by a subsidiary, such transfers were subject to stringent conditions from the British authorities. Nevertheless, they were possible.

In early October, KSF had an outstanding liquidity swap contract with Kaupthing (the mother company) of about €1.4 billion (£1.1 billion). This swap contract was counted among liquid funds in reports from KSF to the UK FSA, which had demanded that KSF keep 95 % of Edge deposits on hand in liquid funds. Kaupthing had also borrowed €1.5 billion (£1.2 billion) from KSF against collateral based on Icelandic assets. However, as the Icelandic currency and asset market tanked in the wake of Lehman's collapse, the margin on the collateral was getting thin. On Friday, October 3, the UK FSA demanded that the swap line be closed and that Kaupthing restore the margin of the collateral loan. This amounted to a €2 billion transfer from the mother company back into Britain, to be executed no later than Monday, October 6.

The British authorities seemed to be obsessed with the thought that the Icelanders were sucking funds out of the UK and into their own troubled financial system. Indeed, this was the main point of discussion when Gordon Brown called his Icelandic counterpart on Sunday, October 5. The British position is to some extent understandable. Three weeks before, on September 12, Lehman Brothers transferred $8 billion from its operations in the UK to the USA just before its collapse, and much to the dismay of the British prime minister.[27]

On Monday, Kaupthing had been granted a €500 million, four-day loan from the CBI with Kaupthing's Danish subsidiary FIH as collateral. That money, however, did not go to the British, but was used to settle

---

[27] Outcry Grows Over Transfer of U.K. Funds by Lehman. (2008, September 22). *Wall Street Journal online version*. http://www.wsj.com/articles/SB122204286442761375

other margin calls facing the bank at the time. The day after the bank had been able to secure an emergency loan from the Swedish central bank (Riksbank) worth about 5 billion Swedish kronor, with Kaupthing's operations in that country as collateral. No such help was forthcoming from the Bank of England. And then, after Haarde asked for God's blessing, the stream of funds out of Kaupthing Edge turned into a flood – just as had happened with the Icesave accounts.

During the deliberations on the emergency legislation in the parliament on Monday night, October 6, both Gordon Brown and Alistair Darling, the Chancellor of the Exchequer, tried to call Haarde, but he declined to speak with either of them. However, as Haarde would soon find out, the British were not going to take silence for an answer.

3

Reykjavik on the Thames

3.1 The Problem with the Banks' Owners

When Iceland separated from Denmark in 1918 and became a sovereign nation with an independent currency, the people were enthusiastically prepared for nationhood. The economic grounds for the separation were shakier. Iceland depended on a single export industry – fishing – and was thus at the mercy of global market fluctuations. For decades afterwards, the fishing sector remained the national breadwinner. It was a shielded if simple life, but it ended in about 1989 when the North Atlantic cod stock collapsed and the fishing sector teetered on bankruptcy. The economic reforms that followed transformed Iceland from one of the most secluded, state-controlled nations in Western Europe to one of the most liberal and open, and it took just over ten years. These reforms – focused on privatization and corporate tax cuts – reaped great rewards through the 1990s in terms of new growth and prosperity.

The new tax revenue paid down debt and led to a steadily declining debt-to-GDP ratio. The republic enjoyed a string of rating upgrades, and jumped from A2 in 1995 to Aaa, awarded by Moody's in 2002. In just a

© The Author(s) 2016
Á. Jónsson, H. Sigurgeirsson, *The Icelandic Financial Crisis*,
DOI 10.1057/978-1-137-39455-2_3

decade, Iceland's remarkable modernization received an extremely warm welcome from the international financial community (Fig. 3.1).

However, even though Iceland liberalized and opened up its economy, no foreign investors appeared with equity or direct investment of any kind. Nor did any foreign bank show much interest; the Icelandic market was just too small, illiquid, and opaque. On the other hand, foreigners were willing to lend to Iceland, on the back of its excellent credit ratings, and from an almost bottomless reserve.

Meanwhile, there were many aspiring domestic multinationals waiting to expand beyond the shores of Iceland in the early 2000s. Most of them mined specialized niches in three oversized industries – health, fishing, and biotech – where most of Iceland's educated class worked with considerable entrepreneurial activity. These companies thrived on pent-up ambition. It is revealing that the Icelandic term for the policy that set it loose on the continent is útrás: a military phrase from the Viking age that literally means an outward attack from a besieged fortress.

Kaupthing was founded in 1981 and became the leading investment bank in Iceland. The bank had explored cross-border investment strategies since 1999, and quickly established its authority as the executer of leveraged foreign acquisitions and buyouts. The timing for a major expansion in this direction was propitious in 2002: the dot-com bubble had burst, stock market multiples were at historic lows, and Iceland had won its Aaa rating.

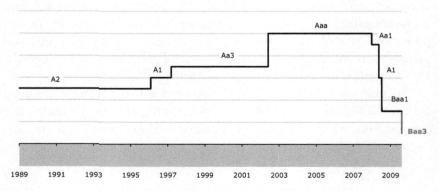

Fig. 3.1 Moody's rating of the Icelandic republic 1989–2009

Kaupthing's targets were usually well-established companies that would deliver both production synergies and market access. The transactions were usually partnerships, with the equity shared between the bank and the aspiring multinational. Transactions tended to be highly leveraged, as the foreign targets would be much bigger than the acquiring domestic companies. Later on, these companies would be listed on the Icelandic stock exchange that helped to fund continued expansion with new offerings.

Gradually, the composition of the Icelandic stock market (ICEX) would change. Investor preferences would turn towards international growth stocks, while boring domestic companies with no growth story to tell would be sidelined. For example, by 2003, practically all fishing companies were delisted from the ICEX, and the total number of listed companies had shrunk to only 23 from 75 in 1999. Simultaneously, the market cap swelled from 60 % of GDP to 180 % as the ICEX index tripled. Now that 70 % of the revenue of ICEX companies came from abroad, the stock market at last could be described as an international entity. On the other hand, it was still a local concern: foreign investors were still not tapping into the ICEX, despite having many internationals to choose from.

In a sense, the early success led to the doom. As international stock markets recovered and production synergies began to materialize, the returns would be enormous for the bottom lines of both the banks and their partners. The success fueled booming confidence. Almost every Icelandic company attempted some kind of útrás strategy: confidence bred exuberance, which turned into hubris. Banks evolved from being facilitators of foreign expansion of other companies into expansionist entities on their own. Their partners became main owners and drivers of continued expansion. There were also significant rewards from the rating agencies that came with developing a larger, more diversified balance sheet.

Kaupthing ("market place" in Icelandic) had been unrated until it merged with the newly privatized Búnaðarbanki ("bank of agriculture") in 2003. The new entity assumed the Búnaðarbanki rating (A3). But this marriage of purely Icelandic retail banking with Kaupthing's investment banking operations, active both at home and abroad, led to an upgrade to

A2 from Moody's. In 2004, Kaupthing acquired the Danish corporate bank FIH. This purchase, which doubled Kaupthing's balance sheet, was financed with the largest-recorded offering ever carried out in the Icelandic stock market: an amount that represented 4 % of Iceland's GDP. Once again, bigger meant better. The acquisition netted an upgrade to A1 from Moody's investors, once again strengthening the funding position of the group (Fig. 3.2).

The FIH acquisition marked a watershed in Icelandic banking. In just three years, Kaupthing had transformed itself from a small, unrated investment bank into the largest bank in the nation, endowed with its A1 rating and an international investment banking platform. The other two Icelandic banks saw the writing on the wall. Both began to emulate Kaupthing's strategy and expanded internationally. The result was one of the most rapid accumulations of banking assets of any nation in history, which lasted from 2004 to 2007.

In the old egalitarian Iceland there was little concentration of wealth. There were no 'super rich' to speak of; the small number of old moneyed

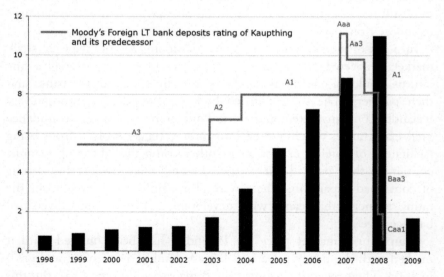

Fig. 3.2 The ratio of bank assets to GDP from 1998 to 2009 in Iceland and Moody's rating of Kaupthing 2003–2009 and its predecessor Búnaðarbanki 1999–2003 (Source: The Central Bank of Iceland and own calculations)

families rarely had the means for substantial corporate investment. Instead, the new shares needed for foreign expansion came from holding companies, which were essentially used as vehicles to transform leverage into equity. Banks channeled cheap, widely available foreign funds into them as loans, made on the value of their stakes in the multinationals.

Thus, the owners and architects of the new multinationals depended on leverage at the outset, since so few funds were available. From 2004, when the banks blazed their expansionary path, this application of leverage was taken to a new level while supported by owners with supersized holding companies. Foreign investors did not prefer the banks to other ICEX companies when it came to buying equity. However, the major international banks were more than willing to lend to the owners of the Icelandic banks on the value of their equity holdings listed on the ICEX.

These arrangements are best illustrated by the development of Exista, Kaupthing's main owner. Exista was founded in 2001 as a holding vehicle for Kaupthing shares owned by savings and loan institutions. In 2003, two brothers, Lýður and Ágúst Guðmundsson, acquired a 55 % stake in Exista. The Guðmundssons had founded an ICEX-listed company named Bakkavör in 1986. They had built their company from scratch, beginning with the processing of roe, but had transformed their vehicle into a leading producer of fresh convenience foods on an international scale. In 1997, they crossed paths with Kaupthing and began their international expansion with a string of leveraged transactions. The first foreign acquisition was made in France in 1997. In 2001, they made the watershed acquisition of the UK-based Katsouris Fresh Foods, a company five times the size of Bakkavör. Four years later they acquired their main British competitor, Geest, which was roughly three or four times the size of their company. By now Bakkavör had become a leader in fresh prepared foods in the UK. After their booming success in the food industry, the brothers turned their attention to financials.

When they became leading owners of Exista, they became owners of Kaupthing as well, as the investment company held a 23 % share in the bank.

Exista and Kaupthing had had cross-ownership from the outset, with the bank owning a 19 % stake in the company. During the Geyser crisis, however, Kaupthing took harsh criticism over this practice and the management devised a clever exit strategy. In a September public offering, Exista was listed on ICEX as an investment company. When Kaupthing paid out its Exista shares as an extra dividend to its shareholders, Exista was endowed with 36,000 new shareholders overnight.

For its part, Exista was intent on becoming a "financial service group," with northern Europe as its core market. The plan was to benefit from the strong cash flow between the company's operating units and its investment arm. The ideal and best-known model of this practice was Warren Buffett's Berkshire Hathaway. Buffett's company uses the "float" provided by insurance operations (a policyholder's money, which it holds temporarily until claims are paid out) to finance its investments. To this end, Exista acquired an insurance company called VIS, which held about 35 % of Icelandic market share, from its partner, Kaupthing, in May 2006.

Exista was the largest, most sophisticated Icelandic investment company to emerge in the stock boom, but there were many other holding companies that transformed themselves into investment bodies by blowing up their balance sheet. In 2006–2007, the aggressive, leveraged giants remained wonderful banking clients who created new fees in both capital markets and investment bank divisions. They frequently established their own hedge fund-type proprietary trading arms for short-term and strategic long-term position-taking in selected companies. Some companies even coinvested with the banks in selected projects. Furthermore, a bigger owner could better support the continued growth of the banks with new equity. The relations had gone far beyond the old model of client-partner: these were symbiotic relationships, or even strategic alliances.

In fact, almost the entire financial system had now become a derivative of the successful foreign expansion of Iceland's three banks. The Savings Bank of Reykjavik (SPRON) was an extremely capable player. In the summer of 2007, its market capitalization was ISK 120 billion ($2 billion at the prevailing exchange rate), which was equal to three times the book value of equity. SPRON had approximately 20,000 customers. Its main asset was a share in Exista, which traded at price-to-book 1.6. The main asset of Exista, meanwhile, was Kaupthing, which traded at up to two times equity. Shareholders in this innocuously named bank were therefore holding the incestuous equity of Kaupthing, at almost ten times book value.

Such deals allowed Icelanders to punch at targets above their weight class. In early 2007, Exista used direct foreign financing to build up a 20 % stake in a Finnish insurance company, Sampo, and an 8–9 % stake in a Norwegian life insurance and pension company, Storebrand (simultaneously, Kaupthing held a 20 % stake in Storebrand). Clearly, the plan was to employ the Berkshire Hathaway model throughout Scandinavia by acquiring insurance companies. By midyear 2007, Exista's balance sheet had swelled to €7.7 billion, with a 37 % equity ratio.

Another main investment company was a spinoff from the national flag carrier, Icelandair. The airline had always stashed summer profits to help tide it over during the slow winter months. In 2004, Hannes Smárason (born in 1967), a distinguished MIT engineering graduate and former McKinsey consultant, took control of the company. He was soon convinced that there was much more money to be made trading stocks than flying customers across the Atlantic, and began to invest the excess in the stock market. In early 2005, the company was officially designated as an investment entity, changed its name to FL Group, and traded at about a 60 % premium to book value at the stock exchange.

At the outset, however, FL Group kept its focus on the airline industry. An early major purchase had been a stake in EasyJet, the UK discount airline, which was sold at a hefty profit. In the final months of 2006, FL acquired a 5.98 % stake in the AMR Corporation – the US holding company that owned American Airlines – and became the third largest shareholder in that entity. AMR had posted a profit in the first two quarters of 2006, for the first time in six years, and its stock price had subsequently appreciated 36 % in the two remaining quarters, which realized another instant profit for FL.

In that same year, during the stock market sell-off at the height of the Geyser Crisis, Smárason grabbed a 30 % stake in Glitnir using a foreign syndicated loan. When the numbers were all in, Smárason could boast a 40 % return on his investments in 2006. It had indeed been his year.

But Smárason had plans far beyond Iceland. In 2007, FL Group cultivated international connections by committing to real estate projects associated with the famous – or infamous – Donald Trump. It invested $50 million in the Manhattan Trump Tower, Trump Soho, and a development in Whitestone, Queens. FL Group had managed this by forming a close relationship with Bayrock Group, the primary Trump Tower developer. The two companies worked jointly on several projects at this time; along the way, the circumstances of the relationship changed. FL's investment in Trump real estate was relabeled as a loan shortly after it became official; this delivered a huge reduction in the tax liability for all parties to the deal. Donald Trump himself signed off on this relabeling of an investment. His participation came to light in 2016, by which time he had all but secured the Republican presidential nomination; the FL–Trump 'loan' raised one of many questions about his business integrity.[1]

FL had been operating like a hedge fund with active proprietary trading, but its modus operandi was to take large enough stakes in its acquisitions to give it a voice on the companies' boards. That voice exhorted managers to undertake "value-adding reforms," and usually it was loud enough to be heeded. Now focusing on banks, FL bought a stake in the German Commerzbank in 2007. When an economic downturn began in the fall of 2007, airlines and banks were among the first casualties. FL Group was hit by a series of margin calls. Smárason was forced to step down as the CEO in the fall of 2007 and his positions were sold at a horrendous loss.

Meanwhile, FL Group continued to pull in its horns. In February 2008, after the US real estate bubble had burst, it announced it was divesting itself of its US real estate projects, including the Trump Tower project. They were moved to a subsidiary of FL Group called FL Bayrock Holdco. This company posted more than $140 million in losses in 2008. The company was declared bankrupt in January 2014, costing investors and creditors nearly $130 million in losses.

A quick rise and precipitous fall: it would not be the last in Iceland. Later on, Smárason and the other high-flying owners of these investment companies would earn the nickname "corporate Vikings" in Iceland. "Viking" in the original language means a "pirate," and it is not complimentary.

---

[1] Sherlock, R., Malnick, E. and Newell, C. (2016, May 26). Donald Trump signed off deal designed to deprive US of tens of millions of dollars in tax. *The Telegraph*. http://www.telegraph.co.uk/news/2016/05/25/exclusive-donald-trump-signed-off-deal-designed-to-deprive-us-of/

Swelling investment companies' balance sheets with direct foreign funding created an extra layer of foreign leverage on the value of the banks' stock prices, to the grave detriment of the Icelandic financial system. The inflated balance sheets crumpled as soon as the foreign banks withdrew their support in response to the international financial crisis. Their sheer weight was almost enough to crush the banks: their main debtors – the too-big-to-fail holding companies – were also their main owners, with their shares used as collateral. It was a very unhealthy relationship that led to perverse incentives in bank–owner relations.

Starting in August 2007, the ICEX felt sell-off pressure, just like other Western stock markets, and it lost about 40 % of its value by January 2008. Lowering stock prices thinned the equity margin of the holding companies and threatened the whole financial system. In early January 2008, the banks attempted to unwind one of the smaller investment companies, Gnúpur, a large shareholder in Kaupthing and an indirect shareholder in Glitnir (through a holding in another investment company, FL Group). A total market panic followed. The Gnúpur episode apparently was a turning point, at which the bank management seemed to have realized that there was no recourse other than gambling for resurrection.[2]

It was, in one sense, an enormous game of dominoes. The banks believed they could not allow any large investment company to fail for fear of toppling all the rest. In reality, they dismantled margin calls as a tool to recover loans made against the value of equity as collateral for these super-clients. Foreign banks, of course, continued to make margin calls. In the first month of 2008, they withdrew much of the funding that had been lent directly to the Icelandic investment companies in 2006–2007, and contributed mightily to the asset bubble. The three banks, again fearing for the safety of the system, became the lenders of last resort for these investment companies, whose assets had been rendered illiquid when the foreign banks withdrew. This placed greater strain on their liquidity position, but every investment company was considered too

---

[2] Baldursson, Friðrik Már, & Portes, Richard. (2013). Gambling for resurrection in Iceland: the rise and fall of the banks. *Available at SSRN 2361098.*

systemically important to be liquidated by an outside margin call. Practically all of these investment companies had large stakes in one of the banks. The banks were bailing out their owners.

By the peak of the 2008 crisis, almost all of these holding companies had become too-big-to-fail in the Icelandic financial system. Important clients inevitably wield power over their lenders, and as the crisis progressed that power would only increase. The banks began to press big clients to sell off their holdings silently, without inciting a panic abroad or awakening the hedge funds.

One of the "corporate Vikings" actually managed to become too-big-to-fail for one of the large international banks. This was Thor Björgólfsson. His stake in Landsbanki, coowned with his father, Björgólfur Guðmundsson, was the bank's largest, and he was the first Icelander to earn a spot (in 2005) on Forbes's list of the world's richest individuals. Often regarded as "Iceland's first billionaire," he ranked 350th on Forbes's list in 2006 and had climbed to 249th just a year later, with a net worth of $3.5 billion. By March 2009, the country's meltdown had reduced his net worth to $1 billion, yet clearly he was still standing.

In 2007, just two months before the crisis hit, Björgólfsson had obtained from Deutsche Bank about €4 billion to fund a leveraged buyout of the Reykjavik-based drug maker, Actavis. As the credit markets froze, the bank was stuck with this debt, which represented its single largest exposure. In his 2015 biography, Björgólfsson claims Deutsche Bank kept him on life support because of its precarious equity position; it simply could not afford the loan loss. "Some bankers even said to us that this could lead to the German chancellor, Angela Merkel, taking the keys to Deutsche bank," he writes.[3] Patience paid off for the bank and Björgólfsson when the US pharmaceutical company Watson acquired Actavis in 2012. As of March 2015, Björgólfsson was back on the Forbes rich list, albeit only ranked 1415th.

But despite upset in the bank–client relationship, credit quality continued to worsen as 2008 progressed, and management could do little but

---

[3] Bjorgolfsson, Thor. (2014). *Billions to Bust and Back: How I made, lost and rebuilt a fortune, and what I learned on the way.* London: Profile Books Ltd.

watch. At their default, the Icelandic banks had about 23 exposures in their loan books larger than 10 % of their equity (between six and ten in each bank).[4] The majority of these were to holding companies or other institutions, individuals who mainly invest in shares, or other venture capital or speculative activities. Some, of course, were large shareholders in the banks.

There is no evidence that this lending concentration was, by itself, a breach of the standards set by either European Union (EU) directives or the Basel framework. They did, however, represent a perversion of the original intent of those standards. Limits were set to allow small local banks to assist local clients in investment tied to production, such as financing for harvesters of other machinery. It was never intended for them to be used by large banks to execute highly leveraged international deals.[5]

The same could not be said of the snowballing lending to holding companies on the value of their own equity that occurred in the months prior to collapse. To keep the dominoes upright, the banks became almost the sole buyers of their own stock. They then attempted to find new homes for the shares by selling them to other investment companies and financing the transaction, but on weakening collateral. Although patterns varied somewhat, similar developments took place at all three banks. These desperate actions in the months prior to the collapse would later lead to criminal investigations and convictions of the banks' top brass for market manipulation (a closer look at the criminal investigations of the banks' top management appears in Chap. 4).

Foreign hedge funds were still eager to short the stocks of the banks or, as a next-best alternative, to short-list companies abroad that had Icelanders as major shareholders, and perhaps force an asset sale. Shorting an Icelandic stock was not just a bet against a particular company but a bet against the currency as well, since all stocks were denominated in ISK. But there was a catch: to short sell a stock one must borrow it first. Since most Icelandic stocks were held domestically, shorting was not such an easy

---

[4] Special Investigation Commission. (2010). *Report of the Special Investigation Commission.*
[5] Jännäri, Kaarlo. (2009, March 30). *Report on Banking Regulation and Supervision in Iceland: past, present and future.*

game for foreigners. However, as the liquidity crisis deepened, it became more lucrative for an Icelandic party to lend stock to hedge funds, since they could realize 30–40 % in annual interest.

Kaupthing's stock was probably the most shorted since it was the most liquid, the largest, and most widely held in the country; it also had a second listing in Stockholm. The pervasiveness of the short position can be demonstrated by the bank's stock being traded at a significant price on the Swedish stock exchange (2 Swedish krona per share, or 4–5 % of the pre-collapse market value) even after it had defaulted. Hedge funds wanting to close short positions kept up demand.[6]

The domino approach to evaluating collateral in stock lending did in fact slow the price decline in the ICEX. By late summer 2008, the banks, Kaupthing in particular, were trading at high multiples compared to their Scandinavian counterparts, especially considering their CDS spreads. But the strategy bought little more than time. The financial system had become hopelessly entangled through cross-lending systemic risk, especially once bank funding replaced foreign direct lending. More and more, the banks looked like Siamese triplets, vitally connected through lending on the value of each other's shares.

3.2   An Act of Terrorism?

Britain was reeling from its own troubles after the Lehman collapse. Despite having a population of 200 times that of Iceland, the UK also had an open economy, its own currency, an oversized international banking system with assets four to five times the GDP, and shaken confidence in its financial sector. Gordon Brown was under fire for not containing the crisis, and the ruling Labour Party's approval ratings had dropped to their lowest point in 20 years. The UK authorities were also extremely worried that the run on the Icelandic banks would spill over to UK counterparts. The Northern Rock episode – the first European bank run in 70 years – lay heavy on their minds. There were many British banks

---

[6] See: Jónsson, Ásgeir. (2009). *Why Iceland?: How One of the World's Smallest Countries Became the Meltdown's Biggest Casualty*. McGraw Hill Professional.

in dire straits, and their leaders held their own emergency meetings with government officials all through the weekend of October 3–5 to prepare some kind of a bailout package. However, when markets opened on October 6 the FTSE 100 index fell by 391 points, a decline of almost 8 % and the largest percentage drop in the UK market since Black Monday in 1987. It was mirrored by sharp falls in Paris, Frankfurt, and New York. And that was only the beginning.

On Monday night, Alistair Darling, Mervyn King, the governor of the Bank of England, and Adair Turner, chairman of the Financial Services Authority, met with the CEOs of the main British banks. Apparently, the banks were disappointed that the British government had not yet pre-pared or committed to a recapitalization package. At this meeting, the "Gang of Three" (Barclays, the Royal Bank of Scotland, and Lloyds TSB) "told Darling to pull his finger out and finalize whatever it is he's eventually prepared to offer on taxpayers' behalf." The meeting was leaked to BBC business editor Robert Peston, who revealed some details the day after on his BBC blog site.[7] That news led to an instant 40 % drop in the share price of the Royal Bank of Scotland (RBS) when markets opened – wiping around £10 billion off the bank's value. This would earn Peston the nickname "market menace" and fuel speculation that the banks were trying to use the media to bounce the government into recapitalization.[8]

On Tuesday morning, Darling took an early flight to attend the European finance ministers' (Ecofin) meeting in Luxembourg. With the meeting in session, he was called out to answer Sir Tom McKillop, the chairman of RBS, who informed him that money was pouring out of the door. He then asked, "What are you going to do about it?" Darling asked how long they could last. "Two to three hours," Sir Tom answered. RBS was a huge bank, with combined assets roughly 1.5 times Britain's GDP. The bank got immediate emergency liquidity assistance from the

---

[7] Peston's Picks: Banks ask chancellor for capital. (2008, October 7). *BBC website.* http://www.bbc.co.uk/blogs/thereporters/robertpeston/2008/10/banks_ask_chancellor_for_capit.html.

[8] Does this BBC man have too much power? Reporter blamed for helping trigger shares fall. (2008, October 8). *Mail Online.* http://www.dailymail.co.uk/news/article-1072549/BBC-reporter-Robert-Peston-blamed-helping-trigger-shares-fall.html#ixzz434xWkFkk

Bank of England, from which it would draw £36.6 billion over the next ten days. Darling expected that HBOS (Halifax Bank of Scotland) would also need a bailout, since "it was in the same precarious position" – which was, indeed, the case.[9]

Later that morning, Alistair Darling made a call to his Icelandic counterpart, Árni Mathiesen. The chancellor wanted a firm commitment that UK Icesave depositors would be paid off from the Icelandic deposit insurance fund. As became clear, the UK minister was very dissatisfied with the answers he received. When Darling was interviewed on BBC Radio, on the morning of October 8, he stated: "The Icelandic government, believe it or not, has told me yesterday they have no intention of honouring their obligations here. [. . .] But I have decided in these exceptional circumstances that we will stand behind those depositors so they get their money back."[10] When the Icelandic authorities released the transcript of the conversation between the two ministers about two weeks later,[11] it became clear that Mathiesen never refused to compensate UK savers. The call was just a pretext for actions already planned.[12]

There were 300,000 Icesave account holders in the UK. These included prominent charities, hospitals, municipalities, universities, the London police and 14 other police forces, pensions, and thousands of private citizens. They were now locked out from their accounts. They wanted their money back, pure and simple, and the government had little

---

[9] RBS investigation: Chapter 4: the bail-out. (2011, December 11). *The Telegraph.* http://www.telegraph.co.uk/finance/newsbysector/banksandfinance/8947559/RBS-investigation-Chapter-4-the-bail-out.html

See also: Alistair Darling. (2013, February 4). A crisis needs a firewall not a ringfence. *Financial Times.* http://www.ft.com/intl/cms/s/0/3d164732-6ec7-11e2-9ded-00144feab49a.html#axzz4311ZfvHa

[10] Extra help for Icesave customers. (2008, October 8). *BBC News.* http://news.bbc.co.uk/2/hi/business/7658417.stm.

[11] For a full transcript of the conversation see: The Darling-Mathiesen Conversation before Britain Used the Anti-Terrorism Legislation against Iceland. (2008, October 23). *Iceland Review.* http://icelandreview.com/news/2008/10/23/darling-mathiesen-conversation-britain-used-anti-terrorism-legislation-against

[12] As reported in the *Financial Times* at the time: "At no point does the Icelandic finance minister state unequivocally that Iceland would not honour its obligations."

Transcript challenges UK position on Iceland. (2008, October 23). *Financial Times online.* http://www.ft.com/intl/cms/s/0/42c0e23c-a153-11dd-82fd-000077b07658.html#axzz43RRr58yd

choice but to pursue the matter or further jeopardize confidence in their own financial sector, as well as their support base.

The UK government seemed to have decided almost instantly to compensate Icesave depositors in the country. Actually, the Financial Services Compensation Scheme (FSCS) guaranteed £35,000 for all banks in Britain. If the bank was foreign, operating under the European Economic Area "passport" system, the host country would pay the minimum, £16,300, with the FSCS picking up the balance. Ironically, the FSCS had raised its guarantee level from £35,000 to £50,000 on Friday, October 3, just the week before. This did not affect the liability of the Icelandic deposit guarantee under the passport system, but it automatically increased the cost to British authorities when Landsbanki collapsed. Nevertheless, they also maintained that the Icelandic DIGF fund was state-guaranteed – otherwise no British savers would have been willing to risk their money on these accounts. Thus, by compensating the Icesave account holders they were in fact lending money to the Icelandic government.

Gordon Brown held a press conference at 9.15 that same Wednesday morning, and unveiled his new plan for saving the British banking system with a £500 billion rescue package, which represented about a third of Britain's GDP at the time. £450 billion was an emergency liquidity provision and £50 billion was an equity infusion. There was more to report than a bailout at home, however. Brown used the opportunity to announce that he was "taking legal action against the Icelandic authorities to recover the money lost to people who deposited in UK branches of its banks."[13] Indeed, he was. Barely one hour later, the British government enacted an antiterrorism law (Landsbanki Freezing Order 2008) that authorized them to seize all assets of Landsbanki in Britain. The freezing order was issued under the 2001 Anti-Terrorism, Crime and Security Act, which passed after the 9/11 attacks. The order was directed not only against Landsbanki but also the Central Bank of Iceland (CBI), Ministry of Finance, Icelandic FSA, and the Landsbanki resolution committee,

---

[13] UK to sue Iceland over any lost bank savings. (2008, October 16). *The Guardian.* http://www. theguardian.com/world/2008/oct/08/iceland.banking

which had just been established by the Icelandic FSA.[14] The application of this law to a bank unconnected to terrorist activities – not to mention a peaceful nation that had been the UK's ally in NATO from its founding – was unprecedented. Later that day, Landsbanki, the CBI, FSA, and the Icelandic finance ministry were listed with other "financially sanctioned regimes" such as Al Qaeda, the Taliban, North Korea, and Burma. (The CBI, FSA and Icelandic finance ministry were later removed, leaving Landsbanki as the lone Icelandic bedfellow of terrorist states.) This action probably did more to revive Brown's popularity than any other.

But they had more in store for Iceland than this. The negative publicity helped turn the outflow from Kaupthing Edge into a flood. On the morning of October 8, the British FSA asked Kaupthing for an additional £300 million infusion to address the deteriorating liquidity situation. When Kaupthing declined, the British FSA seized the Kaupthing Edge deposits (about $4.5 billion), sold them off to ING, and sent KSF into bankruptcy proceedings. Landsbanki's holding, Heritable Bank, was condemned to the same fate. Singer & Friedlander was an independent UK bank, and its bankruptcy did not automatically take down its mother company. But it did breach Kaupthing loan covenants and open up the possibility of an early redemption for bondholders. Management gave up the ghost at midnight. Control of Kaupthing was given over to the Icelandic FSA. In three days, all of the Icelandic banking giants, constituting 85 % of the financial system, had collapsed; and 75 % of the stock market value was wiped out.

As these events unfolded, it was Geir Haarde's turn to make frantic phone calls to his British counterpart. Brown repaid in kind and refused to talk. Haarde was able to speak with Darling, who assured him that relations between their countries would return to normal. Meanwhile, Brown told BBC political editor Nick Robinson, "I've spoken to the Icelandic prime minister, I have told him this is effectively an illegal action that they have taken. We are freezing the assets of Icelandic companies in the UK where we can. We will take further action against the Icelandic

---

[14] Her Majesty's Treasury. (2008, October 8). *The Landsbanki Freezing Order 2008.* (Statutory Instruments 2008 No. 2668. http://www.legislation.gov.uk/uksi/2008/2668/pdfs/uksi_20082668_en.pdf

authorities where necessary to recover the money." This was only partly true: a freezing order for all Icelandic companies in the UK was never issued. However, for a time there was significant confusion among the British banks regarding the freezing order. To be on the safe side, they froze all Icelandic accounts. The British authorities made it clear in a letter to the Icelandic ambassador on October 11 that they were not taking actions against any other companies. The letter was never made public.[15]

Back in Reykjavík, Haarde was dumbfounded. When interviewed by the British media he said, "I told the chancellor that we consider this to be a completely unfriendly act."[16] This was of course just another understatement from the Icelandic prime minister.

3.3 Will the Payment System Collapse?

The freezing order came at a critical time for the Icelanders. The payment system is in essence a web of accounts, between which banks transfer funds. Thus, when a bank fails, a part of this web freezes over. That was indeed what had made the Lehman default so disastrous; the bank was far too interconnected to fail. The bank's tentacles, its counterparty status in trades around the world, the volume of which was gigantic, were now compromised. Most trades, even those slated for "immediate delivery," are actually settled in two or three days; this meant that most of Lehman's deals from the tail end of its last week were frozen by the default, and remained frozen for weeks to come. "Counterparty risk" was now a term laden with frightening consequence: you really could lose your money just by entering a transaction with a bank that was not on a secure footing.

The Icelandic authorities were able to secure the domestic payment system by seizing ISK deposits – with the authority given to the FSA by the emergency act – and place them into new banks. The transfer was seamless, as the deposits were always available upon demand, and could be

---

[15] Special Investigation Commission. (2010). *Report of the Special Investigation Commission.* Vol. 7. Chapter 20 p. 154.

[16] Treasury officials head to Iceland to resolve banking crisis. (2008, October 10). *The Guardian Online.* http://www.theguardian.com/business/2008/oct/10/banking-creditcrunch

used freely to execute transactions within Iceland. Thus, the average Icelander did not really notice any change when his assets and liabilities were moved to a new entity. The same did not apply to foreign transactions. In the eyes of the outside world, the Icelandic banks had defaulted and their accounts abroad were frozen. Moreover, foreign banks with which the Icelandic banks had accounts now had claims against them, and they refused to disburse funds from the accounts before those claims were satisfied. They also feared that they would become liable for compensatory damages if payments were routed to the estate of the bank in question, instead of being delivered to the correct recipient.

Therefore, the CBI had to take over the role of banks concerning cross-border payment intermediation. Each bank would send two or three employees over to the CBI to conduct the cross-border transactions of their bank's clients – chiefly concerning imports and exports – through the Central Bank's payment intermediation system. When the new banks were firmly established, a "detour" was set up in the Central Bank's system, whereby the new banks could enter payment orders directly into the system and the Central Bank would send them out upon approval. Prior to the collapse, the CBI had handled about 300 transactions per month. The number jumped to 30,000 after the Emergency Act.[17] Moreover, it could take days to execute even simple transactions.[18]

However, since the British freezing order was applied not only to Landsbanki and the Icelandic FSA, but also the CBI, this route was also closed, making Iceland a virtual island within the international payment system. As it turned out, most major banks have operations in London, and they are keen on obeying the British authorities. Thus even the CBI could not escape the freeze. In the wake of the order, everything Icelandic became toxic. Regular Icelandic companies that had nothing to do with the banks would not only be unable to get their payments through; they

---

[17] The Central Bank of Iceland. (2009, October 26). *Fjármálastöðugleiki (Financial Stability)*. http://www.cb.is/library/Skraarsafn—EN/Financial-Stability-Report/2009/2009%20enska.pdf

[18] Ministry of Finance. (2011, August 25). *Skýrsla fjármálaráðherra um mat á áhrifum af beitingu Breta á lögum um varnir gegn hryðjuverkum, glæpum og um öryggi fyrir íslensk fyrirtæki, samkvæmt beiðni. (Report of the minister of finance on the impact of the application of the British Anti-terrorism, Crime and Security Act on Icelandic companies, as requested)*. https://www.fjarmalaraduneyti.is/media/utgafa/Skyrsla_fmrh_ahrif_hvl.pdf

would also be denied anything that could be categorized as counterparty risk. Import companies could not get the usual payment extensions on their orders – everything had to be paid in advance. Export companies could not insure shipments sent abroad against both damage and payment shortfalls, as was customary. Everything had to be paid beforehand.[19]

Therefore, to say late October 2008 was extremely stressful for the CBI and the banks is an understatement. It was terrifying. Employees were working around the clock to keep Iceland's foreign trade afloat, to send fuel payments to keep Icelandic flights from being grounded, and to keep other basic services intact.

On October 16, the CBI sought help from European central banks, the US Fed, and the Canadian Central Bank. It wanted to be able to conduct payments and open transactions with all other countries besides Britain. At the same time, J.P. Morgan opened up clearing accounts for the new Icelandic banks; for some months most payments in and out of Iceland would pass through their accounts. The British Treasury issued a Financial Sanctions Notice on October 17 stating that the freezing order applied only to the Landsbanki assets in the UK.[20] However, it was not until October 30 that the British banks would steer Icelandic payments through the channels; some had been frozen for 20 days more. Given that the UK is Iceland's single largest export market, the freezing was a crippling blow to the economy. It would take almost three months to restore normalcy in Iceland's cross-border payment intermediation.

The original stated objective of the freezing order was to prevent funds from being transferred out of Britain. However, that objective could clearly have been reached by other, more benign measures. What was the real reason behind this drastic action? Most likely, there were two. Presumably, both explanations demonstrate that authorities were dead serious about guaranteeing deposits and building a firewall to keep Iceland's problems at bay.

First, the UK needed to stop the run on the Icelandic banks from spreading into the British financial system. It was now time for "shock and

---

[19] *Ibid.*

[20] Her Majesty's Treasury. (2008, October 17). *The Landsbanki Freezing Order 2008.* (Financial Sanctions Notice). http://www.mbl.is/media/24/1024.pdf

awe," Alistair Darling told the CEOs of the British banks in the secret meeting on October 6.[21] In a letter sent to the Icelandic Ministry of Finance, dated February 11 and signed by Clive Maxwell, director of financial stability at the HM Treasury, it is stated that the action was necessary to restore faith in the British banking system.[22]

Second, it quickly became obvious that the British were using the laws to place pressure on the Icelandic government in the protracted dispute over the Icesave deposit guarantees. Hence, the freezing order was not revoked until June 10, 2009, after the Icelandic minister of finance had signed the guarantee. (However, that was not the end of the affair, as will be explained in Chap. 5.)

The country saw the freeze as a deep humiliation. It was almost incomprehensible that Iceland, a nation without an army, was branded a terrorist entity, and by a fellow NATO country that was also its largest trading partner.

While the events were unfolding, a small contingent of specialists from the IMF waited in Reykjavík for the Icelandic government to seek their assistance. No developed country had sought help from the IMF in almost 30 years. Memories of the measures the IMF had taken in the Asian crisis a decade earlier were still vivid. On October 3, Tryggvi Thor Herbertsson, then the economic advisor to the prime minister, was asked on Bloomberg if he thought the nation would seek IMF aid. "We're an industrialized country, the fifth-richest country in the world per capita," he said. "We are working on various measures to provide liquidity to the economy and you'll see that soon, but the IMF is not an option."[23]

Moreover, after almost 15 years of runaway growth and prosperity, Iceland had been emboldened enough to seek membership on the UN Security Council. The foreign ministry and diplomatic corps had been

---

[21] Lehman Brothers collapse, five years on: 'We had almost no control'. (2013, September 13). *The Guardian Online*. http://www.theguardian.com/business/2013/sep/13/lehman-brothers-collapse-five-years-later-shiver-spine

[22] Clive Maxwell. (2009, February 11). *Landsbanki Freezing Order 2008*. https://www.forsaetisraduneyti.is/media/island/frettir/42.pdf

[23] Brogger, Tasneem. (2008, October 3). Iceland Says to Announce Rescue Plan 'Very Soon'. *Bloomberg*.

totally devoted to this objective. To shift away from that campaign – mostly conducted by island hopping in the Pacific – and pick up a beggar's stick at the IMF's door was too profound a humiliation for the political elite to stomach – at least not yet.

On October 7, the Central Bank announced that Russia was willing to lend €4 billion to Iceland on very advantageous terms, and subsequently pegged the exchange rate to the euro at a much lower rate than the prevailing market rate. However, the Russian loan never materialized, and the exchange rate peg lasted for a day. The government finally decided that the IMF was the right negotiating partner. Preparation of a Stand-By Arrangement for Iceland began on October 9.[24]

On October 17, Austria and Turkey handily defeated Iceland in the vote to the council, and a week later Iceland sought shelter with the Fund. On October 24, the IMF announced "an ad referendum agreement" on an economic program supported by a $2.1 billion loan, and under a two-year Stand-By Arrangement. The IMF loan was matched with loans from the Nordic countries and Poland; in total, the sum reached $5 billion – 40 % of Iceland's GDP. The loan was intended to service external financing needs over the next three years.[25] However, the IMF board needed to approve the loan, and both the British and the Dutch vetoed any lending to Iceland unless a government guarantee was provided for the Icesave deposits. A new standoff began.

Iceland had been caught off guard. Its diplomatic brass had been treating representatives from tiny Pacific island states to blueberry pancakes and other Icelandic delicacies to curry favor on the UN Security Council.[26] Meanwhile, it became clear the European community

---

[24] Baldursson, F. M., & Portes, R. (2013, September). Gambling for resurrection in Iceland: the rise and fall of the banks. *Available at SSRN 2361098.*

[25] International Monetary Fund. (2008, October 24). *IMF Announces Staff Level Agreement with Iceland on US$2.1 Billion Loan.* (Press Release No. 08/256). https://www.imf.org/external/np/sec/pr/2008/pr08256.htm

[26] MacFarquhar, Neil. (2008, October 11). A U.N. Charm Offensive Topped Off by Dessert. The New York Times. http://www.nytimes.com/2008/10/12/world/12nations.html. Ministry of Foreign Affairs. (2009, August 8). *Skýrsla um framboð Íslands og kosningabaráttu til sætis í öryggisráði Sameinuðu þjóðanna 2009–2010. (Report on Iceland's candidacy and campaign for a seat in the United Nations Security Council 2009–2010.)* https://www.utanrikisraduneyti.is/media/PDF/Lokaskyrsla_um_oryggisradsframbodid_2008.PDF

would support the British and the Dutch in the Icesave imbroglio, including the Scandinavians, who made it clear that they would not lend money to Iceland unless it guaranteed the Icesave liabilities.[27]

The Icesave coalition had been formed as a matter of principle, and as a means to keep the Common European Market and cross-border competition in financial services intact. Banks were extending their reach throughout Europe, but with their domestic deposit guarantees as the ultimate insurance. If one nation was unable to provide this insurance abroad, there could be more disasters in store, even though a home-nation guarantee was not required in the strict, legal sense. After a year of crisis, the world was no longer willing to risk another systemic collapse or continental bank run because of one outlier's intransigence.

Behind this dispute lay some very simple arithmetic. The number of British account holders was roughly equal to the total number of Icelanders – 300,000. So in a way, all Icelanders would be saddled with their very own British Icesave account to pay back – a significant sum indeed. Then there were about 125,000 Dutch Icesave accounts with a total €1.7 billion on deposit. Icesave's stake in the UK and Netherlands amounted to about $12 billion, or 60 % of the national GDP, in September. When the ISK tanked the following month, the ratio ballooned to 80 %. The minimum foreign amount due was somewhat lower —£2.35 billion in the UK and €1.33 billion in the Netherlands – but even this amount represented between 40 and 60 % of the GDP, depending on the ISK value. It is debatable if any sovereign nation would voluntarily accept such high indemnity, especially if its economy was in the process of tanking. Moreover, in the confusion of 2008 no one really knew if Landsbanki's assets would be sufficient to cover the deposits on its balance sheet – especially keeping in mind that the deposit-to-loan ratio of the bank prior to the collapse was about 70 %.

With dwindling foreign reserves, foreign exchange rationing, and a growing shortage of imports, the island was beginning to suffocate in

---

[27] Parliamentary Committee on Foreign Affairs. (2008, December 5). *Nefndarálit um tillögu til þingsályktunar um samninga varðandi ábyrgð ríkissjóðs á innstæðutryggingum vegna innstæðna í útibúum íslenskra viðskiptabanka á Evrópska efnahagssvæðinu. (Committee report on a parliamentary resolution on contracts for government guarantees of deposit insurance for deposits in branches of Icelandic commercial banks in the European Economic Area.).*

November 2008. The Icelandic government submitted a formal complaint to NATO that a fellow member state had branded them as terrorists. Then, more than 80,000 Icelanders (about a quarter of the entire population) signed an online petition titled "Icelanders are not terrorists," which was sponsored by a grassroots movement called InDefence. Iceland also made it clear that UK patrols in its airspace were not appropriate, given the state of affairs. Subsequently, on November 14, the UK canceled its patrols and defense of the Icelandic airspace for December 2008.

Iceland also turned to the European Commission but to the same effect – nothing could be done for Iceland unless the Icesave deposits were guaranteed.[28] On November 14, the foreign minister of Iceland, Ingibjörg Sólrún Gísladóttir, told the British press: "We are isolated when all 27 EU member states agree that we have to reach an accord on Icesave."[29]

Talks began almost immediately afterwards in Brussels. France, which held the rotating presidency of the European Council, acted as mediator. On November 16, an outline agreement was reached, by which the Icesave deposits were guaranteed.[30] Three days later, Iceland's loan application with Fund was approved.[31]

That was, however, by no means the end of the Icesave dispute. The responsibility for the Icesave accounts, although accepted in parliament, was rejected in two national referendums, on March 6, 2010 and April 9, 2011, as will be discussed in Chap. 5. The British and Dutch governments then brought a formal complaint to the EFTA Surveillance Authority (ESA), which is tasked with insuring that the EFTA states, parties to

[28] Iceland turns to European Commission for funds. (2008, November 10). *Reuters.* http://www.reuters.com/article/eu-iceland-idUSBRU00697220081110
[29] Iceland close to reaching compensation deal for UK Icesave customers. (2008, November 14). *The Telegraph online version.* http://www.telegraph.co.uk/news/worldnews/europe/iceland/3460807/Iceland-close-to-reaching-compensation-deal-for-UK-Icesave-customers.html
[30] Prime Minister's Office. (2008, November 16). *Agreed Guidelines Reached on Deposit Guarantees.* (Press release.) https://eng.forsaetisraduneyti.is/news-and-articles/nr/3229
[31] International Monetary Fund. (2008, November 19). *IMF Executive Board Approves US$2.1 Billion Stand-By Arrangement for Iceland.* (Press Release No.08/296) https://www.imf.org/external/np/sec/pr/2008/pr08296.htm

the European Economic Area, follow the European rulebook. ESA subsequently brought a case against Iceland to the EFTA Court.

According to the emergency legislation, all deposits, whether foreign or domestic, became priority claims. Sure enough, the Icelandic FSA's mission to rescue the banking operations of the old banks only applied to deposits held in domestic branches, which were transferred into the new banks and were always available on demand. Deposits in foreign branches were left frozen inside the old banks and would be paid out as soon as the funds became available from the asset recovery. However, the Icelanders argued that this was not really a matter of discrimination, since the Icelandic depositors were paid in ISK, which could not be converted into other currencies and transferred off the island. The foreign depositors were in fact being reimbursed in hard currency.

Second, Icelanders maintained that the emergency legislation actually benefited UK savers. Not only were there no limits for the payout to each account, corporate and wholesale deposits would also be given priority over other *pari passu* claims, which had not previously been protected by the government. These proved to be powerful arguments in court.

With a ruling on January 28, 2013, the EFTA Court cleared Iceland of all charges, leaving the government with only "first priority claim," the Landsbanki receivership. As it turned out, asset recovery was more than sufficient to pay the Icesave claim. Landsbanki paid its last installment on January 11, 2016, thereby closing the claim.

3.4   Reykjavik on the Thames

On September 7, 2013, just days before the five-year anniversary of the Lehman default, Alistair Darling gave an interview titled, "Britain was two hours away from total social collapse" to thisismoney.co.uk. When describing the moment on October 7, 2008, when the chairman of RBS called to tell him the bank would collapse in a few hours, Darling remarked:

> The risk I have always seen is that people forget just how close we came to a complete collapse and the thing about a collapse of the banks is that it

wouldn't just have been the banks in ruins, it would have been complete economic and therefore social collapse. People without money can do nothing – you can't buy your petrol, you can't buy your food, anything.

It was rather like a nuclear war, you know you think it will never happen. And then someone tells you that a missile's been launched. It was very scary. That moment will stick with me for the rest of my days.[32]

A fundamental principle of fractional reserve banking is that no deposit-funded bank – no matter how well capitalized – can withstand a run without external liquidity assistance, because a maturity mismatch between assets and liabilities is inherent in its business model. The great paradox of the industrial capitalist system is that firms and corporations need a long-term financing horizon to sync with the expected utilization of productive capital for the funding that is required. Simultaneously, savers value liquidity, and are unwilling to surrender their capital for an extended period without some recourse that can kick in at short notice. The paradox is "solved" with fractional-reserve banking, which allows banks to provide longer-term loans to borrowers while providing immediate liquidity to depositors.

However, this solution is built on the premise that the liquidity demands or withdrawals of depositors are uncorrelated, and that they have full confidence in the institution entrusted with their money. Therefore, every banking system is built on unstable foundations and can tip over. The only question is how low the tipping point is.[33]

Public authorities have two means to safeguard the stability of their financial system. On the one hand, they have the power to print money; that is, a central bank that can function as a lender of last resort and inject liquidity into the system by turning on the printing press. On the other hand, they have the power to recapitalize the banks by levying taxes,

---

[32] Alistair Darling interview: Britain was two hours away from total social collapse – Former Chancellor on the crisis that erupted FIVE years ago this week. (2013, September 7). *This is Money*. http://www.thisismoney.co.uk/money/news/article-2415003/ALISTAIR-DARLING-INTERVIEW-Britain-hours-away-total-social-collapse--Former-Chancellor-crisis-erupted-FIVE-years-ago-week.html#ixzz4351QimLm

[33] This is highlighted by the influential article Diamond DW, Dybvig PH (1983). Bank runs, deposit insurance, and liquidity. *Journal of Political Economy, 91(3)*: 401–419.

which can contribute new capital to them or create guarantees based on future taxation.

In 2008, the US and Iceland were at opposite ends of the spectrum concerning both printing power and taxing power. The former is not only the biggest currency area in the world, but the US dollar is also the chief reserve currency for the entire world. With a population and GDP about one-thousandth of that of the US, Iceland is the smallest independent currency area in the world, and its note issues are illiquid offshore. When the CBI prints ISK for the Icelandic financial system, it almost instantly leads to a currency crisis as people attempt to exchange the new money in the currency market (for a more detailed discussion on CBI repo lending prior to the crisis, and the loan losses suffered when the three banks defaulted, see Chap. 8). Therefore, the CBI can only serve as a credible lender of last resort with the aid of either large currency reserves or capital controls (see Chap. 6). Moreover, the US banking system had assets totaling only 115 % of GDP, whereas Iceland's oversized system had assets equal to ten times GDP. Looking through this lens, there is little surprise that Iceland ran aground in the 2008 crisis, while the US stayed afloat.

Most other countries fell between the Icelandic and US financial poles. Continental Europe was vulnerable, because although the ECB has immense printing power, the taxing power is very fragmented and uncoordinated across the EU. Moreover, the European banking model has traditionally relied on wholesale funding and relationship lending; thus, the average size of a European banking system is about 3.5 times the respective GDP.

The test that Britain faced in September–October 2008 was really twofold. First, it was a test of the pound sterling as the reserve currency; second, it tested the national fiscal power against an international banking system with assets roughly equal to —four to five times GDP. In hindsight, it is clear that for the people in charge at the time, the tipping point was dreadfully close in the wake of the Lehman collapse.

Thinking back to Alistair Darling's predicament on the morning of October 7, 2008, it was not clear that RBS was too-big-to-save when facing the prospect of "total social collapse." This was an aggressive investment bank with offices in 50 countries, with 50 % of its revenue made outside the UK, and a balance sheet of £2.2 trillion, or 150 % of British GDP. Moreover, Britain's largest mortgage lender, HBOS, was also in dire straits and in need of government support. Together, these two banks had assets roughly double the British GDP. Ultimately, the UK government responded by placing about £46 billion as equity into RBS, thus purchasing an 83 % share (68 % of voting rights) in the bank. The UK authorities also assisted Lloyds Banking Group's takeover of HBOS by contributing £21 billion of new capital, thereby acquiring a 41 % stake in the banking group.

A week before, on September 29, 2008, the Icelandic authorities had attempted to pull off an almost identical plan by offering to buy a 75 % stake in Glitnir Bank for €600 million. Glitnir was operating in ten countries, with half of its revenue generated outside Iceland, and a balance sheet about twice the Icelandic GDP.[34] This rescue attempt received endorsement from many quarters, including Paul Krugman, who wrote on his *New York Times* blog the day after: "Notice, by the way, that it was an equity injection rather than a purchase of bad debt; I approve."[35]

However, the attempt failed because of the illiquidity of Icelandic króna, the lack of currency reserves, and the lack of international support. The UK Treasury was able to supply RBS with liquidity by just turning on the printing press at the Bank of England. The Icelandic government assumed that a government ownership would open the way for Glitnir to fund itself in the same private credit markets available to the republic. It actually did the reverse: the move closed the governments access to capital markets.

The nationalization of Glitnir exposed the liquidity problems of the Icelandic banks to the world. It also demonstrated the inability of the Icelandic authorities to provide the liquidity needed to support the banks. Although the Icelandic plan looked good to academics, it was simply not credible in the financial market. Not only did it fail miserably, it also triggered rating downgrades and a systemic bank run, as discussed in Chap. 2.

---

[34] Glitnir (2008). *Condensed Consolidated Interim Financial Statements. 30 June 2008.*

[35] Krugman, Paul (2008, September 30). The $850 billion bailout. *The New York Times Opinion Pages.* http://krugman.blogs.nytimes.com/2008/09/30/the-850-billion-bailout/

It is an irony of history that people deciding on the bailout – Prime Minister Gordon Brown and Chancellor Alistair Darling – were both Scots by origin, and that the banks that received their support both had headquarters and deep lineage in Scotland. Paraphrasing a famous quip by Voltaire about the Holy Roman Empire, one could say that RBS was neither Royal, nor a Bank, nor Scottish. Nevertheless, the Scottish financial sector had assets approximately 12 times the national output,[36] and it is quite clear that if Scotland had been independent and backed by its own currency, its international banking system would have collapsed just like Iceland's.

So Britain enacted a national bailout of an international banking system, just like Iceland. The difference was that Iceland's bailout failed. The general measures taken by the UK authorities included temporary semi-nationalization, major equity injections into the banks, and comprehensive debt guarantees, which were not certain to be credible. The total exposure to the state treasury amounted to 75–85 % of British GDP at the high point of the crisis.[37] In fact, market conditions continued to deteriorate after the bailout measures were introduced on October 8, and the week ended with the FTSE 100 dropping 10 % on Friday, October 10. However, fortunes changed over the weekend, as the G7 and IMF opted for this approach on the Saturday, and the EU core countries the day after.

It is clear that these collective decisions followed determined lobbying on behalf the British authorities, most notably Prime Minister Gordon Brown. On October 12, the day before the announcement of his Nobel Prize, Paul Krugman asked in his column: "Has Gordon Brown, the British prime minister, saved the world financial system?"[38] The anonymous Bagehot columnist in the *Economist* wrote: "Can the prime minister

---

[36] Her Majesty's Government. (2013, May). *Scotland analysis: Financial services and banking.* https://www.gov.uk/government/uploads/system/uploads/attachment_data/file/200491/scotland_analysis_financial_services_and_banking_200513.pdf

[37] For an overview see: National Audit Office (2010, December 15). *Maintaining the financial stability of UK banks: update on the support schemes.* (Report by the comptroller and auditor general, HC 676, Session 2010–2011). https://www.nao.org.uk/wp-content/uploads/2010/12/1011676.pdf

[38] Krugman, Paul. (2008, October 12). Gordon Does Good. *The New York Times Opinion Pages.* http://www.nytimes.com/2008/10/13/opinion/13krugman.html?_r=0

who had sunk beneath criticism into ridicule really be the same man who, last week, called for the world to emulate his bank-rescue package, and saw the world obey? Which is the real Mr. Brown?"[39]

This question was answered in the House of Commons on December 10, 2008, during a fiery exchange between Brown and David Cameron, the opposition leader, who claimed that recapitalization of ailing banks had "failed." Brown maintained that Cameron was on the "on the wrong side of history." Cameron retorted that the prime minister was "on the wrong side of mathematics." The Tory benches collapsed into gales of derisive laughter as Brown responded: "We not only saved the world. . ."[40]

3.5   Sound and Fury

After their attempted bailout failed, the Icelandic authorities had to resort to extremes and let the banks fail. However – perhaps paradoxically – the financial system itself did not fail. It continued to function in a smooth and uninterrupted fashion despite the circumstances. People continued to have access to their deposits and the branches never closed. The new banks that were established in the wake of the emergency act were not only much smaller, about 15 % the size of the old banks,[41] they were funded almost entirely in ISK. Therefore, they fell within the scope of the sovereign's powers of money printing and taxation. These powers were further enhanced by the implementation of capital controls, which not only kept liquidity that the CBI placed into the banks from streaming out of the country, it also left depositors virtually no place to go should they

---

[39] The riddle of Gordon Brown. (2008, October 16). *The Economist Online.* http://www.economist.com/node/12427804

[40] Gordon Brown mocked over 'save the world' slip-up in Commons. (2008, December 10). *The Telegraph Online.* http://www.telegraph.co.uk/news/politics/3701712/Gordon-Brown-mocked-over-save-the-world-slip-up-in-Commons.html

[41] According to new banks' initial balance sheets, published at the end of 2009 and the beginning of 2010, their total assets amounted to about €14 billion (ISK 2100 billion), as compared with the old banks' consolidated assets of €96 billion (ISK 14,400 billion) as of mid-2008.

want to leave the Icelandic financial system – unless they hoarded printed ISK notes in their homes!

At the same time, the authorities issued a statement declaring that all domestic deposits were guaranteed – which represented an amount estimated at about €10.6 billion (ISK 1600 billion), or just a bit more than Iceland's GDP.[42] This blanket deposit guarantee could have been extremely expensive for the Treasury, if the Emergency Act had not financed it by defining deposits as priority claims and letting losses fall on general creditors. That group included resident entities, such as Icelandic pension funds, which were large owners of the banks' bonds. But the vast majority of them were foreign institutional investors, who then had to bear the losses. When all is said and done, the Emergency Act represented a transfer from the three banks' general creditors to domestic depositors of the amount of €5 billion, and a similar amount to foreign depositors.[43]

Some of the authorities' actions contradicted the methodology entailed in the Emergency Act in an attempt to lighten the Treasury's guarantees of the banking system. This was true, for instance, of the decision to grant a €500 million loan to Kaupthing on the same day the Act was passed. Despite murmurs about Kaupthing's viability at market close on October 3, 2008, it was clear that the passage of the Act three days later put the last nail in its coffin. The loan was granted, secured by shares in FIH Bank in Copenhagen, and was only collected in part when the CBI sold the Danish bank in September 2010 for a purchase price of €255 million.[44] Ultimately, the Treasury lost €245 million on this loan, or about 2.6 % of GDP. This is approximately equal to the loss that the British treasury might expect to shoulder from the recapitalization of RBS. In August 2015, the UK government sold 5.4 % of RBS at 330 pence per share, for a

---

[42] This statement was never enshrined in law.

[43] Domestic deposits totalled €9.6 billion (ISK 1438 billion), and the recoveries of the failed banks' estates average about 49 %. General creditors therefore compensated domestic depositors in the amount of 51 % of total deposits. The banks' parent companies' foreign loans amounted to the equivalent of some €9.5 billion (ISK 1421 billion).

[44] The Central Bank of Iceland (2010, September 19). *FIH to be sold to a consortium of ATP, PFA, Folksam and CPDyvig.* (Press release No. 26/2010). http://www.cb.is/publications/news/news/2010/09/19/FIH-to-be-sold-to-a-consortium-of-ATP--PFA--Folksam-and-CPDyvig-/.

total of £2.08 billion. The original purchase had been about 502 pence per share, meaning the British taxpayer will sustain a loss of around £1 billion from the sale of the first tranche of shares. Given that UK authorities used about £45.5 billion to recapitalize RBS during the financial crisis, this adds up to a total 35 % loss or £15.5 billion, equal to about 3 % of current UK output – whatever the final outcome will be.

Moreover, the measures taken by the Icelandic authorities have withstood all legal challenges in Icelandic and international courts. The multiple investigations launched by UK authorities into the conduct of the Icelandic banks all closed without any charges. Prime Minister Haarde may have been reluctant to act until he was standing with his back against the wall, but nevertheless most of the choices he made were, in hindsight, the correct ones. Perhaps the most important decision he made was to place matters into the hands of the experts assembled by the FSA.

Just like his counterpart, Gordon Brown, Haarde received no hero's salute, and his party fared poorly in the next election. He was, in fact, on the receiving end of both anger and blame. The collapse of the banks was seen as a major disaster and humiliation by the Icelandic nation. The numbers support that view: the collapse was accompanied by a 50 % drop in the value of the ISK, which was halted only by imposing capital controls, inflation in the range of 10–20 %, with corresponding reduction in purchasing power, 10 % output contraction, and a sharp rise in unemployment. Furthermore, the Emergency Act seemed to be forced upon the unsuspecting nation, since Haarde and his emissaries never conveyed an effective explanation of their actions to the public.

On November 15, a group calling themselves "the voices of the people" assembled in front of the parliamentary house. They made two demands: first, that the government would resign and a new election would be held immediately; second, that three governors of the CBI resign, as well as the director and the board of the FSA. With every passing week, the protest built up steam. Soon, huge masses of people were protesting, marching, and banging pots and pans – hence the protest would be known as the Kitchenware revolution. As one of the participants describes it:

It became evident that the Icelandic banking sector had, with the government's complicity, systematically concealed its vulnerabilities for years and engaged in massive fraud, the ludicrousness and magnitude of which has few parallels. . . . Hatred of the Independence Party and of Davíð Oddsson, head of the Central Bank since 2005, was the core unifying element of this disparate movement.[45]

By January 2009, protests had even turned violent. Although quite tame by international comparison – there was no looting or burned cars – the riots were unprecedented in the tranquil world of Icelandic politics.

The coalition between the Independence Party and the Social Democratic Alliance had an overwhelming majority in parliament, with 43 seats out of 63. The street protest notwithstanding, there were respectful but firm calls for reform. After so much national suffering, there needed to be a charter path to a new and better Iceland. Haarde, the quintessential old establishment insider, was unable to fulfill this demand in a credible way. In early 2009, the popular pressure for action became unbearable for his partnering party, the Social Democratic Alliance. They broke ranks and formed a minority government with the Left-Greens in February. By that time, Haarde had been diagnosed with throat cancer, and he left politics altogether. In the final days of his government, the minister of trade and commerce, the FSA director, and its board all resigned. About two weeks after the new government had taken power, the governors of the CBI were forced out of office.

In the May 2009 election, the Independence Party suffered a huge defeat and center-left parties gained a majority in parliament for the first time in Iceland's post-war history. That was in many ways a Pyrrhic victory. The intellectual left saw its elective majority as an historic chance to implement various changes. Visions that had been stoked endlessly in cafés and parlors all over Iceland, with little practical chance of being implemented, could now see a winning margin in parliament. Thus, the banking crisis of 2008 became a pretext for pushing various reforms in Iceland's society that had nothing to do with banking or stabilization policies. This included a new constitution, the abolition of the quota

---

[45] Thorsteinsson, Vidar. (2016). Iceland's Revolution. *The Jacobin magazine, 20*. https://www.jacobinmag.com/2016/03/iceland-banking-finance-icesave-left-greens/

system in the fishing sector, and various other measures that were bound to create divisions within a nation long accustomed to consensus politics.

Whatever potential those goals may have held, the reform processes went nowhere. They were steered by narrow-minded ideologues happy to side-step expert advice and the usual consensus-building process. This led to confrontations between the government, the business community, and the labor unions, with the latter convinced the government was hell-bent on destroying rather than "creating" jobs. Moreover, taking power at the onset of a great output contraction, it was now up to the left to deal with the gargantuan task of reconstructing a new financial system from the rubble of the old banks. This work had to proceed alongside a harsh fiscal adjustment to a much lower revenue base, as well a severe household debt crisis.

The conditions were sufficient to extinguish any revolutionary flame. The governing parties soon began to splinter, and the majority became insecure halfway through the term. When a new election came up in the spring of 2013, the two coalition partners suffered a crushing defeat as their combined electoral strength went from 51.5 % down to 23.8 % – a record loss in Iceland for any government since independence. That result left the Independence Party back in control – but now with the centrist Progressive Party as a partner.

Prior to the left-wing government taking over in February 2009, the Minister of Justice, Björn Bjarnason, appointed a special prosecutor to investigate and prosecute bankers for financial crimes. (These prosecutions are ongoing, and are discussed in Chap. 4.) In September 2010, the left-wing government evoked an archaic clause in the constitution to convene a special court of impeachment (Landsdómur), a body created in 1905 to try government ministers. Hitherto, it had never been put into action. The court consisted of 15 members – five Supreme Court justices, a district court president, a constitutional law professor, and eight people chosen by parliament. The decision to indict a minister to stand trial is voted on in parliament. This arrangement is in clear contradiction to the generally accepted principle of separated powers (trias politica), which divides branches into a legislature, an executive, and a judiciary. The Icelandic constitution had originally been drafted in 1874, at the time when ministers were appointed by the Danish king and could not be displaced by parliament, as is now customary.

Indictments for Haarde and three other ministers from his cabinet – the minister of finance (from the Independence Party), the minister of trade and commerce, and the foreign minister (the latter two from the Social Democratic Alliance) – were put to a vote on September 28, 2010. Indictments against three of the ministers were dismissed, but the parliament voted 33–30 to indict Haarde on four accounts of gross negligence or malfeasance: neglecting to monitor the activities of the working group on financial stability and insure they were sufficiently effective; neglecting to act to reduce the size of the banking system; not making sure that Icesave interest accounts in Britain were transferred to a subsidiary; and negligence for not holding cabinet meetings when the crisis reached the breaking point. He would face up to two years in prison if found guilty of the most serious offences.

Critics claimed the leftist government was using an old and tricky legal clause to exact political vendetta against one man, especially after indictments against three other ministers were put to the vote in parliament and failed. At its fortieth national convention, on November 17–20, 2011, the Independence Party concluded that "accusations against Geir H. Haarde, the former leader of the Independence Party and former Prime Minister, constituted an abhorrent political trial." The convention declared its unequivocal support for Haarde, while noting the serious precedent the parliament had set with its decision to prosecute.[46]

The trial began in March 2012 and the verdict was delivered on April 23. Haarde was acquitted of the three most serious charges but found guilty for not holding cabinet meetings on important state matters. The lesser charge carried no prison sentence or fine, and all legal fees were paid by the state. Haarde decided, as a matter of principle, to refer the whole case to the European Court of Human Rights in Strasbourg, where a judgment is still pending. With the Independence Party back in power,

---

[46] The Independence Party (2011, November 20). *Drög að stjórnmálaályktun 40. landsfundar Sjálfstæðisflokksins. (Draft political resolution of the 40th national convention of the Independence Party.)* http://www.xd.is/media/xd/landsfundur-2011/Stjornmalaalyktun-loka.pdf

Haarde was appointed Ambassador of Iceland to the United States in 2014.

The whole affair is, unfortunately, a very revealing testament to the political climate in post-crisis Iceland. Letting old banks fail and establishing new ones in their place looks good on paper, as does the ability to regain competiveness in the wake of a crashing currency. But the institutional and social costs have been huge. The banks are the keepers of value and confidence in every modern society, and when they fall the collateral damage is extensive. It is straightforward accounting to tally the lost physical and financial capital, but the drain on social capital is more elusive. The systematic banking failure in October 2008 led the public to lose confidence in main sovereign institutions of the Icelandic republic – and that has proved to be difficult to repair.

"You never want a serious crisis to go to waste. . . . It's an opportunity to do things you could not do before." Attributed to Rahm Emanuel, mayor of Chicago and former White House Chief of Staff, this is the so-called Rahm's Rule of Crisis Management.[47] Social upheaval following a banking crisis opens the door for all kinds of reform agendas with long shelf lives and little political capital. Sometimes, as in a brawl at a local pub, there arises the opportunity to hit a person you have a grudge against, even though he didn't start the fight. And thus a sneak punch sparks a group fight. However, to quote another well-known author, most bar-brawl reforms are full of "sound and fury, signifying nothing."[48]

---

[47] See Bruce Yandle, "Rahm's Rule of Crisis Management: A Footnote to the Theory of Regulation", February 11, 2013, The Foundation for Economic Education. http://fee.org/articles/rahms-rule-of-crisis-management-a-footnote-to-the-theory-of-regulation/#axzz2KizozPJ4

[48] Shakespeare, William. (1623). *The Tragedy of Macbeth*. Act 5, Scene 5.

4

Day Zero

4.1 When the Phones Went Silent

On the morning of Wednesday, October 8, 2008, employees at
Kaupthing Bank's headquarters noticed a banner on the television screen
mounted above them. The banner, from a Bloomberg broadcast, read:
"ING Buys 3 Billion Pounds of Icelandic Deposits." Soon, a large, solemn
congregation stood in front of the screen, staring at the banner. It was the
bank's death sentence, writ large.

That fateful morning, the UK Financial Services Authority (FSA) had
taken over Kaupthing's UK subsidiary, Kaupthing Singer & Friedlander
(KSF), and transferred the bank's deposits – known as Kaupthing Edge –
to the Dutch bank ING. But that was the minor part of the UK
authorities' business that morning. They had also frozen Landsbanki's
assets by invoking the infamous terrorist legislation,[1] and seized the
bank's UK subsidiary, Heritable Bank, into the bargain. The freezing

---

[1] Her Majesty's Treasury. (2008, October 8). *The Landsbanki Freezing Order 2008*. (Statutory
Instruments 2008 No. 2668).

© The Author(s) 2016
Á. Jónsson, H. Sigurgeirsson, *The Icelandic Financial Crisis*,
DOI 10.1057/978-1-137-39455-2_4

order also applied to the Icelandic government, the Central Bank of Iceland (CBI), and the Icelandic Financial Supervisory Authority (FSA), to the extent that their actions were entangled with those of the bank. Landsbanki then joined the HM Treasury's official blacklist of the world's leading terrorist groups.[2]

But why was the Bloomberg headline received as a death sentence in Kaupthing headquarters? KSF was an independent UK bank; its bankruptcy did not automatically imply a takedown of the mother company. But it did breach Kaupthing's cross-default provisions loan covenants and open up the possibility of an early redemption for bondholders. The bank's management spent the rest of the day frantically attempting to persuade bondholders not to act. Some agreed to waive their rights; but others had hedged themselves by shorting the bank in the CDS market, and actually stood to gain from a default.

It was over by midnight. The top management went to the Icelandic FSA and handed the bank over. With Kaupthing down, the government had taken over the last of the three major banks.

When employees arrived at Kaupthing's headquarters on Thursday, they found a totally different world. The bank was dead and silent. In the days leading up to the collapse, the trading room had been hectic. Facing foreign and domestic investors, who wanted to close down their positions and eliminate exposure to Kaupthing and the Icelandic market in general, the traders had lived in an effective bunker. Their calls for counterparties to pay up fell into a void. Most were simply ignored. One of the authors was present at the trading floor at the time, and heard excuses such as some counterparties were at lunch, on holiday, or otherwise disposed, and would call to square the balance directly. Those calls, of course, never came. What was happening was a sort of investment bank run, with liquidity sucked out of trading accounts and never replenished.

---

[2] From October 10 to 22 2008 Landsbanki was put on a list of current regimes of financial sanctions on the HM Treasury website. See for example Figure 1 on p. 6 of: Ministry of Finance. (2011, August 25). *Skýrsla fjármálaráðherra um mat á áhrifum af beitingu Breta á lögum um varnir gegn hryðjuverkum, glæpum og um öryggi fyrir íslensk fyrirtæki.* (*Report by the Minister of Finance on the impact of the application of the British Act on Anti-terrorism, Crime and Security on Icelandic companies.*) https://www.fjarmalaraduneyti.is/media/utgafa/Skyrsla_fmrh_ahrif_hvl.pdf

On Thursday morning the traders' phones were silent. Dead banks pay no bills. Computer screens were black, because except for Treasury bonds and government guaranteed housing bonds (HFF), the Icelandic financial market was also dead. The currency interbank market was down, too: once the banks defaulted, 85 % of the financial sector disappeared.

Landsbanki had been taken over the same night the emergency legislation was passed; Glitnir fell the day after. It was now anticipated that new banks would be carved out of the old ones, though no one really knew how they would operate, or which people would have jobs. But Kaupthing's personnel caught a glimpse of their future on this fateful Thursday, when the New Landsbanki appeared via a restructuring process. It was a chilling future, to say the least.

On Tuesday morning October 7, the day after the FSA takeover, the ministers of finance, trade, and commerce paid Landsbanki a special visit, accompanied by journalists and photographers. In front of the media, they promised there would be no major changes and employees' labor contracts would remain valid.[3] But the UK terrorism legislation, launched the next day, changed everything. With old Landsbanki now branded a terrorist entity, a new bank had to be founded almost instantaneously.

So when Landsbanki employees arrived at work on Thursday, they found an email waiting. It stated that only 1000 of the 1550 employees of the old bank would have jobs at the new one; thus a third of the jobs at Landsbanki dissolved in the default. The new Landsbanki would be a purely domestic retail concern, so the cuts were realized by savaging the investment bank operations, along with foreign relations personnel.[4]

There was more bad news. Iceland's emergency legislation had overwritten the standard bill of rights in EEA legislation, which protected workers from being transferred in the event of default. In other words, neither the old bank nor the new would honor existing labor contracts.

---

[3] Guðbjartsson, Steinþór. (2008, October 8). Bankafólk í kreppu. (Bank staff in a crisis). *Morgunblaðið*

[4] Landsbankinn: Einkabankasvið og Verðbréfasvið lögð af. (Landsbankinn: Private banking and Investment banking discontinued.) (2008, October 9). Viðskiptablaðið. http://www.vb.is/frettir/landsbankinn-einkabankasvi-og-verbrefasvi-log-af/12692/

This had two practical implications. First the new bank staff effectively became new hires, and their old salaries were slashed (the average cut to fix salaries was around 30 %). This was not unexpected, and perhaps tolerable for those happy to still have a job. For those let go, the standard three- to six-month leave of old Landsbanki was disabled.[5] Instead, they needed to file claims on the old bank to have their contracts honored: a dubious proposal when no one yet knew how or when the old bank estates would be divided. The other option was to apply to a special government insurance fund for workers of bankrupt companies. They would receive minimum wage payments that ended after three months.

What followed was reminiscent of the destruction that followed the Lehman default, just three weeks earlier. Confusion led to fury and then despair. As the new management selected workers for the new bank, those given the sack left – often crying – with their belongings in a box. There were wails of genuine agony throughout the day.[6] These were the conditions under which New Landsbanki was founded.

New Glitnir was founded on October 15, through a much more orderly process. The labor cuts were still drastic – also about 30 % – but by this time it was clear that the banks would be sheltered from enforcement action from creditors, although they would not be officially in default. Moreover, hard pushback by the labor unions had led to the reinstatement of paid periods of notice stipulated in their old contracts. However, the old banks refused to pay all other negotiated extra payments to the fixed salaries, such as bonuses. Sacked employees tried to claw back these extras through litigation, with varying success.

At Kaupthing, there was a new twist. Five Icelandic pension funds initiated talks with the government to buy the bank out of the resolution process. This kept bank operations in limbo for a part of October. Its headquarters were filled by young, energetic people left with little to do but worry over their fate. Employees kept showing up to work, where so

---

[5] Fá starfsmenn Landsbankans greidd laun? (Will Landsbankinn staff be paid salary?). (2008, October 9). *Vísir*. http://www.visir.is/fa-starfsmenn-landsbankans-greidd-laun-/article/2008146114965

[6] "Við sitjum bara hérna og bíðum," segir starfsmaður Landsbankans ("We just sit here and wait," says Landsbankinn employee. (2008, October 9). *Viðskiptablaðið*. http://www.vb.is/frettir/vi-sitjum-bara-herna-og-bium-segir-starfsmaur-land/12677/

much of their fortunes now stood on the line. Not only did Kaupthing workers fear for their jobs: a default could well result in many personal bankruptcies. Kaupthing had paid its workers salaries in kind, using shares in the bank along with generous financing, often in some low-yielding foreign currency.[7] Thus, most Kaupthing employees were shareholders, some of them major, who faced the prospect of their main asset being wiped out. Furthermore, to make matters worse, the currency loan from the bank had doubled in size after the collapse of the ISK.

Kaupthing's employee shareholder policy had been a cornerstone of its model from the outset. The aim was to align employee incentives with the bank's success and inspire loyalty through ownership. But the strategy showed signs of backfiring even before the collapse. When the bank faced a run and the stock price (along with the ISK) went south, some employees worried their positions were now precarious. But if anyone wanted to liquidate a position, he or she needed permission from the bank's compliance offer.[8]

As the situation worsened, people became more desperate to sell and threatened to resign, just so they could clear out their positions. The bank at last was forced to respond. In the last board meeting, held on September 25, the personal guarantee to employees of all equity loans granted by the bank was terminated.[9] The decision came from "the view to ensuring that the employees can remain focused to their work within the Bank."[10] This decision was later challenged and then annulled in court, with disastrous consequences for the employees.[11]

While waiting for whatever came next, employees turned to chess, somewhat of a national sport for Icelanders (the country prides itself in having the largest number of chess grandmasters per capita). October at Kaupthing saw endless tournaments between various departments and floors, and plenty of individual competitions.

---

[7] See for example Supreme Court verdicts no. 406/2011, 518/2011, and 176/2012.

[8] Matthíasson, Viðar Már. (2008, November 12). Álitsgerð. (Legal opinion). http://www.visir.is/assets/pdf/XZ672616.PDF

[9] See for example Supreme Court verdict no. 406/2011. http://haestirettur.is/domar?nr=8362

[10] Matthíasson, Viðar Már. (2008, November 12). Álitsgerð. (Legal opinion).

[11] Supreme Court verdict no. 406/2011, October 18, 2012. http://haestirettur.is/domar?nr=8362

However, some employees remained quite busy with banking. A small team of traders was sent to the CBI to handle international payments on behalf of the bank's clients (see Chap. 3). The traders in the capital market division saw to the unpleasant business of gathering the losses of their clients, then making the dreaded call to report on a loss and a balance due to the bank estate.

Lending against the value of a listed equity does not have to carry a higher risk than, say, lending against the value of a house, if the under-lying stock can be sold in a liquid market on short notice. In that case, the bank can just liquidate the position by placing a margin call on the loan and recover the funds. A house or commercial property is much less liquid as collateral, and can only be retrieved after a lengthy legal process.

The Icelandic banks made the loans to investors buying listed stocks on what they considered to be a comfortable equity buffer. They were not unique in this, since the most profitable and fastest-growing segment of banking on both sides of the Atlantic was loans to hedge funds or investment companies. What was unusual was the precarious liquidity of the ICEX. In most cases, a bank could easily liquidate its holding company's client portfolio through a margin call, sell it in the market, and recover its loan. However, the portfolios of all the banks' clients were very similar and therefore highly correlated. That included the banks' most important customers, owners, and managers. When the need arose, liquidating the whole system in an orderly fashion proved impossible. But this arrangement, like much else, worked well until stock markets the world over found themselves in a systemic liquidity crisis after August 2007.

The three Icelandic banks were the first A-rated enterprises to go bankrupt. Between them, they had listed stock valued at €5 billion on the last open trading day, Friday, October 3, 2008.[12] Financial stock constituted about 90 % of the market cap of listed Icelandic equity. With all that value wiped out with a single blow, the average investor's portfolio inevitably cratered.

_____

[12] The closing prices of Glitnir, Kaupthing, and Landsbanki where 3.91, 654 and 19.85 and their number of shares 14,647, 718.7 and 10,910 million ISK respectively, for a market cap of 750 billion ISK, or around €5 billion.

Furthermore, since stock purchases were often leveraged with loans in foreign, low-yielding currencies, the collapse of the ISK constituted a double whammy for the investor base of Kaupthing. On the other hand, the exit from the stocks and run from the banks also meant a flight to safety into the government bond market. Yields dropped to historical lows in the advent of the crisis.

With banking stocks and the ISK declining steadily throughout 2008, Kaupthing's trading book had actively monitored client positions, and with aggressive margin calls. These were, of course, the small clients. The situation in the first week of October, then, was not totally unprepared for, nor was it unexpected. The bank had not followed through with margin calls to the large clients, namely the large holding companies that had become too-big-to-fail (see Chap. 3). It had also stopped making margin calls to employees owning Kaupthing's stock, even though some had actually begged for one so they could liquidate their holdings and pay off their loans. However, the main difficulty lay in settling derivative contracts made to either hedge against risk or to assume risk to benefit from the market volatility. After the collapse, Icelandic courts were kept busy with endless litigation and legal disputes concerning the settlements of these losses.

Also at work in Kaupthing was a group cooperating with the FSA to carve assets for New Kaupthing out of the old bank. The emergency legislation had made deposits priority claims, which enabled the FSA to transfer them from the old banks to new operators. In many respects, these authorizations mirrored those made by the US FDIC, and they comprised a sort of Purchase and Assumption (P&A) agreement of the assets and liabilities of the old banks. However, the Icelandic FSA actions differed from those of the FDIC in that the FSA could not dispose of the banks' assets and liabilities to other existing banks. Therefore, new banks owned by the Treasury were established to undertake this role.

The deposit transfer itself was simple; Prime Minister Geir Haarde declared a blanket government guarantee of all deposits, regardless of holder or size, and they were transferred at nominal value to the new banks. The main difficulty lay in the asset transfer, which had to be done at a "fair value."

But in a country afflicted with a severe banking crisis, collapsing asset prices, double-digit inflation, and an illiquid currency market, "fair value" is fickle, to say the least. It was clear that inflated pre-crash asset valuation would not apply. Huge loan losses were imminent and steep cautionary write-downs were in order – but how large would those be? This was – of course – an urgent matter for the creditors of the fallen banks. Making deposits priority claims constituted a very large loss in itself. Nevertheless, the general insolvency law still applied, to the effect that all appropriated assets exceeding priority claims required compensation to the estates of the fallen banks. Given these crisis conditions, the banks' creditors were a divided and unorganized flock, but that would change as the year drew to its close and hedge funds started to accumulate claims, as will be discussed in Chap. 6.

The task of asset valuation was also of a great importance to the Icelandic government, since at the outset it had decided to transfer both domestic deposits *and* assets to the new banks. In other words, the banks would be partitioned into a purely domestic part, which would be recapitalized, and a foreign part, that would go into default. The government's intention was to find a place for Icelandic households and businesses in a new, living bank, rather than a defaulted estate. As such, asset valuation had two objectives: in the first place, it would determine the size of the banks and the subsequent need for re-capitalization out of state coffers. Second, it would affix a price tag on each domestic asset bought from the defaulted estate and applied to the establishment of the new banking system. Furthermore, it was important for Icelandic authorities to demonstrate that the process was fair and that assets were not being nationalized without compensation.

After discussions with the five pension funds to buy the bank came to nothing, Kaupthing's staff made the first assessment of New Kaupthing on October 22.[13] The new bank had deposits in the amount of €2.8 billion (417 billion ISK) and assets valued at €4.7 billion (700 billion ISK). The old bank would therefore – on behalf of general creditors – have

---

[13] Financial Supervisory Authority. (2008, October 21). *Ákvörðun Fjármálaeftirlitsins um ráðstöfun eigna og skulda Kaupþings banka hf. til Nýja Kaupþings banka hf. (The FSA's decision on the allocation of the assets and liabilities of Kaupthing bank hf. to New Kaupthing bank hf.)* (Reference no. 200810055). http://www.fme.is/media/akvardanir/22.-oktober-2008.pdf

a claim of €1.9 billion on the new bank as an outstanding bond, which corresponded to the difference between domestic deposits and the fair value of the domestic assets. The new balance sheet was a slimmed down version, with assets only about 23 % of the original. This reflected the fact that the old bank's asset base was about 50 % foreign. It also reflected the 80 % write down of the domestic corporate loan book, which creditors vehemently opposed.

The day of reckoning came on Friday, October 24, for Kaupthing employees. The new bank picked its staff and the others left.

4.2   How to Value Assets?

When most of the dust had settled, Icelandic authorities faced the task of deciding how to split the banks. The FSA decided to create purely domestic banking entities. To safeguard deposits and provide some stable funding for the new entities, domestic deposits were moved to the new banks on the liability side. With deposits having priority, assets of the estates would always go towards covering them first. At the parent companies, domestic deposits were only 18 % of Glitnir's total funding, and 14 % of Landsbanki and Kaupthing.[14] No other liabilities would be transferred, as this could also give rise to a dispute of unfounded differentiation of creditors. This did not go well down with the CBI, which had lent the fallen banks the equivalent of €2.3 billion (345 billion ISK) with unsecured bank bonds as collateral and therefore wanted to have its loans transferred to the new banks. However, the CBI had to be categorized as a general creditor and would thus suffer the same loss from prioritization of deposits as others in that category. The CBI proceeded to write off about 20 % of the claims (ISK 75 billion), and at year-end 2008 it sold them to the Treasury for ISK 270 billion. This numbers game was meant to prevent the CBI's equity from turning negative. Immediately after the purchase, the Treasury wrote the claims down by ISK 175 billion, which represented the difference between purchase price and assessed value. This was the direct loss to the Icelandic taxpayer from the repo lending of the CBI.[14]

---

[14] The Icelandic Treasury paid for the purchase of the CBI's collateralized loans by issuing a bond in the amount of ISK 270 billion. See a more detailed discussion in Chap. 8.

On the asset side, it was decided to transfer only domestic assets. The goal here was to create fully operating domestic banks and, hence, keep the banking system from collapsing even if the "old bank" went into winding-up procedure. Therefore, the asset split was generally based on whether the assets were claims on domestic or foreign clients. However, the domestic/foreign partition could not be done on a razor edge. On October 12, 2008, three days after the establishment of New Landsbanki, the FSA issued a decision stating that derivative contracts would not leave the old bank, even if they had domestic actors as counterparties. The derivative contracts were judged to be such a large, open-ended risk for the new bank that it might even be expected to default on them owing to "unforeseeable consequences."[15]

The asset transfer was made at fair value, that is, after precautionary write-downs. The difference between the fair value of assets and deposits naturally belonged to general creditors, according to the Act on Bankruptcy. The first initial fair value assessment was done by the banks themselves. The balance sheets of the new banks were based on this first assessment.

The FSA then hired Deloitte LP, a London-based consultancy, to make its own assessment and another consultancy firm, Oliver Wyman, to review that assessment.

Deloitte's assessment valued assets considerably higher than the transferred liabilities. Therefore, the new banks, other things remaining equal, should have had to issue large bonds to the old banks. The intention of the authorities was to have the Treasury provide equity for the new banks, estimated at €2.6 billion (ISK 385 billion).[16] However, the authorities decided that it was inadvisable to start the new banks with such large debts to the insolvent estates. They presented a new assessment of their assets, which was considerably lower than Deloitte's minimum estimate.

Following negotiations with the estates, the Icelandic assets were written down to this estimated value before being placed on the new banks' balance sheets. When they finally saw the light of day at the end of 2009

---

[15] Financial Supervisory Authority. (2008, October 12). (Reference no. 200810037). http://www.fme.is/media/akvardanir/12.-oktober-2008.pdf

[16] Ministry of Finance. (2011, March). *Skýrsla fjármálaráðherra um endurreisn viðskiptabankanna. (Minister of finance report on the restoration of the commercial banks).*

and the beginning of 2010, the banks' assets amounted to some ISK 2088 billion, whereof the transferred assets were valued at ISK 1762 billion (See Fig. 4.1 in billion euros).

The far left of the figure shows the combined consolidated balance sheets of the old banks, Glitnir, Kaupthing, and Landsbanki, as of the end of June 2008, with assets on the left and liabilities on the right. As the figure shows, the old banks' total assets were the equivalent of €96 billion. The banks' equity was €6 billion, making their total liabilities €90 billion. As the banks' balance sheets are consolidated, they include all the assets and liabilities of their subsidiaries. At year-end 2007, around 41 % of the banks' total assets on a group-wide basis were in their foreign subsidiaries.[17] It was the banks' parent companies that became insolvent, while individual subsidiaries were sold, wound up separately, or continued to operate for a period of longer or shorter duration.

The center of the figure shows the assets and liabilities of the insolvent estates. The estates' "assets" represents the sum amount that the estates have already distributed to priority creditors and the value of those assets remaining to them at year-end 2014. It therefore reflects the assets that remained in the estates upon the establishment of the new banks. As the figure shows, the total assets of the insolvent estates amounted to €23 billion, whereas total claims on the insolvent estates amount to around €55 billion. Of these, €9.5 billion are priority claims, of which €8.6 billion had already been paid at year-end 2014.[18]

The far right of the figure represents the part of the new banks' balance sheets taken over from the old banks. This does not include the initial equity contribution from the Treasury, or debts owed by the new banks to the old ones. The total value of the assets transferred from the old banks to

---

[17] Central Bank of Iceland. (2008, May 8). *Fjármálastöðugleiki. (Financial Stability)*. p. 38.

[18] The intention in presenting the estates' assets in this manner is to obtain an assessment of the value of the assets remaining with the insolvent estates upon the split of the banks. One of the advantages of this presentation is to give a better assessment of the value of the assets than was available at the commencement of their winding-up proceedings. The problem, however, is that these are 2014 price levels, and not those of 2008 or 2009, as are balance sheet figures for the old and new banks in the figure. What are referred to as "liabilities" of the estates, however, are all claims against the estates recognized by their winding-up boards as of year-end 2014, whether they have been paid in full, in part, or not at all. This amount is based on claims lodged against the banks as of April 22, 2009, and therefore on 2009 price levels.

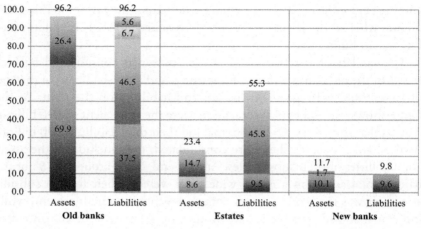

Fig. 4.1 Division of assets and liabilities between the estates and the new banks. The old banks' balance sheets are consolidated balance sheets as of end of June 2008. The estates' assets are priority claims paid on the one hand and their assets at year-end 2014 on the other. Liabilities of the estates are recognized claims as of year-end 2014. The assets and liabilities of the new banks are the part of the assets and liabilities that were transferred from the old banks. Amounts in billion euros at the exchange rate 150 ISK per euro (Source: Six month interim financial statements of Glitnir, Kaupthing, and Landsbanki in 2008, annual financial statements of Glitnir, Kaupthing, and LBI for 2014 and annual financial statements of Íslandsbanki, Arion bank, and Landsbankinn 2008)

the new ones was about €12 billion, and the total value of their liabilities was €10 billion, most of which was deposits. The difference between the value of assets and liabilities was therefore €2 billion, which was made up by bonds issued by the new banks to the old ones, and as equity contributions from the old banks to the new ones.

Various insights can be gained by reviewing the size of the banking system before and after the collapse, recoveries and losses of creditors, and the impact of the emergency legislation on the recoveries of general creditors. In the first place, the new banks' balance sheets, including the initial equity contribution made to them, total around €14 billion; compare this to the old banks' assets of around €96 billion on a consolidated basis. The reestablished banking system was therefore only around 15 % the size of the pre-collapse banking system. From the claims lodged against the insolvent estates and the deposits transferred to the new banks, it can be deduced that deposits comprised around 30 % of the parent company liabilities, divided fairly evenly between their foreign and domestic branches.

4.3   How to Partition the Banks?

There were of course other proposals for partitioning the failed banks. The most common cut-through of failed or troubled financial institutions is the so called "good bank–bad bank" division, by which toxic assets are removed or somehow quarantined from other (good) assets of the bank – most often with some kind of government guarantee to remove any chance of loss. With this methodology, there is no doubt about the good bank's financial health and performance, which might otherwise impair its ability to borrow, lend, trade, and raise capital. This was the aim of the Emergency Economic Stabilization Act enacted October 2008, which called for the US government to purchase up to $700 billion in distressed assets from financial institutions.[19]

Given both the structure and size of the Icelandic banks and the expediency of the crisis, the Icelandic FSA judged this approach impossible to execute. Iceland's primary responsibility was to sustain a fully operational banking system despite the default of the three main banks. The banking system had assets in excess of ten times the Icelandic gross domestic product (GDP), and many of the foreign assets were performing well. Foreign subsidiaries, of course, held a large share of the banks' assets (about 41 % as of year-end 2007).[20] Some, such as KSF and Heritable Bank, had already been taken into liquidation by the British authorities and were of no concern. Nevertheless, the good bank–bad bank methodology would have left Icelandic authorities with a banking system too large to refinance and recapitalize. The cost would have been prohibitive,

---

[19] Division A of Pub. L. 110–343, 122 Stat. 3765, enacted October 3, 2008.
[20] Central Bank of Iceland. (2008, May 8). *Fjármálastöðugleiki. (Financial Stability)*. p. 38.

and the necessary foreign funding was probably unavailable in any event. One government advisor, Professor Friðrik Már Baldursson, later maintained that government action was based on legal grounds, and was meant to avoid violating the property-rights provisions of the constitution and unlawful discrimination between domestic and international creditors.[21]

A variety of "good bank–bad bank" structures use separate portfolios or subsidiaries to segregate troubled assets and save distressed and potentially failing banks. Some have been applied without government assistance.[22] The first limited-life "bad bank," created specifically to handle toxic assets, was the Grant Street National Bank. Created in 1988, it held a $1.4 billion portfolio of low-quality assets and non-performing loans from Mellon Bank in the USA.[23] The assets were transferred to the bad bank at a 47 % discount, and the $640 million purchase was funded by the public sale of two classes of short-term, extendible pay-through notes. Grant Street's common stock was declared a special dividend and was spun off to Mellon shareholders. Subsequently, Grant Street was established as a discrete, unaffiliated entity. The outcome was a success both for the good bank and the bad bank. Mellon bank regained market trust and was able to seek new capital (ultimately it morphed into

---

[21] See p. 92 in. Baldursson, Friðrik Már, & Portes, Richard. (2013). *Gambling for resurrection in Iceland: the rise and fall of the banks.* Available at SSRN 2361098.

[22] Brenna, Gabriel, Thomas Poppensieker, & Sebastian Schneider (2009, December). *Understanding the bad bank.* McKinsey & Company.

[23] There were other similar good bank–bad bank approaches prior to Grant Street National. Frank Cahouet, Mellon's CEO from 1987 to 1998, originally used a variation in 1986 when he was CEO at Crocker National Bank and was brought in to clean up Crocker's asset problems. In the case of Crocker, Britain's Midland Bank PLC, Crocker's parent, down-streamed capital in exchange for $3.5 billion of Crocker's non-performing loans These were transferred to a workout subsidiary of Midland, and were removed from Crocker's balance sheet before Crocker was sold to Wells Fargo. In connection with the 1987 Chemical Banking Corporation acquisition of Texas Commerce Bancshares, the lower quality loans of Texas Commerce were written down and transferred into a stripped-down, existing subsidiary bank of Texas Commerce, that is, a "bad bank," which was then spun off to Texas Commerce's shareholders. See: Bleier, Michael E. (2008, August) *From 'Bad' Bank to 'Good'.* ReedSmith. (Client Alert 08-143). https://www.reedsmith.com/files/Publication/15cda61b-edcc-47dd-a186-cba9a4012fed/Presentation/PublicationAttachment/2e8568c2-06f1-4c05-9641-d2a0a15991ec/bull08143_200809034643.pdf

BNY Mellon asset management).[24] Grant Street was able to deliver the cash flow to pay off all the notes before maturity, and its existence was terminated July 31, 1995.[25]

To determine the fair market value of the assets it transferred to Grant Street, Mellon used a valuation process based on a liquidation scenario, with a forecasted cash flow (using discount rates). The process was developed with the assistance of the Arthur Andersen & Co. accounting firm. The results were checked by Kenneth Leventhal & Company, which reviewed the reasonableness of the assumptions. The last step was a sensitivity analysis done by an independent third party to test the potential effect of variations from the underlying assumptions, with respect to oil prices, economic growth, inflation, and interest rates.[26]

Ultimately, the Icelandic authorities used almost identical methods to establish a fair value estimate of the banks' domestic assets.

The creditors of the fallen Icelandic banks also considered some application of this route. Some sought advice from the authors of this book on how to proceed in early 2009. One option considered was a reverse takeover, in which Kaupthing subsidiary, the Danish FIH, acquired the mother company.

The J.P. Morgan advisors to the CBI (see Chap. 2) seemed to have something similar in mind in October 2008, when they suggested a new approach at a meeting with the CBI and other government officials some days after the emergency legislation became active and after two banks had been divided. The suggestions were not made public, but judging from contemporary news reports, the main theme was that only domestic deposits should be transferred to the new banks, while their assets should be guaranteed by a government-issued bond that used the old banks' estates as collateral.[27] It is, however, difficult to envision how the new banks would

---

[24] Daniel, Richard H. (2004). An alternative approach to government managed companies: The Mellon approach. In Pomerleano, Michael and Shaw, William (Eds.), *Corporate Restructuring: Lessons from Experience*. Washington DC: The World Bank.

[25] Grant Street National Bank (in liquidation) reports results. (1995, January 30). *PR Newswire*.

[26] Eagleson, William R. (1990). How Good is a Bad Bank? *The Real Estate Finance Journal*, pp. 71–75.

[27] Bergsveinsson, Jón Aðalsteinn. (2009, March 17). Ein leið af mörgum valin í endurreisn. (One proposal of many chosen for restoration.) *Markaðurinn*. http://www.visir.is/ExternalData/pdf/mark/M090318.pdf

have assumed regular banking operations with only their customers' deposits on their balance sheets, and not the respective loans or other assets unconnected to the deposit holders. In any event, the FSA did not heed Morgan's advice, and ultimately its strategy proved successful.

Jón Gunnar Jónsson, an alumnus of Merrill Lynch and later a director of the Icelandic State Financial Investments,[28] issued a similar proposal in early 2009. He maintained that in order to limit the government's risk while capitalizing the new banks, the asset transfers should be capped to the amount of their deposits. Thus, the new banks would be smaller and less costly to recapitalize. Furthermore, the new banks would not need to issue bonds to the old banks to cover the difference between the nominal value of the deposits and the estimated fair value of the transferred assets; this could lead to a loss if the real asset value turned out to be lower than the estimate. Jónsson provided no specific guidelines for dividing the asset classes, except that transferred assets should be loans to households and small businesses in the lowest risk category.[29] These proposals were drafted into legislation presented to parliament on July 15, 2009, by the Progressive Party chairman, Sigmundur Davíð Gunnlaugsson (then the opposition leader, but destined to become prime minister in 2013).[30]

However, excepting foreign assets, a second good–bad partition could have been carried out after the initial domestic/foreign partition. Non-performing loans of the three banks could be placed into a special government-sponsored National Asset Management Company (National AMC). This methodology was applied in the Scandinavian banking crisis of the early 1990s, when two National AMCs were founded in Sweden as toxic asset destinations, which were bought by the government at a discount. These were Securum for Nordbanken and Retriva for Gotabanken, two banks that represented roughly 20 % of all

---

[28] The Icelandic State Financial Investments, Bankasýsla Ríkisins in Icelandic, manages the state's holdings in banks.

[29] Jónsson, Jón Gunnar (2009, April 24). Endurreisn án eftirskjálfta. (Restoration without aftershocks). *Morgunblaðið*.

[30] Tillaga til þingsályktunar um endurreisn íslensku bankanna. (Proposal for a parliamentary resolution on the restoration of the Icelandic commercial banks.) (2009). Þskj. 275 – 157. mál. 137. löggjafarþing. http://www.althingi.is/altext/137/s/0275.html

Swedish deposits.[31] This approach is generally considered to have been a great success. Not only did the Swedish government recover costs from their National AMC, it also reaped a small profit. The good banks thus created would later morph into the pan-Nordic bank, Nordea.[32]

The Icelandic authorities gave serious consideration to this option while cooperating with the International Monetary Fund (IMF). A letter of intent, signed on November 15, 2008, at the advent of the joint IMF plan, stated that "a well-reputed expert in banking was appointed to be in charge of managing the bank restructuring process." The expert would head a committee comprised of representatives from the prime minister's office, the FSA, the CBI, the Ministry of Finance, and the Ministry of Commerce, but he would report directly to the prime minister.[33]

This "well-reputed expert" was Mats Josefsson, who had been an assistant director of Finansinspektionen, the Swedish financial supervisory authority, as well as the deputy governor of Riksbanken, in which capacity he had directed banking supervision in Sweden from 1990 to 1994, during the years of the Nordic banking crisis.

The committee delivered a report on February 5, 2009. It strongly recommended that the government establish a national AMC to purchase the "bad investments" of the savings banks, most of which were still in operation at this time but were faced with huge loan losses.[34] The AMC was undoubtedly meant to act as a conduit for a government bailout. The report also encouraged the government to found a national AMC for three new banks. That proposal was met with almost unified opposition by the new banks' management, the creditors, and the Icelandic corporate sector. The new banks were afraid that they would lose potential future clients; the creditors worried this action would lead to appropriation or

---

[31] Bergström, C., P. Englund and P. Thorell. (2002). Securum och vägen ut ur bankkrisen, (Securum and the road out of the banking crisis), SNS, Stockholm.

[32] Jonung, L., (2009, February). The Swedish model for resolving the banking crisis of 1991–93. Seven reasons why it was successful. *European Economy, Economic papers 360*. Brussels: European Commission.

[33] International Monetary Fund. (2008, November 15). *Iceland: Letter of Intent and Technical Memorandum of Understanding.* https://www.imf.org/external/np/loi/2008/isl/111508.pdf

[34] Committee on the restoration of the financial system. (2009, February 5). *Starfsáætlun Nr. 1. (Work schedule No. 1).* https://www.forsaetisraduneyti.is/media/Skyrslur/starfsaaetlun1.pdf

mishandling of estate assets. Icelandic corporations in general – in particular represented by the Employers Union SA – were adamant that banks should handle their affairs, but not in tandem with a government-owned resolution fund.

In the end, new legislation, authored by Steingrímur J. Sigfússon, the Minister of Finance, went before parliament on May 15, 2009. It gave the treasury the authority to found a national AMC. However, the authorization came with a twist. It applied to corporations of "national economic importance," which served such a "vital public and security interest" that their foreclosures would "cause a significant disturbance in the society at large."[35] This was certainly some kind of safety measure, meant to assure ownership of these corporations that they would remain domestic and not be sold abroad during some restructuring process.

The legislation was passed, but the AMC was never established. Some savings banks received government aid, but after some years they were singly taken over by the new banks as the household debt crisis deepened and the number of non-performing loans kept accumulating. The new banks would by themselves found a number of AMCs to handle specific asset classes – mostly in connection with commercial property or equity stakes in companies that they had taken over. A national AMC never materialized.

The key advantage of the good bank–bad bank approach is a renewed confidence in the good bank by the divestiture of lower quality assets, which among other things should provide access to funding markets at a lower cost. The toxic assets are now quarantined in a separate entity – the bad bank – to prevent contamination. In Iceland's case, funding of the three new banks was not really an issue, since they all had deposits with a government guarantee and capital controls prevented their deposit holders from leaving the country altogether. Access to foreign funding was at that time inconceivable.

---

[35] Frumvarp til laga um stofnun hlutafélags til að stuðla að endurskipulagningu þjóðhagslegra mikilvægra atvinnufyrirtækja. (Bill on the establishment of a limited liability company to promote the restructuring of nationally important companies.) Þskj. 1 – 1. mál, 137. löggjafarþing. http://www.althingi.is/altext/137/s/0001.html

Furthermore, the good bank management is freed from being pre-occupied with problem assets. Instead, they can focus on the future, granting new loans and creating new business. Moreover, isolating the collection work within a separate, non-banking subsidiary, whose client was an unaffiliated bank, allowed the collection process to proceed unencumbered by the normal bank desire to protect borrower relationships. For that matter, there would be no personal conflict of interest between the bank's personnel and their clients. Lastly, the segregation of troubled assets would hopefully lead to a strong focus on maximizing net present value. However, this approach deviates from the typical banker mentality "to pursue the last dollar of the problem loan no matter how long it may take."[36]

The main drawback to this approach is also counted among the chief benefits: the bad bank has a finite lifespan and is focused only on collecting the payments as quickly as possible. Future client relationships have no value. Both bad bank examples cited – the Grant Street National and the Swedish AMCs – handled toxic assets that originated from the real estate market and were created around projects that had a finite span. Primarily, this meant building developments or projects attached to easily defined collateral – for example, bricks and mortar. The resolution of such assets is much simpler than handling industrial companies with a large number of employees, complex production processes, and other factors.

This arrangement may suit some debtors quite well, as they have an alternative access to financial services and are perhaps able to bargain for steep write-downs by paying the loans up front. For others, bankruptcy and asset recovery is the option with the highest economic value for society at large. However, if the tasks hinge on balance restructuring of the entire corporate sector, in the wake of an economy-wide debt crisis like Iceland's, another picture may emerge. Wholesale liquidation of the Icelandic corporate sector was probably neither feasible nor desirable.

Furthermore, the incentives of the personnel operating the bad bank or the AMC might be open to question. All the employees of Grant Street National were former Mellon personnel who would return to their former positions as soon as the liquidation was complete. The troubled asset

---

[36] Eagleson, William R. (1990). How Good is a Bad Bank? *The Real Estate Finance Journal*, pp. 71–75.

portfolio was financed with high-yielding short-term bonds, which created a clear focus to speed up the collections.

It is very easy to envision other incentives at de novo bad banks. Their employees might not be keen on speeding up the liquidation in order to prolong their employment or avoid legal risk by taking all conflicts to the courts, especially if their salaries were not connected to a speedy resolution by bonus schemes. That may have been the case concerning the liquidation of the old banks' estates in Iceland, which took far longer than the liquidation of Lehman Brothers, for example. A number of general creditors made complaints to the authors of this book about the prolonged winding-up process, which, among other things, they attributed to the lack of performance bonuses at the estates. Instead, the employees were paid by the hour.

In a cross-country study by Klingebiel (2000), she found that in two out of three cases, corporate restructuring AMCs did not achieve their narrow goals of expediting bank and/or corporate restructuring. In fact, the Swedish AMC is one of the few success cases. However, the Swedish AMCs were only a small fraction of the banking system, which made it easier for them to maintain its independence from political pressures and to sell assets back to the private sector.[37] This suggests that AMCs can be effectively used for narrowly defined purposes, such as resolving real estate-related portfolios.

On March 21, 2009, the largest of the Icelandic savings banks, Reykjavík-based SPRON, was taken over by the Icelandic FSA and its deposits transferred to New Kaupthing (Arion Bank). SPRON's assets were placed in a de novo asset management company – Drómi – which would in turn issue a bond (using these same assets as collateral) to New Kaupthing to match the value of the deposits. This method was chosen was to avoid the same costly and time-consuming problems associated with the asset valuation process, which at this time was ongoing for the three new banks.[38]

---

[37] Klingebiel, D. (2000, February). *The use of asset management companies in the resolution of banking crisis: cross-country experiences.* World Bank, Financial Sector Strategy and Policy Group.

[38] Financial Supervisory Authority. (2009, March 21). Ákvörðun Fjármálaeftirlitsins um ráðstöfun eigna og skulda Sparisjóðs Reykjavíkur og nágrennis. (*The FSA's decision on the allocation of the assets and liabilities of SRPON.*) (Reference no. 2009030080). http://www.fme.is/media/akvardanir/21.-mars-2009.pdf

In this way, the SPRON takeover was an outlier, unlike other applications of the emergency financial legislation, and closer to actions proposed by JP Morgan and the CBI at the advent of the crisis.

In practice, this methodology denied New Kaupthing visibility and control of liabilities of the new deposit holders – outstanding loans, overdrafts, and so on – because they were kept at another entity. Therefore, SPRON's former customers would have to keep up a dual dialogue with two financial institutions: a bank that looked after their deposits and an AMC looking after their liabilities. That, inevitably, led to frustration, not only among the customers but also at New Kaupthing, which was unable to secure the new customer base by providing adequate service. This became critical in the first months after the SPRON takeover. There had been about 250 people employed at SPRON – but only 20 were offered jobs at New Kaupthing. A new and emerging bank – MP Bank – would immediately hire six of the laid-off employees and stage a market push by contacting SPRON clients and urging them to switch over. MP Bank subsequently went forward with plans to hire about 45 SPRON employees and buy the old closed-off branches of the savings banks from the AMC (Drómi). They intended to reopen these branches under the MP name. But at this point, fearing a run on New Kaupthing, the FSA blocked the transaction.

Thus, the SPRON deposit holders turned out to be the only transferees from a failed financial institution to experience a disruption in the financial service provided to them. They would complain that Drómi did not see them as future customers in need of financial service or assistance with their financial positions; instead, they felt they had been treated as mere liquidation cases to be dispatched with minimal costs and maximum short-term return. In 2012, they filed a complaint with the FSA concerning Drómi's allegedly slow, unwilling participation in the government-mandated debt relief programs.[39] By that time, it was the unanimous opinion of the ombudsman for debtors, the CEO of Arion Bank, and the prime minister, that employing Drómi had been a mistake.

---

[39] Financial Supervisory Authority. (2012, November 21). Gagnsæistilkynning vegna athugunar á starfsháttum Dróma hf. (Transparency notification regarding examination of working practices of Drómi hf.). http://www.fme.is/media/gagnsaei/Gagnsaeistilkynning---Dromi-21.11.pdf

4.4   A Troubled Childhood: The Operation of the New Banks

The domestic/foreign partition created a new banking system with a lot of non-performing loans, and at the start about 70 % of the new banks' loan portfolio was in arrears – not exactly trustworthy status. Furthermore, much time and energy had to be spent on legacy problems instead of creating new business. It would take a number of years for the banks to restructure their credit portfolio. How could it be otherwise, given the almost perfect storm hitting the Icelandic credit market in the wake of the banking collapse? Sure enough, there had been a credit bubble during the boom years, as both households and corporates accumulated debt. The main problem, however, was how these debts were designed.

First, it was the indexation. Iceland has a long history of inflation and price volatility, and since 1979 practically all long-term debt was inflation indexed – whether it belonged to households or corporations. The indexing served both the needs of lenders and borrowers. The former would get the hedge needed for making a long-term loan commitment. Iceland moreover has a large, fully funded pension system with indexed benefits, and thus there was huge appetite for long-term indexed debt in the financial market. Corporations and households would face a lower burden of payment, as the indexed real rates were significantly lower than the nominally adjusted real rates, given the relatively high inflation expectations. Moreover, it was also assumed that inflation and nominal wages would move in tandem in the longer term, as the labor unions would sooner or later seek wage compensation for unexpected inflationary shocks. Thus the burden of payment would be stable over the medium term. To ensure this stability, most indexed loans to households were annuities, and thus jumps in the CPI would inflate the principal of a loan – but payments would remain relatively stable.

This form of indexation would of course increase the risk of negative equity on mortgages. Falling housing prices and declining collateral would collaborate with rising inflation and higher principal, since most economic downturns in Iceland are marked by currency depreciation and rising prices on imported goods. Nevertheless, all mortgages in Iceland were underwritten with a personal guarantee, and the households had a track record of a strong willingness to pay. The market just waited for the impending recovery to restore the equity ratio. At least, it did up to 2008.[40]

The second debt factor was currency-linked loans. The 1994 abolition of capital controls and subsequent rating upgrades created the option to substitute indexation for currency linking. Given that Iceland was a small, open economy – with about 40 % of the consumer basket imported and another 10–20 % indirectly imported as factor of production – the inflation indexing and currency linking were close to the same thing. It was just a question of time lags. Given the relatively high real rates of interest prevailing in Iceland at time (indexed real rates for corporations were in the range of 6–8 %) and the very low credit spreads the banks were able to offer on the back of their high credit ratings, currency linking became the corporate funding of choice. And, of course, many companies would be tempted to lower their interest rates even further by switching to low-yielding currency, such the Swiss franc or the Japanese yen.

By 2000, about 50 % of corporate funding was currency-linked. In 2007, the ratio had risen to about 70 %. Currency-linked lending was more frequent among the larger companies, and in terms of head counts the numbers are lower, with only about 44 % of all corporations taking - currency-linked loans. Households would also be tempted to explore currency linking, especially with regard to car loans. After 2006, currency-linked mortgages also enjoyed some popularity. Nevertheless, the currency-linked loans never rose higher than about 15–20 % of household debt in 2007. In terms of a head count, only 6.5 % of all households had currency-linked loans.

In short, the vast majority of bank lending to households and corporations in Iceland was linked to the value of the ISK, either directly or indirectly as inflation indexation (as was the case with about 70–75 % of household debt). Thus, a 50 %-plus devaluation in 2008, a 30 % rise in the price level between 2008 and 2011, and a 10 % output contraction

---

[40] Ásgeir Jónsson,, Sigurður Jóhannesson, Valdimar Ármann, Brice Benaben & Stefaniu Perucci. (2012). Nauðsyn eða val? Verðtrygging, vextir og verðbólga á Íslandi. (Necessity or choice? Indexation, interests and inflation in Iceland). Reykjavík: Icelandic Financial Services Association.

would wreak havoc on the loan portfolios of the new banks. All in all, about 20 % of households went underwater with negative equity, and 15 % of mortgages went into arrears. The numbers were much more staggering for corporations, 70–80 % of which went into a negative equity territory.

The asset transfer to the new banks had, of course, been at a "fair value," with large precautionary write-offs. This gave them an unusually large space to maneuver when responding to these challenges, most of which are not usually open to operational banks that have to protect their slim equity buffers. Nevertheless, if the real value of the transferred assets turned out to be lower than the estimated value, the banks could become insolvent, needing more capital or even another round of restructuring.

In the beginning, each bank had its own strategy for dealing with client debt problems, and each strategy was original. It also has to be kept in mind that although the three banks had collapsed, there were numerous savings banks still in operation, with about a 30 % market share between them in retail banking. These banks were still attempting to guard their limited pool of equity. The lack of uniformity in client relations created great consternation in egalitarian Iceland. People would wonder why they did not receive the same favorable treatment from their bank as their uncle, neighbor, or coworker enjoyed at *their* bank. Some had loans with more than one bank, and did not understand why their experiences could be so different in one bank versus another. In 2010, the government stepped to ensure that all financial institutions applied the same general measures to deal with credit problems. This was meant to ensure equal treatment for all, and it did cause some delay in the restructuring process. By that time, most of the savings banks had been taken over by the FSA, and their assets and deposits were transferred to the three banks.

After some handwringing and debates between the banks, creditors, and the government initiated certain generalized measures for debt restructuring, the bulk of which were implemented in 2011.[41] Household mortgage debt in excess of 110 % of the fair value of each property was written off. Furthermore, specific relief measures (administered by a bank

[41] Matthíasson, Þórólfur. (2013, July). The Icelandic response to the collapse of the financial sector in October 2008. *Institute of Economic Studies Working Paper Series*, (W13), 01.

or a new debtors' ombudsman) were put in place for those that could not service a reduced loan. Low-income, asset-poor households with high-interest mortgage payments got a temporary subsidy from the government. In addition, the government attempted to bolster the bargaining power of individuals against the banks by making bankruptcy overall an easier option, and by allowing claims, as a general rule, to expire only two years after a formal default.

Small- to medium-sized businesses (with total outstanding debt below 1 billion ISK, or €7 million) would go onto a fast track and could apply for debt relief if they could credibly document positive cash flow (EBITDA) from future activities. The firm had to be willing to reengineer its operation to make best use of its assets. Conforming to those conditions, the firm could expect its debt to be written down to equal the discounted value of future earnings or, alternatively, to the amount that the bank or other financial firm could expect, in the best of circumstances, to gain from taking the assets over and realizing their monetary value. About a third of the restructuring involved a convertible loan with a deferred repayment after three years, which the company could buy from the bank at a discount prior to maturity.

Hence, the debt relief programs did not create new equity on the balance sheets of firms or households. As for the larger corporations, the so-called London approach was applied,[42] which was based on principles similar to the fast track for small- and medium-sized businesses. Holding companies and business deemed unviable were simply put into liquidation.

These restructuring efforts were also affected by court decisions. On June 16, 2010, the Supreme Court passed two verdicts regarding loans linked to foreign currency that had profound effects in the years to come.[43] The verdicts simply stated that two particular auto leasing agreements in foreign currency were in fact loans in ISK, linked to the price of foreign currencies, and that this currency linking was a breach of the law

---

[42] See pp. 18–19 in. Laryea, Thomas. (2010, January 26). Approaches to Corporate Debt Restructuring in the Wake of Financial Crises. *IMF Staff Position Note*, SPN/10/02. International Monetary Fund. https://www.imf.org/external/pubs/ft/spn/2010/spn1002.pdf
[43] Supreme Court verdicts no. 92/2010 and 153/2010.

on interest and indexation.[44] The lenders could therefore not demand payments according to the indexation and the loans had to be recalculated.

Early speculation suggested that these verdicts would not be precedents for other types of loans, such as mortgages or loans to companies. But many similar verdicts followed, applying to other types of loans. Furthermore, many court cases would follow where it was disputed between lenders and borrowers whether a particular loan was in foreign currency or just "currency-linked."

The first two Supreme Court verdicts were silent on whether other terms of the loans, such as the interest rate, could be valid if the currency link was invalid. In a verdict in September 2010, the Supreme Court judged that the interest rate was not valid either and a currency-linked loan was to bear a variable interest rate, equal to the lowest interest rate offered by domestic banks each month and recorded by the CBI.[45] There was disagreement surrounding the precedent of this verdict, but the government decided to cut the knot by passing a bill through parliament,[46] which stated that currency-linked loans should be calculated in accordance with the Supreme Court's 2010 judgment.

Although the bill specified use of the "lowest" rates offered by banks, that low rate was very high, as high as 21 % in December 2008 and January 2009. The law mitigated to some extent the effects on the banks' balance sheet. The principal of the loans was lower, but the banks could charge higher interest rates, retroactive from the borrowing day.

The picture changed on February 15, 2012, when the Supreme Court passed yet another verdict on currency-linked loans.[47] This time, the court applied a derogation principle. The verdict stated that if interest had been paid off the loan and the borrower could have expected that the payment was final, the lender could not demand higher interest payments later on. This meant that the foreign interest rate applied to the loan, even though the loan was effectively in króna and not indexed. Thus, the

---

[44] Act no. 38/2001 on interest and indexation.
[45] Supreme Court verdict no. 471/2010.
[46] Act no. 151/2010 on the amendment of act no. 38/2001.
[47] Supreme Court verdict no. 600/2011.

offsetting effect of the higher interest rates on the loans was no longer valid, if the derogation principle applied, which seemed to be the norm for most individuals and small companies. The FSA estimated at the time that the total effect of the verdict on the banks could be up to €1.1 billion.

The banks had provisioned €0.5 billion for possible losses, but now a further €0.6 billion provision was possible. The banks' combined equity at year-end 2011 was €2.9 billion, so the possible additional impairment amounted to 20 % of their equity. However, Supreme Court verdicts later in 2012 stated that some foreign currency loans to domestic borrowers were proper and not a breach of the law of interest and indexation. This reduced the effect of the February verdict on banks' balance sheets to a manageable amount.

By 2012, when the debt restructuring was largely completed, corporate debt worth about 60–70 % of GDP had been written down, but household debt write-downs amounted to about 20 % of GDP, as can be seen in Figs. 4.2 and 4.3.

Recapitalizing an entire banking system with a significant number of non-performing assets of uncertain value entailed a huge risk for the government – if not from loan losses then by litigation by the creditors. As will be discussed in more detail in Chap. 5, the government "sold" its stake in Íslandsbanki (New Glitnir) and Arion Bank (New Kaupthing) at face value to the estates of the old banks in the autumn of 2009. This followed intensive negotiations with creditors, who by that time had organized into a single forum. The government kept only 5 % in Íslandsbanki and 13 % in Arion, but with a shareholder agreement that gave the government-appointed board members veto power on the board of these "privatized" banks regarding certain topics. The government kept 80 % of Landsbanki, and later acquired that bank almost in full.

The creditors accepted the debt measures as essential to the restart of the Icelandic economy. Moreover, given the systematic nature of the debt crisis, there were fears of a debtors' revolt – especially after the large debt relief protests that had been organized in front of the parliament in the fall of 2011. Households might just stop serving their debt (some actually did), while owners and management of the corporations jumped from the sinking ship, and even attempted to strip it of assets beforehand. As it turned out, the creditors' acquiescence was a wise and profitable decision.

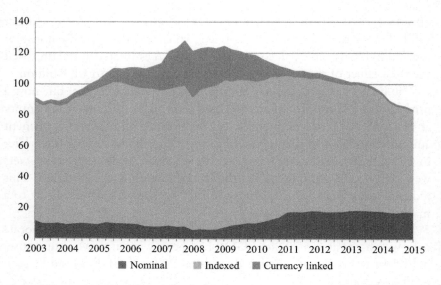

Fig. 4.2 Household debt in Iceland as percentage of GDP from 2004 to year-end 2015 categorized according to contract terms (Source: Central Bank of Iceland)

Despite the huge debt write-off, the real value of the assets transferred from the old banks turned out to be higher than reported on their opening balance sheets. This was probably due to both a conservative asset valuation and an economic recovery that transpired a lot faster than expected (the recovery, especially reliant on a boom in the tourist industry, will be discussed in Chap. 5). Furthermore, the initial rate used to discount the income stream of the loan portfolios was very high, given the high interest rates (both real and nominal) in 2008–2009. As the interest rates came down, the asset valuation would of course be revised upward.

On the other hand, the new banks had the old domestic deposit base transferred to them at booked value without haircuts, and these deposits could not leave the country because of the capital controls. In addition, their deposit base would be further boosted as the savings banks gave up the ghost one by one, and subsequently their deposits were transferred to the banks. The 21 savings banks operating in 2008 varied greatly in size. In total, they held about 33 % of the deposit base. In 2016, the number of

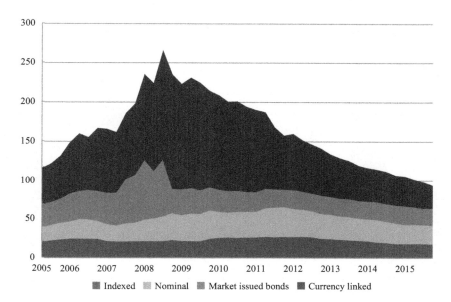

Fig. 4.3 Corporate debt in Iceland as percentage of GDP from 2004 to year-end 2015 categorized according to contract terms (Source: Central Bank of Iceland)

savings banks was down to four, and their share of deposits had shrunk to 3 %. In 2015, the three new banks had between them about 95 % of the total deposit base, and the small commercial bank Kvika had about 2 %. Thus, the new banks had ample liquidity from the start, and were in no need for repo lending from the CBI. Instead they would deposit funds into the CBI.

Thus, the new banks turned out to be quite profitable. Figure 4.4 shows the new banks' profit before taxes in the period 2010–2015, broken down into profits from change in loan valuation; discontinued operations; shares, and other profits. The total profit before taxes in the period is €3.6 billion, which is more than acceptable when compared with their initial equity of less than €2 billion. Of the total profit, around €400 million can be attributed to the net revaluation of their loan portfolio; €200 million from discontinued operations; and €900 million in profits from shares, leaving €2.1 billion in other profits. Thus, about €1.1 billion

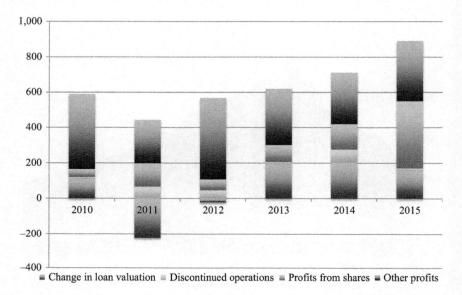

Fig. 4.4 The new banks' profit before taxes in the years 2010–2015. Amounts in million euros (Source: The CBI Financial Stability 2016/1)

of profits have come from revaluations of the loan portfolio and equity stakes transferred from the old banks.

Figure 4.5 shows the new banks' capital adequacy ratio over the period 2009–2015. The initial capital of the banks was set so that the ratio was no lower than 16 % at founding, or twice the legal minimum of 8 %. Since then, the ratio has grown steadily. At year-end 2015 it stood at around 30 % for both Íslandsbanki (New Glitnir) and Landsbanki, and 24 % for Arion Bank. These ratios indicate very strong financial positions for the banks; many bankers would argue that the ratios are far too high.

Despite a traumatic birth and a troubled childhood, the new banks have nevertheless emerged as solid enterprises, financed almost solely by domestic deposits, and with the highest equity ratios among banks in the Western world.

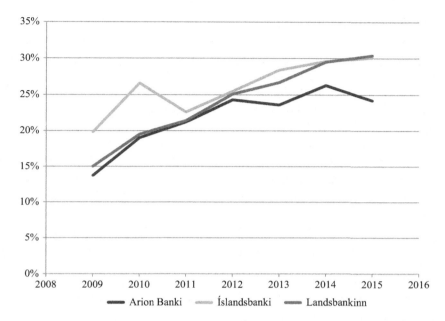

Fig. 4.5 Capital adequacy ratios of the new banks in the period 2009–2016 (Source: The CBI Financial Stability 2016/1)

4.5   Dealing with Blame, Shame and Punishment

During the financial boom, Kaupthing was the standard among the Icelandic trio, the largest and most prestigious company in Iceland: a fast-growing international investment bank with stock that constituted about 40 % of the total ICEX market cap. Kaupthing did not pay the highest salaries – quite the reverse. The bank just assumed that it could have its pick among Iceland's best and brightest, and then, in time, reward them with stock options and the leverage to exercise them. Therefore, stuck in the carcass of the old bank in October 2008, in very tight seating rows, were some of Iceland's top graduates from recent years who could do little but speculate gloomily about their future.

People offered continued employment at New Kaupthing would count themselves lucky, but they faced difficult times ahead as well. New Kaupthing turned out to be quite different from its predecessor. The retail arm was dominant, and water-cooler discussions would often turn to the good old days at the bank. There was a lack of motivation. People showed up later to work than before, and men stopped wearing ties.

Strangely enough, morale was much higher at the old, dead bank. Its operations took up one floor of a building that now housed the headquarters of both old and new Kaupthing. As previously discussed, the emergency legislation authorized the FSA to take over the troubled banks and appoint a resolution committee to assume the powers of the board and administer the banks' assets and operations. Furthermore, on November 24, 2008, the old bank received formal court authorization for a moratorium, which lasted two years.[48] Under these conditions, the failed bank kept its banking license and sustained certain operative functions. It could, for example, grant new loans to existing customers or participate in equity offerings of their existing holdings, if deemed necessary, to maximize the value of assets. (For further discussion, see Chap. 6.)

Nevertheless, it would take several months to separate the operation of the two banks under a single roof. As stated, New Kaupthing had to deal with a domestic asset portfolio that included lots of non-performing loans and angry customers. Kaupthing, on the other hand, morphed into an asset management company of sorts, which oversaw a huge portfolio of assets all over the world, most of which were performing well. The scale of operations at the old bank would grow rapidly in the first months of 2009, and the bank rehired many staff previously laid off. These "new" hires would receive much higher salaries than employees of the new bank, which inevitably led to building-wide tension until the old bank moved out in 2010.

---

[48] Kaupthing Bank hf. (2008, November 24). *Kaupthing Bank hf. granted a moratorium.* http://www.kaupthing.com/home/announcements/all-announcements/2008/11/24/Kaupthing-Bank-hf.-granted-a-moratorium/ Kaupthing Bank hf. (2010, November 22). *Kaupthing formally enters winding-up procedure.* http://www.kaupthing.com/home/announcements/all-announcements/2010/11/22/Kaupthing-formally-enters-winding-up-procedure/

Of the survivors from Kaupthing's investment banking arm, most would leave the new bank within three years of its establishment. Some went to work for one of the old banks, which were conducting large recovery projects on an international scale. Many others would establish or join new investment banking boutiques that sprang up after the collapse, or take positions at non-financial companies.

Overall, the number of people working in the financial sector (excluding insurance companies) decreased by a third, or from 5790 at year end 2007 to about 3900 at year end 2015. Most of that reduction was due to the downsizing of the commercial banks as well as the almost wholesale merger of the savings funds into the banking system. At the end of 2007 there were 4050 people working for five commercial banks and 785 people working for 18 saving funds.[49] In 2015 there were 3005 people working in four banks and 32 people working in four savings funds. On the other hand the number of people in investment boutiques and asset management companies is almost the same.[50] A lot of ex-bankers would just migrate into other sectors; the number of unemployed bankers remained very small.

Surveys also showed a high level of stress among banking employees in the aftermath of the crisis. In a survey made by the bankers' union in 2009 about 50 % of those queried were afraid of losing their job, 83 % feared a disadvantageous transfer within the workplace, and about a third complained of greater anxiety and depression in the wake of the crisis.[51] Moreover, perhaps paradoxically, other independent surveys showed that employees fired or fleeing from the banks after the collapse were, in

---

[49] Financial Supervisory Authority. (2008, September). *Heildarniðurstöður ársreikninga fjármálafyrirtækja og verðbréfa- og fjárfestingarsjóða fyrir árið 2007.* (*Summary of annual financial statements of financial companies and mutual and investment funds for the year 2007.*) http://www.fme. is/media/utgefid-efni/2007_Efnahags-og-rekstrarreikningar-banka-og-sparisjoda,-verdbrefafyrirtaekja-og-verdbrefamidlana,-rekstrarfelaga-verdbrefasjoda,-asamt-ymsum-kennitolum-og-odrum-upplysingum-31_12_2007.pdf

[50] Financial Supervisory Authority. (2016, June). *Fjármálafyrirtæki o.fl. Heildarniðurstöður ársreikninga 2015.* (*Financial companies etc. Summary of annual financial statements 2015.*) http:// www.fme.is/media/utgefid-efni/Arsreikningabok-2015---lanamarkadur.pdf

[51] Snorradóttir, Ásta. (2009). Líðan, heilsa og vinnuumhverfi starfsfólks í bönkum og sparisjóðum. (Well-being, health and work environment in commercial and savings banks.) Reykjavík: Rannsókna- og heilbrigðisdeild Vinnueftirlits ríkisins. http://dev.ssf.is/wp-content/uploads/2013/02/L%C3%AD%C3%B0an-heilsa-vinnuumhv-lokask%C3%BDrsla09_1362860619.pdf

general, happier than those who stayed behind in the post-crisis years.[52] That can be explained in part by the almost society-wide condemnation employees in the financial sector faced in the months and years after the collapse. The Icelanders wanted the banks to forgive their debts, but they were not about to forgive the banks for the crisis.

For those in finance who had achieved celebrity status, the downfall was particularly steep. Kaupthing and its employees went from stardom to being scapegoats as the financial disaster unfolded. It did not take long until demands for criminal investigations and prosecutions gained traction. In particular, there were calls to target bankers for possible market manipulation and agency fraud in the pre-crisis years. Already in mid-October 2008, the FSA demanded that the winding-up committees of the estates conduct thorough investigations of possible lawbreaking at the old banks with the assistance of outside experts. Two months after the crisis hit, on December 11, 2008, a parliamentary action established a special prosecutor's office. Its mandate was to investigate suspected criminal conduct before, during and after the events leading up to the financial crisis.[53] The report following the bill was very telling; it stated that the purpose of the act was to calm the societal rage by bringing people to justice if there was any doubt about their innocence. The special prosecutor's position was opened for applicants the next day, with a December 29 deadline.[54]

Despite the financial hardships in Iceland, the position was not especially coveted. By the deadline there were no applications on file, and it was extended to January 12.[55] After being approached by the minister of justice, one applicant came forward in the second round: Ólafur Þór Hauksson, a 44-year-old magistrate in a small town just outside Reykjavik. He was appointed the same day.

[52] Rafnsdóttir, G. L., Snorradóttir, Á & Sigursteinsdóttir, H. (2014). Vinnufyrirkomulag og líðan í kjölfar kreppu. Yfirlitsgrein. (Work environment and well-being in the wake of a crisis. A summary article.) *Íslenska þjóðfélagið*, 5(2):39–55. http://thjodfelagid.is/index.php/Th/article/view/68
[53] Act on a special prosecutor's office no. 135/2008. http://www.althingi.is/lagas/136a/2008135.html
[54] Department of Justice. (2008, December 12). *Special prosecutor is open for application.* https://www.innanrikisraduneyti.is/media/frettir/Auglysing_serstakur_saksoknari.pdf
[55] Department of Justice. (2008, December 30). *Deadline for the position of special prosecutor extended to January 12.* https://www.innanrikisraduneyti.is/frettir/frettatilkynningar/nr/6593

The office formally started operations on February 1, 2009. In the first few months it was an office of five, but at the peak of investigations the staff exceeded 100. From its founding until January 1, 2016, the office ran on a budget of 5 billion ISK (about €30–35 million). In March a new figure arrived on the scene: Eva Joly, a Norwegian-born former French magistrate and a member of the European Parliament. Joly was well known for her crusade against corruption in France, running cases against both Crédit Lyonnaise and the oil company Elf Aquitaine. Shortly after her appearance, she was hired as a consultant to the special prosecutor and worked with the office for 18 months, when she withdrew to focus on her campaign for the French presidential elections in 2012.

A total of 200 cases linked to the crisis have been investigated, of which 150 have been dropped or merged with other cases. At the time of this writing, charges have been made in 22 cases, 14–16 await decision on prosecution, and 15 are still under investigation. The judicial procedure of wound-up cases has taken up to three years. Based on that record, it can be expected that the last cases linked to the financial crisis will not be decided until 2020.

Of the 22 cases already prosecuted, 71 charges have been lodged against 52 individuals, and 19 cases have been decided in district courts. Of these, 11 have had verdicts before the Supreme Court. One district court acquittal was not appealed, but the remaining seven are pending trial at the Supreme Court.

A final verdict has thus been reached in 12 cases. Those cases include 29 charges against 25 individuals. A guilty verdict has been reached on 23 charges against 22 individuals, who have been sentenced to a total of 59 years in prison; three individuals have been acquitted.

The CEOs of Kaupthing Bank, Kaupthing Bank Luxembourg, Landsbanki, and BYR Savings Bank have all been sentenced to four and a half to five and a half years in prison by the Supreme Court. The chairmen of both Kaupthing Bank and BYR Savings Bank received sentences of four to four and a half years. The CEO of Glitnir Bank has been acquitted of a charge of agency fraud in the Supreme Court, but a district court judged him guilty of agency fraud and sentenced him to five years in prison. That case is pending trial at the Supreme Court.

Some of these cases are not really linked to the crisis. They just came to light during the wide-ranging investigations conducted after the collapse and involved some kind of fraud perpetrated by lower level financial staff; these cases had no systemic importance. Of the cases directly linked to the crisis, almost all of them involve some actions taken in the 12 months before October 2008, and none resulted in personal benefit to those involved. In hindsight, the actions look more desperate than criminal.

The special prosecutor's office has been heavily criticized for its methods, which include subjecting bankers to years of phone taps, public displays, isolation, and confinement for the accused. Those sentenced believe they never had a chance for a fair hearing, with the judiciary in seeming lockstep with public opinion; guilty verdicts have seemed to be a cause rather than the result of objective inquiry. Some of the accused are still in limbo nearly eight years later, still waiting for an investigation or trial to begin and end so they can begin a new chapter in their lives.

There are huge risks involved in criminalizing banking. Blaming failure or losses on bad character or criminal intent belittles the real systemic problems and incentives structures involved in financial intermediation. No matter how many bankers are jailed, these systemic problems remain. The Swedish debt restructuring specialist, Mats Josefsson, brought by the IMF to oversee the reconstruction of the new banks, is a veteran of many banking crises in all parts of the world. In an interview with the *Fré ttablaðið* daily on June 25, 2009, he reported that about 500 charges had been filed in the aftermath of the Swedish financial crisis, of which just a few had led to convictions. The burden of proof in such crimes was too high if a just legal framework was applied:

> *People always show the same reaction to banking crisis all over the world. First, they blame the bank CEOs for the economic collapse. Then the politicians, accountants, regulatory authorities, the Central Bank and the media for having been too soft. But in the end, it is always the boards and the CEOs of the banks who are responsible for the business decisions taken.*[56]

---

[56] Bergsveinsson, Jón Aðalsteinn. (2009, June 25). Bankastjórarnir eru alltaf sekir. (The banks' CEOs are always guilty). *Fréttablaðið*, p. 12.

5

Worthless Currency?

5.1 The Transfer Problem

On November 11, 1918, the Armistice of Compiègne between the Allies and the German Empire was signed.[1] The Great War was effectively over. By 1920, peace would be concluded with the defeated Central Powers (the German Empire, Austria-Hungary, the Ottoman Empire, and the Kingdom of Bulgaria) in five separate treaties at Versailles, Saint-Germain-en-Laye, Neuilly-sur-Seine, Trianon, and Sèvres. According to the treaties, war guilt served as a prerequisite to compel the Central Powers to pay reparations. However, all Central Power states (Austria-Hungary dissolved into the Kingdom of Hungary and the First Austrian Republic in 1918), besides the German state (the Weimar Republic), soon had their reparations cancelled due to poor economic circumstances.

---

[1] It is highly illuminating that, in 1940, the French were made to sign their terms of surrender to the Germans in the same railway carriage, at exactly the same location, in which German officials had signed the 1918 treaty. Hitler himself sat in the same chair that the French supreme commander, Ferdinand Foch, had occupied when he delivered the terms of surrender. Both the chair and the carriage were retrieved from a museum for the ceremony.

© The Author(s) 2016
Á. Jónsson, H. Sigurgeirsson, *The Icelandic Financial Crisis*,
DOI 10.1057/978-1-137-39455-2_5

Germany did not get off so easily. In 1921, the Germans received a very hefty bill from the Allies, in three parts. First, they were expected to pay for damage directly linked to the war; this bill amounted to 20 % of Germany's gross domestic product (GDP). They were also held liable for war debts incurred by France and Britain to the USA, which then amounted to around 80 % of GDP. Special reparations, amounting to 150 % of GDP, were piled on top, in an apparent attempt to keep Germany too heavily taxed to even consider waging war. This massive last straw was not expected to be paid; diplomatic channels got word to the German government that it was meant to placate public anger in the badly damaged Allied states. Meanwhile, there were other real penalties, including the confiscation of colonies, bank deposits, and undertakings. Prior to Versailles, national debt amounted to around 50 % of German GDP. Adding in the war reparations, debt ballooned to about 300 % of GDP.

It should come as no surprise that collecting the debt proved difficult. In 1923, the French and Belgians sent troops to occupy the Ruhr region when Germany defaulted on reparation payments. Afterwards, a now-infamous spate of hyperinflation broke out when the government sought to print money to finance the treasury. The war reparations were subsequently reduced; payments were restructured in 1932. But by then, the Weimar Republic had sunk into a serious financial crisis, and Hitler was a few months away from consolidating absolute power. Historians disagree over how much the Germans eventually paid, but the probable amount was somewhere between 30 % and 40 % of GDP in 1920.[2]

One of the advisors of the British government during the Versailles Conference in 1919 was the Treasury's appointed financial representative, economist John Maynard Keynes. Keynes was adamantly opposed to the eventual treaty, especially the war reparations. Later that same year, he published the book *The Economic Consequences of the Peace* in which he strongly criticized the treaty, saying it would create a huge imbalance in international finance. The book was a bestseller and made the author an overnight star.

---

[2] See Ritschl, Albrecht. (2012). The German Transfer Problem, 1920–33: A Sovereign-Debt Perspective. *European Review of History: Revue européenne d'histoire, 19*(6), 943–964.

When war reparations were discussed at the conference, the debate focused mostly on the capacity of the German state to service its debt. Keynes, however, pointed out that this was only one aspect of the problem. There was also a problem connected to the transfer of value from one currency area to another. The transfer problem in fact demonstrates the double nature of the foreign exchange market, which is a channel both for foreign trade and capital movements. With regard to foreign trade (the trade balance), the exchange rate is a macroeconomic parameter, which reflects domestic productivity and comparative advantage of the state in question within the global market. To that effect, each nation will produce those goods that have the lowest relative opportunity cost due to its financial structure, productivity, and resources. With regard to capital transactions, the exchange rate is only a float on the streams flowing between currency areas, which can be volatile and subject to their own rules.

There are obvious limits on how much capital can be transferred from one currency area to another through the capital account without sending the exchange rate to a level inappropriate to the foreign trade balance. In order for the Germans to be able to transfer so much capital to France, they needed an enormous trade surplus to finance the conversion from German marks to French francs. For this to be possible, the real exchange rate of the German mark would have to be very low, so that German exports would be competitive and imports of foreign consumer goods limited. This would furthermore imply that the German people would have to bear the burden of war reparations with low real wages and poorer living standards. As a result, German citizens would not just be paying higher direct taxes to the state for the war reparations. They would also be subjected to an indirect tax, as a result of higher price levels for imports, which in turn could be traced to the low mark exchange rate after reparations were in place. On the Allied side, the plus and minus signs were reversed. When the victors received such large amounts of German capital, it was bound to result in a current account deficit, a high real exchange rate, lower business competitiveness, and unemployment.

The global ramifications of these imbalances were severe. Together, the war debts owed to the USA and the German war reparations created an imbalance in international capital flows, which made the gold standard unworkable. This is commonly connected to the origins of the Great Depression.

In Keynes's opinion, it was unrealistic to place these colossal demands on the Germans without drastically lowering the living standards of the general public and causing major social upheaval. The Western powers absorbed this lesson, but at an astronomical cost. In the aftermath of World War II, debts incurred by the West Germans were cancelled, and the new nation received assistance in its economic recovery.

To some extent, the transfer problem that arose in Iceland following the 2008 banking collapse draws parallels to that of Germany after World War I. The balance of offshore ISK assets residing in the Icelandic financial system post-collapse was comparable with Iceland's GDP.[3] With the passage of emergency legislation, the Icelandic government effectively severed the link between the sovereign and the banks. The policy and actions taken after the legislation passed protected taxpayers from financial responsibility for the banks. The International Monetary Fund (IMF) subsequently endorsed the policy in November 2008. It was one of three objectives outlined in a press release issued upon the commencement of the economic recovery program agreed upon by the IMF and the Icelandic government on November 19, 2008:

There are three main objectives of the IMF-supported program: To contain the negative impact of the crisis on the economy by restoring confidence and stabilizing the exchange rate in the near-term; to promote a viable domestic banking sector and safeguard international financial relations by implementing a sound banking system strategy that is non-discriminatory and collaborative; and to safeguard medium-term fiscal viability by limiting the socialization of losses in the collapsed banks and implementing an ambitious multi-year fiscal consolidation program.[4]

---

[3] The first person to make this comparison was Jón Daníelsson. See: Danielsson, Jon. (2008, November 12). The first casualty of the crisis: Iceland. *VOX CEPR's Policy Portal.* http//www.voxeu.org/article/how-bad-could-crisis-get-lessons-iceland

[4] International Monetary Fund. (2008, November 19). *IMF Executive Board Approves US$2.1 Billion Stand-By Arrangement for Iceland.* (Press Release No. 08/296). https://www.imf.org/external/np/sec/pr/2008/pr08296.htm

The first test of the policy's soundness came when the emergency legislation prioritized deposits, via a transfer of €10 billion from general creditors to depositors – domestic as well as foreign. The second test came with the capitalization of the new banks, which was to a large extent left to the creditors. They became the majority owners of both New Kaupthing (later Arion Bank) and New Glitnir (later Íslandsbanki) in late 2009. The estimate of a required capital injection from the treasury initially hit €2.6 billion; concurrently, the new banks were to issue €4 billion in debt to the old banks. However, the equity participation of the estates reduced the treasury's capital injection by half and the banks' debt to €1.6 billion. New Landsbanki continued to be a state concern, but as the economy turned to recovery at year-end 2010, equity losses became very unlikely. In fact, it was quite the reverse. All the banks started to churn out profits as assets transferred at depressed prices were revalued.

The third test concerned the Icesave claims. As discussed in Chap. 3, The British and the Dutch sitting on the boards of IMF wanted to block all assistance or loans to Iceland until it agreed to a full guarantee on those claims.[5] The Scandinavian countries chimed in by declaring that they would not provide assistance without an IMF approval. In other words, the Icesave issue had to be resolved first.

The stalemate lasted a few weeks, until November 16. The Icelandic government at last pledged to guarantee the liabilities of the Deposit Insurance Fund (DIF).[6] By European law, this meant the first €20,887 in savings held by private foreign individuals in an Icesave account was covered, up to a collective amount of €4 billion, or 40–60 % of Iceland's GDP depending on the valuation of the ISK. The remainder would be guaranteed under the rules of the other nations. This meant that Dutch and British authorities covered up to a maximum €100,000 and £50,000 (approx. €60,000), respectively.

On November 18, once the IMF Board had approved, the Central Bank of Iceland (CBI) received a collective $4.85 billion injection of foreign

---

[5] Ibison, David (2008, November 11). Iceland's rescue package flounders. *Financial Times*. http://www.ft.com/cms/s/0/ed069984-b022-11dd-a795-0000779fd18c.html

[6] Prime Minister's Office. (2008, November 16). *Agreed Guidelines Reached on Deposit Guarantees.* https://eng.forsaetisraduneyti.is/news-and-articles/nr/3229

reserves. Broken down, this included a $2.1 billion emergency loan facility from the IMF; bilateral funding amounting to $2.5 billion from Scandinavian countries; $200 million from Poland; and $50 million from the Faroe Islands. Customarily, IMF supplies liquidity, or short-term funding, to restore a balance of payment and support the currency. It is not expected to refinance the sovereign; that was the aim of the bilateral loans. The IMF loan was disbursed in seven tranches over three years and each tranche had a term of five years with interest-only payments in the first two years. The Scandinavian loans had a term of 12 years with interest-only payments in the first five years. Both loans carried a 2.75 % interest premium: the IMF loan over the SDR interest rates, as is the standard for loans from the IMF, and the Scandinavian over EURIBOR.

Separately, the UK and Netherlands insisted on lending Iceland £2.2 billion (€2.6bn) and €1.3 billion, respectively. These loans were earmarked for the coverage of the Icelandic minimum deposit guarantees for the UK and Dutch Icesave retail depositors. Similarly, Germany agreed to a €1.1 billion loan, which would cover the Icelandic minimum deposit guarantees for the German Kaupthing Edge retail depositors. The goal was to transform claims on the DIF into Icelandic sovereign debt.

There were about 30,000 savers that had deposited roughly €300 million in Kaupthing Edge in Germany, under an Icelandic guarantee. By February 2009, the Kaupthing estate had secured enough funds to repay them in full. However, repayments were stifled when Germany's DZ Bank seized €55 million as a debt settlement against Kaupthing.[7] This highlighted the peculiar positioning of the old banks' estates at the start of the recovery process. By Icelandic law, they were functional banking institutions, in moratorium but with a valid banking license. The outside world, however, saw the banks as in default. It would take several months to straighten out the mess and return the seized funds to the German depositors. Nevertheless, Germany did not intervene in the Icesave issue, which turned into a huge debacle for the Icelanders.

---

[7] Kaupthing. (2009, February 10). *Kaupthing Bank has secured sufficient funds to pay back the large majority of German Kaupthing EDGE deposits*. (Press release). http://www.kaupthing.com/home/announcements/all-announcements/2009/02/10/Kaupthing-Bank-has-secured-sufficient-funds-to-pay-back-the-large-majority-of-German-Kaupthing-EDGE-deposits/

Foreign relations and domestic politics were both adversely affected by Icesave headaches that lasted for years (see Sect. 5.2). The government guarantee sought by the British and Dutch won parliamentary approval in August 2009, but repayment was conditional, based on Iceland's macro-economic development in the wake of the crisis. The British and Dutch rejected this amendment to the plan. Subsequently, parliament passed two further Icesave bills that accepted the guarantee, but under different payment schedules. Both bills, however, were rejected in national referendums, held on March 6, 2010 and April 9, 2011. This sent the Icelandic republic to a junk status, or BB+, downgrade by Fitch. The British and Dutch then lodged a formal complaint to the EFTA court, which oversees the European Economic Area.

On January 28, 2013, the EFTA court rejected the state's liability for Icesave deposits, which left the two nations only with a priority claim on Landsbanki's estate (LBI). On January 11, 2016, LBI paid the last installment on the outstanding Icesave debt and thereby closed the claim.

So while the state escaped the guaranteed payment trap and debt interest payments, the Icesave tangle did considerable damage to the nation's economy, although indirectly. Landsbanki's assets, which closed the claim, were to a large extent domestic, and had to be converted to pounds sterling or euros to be distributed. The FX transfers were thus financed with export revenues and resulted, other things remaining equal, in a lower ISK exchange rate. The Icesave payments therefore affected Icelanders' standard of living through the effect on the FX market.

Regarding the junk rating on Iceland's sovereign debt, it seems to be a questionable call, regardless of the Icesave debacle. Prior to the crisis, the general government debt ratio had been low, about 28 % of GDP in 2007. Furthermore, the treasury did not carry any short-term foreign debt. The foreign long-term debt amounted to $2.4 billion, or just 16 % of GDP, and 90 % of it carried a fixed interest and no large payments due until late 2011. On the other hand, the Icelandic republic was low on foreign liquidity, with only about €2.5 billion in foreign reserves at the onset of the crisis. One-fifth of that total was loaned to Kaupthing on October 6.

If the British and Dutch indeed wanted a long-term block against Iceland in international capital markets, they failed. Iceland would re-enter the capital markets in June 2011 with an issuance of $1 billion at fixed 5 % interest, which equaled a 3.2 % interest premium. More bond issues followed in the years to come. All the loans taken in relation to the IMF program were repaid in full before year-end 2015: Faroe Islands in December 2012, the Scandinavian countries in July 2014, Poland in May 2015, and the IMF in October 2015.

There was yet a fourth test of the efforts to prevent the socialization of bank losses. This was the unwinding of the once lively carry trade and the liquidation of the very sizable offshore ISK holding left within the Icelandic financial system after the collapse of the currency, commonly referred to as *the overhang*.

In September 2008, the overhang stood at the equivalent of €4.3 billion, or 42 % of GDP. The principal purpose of capital controls in the wake of the collapse was to prevent large-scale capital outflows from burdening the general public via an excessively low exchange rate (see Chap. 7). In 2011, the government started efforts to eliminate the accumulated overhang, which was cut in half by year-end 2015. The CBI's method was to resolve the problem within the scope of the capital account, by creating a special auction market where asset swaps could be conducted at a lower exchange rate than the publicly quoted onshore rate. This not only prevented the reduction from disturbing the real economy by lowering the ISK exchange rate; it also ensured that the trade surplus was not used to convert offshore ISK to foreign currency. In this way, the CBI wound down the carry-trade transactions without impacting the general public. (Sects. 4.3 and 4.4 explain polices implemented to reduce these holdings without a public costs.)

In total, the obligations related to the overhang (€4.3 billion), and €3.9 billion in Icesave claims, produced €8.2 billion in potential government debt. On top of that, €2.6 billion would be needed to capitalize the new banks. The total bill, therefore, reached almost €11 billion, or 110 % of GDP.

And this was just the direct result of the crisis. In addition, the government had to reckon with pre-existing debt; new debt issued to finance a budget shortfall (a result of economic contraction); and any domestic assets left in the old banks' estates that would have to paid out to foreign creditors (these turned out to be substantial, about 40–60 % of GDP).

The financial challenges faced by Iceland were therefore on the same order of magnitude as the war reparations burden on Germany in 1920. The critical difference was that the Icelandic state ultimately did not need to foot the entire bill, despite the severe international pressure to do so.

5.2   The Icesave Debacle

On December 10, 2008, shortly after the Icelandic government agreed to guarantee the liabilities of the DIF, the Dutch central bank began to refund Icesave depositors up to a maximum amount of €100,000 per person. For this operation, DNB hired sixty temporary employees, who were housed on the second floor of the bank's headquarters. The repayment liability for the Dutch state – according to the Dutch minimum deposit guarantee scheme – equaled €1.6 billion, out of a total of €1.67 billion in deposits held by Dutch retail customers, but €1.33 billion of that amount was covered by the Icelandic minimum deposit guarantee liabilities, sourced either to the DIF or the Icelandic state.[8] The repayment liability for the British state – according to the British minimum deposit guarantee scheme – equaled £3.5 billion out of the £4.53 billion held by British retail customers. Of this, the DIF or Icelandic state would cover £2.2 billion.

The new left-wing minority government assumed power in February 2009 and subsequently began negotiations with the British and Dutch governments. A final repayment agreement was reached in the spring, and a bill[9] was presented to the Icelandic parliament in June 2009. Iceland guaranteed payments in the amount of €3.8 billion, at 5.55 % interest, to both UK and Netherlands. With these conditions in place, the British would finally revoke the terrorist act against Landsbanki and the CBI. The agreement stipulated that the payments from the estate would go towards the principal of the Icesave debt. The treasury would pay any balance

---

[8] Meijer, Rien (2008, December 11). Operatie Icesave: 20.000 spaarders moeten formulier nog opsturen! *De Telegraf.* http://www.telegraaf.nl/overgeld/rubriek/sparen/article2771885.ece
[9] Act no. 96/2009.

remaining as of June 6, 2016, and any accrued interest, over the next eight years in equal installments.

Members of Althing responded with skepticism and worry about the effects of such colossal payments in the crisis aftermath. There was particular uncertainty regarding asset recovery at Landsbanki and whether the bank's estate would be able to repay. Thus, the parliament unilaterally added an amendment to the bill, putting a ceiling on the yearly repayments in relation to GDP growth. Specifically, the amendment stated that annual payments would not exceed 4 % of the total growth in GDP from 2008. It also contained legal disclaimers regarding the validity of the claims. The amended bill was passed into law on August 28, 2009, with affirmative votes winning out 34–15, with 14 abstentions.

But the British and Dutch authorities rejected the amendment and thereby voided the agreement.[10] They also resorted to blocking payment on the second tranche of the IMF loans until Iceland passed an agreement that guaranteed full repayment of what it owed.[11] In fact, the annual payment ceiling imposed by Althing is very unlikely to have had any effect on actual payments by the state. It is estimated that the remaining principal on June 6, 2016, to be paid from 2016 to 2024, would have amounted to less than €1 billion, or €125 million a year: far less than 4 % of GDP growth since 2008. The legal disclaimers, however, could have voided the agreement in the EFTA court, as the court later judged that the Icelandic state was not liable for the payments.

New negotiations began and in December 2009, a new bill[12] was presented to the parliament. The bill was in most respects the same as the first: it included the annual ceiling on payments and most of the legal disclaimers. But some issues that the British and Dutch governments thought were unclear in the amendments of the first bill were clarified. The first bill had not clarified whether the debt would be written off if not repaid in full by 2024. The second bill affirmed that the debt would not

[10] British and Dutch stance on Icesave hardening. (2009, September 28). *IceNews*. http://www.icenews.is/index.php/2009/09/28/british-and-dutch-stance-on-icesave-hardening/

[11] PM: Iceland cannot wait much longer for IMF payout. (2009, September 29). *IceNews*. http://www.icenews.is/index.php/2009/09/29/pm-iceland-cannot-wait-much-longer-for-imf-payout/

[12] Act no. 1/2010.

be written off; instead the repayment period would be extended. Annual interest payments were also exempt from the payment ceiling, so interest payments would always be made in full.

This proposal had a narrow passage, with parliament voting 33–30 along strict party lines (excepting two governing party defectors). The new version of the Icesave bill – entitled Act 1/2010 – took the moniker Icesave II. But another roadblock appeared, this time locally sourced. On January 5, 2010, President Ólafur Ragnar Grímsson, refused to pass the bill into law.

UK Financial Services Secretary Lord Myners tartly responded, "The Icelandic people, if they took that decision [not to accept the bill], would effectively be saying that Iceland doesn't want to be part of the international financial system."[13] Fitch Ratings stated that the president's refusal had created "a new wave of political, economic and financial uncertainty," and represented a "step back in the attempts to re-establish normal financial relations with the rest of the world." Such was the reasoning for Fitch's downgrade from BBB- to BB+, or junk status.[14] Both Moody's and S&P announced that Iceland's ratings had been placed on negative credit watch, but neither took rating action.[15]

Understanding President Grímsson's action requires a wider context. Iceland's ascendance to a republic in 1944 did not result in many changes to the Danish constitution, and the Icelandic president became the equivalent of the Danish king. European royalty has a mostly ceremonial role in government, and although the monarch's signature is needed for approved legislation to become law, this is usually mere formality. The new Icelandic republic considered the presidential office as a kind of safety valve: when a president refused to sign legislation, it was automatically sent out to a national referendum. Until Grímsson was elected in 1996,

[13] Iceland leader vetoes bank repayments bill. (2010, January 5). *BBC News.* http://news.bbc.co.uk/2/hi/business/8441312.stm
[14] Fitch Ratings. (2010, January 5). *Fitch downgrades Iceland to 'BB+'/'BBB+'; outlook negative.* http://sedlabanki.is/lisalib/getfile.aspx?itemid=7555
[15] The Central Bank of Iceland. (2010, January 5). *The Sovereign Ratings Company Standard & Poor's has placed Iceland's ratings on CreditWatch with negative implications.* http://www.cb.is/publications/news/news/2010/01/05/The-Sovereign-Ratings-Company-Standard---Poors-has-placed-Icelands-ratings/

the presidential "veto" had never been exercised. Grímsson's first confrontation with a ruling government came in 2004, when he refused to pass a bill that imposed restrictions on the ownership of newspaper and media corporations. As it turned out, his rejection was no ceremonial flourish; parliament backed down and withdrew the bill. Now, in the wake of the crisis, he tested his authority a second time.

Grímsson was a seasoned, skillful, if opportunistic politician, with a British academic pedigree (he graduated with a Ph.D. in political science from the University of Manchester in 1970). He did not retreat after exercising his veto; he guested on UK talk shows and ably held his own against the British political and media elite. It was the first time during the Icesave debacle that the nation had an advocate that could reach the UK's population, and Grímsson's performance did much to restore public confidence back home. Iceland's left-wing government, however, was unmoved. Icesave II went to national referendum on March 6, 2010, and was rejected overwhelmingly, with 93 % opposing and less than 2 % in favor.

The government had lost face during the first two Icesave negotiations, and faced harsh local criticism. The team sent to the UK, composed mainly of government officials and retired politicians, had been so amateurish – or so opponents of the left-wing government claimed – that their British counterparts had an easy time of it. Stung by the rebukes, the next negotiation team was led by Lee Buchheit, a famed legal expert and veteran of many international distressed debt negotiations.

The new bill was approved by parliament and passed into law on February 16, 2011, on a 44–16 vote.[16] 'Icesave III' differed from its predecessors in a few important ways: it involved no direct DIF borrowing from the British and Dutch governments to pay the minimum guarantee, but instead it would reimburse, with interest, what the British and Dutch had paid out to depositors, to the extent that payments from the Landsbanki estate would not cover their outlays. The material components of the treasury payments were similar to those outlined in the first two bills but the main difference was a much lower interest rate: 3 % in

---

[16] Act no. 13/2011.

euros and 3.3 % in pounds sterling, compared to the 5.5 % rate in the previous bills. Also, the first interest date was set at October 1, 2009, instead of January 1. Since the bulk of the treasury's responsibility concerned the interest payments, Icesave III would greatly reduce its outlays, as compared to I and II.

However, President Grímsson again refused to sign, and a second national referendum was set for April 9, 2011. About a month before the vote, the Landsbanki estate published a quarterly financial status, where its total recovery of assets was estimated to equal roughly 96 % (ISK 1263bn/1319bn) of all priority claims towards the estate, which implied that full repayment of all minimum deposit guarantees might be accomplished by the end of 2013.[17] Thus, Icelandic taxpayers would be liable only for the accrued 3–3.2 % interest related to the delayed repayment of minimum deposit guarantees between 2009 and 2013. It is now estimated, after the fact, that the bill would have resulted in payments by the state of €300 million, amounting to 2.7 % of GDP.

Despite these improvements, Icesave III was rejected in the referendum. It was a closer vote, but 58 % opposed the deal, with 40 % in favor.

The UK Treasury Minister Danny Alexander described the decision as "obviously disappointing . . .. we tried to get a negotiated settlement. We have an obligation to get that money back, and we will continue to pursue that until we do. . . We have a difficult financial position as a country and this money would help."[18]

The matter was now put before EFTA Court. The oral hearing took place on September 18, 2012. The judgment delivered on January 28, 2013 cleared Iceland of all claims, leaving the foreign governments with only "first priority claim" to the Landsbanki estate.[19] A *Financial Times* editorial called the court's ruling "a victory for law and economic

---

[17] Landsbanki Íslands hf. (2011, March 2). *LBI financial information 2010.* https://lbi.is/library/Opin-gogn/skyrslan/Q4%20Financial%20Information%20-%20open%20side.pdf
[18] UK 'disappointment' as Iceland rejects repayment deal. (2011, April 10). *BBC News.* http://www.bbc.co.uk/news/world-europe-13022524
[19] EFTA Court. (2013, January 28). *Judgment of the Court in Case E-16/11 – EFTA Surveillance Authority v Iceland.* http://www.eftacourt.int/index.php/cases/case_e_16_11_efta_surveillance_authority_v_the_republic_of_iceland

sense."[20] On January 11 2016, LBI, the old Landsbanki estate, paid the last installment to the outstanding Icesave debt and closed the claim.

5.3   The Carry Trade Hangover

The CBI embraced inflation targeting in 2001. This policy is built on the premise that a central bank should keep inflation at a given target number by adhering to a Taylor rule, which automates interest rate hikes in response to expectations of rising inflation. In 2003 and 2004, the Icelandic economy was hit by several large demands shocks, which led to overheating on a grand scale. The CBI had to respond with significant policy rate increases.

First, in 2003, the Althing approved plans to double the electric production capacity of the country to support the power needs of the aluminum industry. Alcoa had a new aluminum smelter on the eastern side of the island, while on the west side Century Aluminum had another smelter that needed to be enlarged. Both were gigantic, capital-intensive projects. In the west, the power was generated through geothermal means, by drilling holes deep into the volcanic hotbed of the country and releasing steam that would turn power generators. In the east, a new, 54-square kilometer lake was filled with glacier water trapped by the largest gravel dam in the world. The water passed through underground tunnels to the power generator. Together, the project cost would equal roughly 35 % of Iceland's GDP.

Stress on the labor market was mitigated when one of the general contractors, Italy-based Impregilo, imported workers from Portugal and China to complete the hard labor in the highlands. Not overly concerned with Icelandic labor laws or regulations, Impregilo built a "mining town" for its Sino-Portuguese workforce, which remained isolated from society at large. Dubious practices aside, projects on this scale generate abundant economic heat.

---

[20] Saga ends with Icesave redemption – Ruling vindicates Iceland's policy over rest of Europe's. (2013, January 29). *Financial Times.* http://www.ft.com/cms/s/0/78b96684-6a21-11e2-a80c-00144feab49a.html

Second, there was the heat generated by the privatization of the banking system and its subsequent foreign expansion. The aggressive positions of the banks provided intensive economic stimulus, through both the labor and asset market. The short-handed banks splashed into the limited Icelandic talent pool, which drove up the wage levels for educated workers. Rising asset prices – especially in the stock market – also created wealth effects that spilled into consumption. Moreover, higher ratings and increased competition would also translate into lower credit spreads among the banks and tempting loan offers in foreign currency. All in all, the interest rate margins (between the average funding and lending rates) went from being about 400bp in 2003 to about 200bp in 2007.

Last, emboldened by a rating upgrade after its acquisition of FIH in Denmark, Kaupthing began in August 2004 to offer mortgages at the same rate as the government-guaranteed Housing Financing Fund (HFF) (4.15 % real plus inflation indexation to 40 years) but allowing up to 80 % loan-to-value ratio. The bank had several motives for this move. First, Kaupthing had the lowest market share in consumer lending, but its retail branch network was as developed as those of the other two banks and the savings funds. Therefore, using the same branch system, a higher market share and more services sold would create almost costless revenues for the bank. Moreover, transforming the largely unsecured consumer loan portfolio into housing debt would also lower the bank's capital charges, according to the international capital adequacy ratio rules, and facilitate better funding in the future. It was also an important PR move for Kaupthing. The bank's management was keen to share the fruits of their international expansion with the Icelandic nation by offering cheap real estate loans.

Kaupthing initiated no less than a paradigm shift in the housing market. It reaped great success and a flock of new customers, who happened to be the very customers every bank wants: high-income households unhappy with the credit rationing of the HFF. The other two banks had no choice but to follow suit. With the last vestiges of the credit controls now abolished, housing prices skyrocketed.

The CBI, still slow to respond, began to raise interest rates cautiously in May 2004. It became more aggressive as the signs of overheating became visible. At the end of 2005, the CBI's policy rate stood at about 10.5 %. Hiking interest rates in a small, open economy in response to overheating is in some ways counterproductive, especially if the rates are raised significantly higher than those of neighboring countries; this will attract foreign funds and appreciate the currency. An overvalued currency in turn creates false wealth effects. Households can buy foreign goods at great bargains, and even domestic companies can acquire foreign assets at prices that seem extremely cheap. Eventually, both firms and households would attempt to circumvent the punishingly high domestic interest rate by turning to foreign currency financing. This had actually started soon after the capital controls had been abolished in 1994; by 2003, about 50 % of all corporate loans were currency-denominated (see Chap. 4). In 2007, that ratio had jumped to about 70 %. Companies in every corner of the economy, producers of tradable and non-tradable goods alike, had taken currency risk that was essentially unhedged. Ordinary domestic business in Iceland had only two choices: to accept the punishing double-digit domestic interest rates or turn to unhedged foreign currency financing. Either way, the financial risk was huge.

The double-digit interest rates made Iceland an instant favorite among carry traders. Investors who use the carry trade will take loans in low-yielding currencies (such as the Japanese yen or the Swiss franc), invest the money in high-yielding currencies (such as the Turkish lira, the South African rand, or the Icelandic króna), and pocket the spread. Most high-yielding currencies are traded in small, illiquid currency markets; this often means that carry traders survive turmoil by stampede, their investments gored by severe depreciation. Most of these currencies show steady appreciation for a year or two before their inevitable decline. Not surprisingly, carry traders are a nervous, jumpy lot, always poised to withdraw their money if they detect the slightest disturbance in a country. Inevitably, their mere presence creates volatility, and it can blunt the effectiveness of monetary policy, especially in a small and open economy like that of Iceland.

Typically, carry traders worked at hedge funds and proprietary trading desks of banks. In 2005, however, the carry trade quantum-jumped when foreign banks began to issue the so-called "glacier bonds," which were denominated in ISK but sold to investors outside the country. The concept behind these bonds, like other Eurobonds issued in high-yielding currencies, was simple. The issuer would buy Icelandic bonds or secure Icelandic interest rates with some kind of a swap contract, then bundle it to issue a new bond denominated in ISK that would be guaranteed by a bank, or another party with a high AAA rating. The new bond would earn 2–3 % lower interest than the underlying Icelandic assets, and the issuer would thus receive a fat spread.

About 60–70 % of all glacier bonds issued were arranged by the London branch of the Canadian bank Toronto Dominion (TD), which actively peddled bonds of various high-yielding currencies on both sides of the Atlantic, carrying hefty fees. The glacier bonds would then be sold to retail clients – Belgian dentists, Italian widows, etc. – who had at best a vague idea of what exchange rate risk meant, but who were delighted to receive high interest with AAA rating. The glacier bond issuing began in August 2005, and became quite ferocious. The stock of outstanding bonds reached a high of about €5 billion, or 30 % of GDP, in August 2007. Demand drove the króna up to levels never seen before. But sooner or later, these speculators would try to escape en masse through the narrow corridor of the currency market, sparking a crisis.

Towards the end, the CBI attracted even more carry trade by adopting a de facto implicit exchange rate policy. The CBI issued not only predictions for inflation and interest rates; it also predicted exchange rate paths consistent with its inflation forecast. Its policy statements did nothing to stem the tide, either. The bank often discussed a possible devaluation of the króna by declaring it would 'respond firmly' should the currency fall, to keep consistent with its inflation target.[21] Plantin and Shin (2011) wrote that Iceland in the run-up to the 2008 financial crisis was "[p]erhaps the poster child for the perverse interaction between monetary policy and carry trade inflows."[22]

---

[21] Baldursson, F. M., & Portes, R. (2013). Gambling for resurrection in Iceland: the rise and fall of the banks. *Available at SSRN 2361098.*

[22] Plantin, G., & Shin, H. S. (2011). Carry trades, monetary policy and speculative dynamics.

For a wide-ranging empirical study of carry trade and its determinants, see Anzuini, A., & Fornari, F. (2012). Macroeconomic determinants of carry trade activity. *Review of International Economics, 20*(3), 468–488.

For a model of the interdependence between the carry trade, monetary policy and the real economy, see Truempler, K. (2013). On the Carry Trade in Small Open Economies.

There was a very curious interaction between the banks and carry traders. First, the banks explored the possibility of issuing glacier bonds themselves, but quickly gave up on the prospect since the buyers of these bonds were essentially retail investors who could not be reached without an extensive sales network. The banks had no such network and it was too expensive to build. Instead, they became counterparties to the issuers of the glacier bonds via swap contracts. This was equivalent to depositing ISK into the banks but at lower interest rates than the banks would have to pay in the interbank market; thus they could bolster their interest rate margins. However, toward the very end the banks saw a reverse carry trade as a way to offload currency risk on the foreign speculators, in effect by shorting the ISK.

By 2007, the three Icelandic banks were international entities with large profiles abroad. Their domestic lending was also to a large extent done in foreign currency, which meant 60–70 % of their balance was either foreign or currency-linked. However, by Icelandic law their equity had to be in domestic currency. The banks would, of course, attempt to hedge currency risk by matching foreign assets and liabilities on balance sheets. However, such hedging may be illusory, since if the bank's capital is denominated in domestic currency it will stay fixed, while the relative value of the foreign component of the balance sheet fluctuates with the exchange rate. Thus, an appreciation of the ISK will decrease the relative value of foreign assets and liability and bolster the equity ratio; depreciation will do the reverse.[23] Therefore, rising policy rates and the surging value of the ISK would actually increase the equity ratio of the banks, and give an added impetus for further growth. However, the eventual disastrous downfall reduced their equity ratio below the regulatory minimums.

A clear risk manifested when ISK dropped during the Geyser mini-crisis in early 2006 (see Chap. 2). The current legislation – adopted as an EU directive through a membership to the European Economic Area – allowed Icelandic companies to switch their operating currency into some foreign denomination. This is what one Icelandic investment bank, Straumur-Burðarás, actually did at the end of 2006. Davíð Oddsson, the CBI governor at the time, lambasted the move on December 21, on the grounds that laws allowing for using a foreign operating currency did not apply to

---

[23] Danielsson, Jon and Jonsson, Asgeir (2005) „Countercyclical Capital and Currency Dependence" Financial Markets, Institutions & Instruments, Vol. 14, No. 5, pp. 329–348, December 2005.

banks.[24] On February 14, 2007, the Ministry of Finance published a directive requiring all financial accompanies to win CBI approval to switch operating currency.[25] That approval was not forthcoming. The CBI never stated clearly why it opposed using any other operating currency besides ISK. Most likely, it worried that this type of currency substitution would render its monetary policy impotent if the banks ever switched to euros for operating, although the argument was not overtly stated.

Whatever the reasoning, Kaupthing and the other banks were stuck with ISK and no recourse beyond hedging their equity ratio through a reverse carry trade. And so they did. In late 2007, the banks began to worry about the pending depreciation of the ISK, since sooner or later the carry trade would fall apart and equity ratios would automatically drop. They subsequently began to hedge their equity with forward contracts – in other words, they shorted the ISK. This was more or less accomplished in January 2008, when the outstanding net forward currency position, as measured by the CBI, would be €9 billion, or about 60 % of GDP, a bit higher than the €8 billion book value of their equity. The banks would also offload currency risk through forward contracts with domestic parties like fishing companies, which essentially sold their future earnings in forward contracts and the pension funds hedging their foreign assets.

Thus, when the currency market eventually did move south in March 2008 (to the tune of about 20 % depreciation of the ISK), the equity in the banks was fully hedged and their capital ratios remained constant. Otherwise, a currency depreciation and rising value of foreign assets denominated in ISK would have created the need for new capital, and perhaps brought the banks down about six months earlier than actually happened. However, there were other ways to look at this currency hedging. One could argue the banks actually gained at the expense of the carry traders, as the currency hedge delivered profits that increased the value of the equity in domestic currency. Or, perhaps the banks were simply shorting their own currency, and would now have profit incentives that would go against the interest of

---

[24] Einarsson, Kristján Torfi & Björnsson, Björn Jóhann. (2006, December 22). Davíð gangrýnir ákvörðun Straums. (Davíð criticizes Straumur's decision). *Morgunblaðið*. http://www.mbl.is/vidskipti/frettir/2006/12/22/david_gagnrynir_akvordun_straums/

[25] On February 14, the minister of finance adopted regulation no. 10/2007 where it states that before a financial institution can change its operation currency it needs to seek the opinion of the CBI.

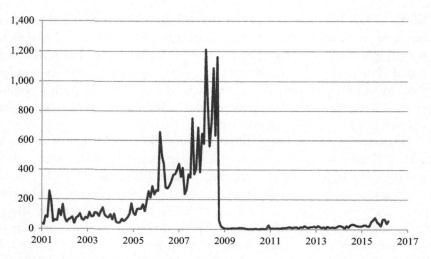

Fig. 5.1 Monthly turnover on the interbank foreign exchange market. Amounts in billion ISK (Source: Central Bank of Iceland statistics)

the general public. These conspiracies stayed alive and generated investigations before and after the banking collapse, but all came to naught.[26] Nevertheless, the public came to see the collapse of the ISK as the work of reckless bankers shorting the currency to the detriment of the common people – which later would have large political consequences, as will be explained in the last section.

With their equity fully hedged in early 2008, the banks withdrew from the carry trade game. Desperate to support the value of the ISK, the CBI raised rates up to 15.5 % and lobbied the treasury to initiate a new, short-term bond issue to serve as a vehicle for carry traders. These efforts were moderately successful, and the ISK would remain relatively stable up until bank runs of September 2008. However, when the reversal came, the carry traders would not have much time to run. On September 24, 2008, after the US Fed denied requests from the CBI for a currency swap – comparable to those extended to the other Scandinavian countries – the currency market dried up and choked off the carry trade (Fig. 5.1). Left frozen inside the Icelandic currency area was €4.3 billion (ISK 650 billion) worth of short-term ISK

---

[26] Special Investigation Commission. (2010). *Report of the Special Investigation Commission.* Chapter 13.

monetary assets, about 42 % of GDP. Since much of this position had been built up by the issuance of glacier bonds, it can quite fittingly be referred to as the "snow overhang".

5.4   The Current Account and the Capital Controls

Iceland is the smallest currency in the world with its own independent monetary policy.[27] As would be expected, all the foreign money heading into the country after its AAA rating in 2002 – whether due to foreign currency lending by the banks, carry traders lured by high interest rates, or foreign direct investment (FDI) heading for aluminum smelting – swelled the economy to the point of bursting. The currency would of course appreciate, which would boost the purchasing power of households when spending their ISK-denominated salaries. Iceland imports most of its tradable consumption, and all of its durable goods consumption.

Thus, a higher currency translated into cars, flat-screen TVs, design furniture and other imports, bought on the cheap. Or you could just take quick trip to London, New York, or coastal Spain to put that super charged purchasing power into use. The US dollar was relatively weak during this time period, and thus the streets of Reykjavík would soon be crowded up with American SUVs bought for ridiculously low prices. As a result, the current account deficit would be in excess of 20 % of GDP during 2006–2007 (see Fig. 5.2).

Some of this deficit would be self-correcting. The smelter projects were bound to increase the country's foreign debt and trade deficit until their slated 2008 completion; but it was expected that aluminum exports would correct the imbalances. There was also widespread belief that the ISK would depreciate within in a relatively short period – and thus there was ever more reason to buy that SUV next week rather than next year. The correction, of course, was much sharper and deeper than anticipated:

---

[27] The Central Bank of Iceland. (2012, September). *Valkostir Íslands í gjaldmiðils- og gengismálum. (Iceland's options regarding currency and foreign exchange.)* (The Central Bank's special publication no. 7).

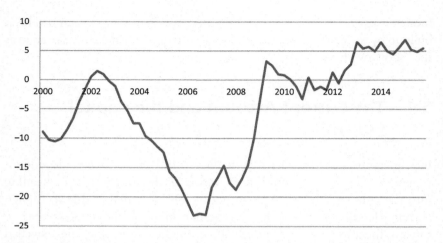

Fig. 5.2 Iceland's current account in 2000–2015. Quarterly figures as percentage of GDP (Source: Central Bank statistics)

the ISK depreciated by 50 % in 2008 before being stabilized with the use of capital controls. Imports of goods and service reduced by 20–25 % at real value between 2008 and 2009, and private consumption fell by 15 %. This would be sufficient to turn the current account into a positive territory. The import of consumption goods – especially durables – would remain modest in the post-crisis years, and very few new cars were shipped to Iceland. At the time of this writing, the traffic in Reykjavík is still dominated by 2006–2008 car models.

The export side of the current account was much slower to adjust. The main export industries of Iceland are fishing and aluminum smelting, and both faced quantity restriction. Government-issued quotas, based on the estimated size of fishing stocks, determine how much fishing firms are allowed to catch. Thus, the marine output of the country is determined by biology, not the export prices. There were a few lucky draws. Due to global warming and rising sea temperatures, a new fish species – mackerel – has migrated into Icelandic waters, much to the anger of Norway and the UK, which maintain mackerel are still theirs to catch. The nations have yet to agree on how that fishing stock should be shared. Of course, the fishing firms received higher prices for the fish denominated in ISK, but foreign revenue remained relatively stable.

The same would apply for the aluminum smelter. The new Alcoa smelter began operating in 2008, and the smelters always run on full and stable capacity, regardless of currency movements. With no FDI arriving and domestic investment at a historical low in post-crisis years, the export base is largely unchanged, although a lower currency gave a new edge in competitiveness.

But the export equation did not change markedly until tourism took off, almost 5 years after the crisis. In 2013, Iceland received about half a million foreign visitors; by 2015, the number of visitors had more than trebled to 1.6 million. The tourist industry subsequently became the leading driver of the economy in terms of export earnings, real estate prices and job creation. As can be seen from Fig. 5.3, service exports now dominate the current account, while the merchandise trade balance has turned negative.

There is no single explanation for the tourism explosion. The likeliest, of course, is the exchange rate depreciation, which made Iceland a lot cheaper for foreign visitors. However, even though a cheaper currency would stimulate spending of those visitors that came to Iceland, about 4–5 years would pass from the depreciation before their number would actually start to increase. The infamy related to the banking collapse probably is also part of the answer. The 2010 Eyjafjallajökull eruption, which blocked flight traffic over the North Atlantic for weeks, may also have renewed interest in the country's geology and landscapes. But social media, which is used extensively to stream images and footage of Iceland's unique landscapes, also has been important. There is further benefit from Reykjavík's rapid development as a transatlantic flight hub thanks to the expansion of Icelandair, the flag carrier, and Iceland's popularity as a tourist destination. 27 airlines now use Keflavik International Airport; a decade ago there were only two or three.

Whatever the reasons for its sudden popularity, Iceland the tourist destination caused a northward shift of the current account and finally gave the CBI the chance to replenish its foreign reserves. Since 2014, the CBI has purchased about 50–70 % of all currency offered in the interbank market and accumulated €3.3 billion (500bn ISK) in reserves.

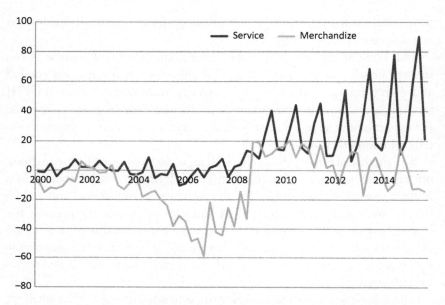

Fig. 5.3 The Merchandize trade balance and the service trade balance in Iceland from 2000 to 2015, quarterly numbers in billion ISK (Source: Central Bank of Iceland statistics)

The sudden and unexpected tourism boom was an economic *deus ex machina* in 2013. Up until that time, the balance of payment situation was very tight, and the ISK was on veritable life support. Controls were tightened and the CBI intervened when necessary, selling small amounts of the currency to prevent it from depreciating below 165–170 versus the euro. Of course it had been worse: the offshore rate hovered between 200 and 250 – after touching 300 – in the wake of the 2008 collapse.

The CBI had to curb the offshore market that was more active than the onshore during the winter of 2008–2009. In the fall, it finally took action by founding a special division of foreign currency control. It rounded up the main traders of the offshore dealings and charged them for illegal trading. Moreover, the offices of the largest fishing company – Samherji – were raided in 2012, on the basis of an allegation that they were breaching the capital controls through intra-firm exchange between the home office and foreign subsidiaries. The enforcement of the capital control regime is discussed in more detail in Chap. 7.

All these cases were dismissed, but they would serve as a deterrent. By applying these coercive measures, the CBI had established the onshore market as a real trading place. Over the next few years controls would be tightened to further safeguard the onshore trading. That left policymakers with the task of somehow clearing away the carry trade overhang from the Icelandic financial system.

5.5   The Currency Auctions

After stabilizing the onshore market through foreign currency control, the CBI attempted to control the offshore market by organizing auctions. All in all, the CBI held 25 currency auctions between June 2011 and February 2015. The auctions were two-legged, where the CBI offered to buy euros for ISK in one leg and sell euros for ISK in the other. The first leg (buy-leg, where the CBI bought euros) was further split into two parts: the Investment Programme (IP)[28] and the Treasury Bond Programme.[29] In the former part, the auction participants got ISK that could be used for long-term investments in the Icelandic economy; in the latter, they received a 20-year, index-linked treasury bond. In the second leg (sell-leg, where the CBI sold euros) the auction participants exchanged offshore ISK for euros.

The first five auctions were single-leg, with the CBI offering to either buy or sell euros in each auction. In the first two auctions, a sell-leg held in early June and a buy-leg in late June 2011, the amounts and prices in the two legs matched, leaving a spread of 9 króna (kr.) per euro for the CBI. In the next two, held in July and August 2011, there was a great mismatch. The CBI sold €69 million in the sell-leg in July, but only

---

[28] The Central Bank of Iceland. (n.d.). *Terms of Auction for the purchase of foreign currency by the Central Bank of Iceland according to the Investment Programme. Transaction date: 10 February 2015.*
[29] The Central Bank of Iceland. (n.d.). *Terms of Auction for the purchase of foreign currency by the Central Bank of Iceland in exchange for Treasury securities. Transaction date: 10 February 2015.*

got offers for €3 million in the buy-leg in August. The CBI then held another buy-leg auction in February 2012, where it bought €141 million at the second highest price recorded in all the auctions: 240 kr. pr. euro. (This action now seems somewhat desperate.) After that, all the auctions were double-legged, in which the CBI matched the amounts and price of each leg, often with a small spread (in the range of 6–17 kr. per euro).

The purpose of the auctions was to replace the overhang of presumably impatient short-term deposits and treasury bonds with long-term investments in the Icelandic economy. The bank then found out – almost surprisingly – owners of the offshore ISK were in no special hurry to dispose of their funds. For this there were several reasons.

First one has to keep mind that Icelandic controls were *capital controls* that prohibited capital account transfers. Current account transfers, however, were unrestricted through the onshore market, despite the obligation to repatriate foreign currency. The overhang ISK earned interest, whether on deposit with banks or invested in bonds. Interest payments are defined as factor income, i.e., income arising from use of factors of production, which is included under the current account. Owners of the overhang ISK had extensive authorizations, right up until March 6, 2015, to purchase Icelandic bonds and had been able to convert interest paid on them at onshore rates as soon as they were obtained.[30] Icelandic nominal interest rates were especially high at the beginning of the period of controls, and although the principal was locked in, they paid a high return. In this sense, the offshore ISK locked in by the controls could be regarded as a perpetuity, which pays only interest while the principal never falls due. A similar example can be found in the British Consols, which have occasionally been issued to finance war operations. If Iceland had turned into a prison for carry traders after the collapse, it had golden window bars.

Second, it is important to remember that ISK exist nowhere but in Iceland, so all offshore ISK are either in deposit accounts in Icelandic

---

[30] Owners of offshore ISK were prohibited from purchasing other assets than treasury bills and one treasury bond series, RIKB 15 0408. See: The Central Bank of Iceland. (2015, March 6). *Undanþágulistum og reglum Seðlabanka Íslands um gjaldeyrismál breytt. (Exemption lists and the Central Bank's rules on foreign exchange changed).* (Press release no. 7/2015). http://www.sedlabanki.is/utgefid-efni/frettir-og-tilkynningar/frettasafn/frett/2015/03/06/Undanthagulistum-og-reglum-Sedlabanka-Islands-um-gjaldeyrismal-breytt/

banks or invested in treasury securities. During the CBI auctions, the ISK never left the country; it only changed ownership. If an investor wishes to recoup the principal of a perpetuity, he simply sells the bond to another investor. Similarly, owners of offshore ISK could easily sell them to other foreign investors – without the intermediation of the CBI – on a securities market abroad. It seems that there was a very active market abroad with these high yielding, Consol-like ISK assets locked in the capital controls, and that the ownership became very concentrated. Just four hedge funds dominated the holdings.[31]

The increased concentration of offshore holdings affected the auctions – as the selling side of ISK gradually became better organized, attempts were made to raise the auction price. In the first auctions, in June and July 2011, bids were received to sell ISK amounting to ISK 61 and 52 billion, respectively. In the next three auctions held after the last single-legged auction in February 2012, bids were received totaling ISK 25–29 billion. After that, the amounts offered for sale dropped substantially, generally ranging from ISK 7–20 billion per auction, which only represented 2–7 % of the total outstanding stock.

At the same time, the ISK exchange rate applied in the auctions rose significantly, moving closer to the onshore rate. This is evident from the fact that in the first half of 2012, the auction exchange rate was around ISK 240 per euro; by the latter half of 2014, it had risen to ISK 180 per euro. Admittedly, the trend was reversed in the last auction on February 10, when bids totaling around ISK 58 billion were received. At the same time, the auction exchange rate dropped to ISK 200 per euro.

It is debatable what conclusions should be drawn from that auction, as it was both the final one and the first time that foreign creditors who had received payment of priority claims were allowed to participate. These claims totaled around ISK 24 billion. Discussion of a possible exit tax may well have prompted investors to leave the country. However, the group of investors wishing to transfer capital to Iceland in this auction was

---

[31] Minister of Finance. (2015, March 18). *Framgangur áætlunar um losun fjármagnshafta. (The progress of the program of capital account liberalization).* In the report it states that "ownership of these ISK assets has become highly concentrated." https://www.fjarmalaraduneyti.is/media/frettatengt2015/Framgangur-aaetlunar-um-losun-fjarmagnshafta-18.3.2015.pdf

comparatively smaller, as bids to purchase ISK totaled only around ISK 12.2 billion.[32]

The bidding side was mostly Icelandic. Many Icelandic expats abroad would jump on the opportunity to get hold of ISK at a reduced price to buy a house or an apartment in Reykjavík, or even a company. Many residents, who had accumulated foreign assets abroad, while the capital account was open, brought the funds home through this option. The CBI imposed a five-year lockup period for investments under the Investment Program, and any payments from the investment in that time had to be reinvested according to the IP rules. According to information from the Ministry of Finance, around 35 % of the buyers of ISK in currency auctions were residents, while 65 % were non-residents.[33]

The CBI was able to reduce the carry trade overhang by half through these auctions – from about €4 billion (600 billion ISK) in 2008 to around €2 billion (300 billion ISK) when the last regular auction was held in February 2015. Being very short on foreign currency during most of this period, the CBI could not serve as counterparty seller of FX in these transactions. That role had to be taken by other private parties willing to invest in the Icelandic economy for the longer term. That methodology would create some discontent at home, as many domestic investors – who unfortunately had not transferred their funds out of the country prior to the crisis – would claim that they were discriminated against. On other hand, those who had run away were now getting a red-carpet welcome and the opportunity to buy up Iceland at a discount. Same complaints could be heard from the real estate market – where expats would allegedly bid up the price with funds from the auctions.

So does the remaining ISK 300 billion (€2 billion) of offshore ISK create a problem for Iceland? The answer depends on how you view the

---

[32] Arion Bank. (2015, January 13). *Mun snjóhengjan minnka í febrúar? (Will the overhang decrease in February?)* https://www.arionbanki.is/markadir/greiningardeild/greiningardeild-allar-frettir/2015/01/13/Mun-snjohengjan-minnka-i-februar/

  Arion Bank. (2015, March 11). *Snjóhengjan minnkar um 12 milljarða. (The overhang decreases by 12 billion.)* https://www.arionbanki.is/markadir/greiningar-deild/greiningardeild-allar-frettir/2015/02/11/Snjohengjan-minnkar-um-12-milljarda/

[33] Eyjólfsson, Þorgeir. (2014, January 27). Af gjaldeyrisútboðum Seðlabankans. (On the Central Bank's currency auctions). *Morgunblaðið.* http://www.sedlabanki.is/utgefid-efni/frettir-og-tilkynningar/frettasafn/frett/2014/01/28/Af-gjaldeyrisutbodum-Sedlabankans/

question. It is not at all abnormal for foreign investors to hold Icelandic financial assets, such as bonds. In fact, it is desirable. But it would be most suitable if these were long-term assets. In addition, the current owners of the overhang do not seem impatient: they can still sell ISK to other foreign parties without going through the Icelandic FX market. In this light, the overhang can easily be viewed as foreign investment. On the other hand, the fact remains that the overhang as a whole is either in short-term deposit accounts or highly liquid treasury bonds, and therefore it could exit the country at any time. From this perspective, it is the sword of Damocles that hangs over the FX market. This, apparently, is the point of view of the Icelandic authorities.

In June 2015, in accordance with the plan for the resolution of the estates, it was announced that a final currency auction would be held later that year, at which the overhang remains would be resolved. The auction was repeatedly postponed and finally held a year later, on June 16, 2016.[34] Holders of offshore ISK were given the option to exchange them for euros at an exchange rate in the range of 190–210 kr. per euro. At the time the official onshore rate was 140 kr. per euro. Any offshore ISK not dispatched by the auction would be stuck in locked, non-interest bearing accounts. The auction was meant to be the final attempt to melt the overhang, which was estimated to stand at €2.1 billion (320 billion ISK).

The auction setup was special in that bidders would not submit their bid price but only their bidding amount. The auction price would depend on the overall participation in the auction, but in the reverse from the usual relation between price and volume: the higher the total volume, the lower the price. If auction participation exceeded €1.2 billion, the exchange rate would be set at 190 kr. per euro; it would rise in steps up to a high of 210 kr. if participation was less than €330 million.

The authors could not evaluate the success of this strategy, since the auction had not occurred at the time of this writing. However, most of the overhang had concentrated in the hands of just a few owners, with majority being held by four US investors, hedge funds Discovery Capital and Autonomy Capital and government bond funds controlled by Eaton

---

[34] Central Bank of Iceland. (2016, May 25). *Central Bank of Iceland foreign currency auction 16 June 2016.*

Vance and Loomis Sayles. When the auction was announced, the latter two declared they had no interest in participating in it.[35]

5.6   The Political Fallout

By and large, the Icelandic authorities avoided a transfer problem stemming from the unwinding of the carry trade, as did post-war Germany. The auction methodology was possible because of the controls, which divided the FX market in two: an official, onshore market for transfers within the current account, and an offshore, auction market for capital account transfers. Such a separation is naturally impossible on a free FX market, where only one exchange rate exists and capital account movements immediately infect the current account through exchange rate movements. This separation served the original purpose behind the imposition of controls: to be able to clean up after the financial bubble before unrestricted foreign currency trading began. The imposition of capital controls in the wake of the 2008 collapse was meant to prevent large-scale capital outflows by burdening the general public with an excessively low ISK exchange rate. The CBI resolved the problem within the scope of the capital account by creating a special auction market, where asset swaps could be concluded at a lower exchange rate than the publicly quoted onshore rate. This not only prevented the reduction from disturbing the real economy, it also ensured that the trade surplus was not used to convert offshore ISK to foreign currency.

The Icesave issue resulted in half a victory. The government guarantee was avoided, but since Landsbanki's estate assets were to some extent domestic, they had to be converted into euros or pounds to the settle the claims made by the Dutch and British. This put excessive pressure on the currency market before the country rebounded, thanks to the flood of foreign currency generated by the tourist boom.

But there are permanent scars left over from the debate. There is deep bitterness against the British authorities after what Icelanders perceive as

---

[35] Wirz, Matt. (2016, May 27). Iceland Puts Freeze on Foreign Investors. *The Wall Street Journal*.

ruthless tactics deployed in trying to collect the Icesave claim from the Icelandic taxpayers, tactics that were supported by complicit actions of the Scandinavian countries.

Also, the Icesave debate pitted the educated, internationally minded elite against the more conservative, nationalistic elements of the populace. The internationalist wing supported the Icesave negotiations, while the nationalists accused them of subservience to foreign domination. In the end, the Icesave skeptics were vindicated and the Icesave supporters humiliated, which resulted in a more isolationist bent in Icelandic politics. That would, among other things, become one of the chief factors stifling and then breaking off negotiations for EU membership, which were in session at the same time.

Last, the whole Icesave affair had a huge effect of how the Icelandic authorities would deal with general creditors of the default estates. A tough stance against foreign creditors was clearly favored by the electorate, and it galvanized the nation's future leadership. In October 2008, in response to Britain's terrorism gambit that froze the nation's banking assets, a grass-roots organization formed under the name InDefence. The campaign organized a UK-media campaign with the slogan "Icelanders are NOT terrorists." It also collected 75,000 signatories for a petition handed to the British Parliament on March 17, 2009. InDefence's spokesperson, Sigmundur Davíð Gunnlaugsson (born 1975), ascended to the chairmanship of the Progressive Party on January 18, 2009.

Under Gunnlaugsson's stewardship, the Progressive Party led the charge against all three Icesave versions, both in and out of the parliament. The EFTA court ruling in January 2013 scored him a huge personal victory. In its wake, he brought forth a new general debt reduction program that would apply to all debtors, regardless of their income or other ability to service these debts. As explained in Chap. 3, the new banks, in unison with the left-wing government, had carried out an extensive credit reduction program, mostly completed in 2012, by which mortgage debt in excess of 110 % collateral value would be written down; state subsidies were paid to those having trouble in serving these debts.

On top of that, the currency-linked loans had been ruled illegal by Supreme Court in 2010, which led to their revaluation back to their original, pre-crisis ISK value. Also, in 2013 an economic recovery was well underway and real estate prices had turned upwards. There was no debt crisis in Iceland, if measured by number of underwater households, or delinquent loans, as it is framed in the USA and other countries.

Gunnlaugsson maintained that the sharp depreciation of the ISK in 2008 and the resulting inflationary shock was caused by the banks – their reckless behavior and the shorting of the ISK – and thus constituted a "breach of conditions" for people who had seen the principal of their indexed loans mushroom. In other words, Icelandic households in general had lost equity because of the banks, and many believed they should be compensated for that, regardless of their ability to serve their loans or the underlying collateral. The cost of the compensation should, went the thinking, be borne by the perpetrators – the old banks – and be delivered via a special tax levied on the default estates.

These arguments contained numerous flaws and contradictions, and could be considered pure populism in many ways. The devaluation was undeniably a correction of a hugely overvalued currency kept up by carry traders, who essentially funded a current account deficit to the tune of 20–25 % of GDP. Moreover, if the old banks were indeed to blame for the currency collapse, the shareholders had long since been wiped out. It sounded counterintuitive to make the creditors, who already had taken grievous losses, pay twice. Besides, it was doubtful if it was possible to tax a defaulted estate in this manner.

Gunnlaugsson countered these arguments by simply maintaining that the original creditors hit with losses at default had already sold out. In their place were vulture funds, which had acquired the claims at a fraction of their original price (he was partly right, as will be explained in Chap. 6). There was nothing wrong with making the vultures share some of their profits with the Icelandic households.

Whatever logical merits Gunnlaugsson's proposals had, they struck a chord with the middle class. An article written by a young engineer, Karl Sigfússon, and published in the most widely circulated newspaper on November 10, 2011, demonstrates that resonance. The article was titled, "I am an oppressed middle class fool." Sigfússon declared: "It is a fact that all the options available to solve the current household debt problems imply an extensive and unfair discrimination. These options reward the financially irresponsible at the expense of the economical and responsible. Those who did leverage their house to the top get their loans written off while others who used their savings to buy their home and limited their use of leverage have just seen their savings and equity burn. . . . I feel that I have been made a fool of for just wanting to stand by all my obligations despite changed economic conditions. What message is being sent to me and my descendants concerning justice, responsibility and fairness as main founding principles of a democratic society?"[36]

The program ensuring general household debt relief landed the Progressive Party an impressive victory in the parliamentary election the spring of 2013. Afterwards, Gunnlaugsson became the prime minister in the coalition of the Progressive and Independence parties. His debt relief program was implemented in 2014, and would reach 100,000 households (out of about 180,000).[37] Emboldened by his victory, Gunnlaugsson would also appoint his InDefence cohorts as advisors to deal with a new transfer problem emerging from the old bank estates, which, through the wind-up process, had accumulated about €6 billion worth of domestic assets, and is the subject of Chap. 6.

[36] Sigfússon, Karl. (2011, November 10). Ég er kúgaður millistéttarauli! (I am an oppressed middle class fool!). *Visir.is.* http://www.visir.is/eg-er-kugadur-millistettarauli!/article/2011711109981
[37] Ministry of Finance. (2014, March 26). *Debt Relief Will Reach 100,000 Households.* https://eng.fjarmalaraduneyti.is/news/nr/17835

6

Meet the Hedge Funds

6.1 The Sir Philip Moment

"It is like all the vultures of the world are congregating on Reykjavik to buy assets at rock bottom prices." These were the words of an unidentified Icelandic businessman reported by *Icelandic Business Weekly* (*Viðskiptablaðið*) on October 15, 2008. The article also claimed that 100 vulture capitalists had descended on the island the day before, with the intent of wringing assets out of the just-fallen banks at fire sale prices.[1] The banks' carcasses had been severely mauled, first during the passage into receivership and then through the UK terrorism legislation, which froze Landsbanki's assets and pulled the banks' UK subsidiaries into liquidation. Gordon Brown, meanwhile, threatened that other Icelandic assets could be seized as well. That did not happen, but British banks did freeze all payments belonging to the Icelandic entities for the rest of the month (see Chap. 3). This, of course, froze out UK customers as well as

---

[1] Allir hrægammar heimsins safnast saman í Reykjavík. (All the vultures of the world congregating on Reykjavik). (2008, October 15). *Viðskiptablaðið*. http://vb.is/frettir/allir-hrgammar-heimsins-safnast-saman-i-reykjavik/12451/

© The Author(s) 2016
Á. Jónsson, H. Sigurgeirsson, *The Icelandic Financial Crisis*,
DOI 10.1057/978-1-137-39455-2_6

Iceland's business interests. The most severe effects fell on the UK retail sector, where the three banks had been very active lenders and partners in leveraged buyouts. "In just 10 days, Iceland's economy has been devastated. The reverberations are set to engulf the British high street," The *Guardian* UK would exclaim.[2] Of course, the troubles of one group are the opportunities of others.

One of the early arrivals in post-collapse Reykjavík was the British retail fashion mogul and Top Shop founder Sir Philip Green, who was looking to buy the debt of Baugur Investment Group. He reportedly wanted to inject some new equity into the group, bail it out, lift it from the British freeze and thereby save some British jobs. Baugur, whose chief owner was Jón Ásgeir Jóhannesson, was the biggest Icelandic holding company, and it had large indirect holdings in Glitnir through its associated companies. Baugur's investments in the UK economy were vast: the frozen food supermarket chain Iceland; the jewelers' group Aurum Holdings (which owns Goldsmiths, Mappin & Webb, and Mosaic Fashions); a fashion group with ownership of eight brands, including Coast, Karen Millen, Oasis, and Principle and Warehouse; the department store chain House of Fraser; and Hamleys toy store. All told, about 53,000 UK workers could trace their employment back to Baugur and its fortunes.[3]

Baugur was heavily leveraged, and it was all too clear that whoever owned its debt would control it. For Sir Philip, this presented the opportunity to slice and dice Baugur's retail assets and fit them into his own empire.

Sir Philip and Mr. Jóhannesson knew each other well. In addition to their co-ownership of so many premium UK brands, the pair had also cooperated in a number of ventures. Baugur owned the Top Shop franchise in Iceland, and Sir Philip ran concessions in the Icelandic controlled House of Fraser. In 2002, Baugur had struck a deal with Sir Philip to swap its stake in Arcadia for the Top Shop, Top Man, and Miss Selfridge brands – after its own bid failed. However, the deal collapsed

---

[2] Wood, Zoe. (2008, October 12). From hero to size zero: the Baugur crisis. *The Guardian online.* http://www.theguardian.com/business/2008/oct/12/iceland-baugur-philip-green

[3] Davey, James. (2008, October 11). Philip Green in talks to take on Baugur debt. *Reuters.* http://uk.reuters.com/article/uk-financial-iceland-green-idUKTRE49A0GO20081011

after it emerged that Icelandic police had raided Baugur's headquarters, chasing down a fraud allegation.[4] Determined to claim a piece of the action, Baugur sold its shares to Sir Philip and banked a £65 million profit,[5,6,7] which helped finance a spending spree that garnered the long string of UK retailers.[8] Sir Philip went on to make billions by turning Arcadia around. All the while, he remained in regular social contact with Jóhannesson. They would allegedly attempt to outdo each other at the British retail industry's annual fundraising dinner – bidding hundreds of thousands of pounds in the charity auctions.[9]

Reykjavík airport, once crowded with private jets, was virtually empty when Green's 16-seat private plane landed on Friday, October 10. A waiting car whisked him to the 101 Hotel, which was adjacent to Reykjavík's main shopping street (and which had received a modern, glittering facelift designed by Ingibjörg Pálmadóttir, Jóhannesson's wife). The UK *Telegraph* described the 101 as "a pebble-dash prison from the outside,"[10] but it was nevertheless the most expensive hotel in town, and a favorite hangout and watering hole for bankers and financers during the boom years.

---

[4] Baugur Group hf. (2002, August 29). *Tilkynning vegna húsleitar.* (*Announcement regarding a dawn raid.*) OMX The Nordic Exchange. http://news.icex.is/newsservice/MMIcexNSWeb.dll/newspage? primarylanguagecode=IS&newsnumber=18286

[5] Baugur Group hf. (2002, September 5). Possible offer for Arcadia. OMX The Nordic Exchange. http://news.icex.is/newsservice/MMIcexNSWeb.dll/newspage?primarylanguage code=EN&newsnumber=18400

[6] Baugur Group hf. (2002, September 6). *Stjórn Arcadia samþykkir væntanlegt yfirtökutilboð Philips Greens.* (*Arcadia's board of directors accepts Philip Green's forthcoming takeover bid.*) http://news.icex. is/newsservice/MMIcexNSWeb.dll/newspage?primarylanguagecode=IS&newsnumber=18412

[7] Baugur Group hf. (2002, October 16). *Taveta Offer for Arcadia.* OMX The Nordic Exchange. http://news.icex.is/newsservice/MMIcexNSWeb.dll/newspage?primarylanguagecode=EN& newsnumber=18842

[8] Baugur Group hf. (2002, October 24). *Acquisition of a strategic stake in The Big Food Group plc.* OMX The Nordic Exchange; Baugur Group hf. (2002, November 7). *Baugur takes 4.54 % stake in House of Fraser plc.* OMX The Nordic Exchange; Baugur Group hf. (2002, December 20). *Baugur-ID kaupir 2,95 % hlut í Somerfield PLC í Bretlandi.* (*Baugur-ID buys a 2.95 % stake in Somerfield plc.*) OMX The Nordic Exchange.

[9] Fletcher, Richard & Mason, Rowena. (2008, October 12). Sir Philip Green poised for Baugur bailout. *The Telegraph.*

[10] Fletcher, Richard & Mason, Rowena. (2008, October 12). Sir Philip Green poised for Baugur bailout. *The Telegraph online.* http://www.telegraph.co.uk/finance/newsbysector/retailandconsumer/ 3185137/Sir-Philip-Green-poised-for-Baugur-bail-out.html

Sir Philip met with government officials to lodge his bid for Baugur's debt.[11] He left the next day to return to Monaco – where he was said to usually spend weekends with his family.[12] His bid had been outrageous: allegedly he was willing to buy Baugur's debt at a 95 % discount.[13] It received a prompt rejection. Baugur's subsidiary holding most of its UK investments was placed into administration on February 6, 2009, at the request of the Landsbanki estate, which would subsequently assume control of its assets.[14]

Iceland's battered financial community viewed Sir Philip's appearance and his indecent proposal as insult after injury. Had Iceland really sunk so low that investors could gobble up banking assets for a few pence on the pound? Jóhannesson, sensing that the whole affair was a PR disaster for Baugur (and a personal one, too), apologized in an interview with the *Financial Times* three weeks later. Pleading with his old friend for help had been simple 'day-after panic'. Following the asset freeze, "we thought, 'Shit, they are probably going to freeze all the Icelandic assets in the UK.'"[15]

Other venture capitalists were soon to arrive at the scene. A number of private equity funds from the USA – such as Alchemy and TPG – arrived a few days later.[16] Soon British banks were knocking on the door to buy Kaupthing's UK loan book. "All roads lead back to Kaupthing," exclaimed one senior industry banker in the British media.[17]

---

[11] Kleinman, Mark & Mason, Rowena. (2008, October 11). Iceland crisis lures Topshop boss Sir Philip Green to Baugur deal. *The Telegraph.*

[12] Fletcher, Richard & Mason, Rowena. (2008, October 12). Sir Philip Green poised for Baugur bail-out. *The Telegraph.*

[13] Green vildi kaupa skuldir Baugs með 95 % afslætti. (Green wanted to buy Baugur's debt at a 95 % discount.) (2008, October 14). *Morgunblaðið.*

[14] LBI hf. (2009, February 6). *BG Holding ehf placed into administration.* http://lbi.is/home/news/news-item/2009/02/06/BG-Holding-ehf-placed-into-administration/

[15] Braithwaite, Tom. (2008, October 31). Chastened Baugur hopes to navigate debt crisis. *Financial Times.*

[16] Braithwaite, Tom. (2008, October 15). Green faces battle with TPG for Baugur's assets. *Financial Times.* http://www.ft.com/intl/cms/s/0/5e0c23f6-9a52-11dd-bfe2-000077b07658.html#axzz46wtmyqAJ

[17] Wood, Zoe & Mathiason, Nick. (2008, October 12). Philip Green steps in to save Baugur. *The Guardian online.* http://www.theguardian.com/business/2008/oct/12/philip-green-baugur

As previously discussed, the emergency legislation authorized the Financial Services Authority (FSA) to take over the troubled banks and appoint a resolution committee to assume the powers of the board and administer the banks' assets and operations. Selected right after the banks' collapse, the committees were mainly comprised of attorneys and CPAs; three members were independent, and two were former employees of the bank. All banks subject to the legislation kept their banking license but were sheltered from enforcement actions from creditors.

While the resolution committees took over the function of the boards, they kept in close contact with the FSA during the first days. Gradually, however, they assumed their roles as stand-alone operators of the fallen banks. On November 24, the banks got formal court authorization for a moratorium. The committees were to ensure proper handling of the banks' assets and maximize their value. In general, they were not expected to pay or settle any claims against the banks, but they had authority to do so if they deemed it appropriate and favorable to the estate. In many ways, the operations of these committees and, later, the winding up boards, were similar to US Chapter 11 proceedings.

Retaining the banking licenses while the moratorium was in effect was a move meant to prevent asset fire sales. For the most part, the resolution committees were able to hold the line. Sometimes they had assistance, as in the UK. Despite the freezing-via-terrorism order, the UK authorities did not impede with the recovery process. On the contrary, the UK Treasury actually granted the estate a loan (collateralized with the estate's assets) so it would be able to extend liquidity to British companies that had been former Landsbanki customers, or were owned by Icelandic holding companies such as Baugur.

The British insisted that no funds would be transferred out of the country; instead, they would be kept in (interest-free) accounts with the Bank of England. Advisors from Ernst&Young would monitor the recovery process. Thus, the much anticipated fire sale on British High Street never came to be – without a doubt to the disappointment of many investors.

Even though the British freezing order caused a lot of collateral damage to the Icelandic economy, the UK authorities nevertheless always operated within limits of the law and Landsbanki's resolution committee was always in control of the estate's assets in Britain. The same did not apply to the other Icesave country – the Netherlands – where Landsbanki had offered its online accounts under the slogan *de transparante spaarbank* – the transparent savings bank – and attracted about 125,000 customers, who deposited €1.7 billion. When the bank collapsed, the Dutch Central Bank (De Nederlandsche Bank) got emergency court order to seize control of the Dutch branch of Landsbanki and appointed administrators to handle the affairs of the branch, including all assets and dealings with customers.[18,19] The court order was limited to an 18-month period and was obtained on the grounds that Landsbanki's banking license had been revoked, which was in fact not true; the failed banks would keep their licenses for about two to three years in moratorium after their default. Nevertheless, it would not be until after the 18-month court order period had expired that the resolution committee would get control of the assets in the Netherlands despite arguing that the ruling infringed the jurisdiction of Iceland and was thus a breach of Directive 2001/24/EC.[20,21]

In the first few weeks of operations, the resolution committees had to address some urgent issues regarding the estates' assets, while their subsidiaries were often held for ransom. As Glitnir collapsed, its Norwegian subsidiary (BN Bank, renamed Glitnir ASA after Glitnir's acquisition) was granted a liquidity loan of €590 million (NOK 5 billion) from the Norwegian deposit insurance fund. The loan had a duration of seven days. Wanting to preserve the subsidiary's value, Glitnir's resolution committee asked to prolong the loan, but was turned down. Under strong pressure from the Norwegian deposit insurance fund, Glitnir ASA was sold for €35 million (10 % of equity) to a consortium of Norwegian savings banks under the leadership of the CEO of Sparebanken SMN. A

---

[18] The District Court of Amsterdam. (2008, October 13). *Decision in the District Court of Amsterdam. Private Law Sector. Petition number HA-RK 08.668.* https://www.forsaetisraduneyti.is/media/island/frettir/13.pdf

[19] The District Court of Amsterdam. (2008, October 14). *Rectification of this Court's decision of 13 October 2008 on the petition with number HA-RK 08.668.* https://www.forsaetisraduneyti.is/media/island/frettir/13.pdf

[20] Þorsteinsson, Loftur Altice & Valdimarsson, Pétur. (2011, June 25). *Complaint to the Commission of the European Union.*

[21] Þorsteinsson, Loftur Altice & Valdimarsson, Pétur. (2011, September 25). *Complaint No. CHAP (2011) 2011 to the Commission of the European Union.*

month later, Sparebanken estimated the purchased bank (again named BN Bank), to be worth €236 million in its annual report.[22] The CEO of Sparebanken also served as chairman of the board of the Norwegian deposit insurance fund. He did not, however, participate in the denial of liquidity assistance.[23] In January 2009, the Norwegian CEO in question went on record to confirm, "We knew BN Bank well and knew it was a good bank."[24] BN Bank is still operating in Norway. Hence, some claimed that the Norwegians had exploited their position to pocket €200 million.

Kaupthing had operated a number of subsidiaries – such as KSF in Britain, FIH in Denmark, Kaupthing Bank Sverige AB in Sweden and others in Norway, Finland and Luxembourg. The parent company's assets constituted only about 30 % of the total balance sheet prior to the collapse. Afterwards, the fortunes of each subsidiary depended on the response from its respective host country. Some, like the UK's KSF, were liquidated directly. Kaupthing Bank Sverige was sold (for SEK 414 million) to the Finnish Alandsbanken in February 2009; the Danish FIH was sold in 2010 to a group of Swedish and Danish investors. Others were restored, like Kaupthing Luxembourg, which was restructured with the aid of both Luxembourg and Belgium (KL now operates as Banque Havilland).[25]

Considering what we know now, it seems likely that KSF would still be a going concern in the UK if it had had anything but an Icelandic owner. It would have benefitted from UK-sponsored liquidity support, with estimated recoveries of 85–86 pence in the pound.[26] The same holds for Heritable Bank, the former subsidiary of Landsbanki, where

---

[22] Fadnes, Ole Morten. (2009, January 16). Sparebankenes røverkjøp. (Sparebanken's bargain). *Dagens Næringsliv.* http://www.dn.no/nyheter/2009/01/16/sparebankenes-roverkjop

[23] Júlíusson, Þórður Snær. (2009, January 21). Seldur á brot af raunvirði. (Sold for a fraction of real value). *Morgunblaðið,* p. 4.

[24] Fadnes, Ole Morten. (2009, January 16). Sparebankenes røverkjøp. (Sparebanken's bargain). *Dagens Næringsliv.* http://www.dn.no/nyheter/2009/01/16/sparebankenes-roverkjop

[25] European Monitoring Centre on Change. (2012, May 21). *Banque Havilland, Luxembourg.* http://www.eurofound.europa.eu/observatories/erm/restructuring-in-smes/banque-havilland-luxembourg

[26] Ernst & Young. (2015, November 5). *Kaupthing Singer & Friedlander Limited (in Administration) Joint Administrators' Progress Report to creditors for the six month period from 8 April to 7 October 2015.*

non-secured non-preferential creditors have already received payments of 98 pence in the pound.[27]

As previously noted, the Icelandic banks had been very active in the UK real estate sector, and in 2008 the UK was heading for its worst recession since World War II. The British economy suffered a 6 % contraction in GDP from Q2 2008 to Q2 2009, while unemployment would rise to about 8.3 %. This did not spell good tidings for the UK retail sector. One unidentified British observer told the *Financial Times*, "The Icelandic banks highly leveraged their borrowings to holding companies to make leveraged acquisitions of companies that were dependent on leveraged consumers and that's why it unraveled so quickly."[28]

So while the fire sales for the most part were avoided, claims on the Icelandic banks would suffer a sort of "Sir Philip's" pricing, which reflected the poor standing of Iceland and its financial sector in the eyes of the world at large. The low pricing would open the door for new owners to obtain control of the old banks.

6.2   Business at the Old Banks

Even in moratorium, operations at the banks' estates were complex. Iceland's big three all ranked in the top ten largest bank defaults in history, in terms of pre-default asset values: Kaupthing took fifth place, Landsbanki ninth, and Glitnir tenth. Perceived as a single entity, they would rank third, behind only Lehman Brothers and Washington Mutual.

Operations primarily focused on recovering assets and converting them into cash. The aim, of course, was to maximize asset value instead of converting them rapidly through fire sales. The estates kept their banking license and sustained certain operative functions. They could, for example, grant new loans to existing customers, or participate in equity

[27] Ernst & Young. (2015, September 6). *Heritable Bank Plc. (in Administration) Administrators' Nineteenth Progress Report to Creditors.*

[28] Braithwaite, Tom. (2008, October 31). Chastened Baugur hopes to navigate debt crisis. *Financial Times.*

offerings of their existing holdings, if they deemed it necessary to maximize the value of their assets. The winding-up boards also revoked some payments the banks had made in the last few months before default, and sued some former employees and customers for damages.

Early on, the resolution committees also labored over negotiations with the government on the establishment of the new banks. Initial valuations of the assets assumed by the new banks (and carried out by Deloitte London LP) indicated that the asset values far exceeded the value of the transferred deposits. If the new banks were formed on the basis of these valuations, they would need to issue large amounts of debt to the estates, or up to €4 billion. In addition, they would need initial capital of up to €2.5 billion from the treasury. Furthermore, the asset evaluation process did not satisfy some creditors, since it was performed unilaterally at the request of the Icelandic authorities. Creditors also maintained that the valuation was both non-transparent and one-sided.

The government, in turn, upheld the 'bad case scenario' asset valuation principle, but it was willing to let the estates share in whatever upside occurred, in terms of equity stakes, conditional debt instruments or performance bonds. So agreed, Glitnir acquired a 95 % stake in Íslandsbanki (New Glitnir), and Kaupthing acquired 87 % of Arion Bank (New Kaupthing) and a conditional bond that could deliver payments of up to €300 million. However, default estates cannot legally be controlling owners of financial institutions. Thus the transfer of ownership had to go through holding companies (ISB Holding for Íslandsbanki and Kaupskil for Arion Bank), which were in turn controlled by the estates. Old Landsbanki acquired a 19 % stake in Landsbankinn, a performance bond of up to €600 million and a conventional 10-year bond of €1.65 billion that was denominated and repayable in foreign currency. The 10-year bond was the only conventional debt assumed by the new banks. If the performance bond was paid in full, the estate's stake in Landsbanki would be transferred to the Treasury.[29]

These negotiations thus severely reduced both the debt of the new banks (from the estimated €4 billion to €1.6 billion), and the treasury's

---

[29] Ministry of Finance. (2011, March). Skýrsla fjármálaráðherra um endurreisn viðskiptabankanna. (Minister of finance report on the restoration of the commercial banks).

capital contributions (from the estimated €2.5 billion to €1.3 billion). As it turned out, both performance bonds were paid to the maximum and the treasury acquired Landsbanki in full, apart from a minor share distributed to employees of the bank. As detailed in Chap. 7, the estates' equity stakes in the new banks would later be considered a threat to economic stability in Iceland. Glitnir wound up delivering its entire stake as a stability contribution to the state in early 2016, and Kaupthing pledged a considerable part of its stake for the same purpose.

The estate of old Landsbanki was under special scrutiny from the public and the government because of the Icesave debacle. In the resolution committee's (RC) first assessment of the estate's assets, in February 2009, the assets were valued at €8 billion (1195 billion ISK). Priority claims, mostly Icesave deposits, were estimated to be €8.9 billion (1330 billion ISK), so it was estimated that the assets covered 90 % of priority claims. In June that year, the RC lowered its estimate to €7.3 billion, or 83 % of priority claims. This is the estimate that was available when the first Icesave bill was put forth in parliament. The shortfall of assets to priority claims was therefore €1.6 billion, over half of which would be the treasury's liability if the Icesave bill was accepted and the value of the assets did not increase. The valuation would remain largely unchanged until it began rising in 2011, and it then kept rising steadily until year-end 2012. Valuation mostly remained constant from 2013 until composition at year-end 2015. A milestone was reached at year-end 2011, when the asset value reached the amount of priority claims. At that point, no principal payments would fall on the state should it be deemed responsible for paying the minimum guarantee of Icesave deposits (Fig. 6.1).

The improved asset position of the old banks' estates was mostly driven by UK economic recovery that began in the second half of 2009 and gathered steam in 2010. The retail sector also rebounded, and actually started to steam ahead in 2012. Riding this change in fortune, the estates of the old banks were able pull through several successful deals in which the equity stakes in the British retail chains – including the main holdings of Baugur, which Sir Philip had been so eager to grab in October 2008 – were sold for a very high price. This clearly demonstrates the usefulness of the policy of allowing the estates to continue banking operations so as to maximize asset return.

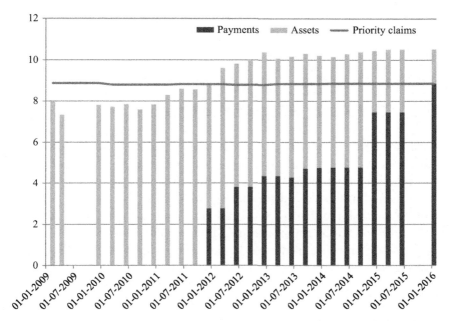

Fig. 6.1 Estimated value of LBI's assets and payment of priority claims. The light gray columns show the estimated value of LBI's total assets, the dark gray shows cumulative payments of priority claims, and the light grey line shows the estimated amount of priority claims at each time. Amounts in billion euros (Source: Announcements from LBI's resolution committee and LBI's quarterly financial information)

UK frozen food retailer Iceland Foods – one of Baugur's most prized possessions – is a good example of this beneficial flexibility. The Landsbanki estate had a 67 % stake in the company; Glitnir's estate held 10 %; owner and founder Malcolm Walker, and the company's management, held the remaining shares. The estates put their combined stake up for sale in early 2011 and received bids from a few groups. After two rounds the highest bidders were the investment funds Bain Capital and BC Partners, but Walker and the management had pre-emptive rights as shareholders, and they waited to strike a deal in February 2012. The selling price was £1.55 billion, the equivalent of €2 billion, of which LBI got €1.74 billion. Before the sale the stake was valued at €1.17 billion, so the sale increased the asset valuation by €0.57 billion. Riding this success, the asset valuation of Landsbanki estate jumped in the first quarter of 2012 to about 10 % over the amount of priority claims.

6.3   The Asset Base of the Estates

Shortly after being appointed by the court, the winding-up boards of the three estates called for claims, and the deadline to lodge a claim was set for October-December 2009. Taken together, a total of almost 50,000 claims were lodged against the three estates, amounting to over €112 billion. Only about half the claims – €55.3 billion – were accepted (see Table 6.1).

In addition to the claims accepted by the winding-up boards, deposits in domestic branches of the old banks, amounting to €9.8 billion, were transferred to the new banks. Total claims against the old banks therefore amounted to €65.1 billion, whereas general claims amounted to €45.8 billion. At the time of composition at year-end 2015, the total recovery for general creditors was estimated by the estates to be €11.9 billion, after the estates had paid stability contributions. The mean recovery of general claims was therefore 26 %, whereas the mean recovery of all claims, general and priority, was 48 %. The total deposits of the banks' parent companies amounted to €19.3 billion. Instead of receiving 48 % of this amount – €9.3 billion – depositors received full recoveries, so the emergency legislation effectively transferred €10 billion from general creditors to depositors (see Table 6.2).

Table 6.1 Number and amounts of claims lodged, the amount accepted and amount of priority claims for each estate. Amounts in million euros

	Number lodged	Lodged amount	Accepted amount	Thereof priority
Glitnir	8,685	22,907	15,940	527
Kaupthing	28,167	48,773	18,667	93
Landsbanki	12,000	40,833	20,693	8,853
Total	48,852	112,513	55,300	9,473

Source: Announcements from the winding-up boards and financial information of the estates

Table 6.2 Ultimate recoveries by the creditors of the estates, showing domestic deposits transferred to the new banks, foreign deposits which were priority claims on the estates, and general claims on the estates. Amounts in million euros

	Claims	Recoveries	Recovery %
Domestic deposits	9,813	9,813	100
Foreign deposits	9,473	9,473	100
General claims	45,827	11,927	26
Total	65,113	31,213	48

Source: Initial balance sheets of the new banks and annual financial statements of the estates for 2015

There is some variation in the average recovery figures of the banks. It was lowest for Kaupthing's estate (40 %), while the estates of Glitnir and Landsbanki recovered 44 % and 58 %, respectively. Recoveries for general creditors were lowest on Landsbanki's estate (14.38 %), which can be attributed to the large amount of priority claims due to Icesave. The final payout for general creditors of Kaupthing and Glitnir were 30 % and 30.2 %, respectively.[30] These statistics refer only to the parent companies; given the high recoveries of the banks' subsidiaries (e.g. KSF, with at least 85 % and Heritable bank with about 98 %), the recoveries on a consolidated basis are higher.

The variation in recovery rates can be explained partly by differences in the banks' structures and the jurisdiction where their foreign assets were controlled. As a rule, foreign recovery was much better abroad than at home, as domestic assets were engulfed in the financial crisis. Kaupthing was organized into a number of subsidiaries. In contrast, foreign lending at Landsbanki was to a much greater extent carried out from the mother company in Iceland. Hence, the resulting assets came under Icelandic jurisdiction, which led to an overall higher recovery ratio for Landsbanki than the other banks.

As was discussed in Chap. 4, the FSA used its authority to partition the banking system into domestic and foreign parts. Of course, deposits of the domestic branches of the failed banks were considerably less than their

---

[30] See announcements from the Reykjavik District Court in the Icelandic Legal Gazette (Lögbirtingablað) on the ratification of composition agreements for Glitnir (2015, November 25), Kaupthing (2015, November 27) and Landsbanki (2015, November 30).

domestic assets, due to large-scale wholesale funding. On a parent company basis, domestic deposits were 18 % of Glitnir's total funding, and 14 % of Landsbanki's and Kaupthing's.[31] Half of the banks' wholesale funding was foreign, and the banks subsequently re-loaned this to Icelandic and foreign corporations (this is reflected by the fact that at the beginning of 2008, around 68 % of total bank lending to Icelandic corporations was in foreign currency, or currency-linked).[32]

According to general insolvency law, all assets exceeding priority claims are held for the benefit of general creditors. Therefore, given the low deposit-to-loan ratios of the banks and their extensive use of wholesale funding in lending to domestic parties, a considerable amount of Icelandic assets remained the property of the insolvent estates – ultimately, there could not be a complete separation of domestic and foreign assets. In addition, due to FSA controls, some domestic assets were not transferred to the new banks. Examples include derivatives resulting in claims against domestic parties[33]; subsidiaries kept off the balance sheet, such as Kaupthing's mortgage fund, which was issuing housing mortgages; and assets moved to foreign special purpose vehicles (SPVs) (used, for instance, as pledges to the Luxembourg Central Bank).

At year-end 2014, a large share of the estates' assets had been converted to cash. The biggest exception was their holdings in the new banks. At that time their stakes, in the form of share capital or bonds, amounted to around €3.5 billion. A total of 69 % of Glitnir's assets, 50 % of

---

[31] On a group-wide basis, including foreign subsidiaries, deposits of domestic branches were a very small portion of the old banks' funding: 14 % for Glitnir, 13 % for LBI and 7 % for Kaupthing. According to the new banks' initial balance sheets, Arion Bank's deposits amounted to ISK 442 billion, those of Íslandsbanki to ISK 496 billion and those of Landsbankinn ISK 501 billion, or a total of ISK 1438 billion. According to the last interim financial statements of the old banks, from June 2008, total liabilities of Kaupthing were ISK 6166 billion, of Glitnir ISK 3662 billion and of LBI ISK 3769 billion.

[32] Statistics, Central Bank of Iceland, Lending to households and corporates. At the beginning of 2008, total lending by commercial banks to corporates amounted to ISK 1322 billion, of which ISK 899 billion was in foreign currencies.

[33] The FSA's first decisions provided for the transfer of derivative contracts with domestic parties to the new banks, but this was altered in later decisions as the contracts were considered too risky for the new banks.

Kaupthing's, and 25 % of LBI's were liquid funds.[34] In addition, the estates had already distributed a considerable amount of liquid funds to priority creditors; this means that around 79 % of LBI's assets and 71 % of Glitnir's had already been converted to liquid funds. Obviously, conditions for starting distributions towards general creditors were satisfied.

As shown in Table 6.3, the three estates held foreign assets valued at €8.8 billion. These were assets residing outside of Iceland, and their distribution to foreign creditors had no effect on Iceland's balance of payments. This was so despite the fact that the insolvent estates were domestic parties, making all of their assets, including the foreign assets, subject to capital controls. However, the estates retained around €6 billion in domestic assets that could create a transfer problem when distributed to foreign creditors. In this regard, however, not all of the estates' domestic assets were the same. Icelandic banks held foreign liquid assets to cover all deposits in foreign currencies, and therefore the estates' domestic deposits in foreign currencies, which were equivalent to around €1.1 billion, were fully financed and their distribution would not have to go through the FX market.[35] In addition, some of the estates' other domestic assets were secured with foreign assets, which could cover the payments and therefore would not impact the FX market, although they would affect the balance of payments. Aside from these assets, however, the estates still retained a large portion of domestic assets, most of which would find their way into the FX markets if distributed to creditors.

In other words, the domestic asset recovery of the estates in Iceland had added a new dimension to the transfer problem. The creditors of the estates were mostly foreign residents, and thus the ISK holdings had to be exchanged into foreign currency when the assets of the estates were distributed.

---

[34] Annual financial statements of Glitnir and Kaupthing for 2014 and financial information from LBI for Q4 2014.

[35] Part of these deposits of the estates results from the sale of foreign assets for foreign currency, and as a result has never had any effect on the domestic FX market, while some part of them results from payments made by domestic parties on foreign-denominated loans, some of which had no income in foreign currency, and this has already had its impact on the FX market.

Table 6.3 Breakdown of the assets of the three estates at year-end 2014. Amounts in billion euros

	Glitnir	Kaupthing	LBI	Total	%
New Banks' shares and bonds	1.2	1.0	1.3	**3.5**	24
ISK-denominated domestic deposits	0.5	0.0	0.2	**0.7**	5
Foreign-denominated domestic deposits	0.2	0.3	0.6	**1.1**	7
Foreign-denominated deposits abroad	3.7	2.3	0.0	**6.0**	41
Other ISK-denominated domestic assets	0.4	0.0	0.1	**0.6**	4
Other foreign-denominated domestic assets	0.0	0.1	0.0	**0.2**	1
Other foreign-denominated assets abroad	0.4	1.5	0.8	**2.7**	18
Total assets	**6.4**	**5.3**	**3.0**	**14.8**	**100**
Total domestic assets	2.3	1.5	2.2	**6.0**	41
Total foreign assets	4.1	3.9	0.8	**8.8**	59
Total deposits	4.4	2.7	0.7	**7.8**	53

Source: Annual financial statements of Glitnir and Kaupthing for 2014 and financial information from LBI for Q4 2014
LBI did not provide a breakdown of assets in foreign currency between foreign and domestic parties. From Landsbankinn's 2014 annual financial statements, however, it can be concluded that the largest portion of LBI's FX deposits were with Landsbankinn. It is assumed here that practically all of LBI's FX deposits were with domestic banks while its other FX assets, with the exception of Landsbankinn's bonds, are assets abroad

6.4   Hedge Funds as Bank Owners

Auctions to settle outstanding credit default swap (CDS) contracts on the old banks' bonds were held in London in early November 2008. These auctions had a twofold purpose: to facilitate physical settlement of the contracts, and to get a reference price for underlying bonds to be used in cash settlement of CDS. The final prices for senior unsecured bonds in the auctions where 1.25 % for Landsbanki, 3 % for Glitnir, and 6.625 % for Kaupthing.[36,37,38]

[36] CreditFixings, 2008. *Landsbanki Íslands hf. CDS Auction Results, Thursday 4th November 2008.* http://www.creditfixings.com/information/affiliations/fixings/auctions/2008/landsb-res.shtml
[37] CreditFixings, 2008. *Glitnir Banki hf. CDS Auction Results, Thursday 4th November 2008.* http://www.creditfixings.com/information/affiliations/fixings/auctions/2008/glitni-res.shtml
[38] CreditFixings, 2008. *Kaupthing banki hf. CDS Auction Results, Thursday 6th November 2008.* http://www.creditfixings.com/information/affiliations/fixings/auctions/2008/kaupth-res.shtml

The auction prices were just a fraction of the eventual payout on general claims on the estates after composition – 14.38 % for Landsbanki, 30.2 % for Glitnir, and 30 % for Kaupthing according to their composition agreements. Considering the size of the financial cataclysm, such undervaluing is not surprising. The crisis had left little certainty about the value of the banks' assets, and Icelandic authorities were still retroactively amending the laws that would govern their distribution to stakeholders. Therefore, trading in the old banks' bonds was scarce at first. Soon, though, investors who prey upon the distressed debt of companies and sovereigns – "vulture funds" – picked up the scent, and trading picked up. However, it would be more than a year, in late 2009 or early 2010, after claims had been lodged, that the creditors' real identity came to light.

The main creditors of the banks had originally been European banks (about 50 % of the loans came from Germany) and institutional investors. In late 2009 and early 2010 the winding-up boards published official lists of claims, and these confirmed the speculation that many of the creditors were indeed hedge funds. On the first lists, the funds with the largest claims were the hedge funds Baupost, Davidson Kempner Capital Management, York Capital Management, Anchorage Capital Management, Centerbridge Partners and Angelo Gordon & Co.[39] These funds acquired the claims through shelf companies and sub-funds, and in some cases they managed to dodge the media's radar almost completely. The majority of the shelf companies could be traced to their original owners through documents from the United States Securities and Exchange Commission (SEC) and Luxembourg's company register. Davidson Kempner's Burlington Loan Management ended up being by far the best known of these funds, due to both the large amount of claims it had accumulated and its oversized public presence.

At first there were remarkably fewer hedge funds amongst Landsbanki's creditors than there were at Glitnir and Kaupthing. The reason is probably that general creditors were not expected to receive a penny because of the huge amount of priority claims, which were mostly Icesave deposits. As discussed above, it was late 2011 before it was finally clear that the estate's

---

[39] Glitnir. (2009, December 8). *List of Claims.*

assets had risen enough in value for regular creditors to get at least some compensation. This news brought more hedge funds forward to buy Landsbanki claims, and those acquisitions turned out to be very profitable.

Figure 6.2 shows the ten hedge funds with the highest amounts of registered claims, in terms of value, following the end of the registration process.[40] What might be surprising is that despite grabbing headlines at the time, Davidson Kempner was only the third largest creditor. Baupost's claims, worth €733 million, were double DK's. The nominal value of Baupost's claims was €3 billion, with €2.3 billion in Kaupthing claims and €0.7 billion in Glitnir claims. The fund acted through numerous shelf companies, many named after famous Icelandic landmarks, such as Þingvellir National Park, Gullfoss waterfall and Geysir.[41] This network of sub-funds obscured the big picture activity.[42] The shelf companies were nearly untraceable until documents from Luxembourg revealed the true owners in the fall of 2011.

Amongst other large hedge fund creditors were York Capital Management, Eton Park Capital Management, Centerbridge Partners, and Anchorage Capital Group. Funds such as Arrowgrass Capital Partners and Third Point LLC had substantial claims on the old Landsbanki in nominal terms,[43] but the value of those claims was very low at the time.

During the winding-up process, some of the hedge funds were able to pad their bank claims substantially, and many more joined the fray. Among the hedge funds who became major creditors later on were Taconic Capital Advisors, Solus Alternative Asset Managers, Abrams Capital, Och Ziff Capital Management and HBK Capital Management. As demonstrated with hypothetical examples below, the level of success of their investment is up for debate.

Two famous players took longer to pounce on Iceland; Glitnir became their primary target. Quantum Partners, owned by George Soros, one of

---

[40] The numbers are based on Glitnir's, Landsbanki's and Kaupthing's first lists of claims in the end of 2009 and beginning of 2010.

[41] Official Journal of the Grand Duchy of Luxembourg: Recueil des Societes et Associations. (2011, September 3).

[42] Some of the shelf companies cannot be explicitly linked to Baupost but substantial evidence suggests that the fund is indeed their real owner.

[43] LBI (2009). *List of Claims.*

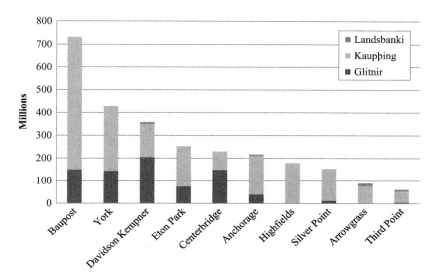

Fig. 6.2 Largest creditors of the Icelandic banks in terms of value according to the first available lists of claims. Amounts in million euros (Source: Glitnir List of Claims December 2009, LBI list of Claims November 2009, Kaupthing List of Claims January 2010)

the richest men on earth,[44] appeared on Glitnir's register in late 2014 with claims of €145 million in nominal value. By the time the composition agreement was signed, he had raised his stake to €840 million.[45] Notable is the fact that Quantum has acted as the sole manager for the Soros family's personal wealth since 2007.[46]

In May 2013, a subsidiary of Paulson & Company also appeared on Glitnir's creditor list. Managing partner John Paulson had become an overnight sensation in the financial sector in 2007, after a successful bet against sub-prime mortgages.[47] His subsidiary claimed €134 million at nominal value. The amount eventually increased to €583 million. Paulson

---

[44] Forbes. (2016). *The World's Billionaires.*

[45] Glitnir Lists of Claims November 2014 to November 2015.

[46] McCrum, Dan (2011, July 26). Soros to close Quantum fund to outsiders. *Financial Times.*

[47] Power, Helen (2008, April 18). John Paulson becomes $3.7bn hedge fund king betting against sub-prime. *Telegraph.*

& Co. sold off all claims a month before the voting on the composition agreement.[48] Additionally, Paulson & Co. had claims on Kaupthing of €97 million at nominal value but would liquidate that position before the composition.

Interestingly, Paulson briefly managed, purposefully or not, to trick the media into believing that he sold his claims a bit earlier by transferring claims between shelf companies,[49] although the press soon caught wind of the transfer.[50] Soros also transferred his position to another fund, called QPTF LLC.

Composition agreements were struck in November 2015. By that time, the largest claim holders were a mix of early and late arrivals. Many of the funds had not bought all their claims at once, and many gradually increased or decreased their stake over time.

At the agreement finish line, Anchorage Capital had the highest share of accepted claims, with total worth €571 million in real terms. The majority were claims on the old Landsbanki, but somewhere between the bank's list of claims in September 2015 and the November vote, the fund had almost tripled its stake, after having gradually increased it from 2009.[51]

The voting lists reflect only *accepted* claims. In the cases of the old Landsbanki and Kaupthing, some funds also held claims through Deutsche Bank Trust Company Americas (DBTA), which came under a different registration category (at least some of them registered as rejected bond claims). DBTA registered nominal claims of €3.2 billion on Kaupthing's voting list, and €2.0 billion on LBI's; because of this, the results in Fig. 6.3 represent the lower end of the funds' position at the time of composition. Other large funds represented were Solus Alternative Asset Management and Davidson Kempner at Glitnir, and Abrams Capital and York Capital at Kaupthing. In some cases, the funds had partially

---

[48] Glitnir Lists of Claims May 2013 to November 2015.

[49] Júlíusson, Þórður Snær (2014, December 4). Sjóður eins ríkasta manns heims búinn að selja allar kröfur á Glitni. (The fund of one of the richest men in the world has sold all its claims on Glitnir). *Kjarninn*.

[50] Júlíusson, Þórður Snær (2015, January 12). Paulson enn tengdur inn í kröfuhafahóp Glitnis. (Paulson still connected to Glitnir's creditor group.) *Kjarninn*.

[51] LBI Lists of Claims December 2009 to September 2015 and LBI Voting List November 2015.

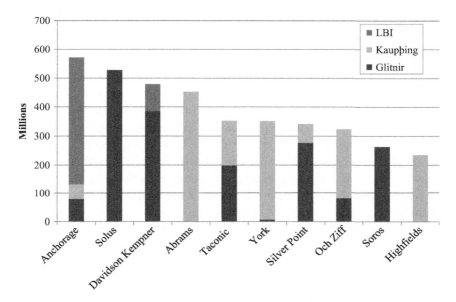

Fig. 6.3 The largest hedge funds at composition agreements in real terms. Amounts in million euros (Sources: Glitnir, Kaupthing and LBI voting lists November 2015)

or completely cleared their position, including Anchorage's case at Glitnir and Davidson Kempner's at Kaupthing.

6.5   What Kind of Resolution?

Under Icelandic law on financial undertakings, there are three options to conclude a winding-up process: (1) returning the estate to the shareholders, (2) reaching a composition agreement with creditors, and (3) liquidation through bankruptcy. Option 1 is only viable if all claims against the estate are paid in full. As the assets of the old banks' estates were nowhere near covering claims on the estates, that left 2 and 3 as options.

Option 2 implies that a specified majority of creditors agree to an offer from the estate to reduce their claims, or more correctly to waive debts. In order to strike such an agreement, it must be approved by a proportion of votes equal to the proportion of claims waived, but with a minimum of 60 % of both the votes weighted by the amounts of the claims and the number of voters. This means that since the estimated recoveries in the estates of Glitnir and Kaupthing were 30 %, some 70 % of general creditors had to accept the composition. The general creditors' recoveries were around 15 % in the Landsbanki winding-up, so 85 % of general creditors were needed to accept Landsbanki's composition.

After acceptance, a court has to ratify the compositions.[52] In a legal sense, a composition implies that the debtor's financial situation has been re-established, and it becomes solvent, usually by write-down of claims.

Upon ratification, the estate becomes a conventional limited-liability company. In most cases, by far, a composition requires creditors to convert a small portion of their claims to equity. Thereby they become shareholders in the company and can take over its management, just as shareholders do in any other limited-liability company. That portion of the claims not paid in cash soon after the ratification, or converted to share capital, is then paid with some type of debenture, after the necessary write-down of claims; in this case, creditors therefore receive cash and transferable securities in place of their claims.

Composition agreements of private enterprises include safeguards against holdouts. When a majority of creditors approve a composition agreement, it is binding for all creditors, whether they accept it or not. This can keep a minority of creditors from refusing to waive the debts that may be needed to maximize recoveries. This does not hold in general for agreements of debt reduction. Even though a majority of creditors can privately agree to reduce their claims to keep the debtor afloat, once the agreement is struck, creditors not parties to the agreement – hold-outs – are not bound by the agreement, and can demand full payment on their claims.

With Option 3, the insolvent estate is settled and its assets or proceeds of asset sales are distributed to creditors. An appointed liquidator handles the affairs of the insolvent estate and ensures equal treatment of creditors and payment of claims. Creditors therefore have no more direct control of

---

[52] See further the Act on Bankruptcy etc., No. 21/1991.

the estate than they do during winding-up proceedings. If this route had been taken for the estates, their ISK holdings would have fallen to the creditors, who subsequently would have disposed of them depending upon their financial status, circumstances and applicable Icelandic law.

When the capital controls were put in place in November 2008, the estates were exempt from them. Thus they could distribute their cash to creditors in domestic or foreign currency and to domestic and foreign creditors alike. The estates used this exemption to distribute payments to priority creditors like foreign deposit holders. In late 2011 and early 2012 the CBI analyzed the legal and economic position of the capital controls and realized that this exemption could jeopardize economic stability, given the extensive ISK holdings of the estates. Based on this analysis, a legislative bill revoking the estates' exemption was prepared and passed as legislation from Althing on March 12, 2012.[53] After the amendment, the estates could not make any payment to foreign creditors or distributions to domestic creditors in foreign currency without special exemption from the CBI

Before the amendment, the winding-up proceedings would have resulted in compositions or even liquidation without any intervention by the authorities. In fact, one small estate, ALMC, the estate of Straumur Investment Bank, had already gone through composition in 2010 without public oversight. After the amendment however, distributions to creditors, which accompanied composition or liquidation, could not commence without the CBI granting an exemption from the capital controls. This gave Icelandic authorities the means to influence the terms of composition by setting forth conditions and thereby apply their touch to winding up the ISK problem (see Chap. 7).

The winding-up boards of the estates always maintained that composition was the proper way to conclude the process. It was more flexible than liquidation, and likelier to maximize value for creditors. As soon as conditions for composition had been reached (such as payments of the bulk of priority claims), the winding-up boards of both Glitnir and

---

[53] See parliamentary document 966, 140th legislative session, Item 608: foreign currency matters (tightened rules on capital transfers). Act No. 17, of 13 March 2012. http://www.althingi.is/altext/stjt/2012.017.html

Kaupthing requested exemptions from the capital controls to conclude composition. Kaupthing's board submitted its exemption request to the Central Bank of Iceland (CBI) on October 24, 2012, but the CBI never replied to this or to subsequent proposals.[54] Glitnir's request was filed on November 28, 2012. It did not receive a formal reply until almost a year later.[55] The reply stated that such an exemption would be granted only "if it did not, in the bank's opinion, upset stability in exchange rate and monetary affairs." However, it also stated that "a detailed analysis of the estates' assets and recoveries, with regard to the impact of their distributions to creditors on Iceland's balance of payments," was not available: "[For] this reason a decision cannot yet be taken on the request for exemption." Glitnir's winding-up board subsequently presented the CBI with several more proposals for how distributions could be made in order to obtain an exemption. Like Kaupthing, it never received a reply.[56]

The option of forcing the estates into liquidation was subject to much public discussion. The appeal of this option may originate from a strict reading of the Act on Bankruptcy that suggests all claims would have to be paid in ISK upon liquidation. If the insolvent estates were liquidated, then they would be forced to deliver their foreign currency assets to the CBI in exchange for ISK at the onshore exchange rate. After such action, the domestic assets of the estates would have grown by the equivalent of €8.8 billion or so, while the estates would have no remaining foreign assets. Foreign creditors would therefore have to sit in the waiting room along with the carry-trade investors, and submit their bids to repurchase foreign currency at a considerably lower auction exchange rate. The intent here appears to have been to prod the estates into providing foreign currency

---

[54] Kaupthing. (2014, May 19). *Announcement from Kaupthing's Winding-up Committee.* http://www.kaupthing.com/home/announcements/all-announcements/2014/05/19/Announcement-from-Kaupthings-Winding-up-Committee

[55] The Central Bank of Iceland. (2013, September 30). *Svar til slitastjórnar Glitnis. (Reply to Glitnir's winding-up board).* http://www.sedlabanki.is/utgefid-efni/frettir-og-tilkynningar/frettasafn/frett/2013/09/30/Svar-til-slitastjornar-Glitnis-hf/

[56] Glitnir. (2013, November 18). *Announcement from the Winding Up Board of Glitnir Hf.* http://www.glitnirbank.com/press-room/548-announcment-from-the-winding-up-board-18-nov2013.html

for the state and positively impact the balance of payments. This was referred to as the *liquidation route* in general discussion.[57]

The center-right coalition that took over following the parliamentary elections in April 2013 put liberalization of capital controls high on the agenda. A Ministerial Committee on Economic Affairs, led by Prime Minister Gunnlaugsson, was responsible for policy on the subject. The Minister of Finance, Bjarni Benediktsson, headed a Steering Committee on Liberalization, which reported to the Ministerial Committee.[58] On November 27, 2013, Prime Minister Gunnlaugsson appointed a group of six advisors to the Ministerial Committee, which was to examine options in the removal of controls and conclusion of winding-up.[59] Some members of the group had been prominent in InDefence's battle against assuming the Icesave debt. Benediktsson's senior advisor on the capital controls, Benedikt Gíslason, worked with the group. The group delivered its proposals in March 2014, which laid out several options, but they were never made public. Part of the group subsequently held meetings on their own initiative with the authorities, parliamentary committees, and stakeholders in April; at these meetings, the liquidation route was presented.[60]

On July 9, 2014, the Ministry of Finance announced that it had formed a task force on the liberalization of capital controls, consisting of four advisors that reported to the Steering Committee.[61] It was also

---

[57] It appears that a Progressive Party MP, Frosti Sigurjónsson, first set forth this opinion in print in an article in *Morgunblaðið* on 26 July 2012.

Sigurjónsson, Frosti. (2012, July 26). Losun hafta: Þrotabú bankanna greiði alfarið í ISK (Removal of Controls: The banks' estates make payments exclusive in ISK). *Morgunblaðið*. http://www.mbl.is/vidskipti/pistlar/frostisig/1250825/

See also the article by Supreme Court attorney Reimar Pétursson in *Morgunblaðið* on 5 October 2013: Pétursson, Reimar. (2013, October 5). Talsýn um nauðasamning (An Illusion Regarding Composition). *Morgunblaðið*.

[58] Other members of the Steering Committee were the Governor of the CBI and officials from the Prime Minister's Office and Ministry of Finance.

[59] See the Prime Minister's reply to a question in parliament from opposition MP Össur Skarphéðinsson, Parliamentary Document 934, Item 385. http://www.althingi.is/altext/143/s/0934.html. The six advisors were investor Sigurbjörn Þorkelsson, engineer and economist Jón Helgi Egilsson, engineer Jón Birgir Jónsson, attorney Eiríkur Svavarsson, economics professor Ragnar Árnason and Supreme Court attorney Reimar Pétursson

[60] See, for instance, the discussion in *Kjarninn* on 10 April 2014, p. 15.

[61] The four were Benedikt Gíslason, senior advisor to the minister of finance on capital controls, Supreme Court attorney Eiríkur Svavarsson, Freyr Hermannsson, head of the Central Bank's treasury

announced that the government had contracted with the legal office Cleary Gottlieb Steen & Hamilton, LLP, Anne Krueger, former first deputy managing director of International Monetary Fund (IMF) and World Bank chief economist, and the consultancy firm White Oak Advisory, LLP, as external advisors working with the task force and the Steering Committee. Lee Buchheit, who had become a household name in Iceland after his involvement in the Icesave dispute, was the main advisor from Cleary Gottlieb. A news item in *Morgunblaðið*, which appeared that same day, stated that the government had "taken a decision on engaging four experts to form a special executive committee on removal of capital controls," which furthermore was intended ("according to *Morgunblaðið's* sources") to find an application for ideas of the previous committee. The work of the task force was mostly confidential, but the public discussion it generated suggested that the liquidation route was definitely being considered. Very little official information was available, however, at the time. It would later emerge that the task force gave no less credence to possible taxation of the estates.

The debate surrounding the liquidation route was lively in both financial markets and politics; both authors of this book observed and participated in the debate. But few details leaked through to the public. The principal points of the discussion are therefore presented as the authors witnessed them.

Proponents of liquidation maintained that it complied with Icelandic legislation, and the government therefore had no need to fear becoming liable for an agreement with creditors.[62] This was the route, some maintained, which would deliver the best results for the nation, in part by increasing foreign currency reserves many times over. With such reserves in hand, all of the country's transfer problems – arising from the overhang and the insolvent estates, and even the accumulated foreign investment needs of domestic parties – could be resolved at once.

The counter-arguments were particularly concerned with legal uncertainty. There were reasonable doubts as to whether Icelandic courts shared

---

section, and Glenn Kim, who led the team. See: Ministry of Finance. (2014, July 9). Agreement with Advisors to Work on Removal of Capital Controls. https://www.ministryoffinance.is/news/2014

[62] See for instance the article by Supreme Court attorney Reimar Pétursson: Pétursson, Reimar. (2013, October 5). Talsýn um nauðasamning (An Illusion Regarding Composition). *Morgunblaðið*.

the interpretation of the insolvency legislation advocated by attorneys who favored the liquidation route. If in fact the courts disagreed, the estates would have to convert all their assets to ISK before making distributions. Second, there were questions as to whether this methodology would meet international acceptance. It was argued that it could possibly be viewed as an appropriation of private property. The insolvent estates would be forced to convert their assets – which still were in liquid, globally traded currencies in foreign bank accounts – to an illiquid micro-currency which was, on top of that, locked in by capital controls. And as if that were not enough, the currency conversion would be asymmetrical: the conversion from foreign currencies to ISK would be made at the official, controls-steered rate, while the reconversion would be made at a considerably lower auction or offshore rate. As such, it was argued, this represented an obvious appropriation of creditors' assets.

From an economist's perspective, the liquidation route was interesting because the country's money supply would almost double when some €8.6 billion (ISK 1,300 billion) were delivered to the three estates in return for their foreign currency assets. This would therefore amount to printing money on a scale hitherto unknown. These new ISK assets would then most likely be locked into interest-free accounts with the CBI, or prevented by some other maneuver from infecting the economy with the resulting over-expansion and inflation. It would be very difficult to wring this amount of offshore ISK out of the financial system once more, without very strong impingements on foreign investors' property rights.

As enlightening as these debates were, they came to rest after the Supreme Court's judgment on November 10, 2014, in the case *Kaupthing hf. v Aresbank SA*. The Court's interpretation clearly stated that although all claims of insolvent Icelandic estates should be calculated in ISK, the country's legal tender, there was no obligation to make payment of these same claims in ISK. Instead, disbursements had to be made in the manner which best served the creditors' interests, whether payment was made in ISK, in foreign currencies or in kind.[63]

---

[63] The said judgement states verbatim: "Should the insolvent estate, however, upon the conclusion of liquidation still own funds in foreign currency, the provisions of Act No. 21/1991 do not prevent, although there is no obligation to do so either, an administrator from making distributions to

Changes were made to the task force in January 2015, when representatives from the CBI were added.[64] The task force consulted with creditors and their advisors between March and June 2015, after which the Icelandic authorities issued proposals for resolution of the estates. The proposals included threefold stability conditions the estates had to meet to become exempt from capital controls and free to form composition agreements with creditors. Otherwise, a 39 % stability tax would be levied on the estates. This condition was meant to put pressure on creditors and coerce their support for the proposals (see Chap. 7 for further discussion). Thus, the exemption became the carrot alternative to the stability tax stick.

Ultimately, hedge funds chose the carrot. They supported the estates' fulfillment of the stability conditions and entrance into composition in 2015. The CBI then granted them exemptions from the capital controls, on the condition that most of the estates' domestic assets would be surrendered to the Icelandic government. For Glitnir and Kaupthing, that amounted to about a 24 % and 16 % haircut, respectively, on the total assets of the estates. The number for Landsbanki was lower, at 10 %.

---

creditors holding claims which were originally in a foreign currency in that currency or another upon conclusion of liquidation. The underlying determination of such a distribution would as usual be made in ISK, and by converting the assets of the insolvent estate in foreign currency to ISK based on the quoted exchange rate at the time and the distribution to the creditors concerned similarly. Furthermore, the administrator of an insolvent estate which holds assets exclusively in domestic currency can act to benefit its creditors in excess of its obligations upon conclusion of liquidation by purchasing foreign currency on the market for a distribution to them, however, which is determined in ISK. Such purchases would be, by their nature, be based on the exchange rate of the currency which applied on the date of payment. Having regard thereto, there is no legal basis for calculating the amount of payments to creditors of an insolvent estate, made in foreign currencies for either of the two above-mentioned reasons, according to the quoted exchange rate on the date of the Ruling on liquidation." http://www.haestirettur.is/domar?nr=9950

[64] The members of the new task force were Glenn V. Kim as chairman, Benedikt Gíslason and Sigurður Hannesson as vice-chairmen, Jón Þ. Sigurgeirsson and Ingibjörg Guðbjartsdóttir from the CBI and Ásgeir H. Reykfjörð. Lilja Alfreðsdóttir worked with the group. Eiríkur Svavarsson left in February 2015. https://www.fjarmalaraduneyti.is/frettir/nr/18876

6.6 Asset Return at Composition

The hedge funds who invested in Icelandic bank debt can be divided into three main categories: (A) those who bought in early and kept their position until the composition agreements in late 2015, (B) those who bought in early but got out of their position by selling their claims, and (C) those who came in later and stayed until the composition agreements.

The funds in category B were in most cases the ones who profited the most on an annual basis, as the price of claims did not change drastically in the later years. For this reason, it can be argued that many of the funds that arrived late made little if any profit from their investment, and perhaps even suffered a loss.

Figure 6.4 shows the estimated evolution of the claims' prices, starting at the CDS auctions and ending with the composition agreement. In the case of Glitnir and Kaupthing, prices did not change significantly from the second half of 2010 until the composition, although both experienced a slight dip in the second half of 2011. With Landsbanki, the winding-up board estimated returns of 14.38 %,[65] which was more than quadruple the price of claims in the second half of 2011, or about the time trading became more active. Glitnir estimated returns of 31.5 % to its creditors at the time of composition, but 30.2 % after discounting future cash flows.[66] Kaupthing returns were estimated at 24.6 % by dividing composition liabilities with accepted claims.[67]

Using this data, we can set up the hypothetical annual return of the three types of funds mentioned above. The results can be seen in Table 6.4. Hypothetical Fund A acquired claims at the CDS auction and kept them until the composition agreements; Fund B acquired claims at the CDS auction and kept them until the end of 2012; and Fund C acquired claims in the beginning of 2012 and kept them until the composition agreements.

It is highly unlikely that every fund appearing on the banks' first lists of claims participated in the CDS auctions in November 2008. The actual

---

[65] LBI. (2015, November). *Composition Agreement.*
[66] Glitnir. (2015, November). *Composition Agreement.*
[67] Kaupthing. (2016). *Financial Statements for the year ended 31 December 2015.*

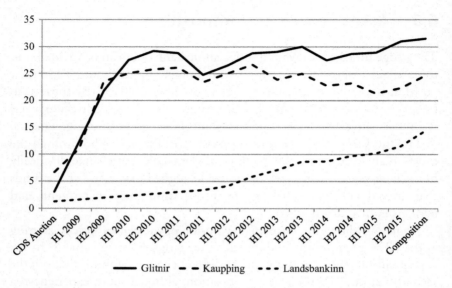

Fig. 6.4 Prices of Glitnir, Kaupthing and Landsbanki claims in cents on the dollar (Source: Moelis & Company, Birwood, and Keldan.is)

time of purchase for their liabilities is therefore open for speculation. Investment bank Moelis & Company performed a detailed analysis of trading activity in Glitnir claims, at the request of the bank's winding-up board.[68] According to this analysis, 64 % of claims by value at the time were held by creditors who had for the most part acquired them sometime before the publication, with an average acquisition price of 28 cents to the euro. The price on Glitnir's claims had remained around this level for the four years prior to publication. Creditors who had acquired claims up to a year after default represented just 1 % of the total creditors, and they held onto 7 % of Glitnir's claims by value. The estimated average acquisition price in the period before claim deadline was 14 cents on the euro, but prices for Glitnir and Kaupthing liabilities had risen steadily in the year following the CDS auction (see Fig. 6.4).

Funds A and B in the hypothetical example therefore presume a best-case scenario regarding the time of purchase. As the table shows, funds

---

[68] Glitnir. (2013, November 16). *Analysis of trading activity in Glitnir hf. claims.*

Table 6.4 Annual return (IRR) on claims purchased on the banks under three different hypothetical scenarios

	Glitnir (%)	Kaupthing (%)	Landsbanki (%)	All banks (%)
Fund A	40	21	42	31
Fund B	76	42	47	54
Fund C	4.4	−0.4	37	6.1

purchasing claims in early 2012 got meager returns in the case of Glitnir, and a negative return in that of Kaupthing. This result would not be very different if claims had been purchased at any time after the end of the registration period. Only in Landsbankinn's case would it have been profitable to purchase the claims later in the process.

Funds that acquired claims at the CDS auctions, or shortly thereafter, will remember their bets on Iceland fondly. Massive profits were possible for those that chose to exit their position early enough. Others spent up to three more years stuck behind capital controls, while prices stayed the same, and suffered substantial opportunity costs.

Baupost and Davidson Kempner, have a different story to tell, despite the fact that they were both among the larger creditors from the start. Their story demonstrates the thin line between success and disappointment. Table 6.5 shows a comparison of the annual return of the funds (IRR) and the net present value (NPV) of their investments, in million euros and assuming a 15 % discount rate. These numbers are only an approximation, since the exact timing of cash flows could not be determined, but they serve as a reasonable estimate of the returns these funds managed to obtain.

What accounts for such major differences in returns? Baupost is believed to have acquired its claims in late 2008, at the CDS auction or shortly thereafter, when prices were still very low.[69] Davidson Kempner is believed to have acquired its claims in 2009,[70] which is supported by the fact that the shelf company holding most of the claims, Burlington Loan

---

[69] Willmer, Sabrina (2015, September 25). Former Baupost Managing Director Fidalgo Said to Plan Hedge Fund. *Bloomberg.*

[70] Burton, Katherine, Kelly Bit and Omar R. Valdimarsson (2013, November 14). Paulson to Taconic Frozen in Iceland Bet Five Years After. *Bloomberg.*

Table 6.5 Comparison of the returns of Baupost and Davidson Kempner in terms of internal rate of return (IRR) and net present value (NPV) in million euros

	IRR (%)	NPV
Baupost	36.4	€197 million
Davidson Kempner	13.5	−€19 million

Management, was incorporated on April 24, 2009.[71] So if the fund bought the claims after that time, it had to pay a substantially higher price. To give an example, according to the analysis of Moelis & Company, Glitnir claims were up from 3 to 14.3 cents on the dollar in April 2009.

Baupost also vacated its position earlier than Davidson Kempner, which only got rid of its Kaupthing claims before the composition agreements. This shows that even the funds that became creditors at the beginning were not necessarily hugely successful. It was very important to buy the claims early, but the three extra years of capital controls that followed the first attempt at a composition agreement had a very negative effect on annual returns and net present value.

6.7 Sharing the Profits with the Public

Hedge funds were relatively quick to take control of the estates of Glitnir and Kaupthing: they managed to stake positions about three to six months after the crisis. By spring of 2009, they created a forum to negotiate the purchase of the new banks from the government. When the first claim registries appeared in November 2009–January 2010, approximately 23.5 % of claims to Glitnir were owned by the major hedge funds; the figure was 30 % for claims on Kaupthing. The number for Landsbanki was much lower – just 11 % – because it was not anticipated that bank assets would cover priority claims (i.e. the Icesave deposits). Thus, the return to general creditors would be zero. The hedge funds' total positions would continue to grow in following years, as German banks – like small savings funds or Landesbanks – sold their

---

[71] DueDil. (n.d.) BURLINGTON LOAN MANAGEMENT LIMITED. Retrieved on May 1 from https://www.duedil.com/company/IE470093/burlington-loan-management-limited

claims one by one. However, as reported above, there was active trading among the funds themselves, as some bought and some sold through the winding up period. At the time of composition, hedge funds owned approximately 70 % of claims to Glitnir and 50 % of Kaupthing's. For Landsbanki the figure had risen to 80 %, since the Dutch government had by then sold the remainder of the Icesave claim.

There had been substantial hedge fund activity in Iceland before the collapse, mostly in the form of packs shorting the currency, the stock market, and the banks. The main pack was an informal club of about 50 macro hedge funds organized through Drobny Global Advisors, a research firm based in Manhattan Beach, California. One Drobnite, Hugh Hendry, the manager of Eclectica Asset Management, told the British Times in the summer of 2006 that he wanted to be "known as the man who bankrupted Iceland." He went so far as to compare himself to his hero, George Soros, whose bets helped to force the pound out of the EMS-fixed exchange rate mechanism in the 1990s. In the same interview Hendry claimed that he was "a Joan of Arc–type manager; I hear voices in my head."[72] Whether or not the voices advocated the shorting of Iceland is unclear. But the Drobny funds held their biannual 2006 meeting in Iceland on October 12 and 13, 2006. They invited CBI's chief economist to the party, and granted him his own Drobny Award "for best defense of currency," complete with a mock ceremony.

Various other credit funds had shorted the banks as well. In January 2008 – at the trendy 101 Hotel – another hedge fund manager brought in by Bear Stearns boasted that Iceland would be the "place for the second coming of Christ, a new financial Armageddon".[73] In March 2008, Prime Minister Geir Haarde threatened direct intervention in the currency and stock markets. "We would like to see these people off our backs and we are considering all options available," he said in an interview. He threatened to set a bear trap for the hedge funds – referring to the successful direct

---

[72] Hosking, Patrick. (2006, July 8). 'How do I pick my stocks? I hear voices'. *The Times*. http://www.thetimes.co.uk/tto/business/columnists/article2621796.ece
[73] See pages 113–114 in. Jónsson, Ásgeir. (2009). *Why Iceland?: How One of the World's Smallest Countries Became the Meltdown's Biggest Casualty*. McGraw Hill Professional.

intervention undertaken by Hong Kong authorities in the Asian crisis of 1998, during which speculators had also attempted systematic destabilization through shorting currency and stock market.[74]

But the hedge funds pack that took control of the estates went long on Iceland, not short. They also kept egos in check and followed a completely different media strategy. The quintessential example of this modest demeanor was "Mister Iceland," Britain's Jeremy Clement Lowe, Davidson Kempner's Burlington Loan Management manager. He won his nickname because of his influence and presence in the post-crisis years, yet curiously, Icelandic media could find no photos or any personal information about him at all. A number of journalists made repeated efforts to interview Lowe, but were unsuccessful – although at last they were able to get hold of a photo of him, taken at a closed meeting in London in early 2015. He would become a legend of sort, surrounded in mystery and described by the media as a "shadow manager" who preferred to lay low at creditors' meetings, but who could be tough when he needed to be.[75]

The old banks' original creditors received a great deal of sympathy from Iceland following their abhorrent losses in the banking collapse. There were also abundant feelings of shame. It took time for the media and public to realize that hedge funds were gradually taking the place of the banks. And it should come as no surprise that when the shadowy hedge funds came into light as the new bank owners, they were greeted with skepticism. Margeir Pétursson, the chairman of the small MP Bank, wrote a piece in the leading newspaper *Fréttablaðið* in December 2009 claiming that the owners of the new banks were "'vulture funds looking for a quick profit."[76] Guðmundur Franklín Jónsson, a former stockbroker at Burnham Securities, New York, and founder of a small political party called the Right Wing Green Movement, claimed that these funds had been given 'hunting permits' on Icelandic households and companies by

[74] Mortished, Carl. (2008, April 3). Iceland puts the freeze on krona speculators as economy boils over. *The Times*. http://www.thetimes.co.uk/tto/business/economics/article2147241.ece

[75] Ægisson, Hörður (2013, December 12). "Herra Ísland" ræður ferðinni. ("Mister Iceland" calls the shots.) *Morgunblaðið*.

[76] Pétursson, Margeir (2009, December 21). Einn heilbrigður banki á Íslandi. (One sound bank in Iceland). *Fréttablaðið*.

the reigning authorities.[77] The funds also earned the vulture label in the Icelandic parliament, this time courtesy of the Progressive Party's MP, Eygló Harðardóttir.[78]

However, because of the high-profile Icesave dispute, the funds received very little media attention in the first few post-collapse years. The "super salaries" of the winding-up boards engendered more comment than any hedge fund. It would not be until the funds were preparing to leave the country with their vast assets that hostilities fully emerged.[79] Not until the winding-up boards requested exemptions from capital controls to proceed with creditor payouts, in mid-2012, did the national mood shift. Then, the next "Sir Philip" vulture moment arrived. The banks' estates were subsequently locked in by capital controls; their owners became subject to negative press coverage while their reputations became political punching bags.

The hedge funds punched back in an attempt to influence Iceland's decision-making process. They deployed a legion of foreign and domestic advisors. Amongst the most influential was American lawyer Barry Russell, from the Bingham McCutchen law firm (and later Akin Gump), who was the chief legal advisor for the majority of creditors of all three estates. The Icelandic law firm Logos was Akin Gump's local partner.[80] Creditors had their advisors on the banks' Informal Creditor Committees (ICCs), which had no official power but maintained powerful influence over the proceedings. The creditors also hired a number of Icelandic public relations officers to get their points across, as well as numerous Icelandic legal advisors. That led to some paranoia among the Icelandic leaders who at one point worried that their mobile phones might be tapped by the hedge funds or their representatives.[81] (The consultations between the

[77] Jónsson, Guðmundur Franklín (2011, May 30). Í þumalskrúfu vogunarsjóða. (In hedge funds' thumbscrew). *Morgunblaðið*.
[78] Hermannsson, Guðmundur Sv. and Pálmason, Rúnar (2011, November 16). Umdeildir eigendur að bönkunum. (Controversial bank owners.) *Morgunblaðið*.
[79] Þórðarson, Þorbjörn (2010, August). *Vísir.is*.
[80] Ægisson, Hörður (2013, December 13). Hagsmunaverðir og ráðgjafar kröfuhafa. (Creditors' lobbyists and advisors). *Morgunblaðið*.
[81] Ægisson, Hörður (2015, February 20). Óttast símhleranir erlendra kröfuhafa. (Fear wiretapping by foreign creditors.) *DV*.

government and the hedge funds – and the results of them – are discussed in detail in Chap. 7.)

The returns of the funds depended greatly on the timing of their entry and exit into the trade. Some made a very good profit – others would not do much more beyond recovering their capital. The hedge funds proved willing to meet the stability conditions set by the authorities to facilitate a quick distribution of the foreign assets. They had bought their claims at discounts, and ultimately were willing to share some of their profit with the Icelanders to reach a settlement. It is doubtful that the original claimants, the ones that took the loss from the collapse of the three banks in October 2008, would have been so acquiescent.

7

The Faustian Bargain of Capital Controls

7.1 Would You Like to Own a Stake in Deutsche Bank AG?

Monday, January 3, 1994, marked a turning point in Iceland's economic history. This was the first business day on which the nation conducted affairs under the auspices of the European Economic Area (EEA) Agreement.

EEA membership, for Iceland, effectively provided backdoor access to the greater European Union. The flow of goods, labor, capital, and services among member countries was unimpeded; in turn, members worked EU directives and regulations into their legal frameworks. EEA gave Iceland access to the common European market without subjecting the nation to conditions of full EU membership.

This first Monday of 1994 also marked the first day, after 62 years, on which foreign exchange transactions were permitted without any restrictions. By joining EEA, Iceland had opened up its capital account. So ended a long period of economic isolation, which had begun in 1931 in

© The Author(s) 2016

Á. Jónsson, H. Sigurgeirsson, *The Icelandic Financial Crisis*,
DOI 10.1057/978-1-137-39455-2_7

response to the collapse of Íslandsbanki, a foreign-owned bank, a year before.[1]

Despite its significance, the EEA membership passed with little comment in Iceland, or at least with no public celebration. The next day's newspapers ignored the event. The one exception was a headline in one of the smaller papers, which referred to the free movement of capital within the context of the EEA agreement.[2] The only harbinger of new times was an advertisement from the Swedish fund, Skandia Investments. Gracing page 5 of Iceland's most circulated daily (*Morgunblaðið*), the ad asked Icelanders, "Would you like to own a stake in Deutsche Bank AG?"

This quiet end to the 60-year old controls was the product of external pressures. After such a long regime, opposition to the capital controls had evaporated inside Iceland; by 1994, the public was not lobbying for their removal. It took demands from the European Union (EU) for the controls to be lifted, demands that ran concurrent with Iceland's membership in the common European market.

The opened capital account was not the only change on that fateful Monday, and may not have been the most significant. The free flow of service also applied to financial services, which provided the nation's banks with a 'European passport', as citizens of the common market. Now, they could move throughout the EU and acquire subsidiaries and branches. The subsidiaries remained under the host country's supervision, but Icelandic authorities supervised the branches and the consolidated company in accordance with the EEA's Home Country Control Principle. Iceland also bore responsibility for most of its banks' operations: deposit guarantees for the banks' branches, lending regulations, provision of lender of last resort facilities, re-capitalization, and so forth.

In other words, Icelandic banks won European freedom, but they operated without a European safety net. Of course, the long-tested principle of cross-border banking continued to hold: international banks are only international when alive – when they get in trouble or die, they

---

[1] See chapter 2 of: Ásgeir Jónsson. (2009). *Why Iceland?: How One of the World's Smallest Countries Became the Meltdown's Biggest Casualty*. McGraw Hill Professional.

[2] Björgvinsson, Sigurður Tómas. (1994, January 4). Endurmat á framtíð sem fortíð. (A reassessment of the future and the past). *Alþýðublaðið*.

become a domestic concern. The full import of that principle was not revealed to the Icelanders until the first week of October 2008.

Moreover, incorporating EU directives – which the Icelanders did diligently – effectively led to financial deregulation, which began without much open discussion or risk assessment. Until 1994, capital controls had created a tightly regulated financial market. The main banks were state-owned, with limited separation from the political arena. Now, all of a sudden, the financial market was completely open. Bankers could now walk freely into the financial centers of Europe to conduct business through any number of channels.

It took some time for the industry to discover the breadth of opportunities. The first Icelandic office on the continent did not open until 1998, when Kaupthing established an outpost in Luxembourg, mainly to serve the growing Icelandic diaspora in Europe. Meanwhile, Europeans had found Iceland. The first were German bankers who loaned directly to the Icelandic banks; in turn, the banks would intermediate the funds to their clients as currency-linked loans paying a fixed spread on LIBOR. Icelandic corporations jumped at this opportunity, since ISK was subject to very high domestic rates at that time.

Corporate debt, measured as a ratio of Iceland's gross domestic product (GDP), doubled between 1998 and 2003, and the net foreign debt of the banks went from 33 % of GDP to roughly 55 %.[3] The new debt was to a large extent currency-linked. The banks were still reluctant to lend in foreign currency to households, with only about 4 % of household debt being denominated in foreign currency in 2003, even while the figure for corporations pushed 60 %. An International Monetary Fund (IMF) study, published in 2005 but using 2003 numbers, also displayed that the median Icelandic corporation had attained the debt-to-equity ratio of 150–200 %; by contrast, a comparable company in Scandinavia maintained a leverage ratio of about 50 %. The study maintained that "while the banking sector is fairly well developed in Iceland, the stock market is not," and "firms trying to raise funds by issuing equity may face more difficulties than firms issuing debt."[4]

---

[3] See data on the CBI website: http://www.cb.is/statistics/statistics/2016/06/23/Miscellaneous-credit-undertakings/?stdID=12

[4] International Monetary Fund. (2005, October). *Iceland: Selected Issues.* (IMF Country Report No. 05/366).

This difference in leverage bore witness to the hard lessons learned by the Scandinavian countries, but not the Icelanders. The other Nordic countries had opened up their capital accounts and liberalized about a decade earlier in the early eighties. This created a real estate boom and a subsequent bust in the early 1990s. This led to a rapid deleveraging in the late 1990s.

By contrast, the problems in the Icelandic financial sector that coincided with the Scandinavian crisis were traced directly to the collapse in the fishing industry. To Scandinavians, the crisis was rooted in speculation; Icelanders saw it as the result of outmoded, inefficient, and corrupt allocation of capital from the state banks. When the Icelanders opened up their capital account in 1994, the sea had calmed and they saw only opportunities on the horizon.

Being a nation of fishermen and seafarers, Icelanders usually refer to their economy as the 'national schooner'. The name reflects the fatalism inherent in their national character. On a schooner, you never know exactly where the winds and waves will carry you – or when a storm will break. It is quite clear the Icelandic national schooner encountered strong tailwinds in the capital markets after entering the EEA, which enabled a rapid open-sea voyage that would last 14 years, until the shipwreck in the autumn of 2008. It appears that until the ship broke up on the rocks, the Icelandic people were mostly unaware of the risks accompanying free capital movements, not to mention the risks accompanying attempts to build up an international financial center.

As can be seen from Fig. 7.1, foreign capital started to flow into the country directly after the financial liberalization. It reached commanding heights after the Icelandic republic was awarded an Aaa rating from Moody's in 2002. The capital flows came to a complete stop in 2008, and the resulting financial crisis prompted the Icelandic government to seek assistance from the IMF and the Scandinavian countries (see Chap. 3).

In a small, open economy, a banking crisis and a currency crisis are twins.[5] Funds withdrawn from the banking system usually try to escape the country through the currency market – leading to a sharp devaluation. One way to stop the twins is to raise interest rates and cut fiscal spending

---

[5] Kaminsky, Graciela L. and Carmen M. Reinhart (1999). The Twin Crises: The Causes of Banking and Balance of Payments Problems. *American Economic Review*, 89(3), 473–500.

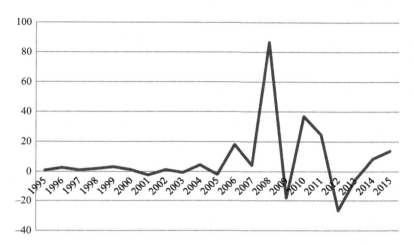

Fig. 7.1 Iceland's Capital Account balance 1990–2015, annual figures as % of GDP (Source: Central Bank of Iceland)

in an attempt to stabilize the balance of payment. This was indeed what the Scandinavians did in the 1990s. In Sweden, interbank rates went up to 35 % and the Swedish Riksbank raised the repo rate up to 500 % for a few days in September 1992, to punish speculators trying to take down the Swedish krona.[6]

The Asian crisis of 1998 followed a similar pattern, although the causality was probably different. The Asian 'tigers' in question were running very large currency deficits financed by short-term borrowing; thus what began as a balance of payments problem soon became a banking problem.[7] In any case, when the 'tigers' were forced to seek help from the IMF, the fund insisted on the same policies followed in Scandinavia – interest rate hikes and cuts in public spending. This policy mix was effective, in the sense that the exchange rate stabilized and recovery was quick, although very painful. Interest rate hikes and fiscal austerity were

---

[6] Redburn, Tom. (1992, September 17). But Don't Rush Out to Buy Kronor: Sweden's 500 % Gamble. *The New York Times*. http://www.nytimes.com/1992/09/17/news/17iht-perc.html

[7] Heikensten, Lars. (1998, July 15). Financial Crisis – Experiences from Sweden. *Seminar organized by the Swedish Embassy in Korea*. http://www.riksbank.se/sv/Press-och-publicerat/Tal/1998/Financial-Crisis----Experiences-from-Sweden/

bound to lead to an even sharper output contraction, rising unemployment and political unrest. One casualty, Malaysia, withdrew its application to the Fund and implemented capital controls instead (see Sect. 7.3).

The Fund also tried to follow through with structural reforms: the abolition of monopolies, the break-up of conglomerates, the sale of state assets, eradication of corruption, and other free market reform measures. Many of the countries objected strenuously. They felt the IMF was infringing on their sovereign rights to such an extent that it was attempting an effective re-colonization. But the fund took harsh criticism from outside observers as well, most notably Nobel laureate Joseph E. Stiglitz, in his book *Globalization and Its Discontents* (2002). Among other things, he characterized the IMF staff as "third-rank economists from first-rate universities" attempting to preach market fundamentalism – or the so-called Washington consensus – all over the world. Thomas C. Dawson, Director of External Relations at the IMF, counted 340 criticisms of the IMF in Stiglitz's book, which worked out to more than one alleged IMF mistake per page.[8]

For a nation accepting so much foreign capital and being such an active partner in the carry trade, as Iceland was, capital flow reversal should have been expected. In hindsight, it was obvious that the national schooner was heading for the rock. However, for almost 14 years, the flow continued almost unabated. The 2000 bursting of the dot-com bubble proved to be a small, short-lived hiccup. The same applied to the Geyser Crisis of 2006 (see Chap. 2).

When Iceland's reversal came, it was part of an international financial crisis. Scandinavia of the 1990s was fortunate to suffer its crisis in isolation. Furthermore, its banks had not held EU passports. They were therefore relatively small and domestic in scope, and it was well within the capacity of their respective governments to bail them out.[9]

In Iceland, the capital flow reversal was so violent that the currency market was just knocked unconscious after the US Fed froze out the CBI

---

[8] Dawson, Thomas C. (2002, June 13). *Stiglitz, the IMF and Globalization*. A speech to the MIT Club of Washington. https://www.imf.org/external/np/speeches/2002/061302.htm

[9] Honkaphohja, Seppo. (2009). The 1990's financial crises in Nordic countries. *Bank of Finland Research Discussion Papers*. 5. http://www.riksbank.se/Upload/Dokument_riksbank/Kat_foa/2009/6_8nov/Honkapohja.pdf

on September 26, 2008. Trading halted in the interbank market. On October 10, 2008, the Central Bank adopted rules on 'temporary modification' of foreign currency outflows, which basically meant that the failed banks should rank their trades according economic importance, and ration out currency to fulfill necessary transactions, such as the import of food, medicine, factor input and the like. There was to be a refrain on all other currency trades.[10] Though drastic, this was seen as a temporary measure, necessary only until Iceland established a stand-by agreement with the IMF. However, while the official currency (interbank) market was inactive, there was still fierce trading going through the Reuters trading system. Here, smaller financial institutions (that were yet to fail) worked as intermediaries between desperate carry traders wanting to exit Iceland, and a diverse group of domestic players with foreign assets who were ready to jump at a bargain. In these trades, as recorded on the Reuters trading system, the ISK was trading at 300 against the euro, or only about 25 % of its pre-crisis value (around 88–90 ISK to the euro).

As is discussed in Chap. 3, British and Dutch authorities blocked Iceland's application for assistance with the IMF at the board level. Their goal was a government guarantee of payment on the balance of Icesave online accounts. A letter of intent was signed on November 16, and three days later the application was approved. This yielded a $4.85 billion war chest in foreign currency reserves, and a policy rate raise to about 18 %. Then, it was widely expected, the currency market would be opened with the conventional shock therapy. This, however, did not come to pass.

Around 8 p.m. on November 27, 2008, one of the authors (in the capacity as chief economist of New Kaupthing) received a phone call from the parliament. He was asked to come 'right away' to testify for the committee of economic and trade affairs. Representatives of the Central Bank of Iceland (CBI) and IMF also arrived when the meeting convened later that evening. They had come to present legislation re-introducing capital controls.

---

[10] Central Bank of Iceland. (2008, November 28). *New foreign exchange regulation*. (Press release No. 44/2008). http://www.cb.is/publications-news-and-speeches/news-and-speeches/news/2008/11/28/New-foreign-exchange-regulation-/

A very harsh debate assumed. Representatives from the labor unions and the employer's federation voiced loud opposition to the controls. They argued that once in place, the controls would not be removed. The representatives from the CBI and the IMF asserted that the proposed measures were merely temporary, and would be lifted in two years. Until then, however, it was necessary to impose stringent restrictions, so that all actions taken thereafter would be in the direction of liberalization.[11] Without these measures against free trade, there was the risk that the ISK would drop to extremely low levels and stay there indefinitely, which would reduce household purchasing power to the level of subsistence for many families. Moreover, it would be impossible to restore the banks with the capital account open. Objections continued, but CBI and IMF officials just maintained that this was the Fund's will, and it had to be implemented. The proposal was accepted by the parliament just before 5 a.m. on November 28. The capital account was now officially closed.

So arose a contradiction in terms. Iceland was both the first developed country to seek help from the IMF since 1979, and the first developed country to impose capital controls for a similar length of time. The IMF's participation in Iceland's economic program represented a radical change of policy on the fund's part.[12] Not only would the IMF levy its approval; it would actually draft the capital controls regime for the nation's authorities. The IMF's new policy was later to be formally introduced in a report entitled *The Liberalization and Management of Capital Flows: An Institutional View*, which was published November 14, 2012. The report also renamed capital controls – they now were 'Capital Flow Management', which could be applied temporarily in a crisis.

This was not, however, the only way Iceland was treated differently from developing countries and former IMF clients. There was no call for Iceland to adopt sharp austerity measures at the inception of the joint economic plan. Instead, the government would be allowed to maintain

---

[11] See the Letter of Intent from the Icelandic authorities to the IMF, which was published as an attachment to the *IMF Staff Report* in November 2008.

[12] International Monetary Fund. (2012, November 14). *The Liberalization and Management of Capital Flows: An Institutional View*. The following is stated on page 25: "In crisis situations, or when a crisis may be imminent, there could be a temporary role for the introduction of CFMs [Capital Flow Management Measures] on outflows."

large public deficits in the first year – 2009 – allowing fiscal multipliers to counteract the output contraction that was underway. Iceland also was not asked to downsize its Scandinavian-type welfare system. Thus, by use for fiscal policy, the immediate output contraction was mitigated to just 10 % from 2008 to 2010, given the extensive overheating and the accumulative 30 % GDP expansion from 2003 to 2007.

The heterodox approach applied by the IMF in the Icelandic program can probably be attributed to past criticism and the fund's capacity for reflection. It is also very likely that the IMF wanted a role beyond just being a lender of last resort for emerging market economies. It wanted to be a developing world partner in resolving the ongoing financial crisis. To that end, it needed a methodology beyond the free market activism previously employed.

The new strategy was more or less successful. Iceland would graduate from the IMF program in 2011 with flying colors. The prime minister's office declared that the 'successful collaboration' had drawn 'considerable attention'.[13] At that time, the IMF had become part of the troika (with the ECB and EU) committed to solving Europe's debt problem.

Nevertheless, after IMF's departure, the controls were still in place, which strangely enough did not seem to cast any shadow on the success of the plan, at least from IMF's vantage point. In fact, instead of loosening controls, the CBI had gradually tightened them, which reflects the relatively tight situation in the Icelandic currency market (see Chap. 4). Iceland would not keep a single dime of the loans provided by the fund: they were all repaid in full before year-end 2015.

It is said banks only lend to people who do not need the money. Thus, having loans from the fund on reserve might have contributed to Iceland's successful re-entrance into private financial markets in 2011. However, that did come at a price. The loans bore the standard, plain vanilla IMF interest rate which amounted to a 2.75 % premium over interbank rates; assuming the Central Bank drew on half the available funds, $2.5 billion, and got interbank rates on its foreign reserves, the interest premium on the loans

---

[13] Prime Minister's Office. (2011, August 26). *Iceland completes IMF Programme.* https://eng. forsaetisraduneyti.is/news-and-articles/nr/6864

amounted to as much as $0.4 billion in total, a large drain on the treasury during the years of economic contraction.

The Central Bank of Iceland was able to reach a number of macro objectives on the back of the capital controls from 2008 to 2011. It stabilized the ISK and reduced inflation from 18 % to about 4 % between 2009 and 2011. It cut the policy rate from 18 % to about 4.25 % during the same period. And behind controls the new banks were able to work through their huge portfolio of non-performing loans and implement debt relief without the risks of an open capital market.

These successes minted Iceland as the poster boy for capital controls. The nation had used them to help engineer an economic recovery.[14] That success did, of course, come at a cost, as will be discussed in Sect. 7.6.

Beyond their merits as a macroeconomic tool, capital controls had other uses. They could also be applied to prevent the socialization of losses stemming from the transfer problem (introduced in Chap. 5) created by the ISK assets of the estates of the old banks. The controls forced direct contributions from the estates, which amounted to about 10 %, 16 %, and 24 % haircuts on the creditors of Landsbanki, Kaupthing, and Glitnir respectively, as well as other indirect measures. In 2015, the banks were forced to relinquish their control of domestic assets in the estates in order to secure the foreign assets. Thus, a lot of heavy baggage was thrown out of the Icelandic national schooner in this arrangement. Controversy aside, when the IMF recommended controls in 2008, it handed the Icelanders a powerful bargaining tool, which in the end netted them ISK denominated assets worth €4 billion, or 26.8 % of GDP.

---

[14] See, for example: Paul Krugman. (2010, June 30). The Icelandic Post-Crisis Miracle. *New York Times* http://krugman.blogs.nytimes.com/2010/06/30/the-icelandic-post-crisis-miracle/?_r=0

7.2   The Operation of the Controls

The capital controls are obviously in contravention of the EEA rules on the four freedoms, one of which is free movement of capital. However, the EEA Agreement does authorize temporary imposition of capital controls.[15] And Iceland was not alone. Other EEA member states have found it necessary to take similar steps. On March 27, 2013, capital controls were imposed in Cyprus, with the consent of the IMF. These included measures prohibiting Cypriots both from spending more than €5000 per month on their credit cards outside the country, and from withdrawing more than €300 per day from their bank accounts. Cyprus is both an EU member state and a member of the Eurozone; like Iceland in 2008, it had a banking system several sizes too large for the country. (The Cypriot banking system had assets totaling seven times the country's GDP, while Iceland's banking system assets amounted to ten times Iceland's GDP.) As in Iceland, the banks transformed quickly from being too-big-to-fail to being too-big-to-save. A run ensued, and could only be stopped by shutting down the banks' capital outflows. In Iceland, this was achieved by closing off exits via the foreign exchange market. In Cyprus, restrictions were placed on withdrawals and money transfers between the banks themselves.

Countries with capital controls can be placed in one of three roughly defined categories:

(a) Countries where market freedom is limited or non-existent, and/or ownership rights are not respected. In such countries, the capital account is closed to ensure that all other restrictions and directives within the economy hold; otherwise, capital would flow out into a freer environment.

Iceland was in this category during the former capital controls regime, in the period from 1931 to 1994, as the capital controls prevented general capital flight due to a lack of freedom in the capital market, negative real

---

[15] With a judgment on December 14, 2011, the EFTA Court concluded that the capital controls were compatible with the EEA Agreement, as both EU member states and EFTA states could adopt protective measures in the event of balance of payments problems. EFTA Court Case E-3/11.

rates, and so forth. At present, this category is populated by many extremely underdeveloped countries. It also contains a number of countries undergoing rapid economic development – countries that are gradually moving towards freedom and lifting their controls in stages.

(b) Countries where moderate controls are part of macro prudential policy, where various restrictions are placed on flows of hot money into and out of the financial system, so as to create stability. This group includes countries such as Chile, Brazil, Turkey, and South Korea, where attempts are usually made to restrict inflows of capital and appreciation of the domestic currency with measures such as taxation, term requirements for deposits, and so forth. Controls of this type have gained acceptance in recent years, and it is highly likely that Iceland will belong to this group of countries in the future.

(c) Countries that impose temporary restrictions in response to a financial crisis. The objective here is to use controls to gain time to restructure the financial system, chip away at overhangs, and re-establish economic equilibrium before restoring free movement of capital. In such instances, capital controls are not a permanent shelter but an interim measure designed to provide room for maneuvering. Countries in this category include Malaysia (1991–2001), Cyprus (2013–2015), and presumably Iceland (from 2008 onwards).

It has been maintained that Iceland's current capital controls fall into Category C, that is, they are a *temporary* crisis management measure. But how long before this management is no longer 'temporary'? In Cyprus, the controls were lifted in full on April 6, 2015, two years after they were imposed. In Malaysia, capital controls also remained in effect for two years. In Iceland, however, the capital controls were in place for eight years after their establishment and have only be partially lifted.

It is worth noting that the capital controls imposed in 1931 were introduced at the request of Landsbanki, which was then the central bank of Iceland. Then, too, the controls were supposed to be only a temporary crisis response. But for more than 60 years, the right moment to lift them never came.

Initially, the capital controls blocked both capital outflows and inflows. On October 31, 2009, the CBI opened the capital account for new foreign investments, and announced that the abolition of the controls had begun.[16] After every interest rate decision, the CBI governor has announced that the abolition of the controls is just around the corner. But in truth, the CBI has been pre-occupied with stopping leakages and *tightening* the controls, rather than removing them.

Why has this been the case? First, it was difficult to make the controls actually work. They banned activity – buying or selling ISK for foreign currency – that had been pretty standard for a long time and still seemed rather innocent. Now, the law stated FX trading was punishable by up two years in prison. But there was no enforcement mechanism in place, and many export companies were eager to sell their foreign earnings at 30–50 % above the official market rate. One of the authors was – as an employee of New Kaupthing (Arion Bank) – appointed to a special task force to form a policy for the banks to conform to controls, which was indeed daunting work. The banks were swamped with companies and individuals presenting all kinds invoices for imported goods, for which they needed to buy foreign currency at the official rate. There were many invoices for expensive items – diamonds, luxury cars, etc. – and it was impossible to tell if they were legitimate purchases. Teenagers would show up at bank branches with bundles of bank notes, with the intention of depositing them into foreign accounts that allegedly belonged to overseas charities exempted from the controls.

The banks had no desire to play control enforcers by verifying all these invoices. Where would it end? New banks were operating with 30 % less staff than the old banks, and running down invoices was labor-intensive. This was police work. The banks of course reported anything suspicious, and there was plenty that was suspicious in the invoices. But the complaints simply piled up. Later on, the banks established what would be

---

[16] Central Bank of Iceland. (2009, October 31). *First stage of capital account liberalisation*. (Press release No. 33/2009). http://www.cb.is/publications/news/news/2009/10/31/First-stage-of-capital-account-liberalisation-/

described a circle of trust; they gave known, trustworthy clients relatively free rein to conduct their foreign trade without hassle.

Second, there was a lot of grey area around capital control legislations. The law only applied to domestic residents, who were forbidden to buy or sell their ISK holdings for FX. However, non-residents could continue to trade unabated without having to worry about judicial interference. Of course, the London banks continued to trade in ISK despite the fact that this activity was off limits to Icelanders.

During the first month of the controls, it seemed there was more flow through the offshore than onshore markets; as a result the spread between the two rates would narrow down. The offshore rate would go from 250 to 300 ISK per euro to about 200–220. Simultaneously, the onshore rate would depreciate 15–20 %, to about to about 180–190, as can be seen from Fig. 7.2.

In the fall of 2009, the CBI finally took action against potential abuses. It founded a special Capital Control Surveillance Unit on September 18. A lawyer – Ingibjörg Guðbjartsdóttir – assumed command. She had worked for Straumur-Burðarás, an investment bank and the nation's fourth largest, which had survived five months longer than the big three but was nonetheless taken over by the FSA in March 2009. During the five-month gap, Straumur-Burðarás had been active in currency trading, since it was the only large counterparty still available.

Shortly after the Capital Control Surveillance Unit was founded, the CBI filed a complaint to the FSA about four of Guðbjartsdóttir's former colleagues at Straumur-Burðarás's currency trading desk. They had, after the collapse of bank, founded their own company in Sweden, called Aserta, which continued the FX trading. The FSA referred the complaint to the economic crime unit of the state police, Helgi Magnús Gunnarsson.[17]

On January 29, 2010, the FSA and the economic crime unit called a joint press conference, which was also attended by Guðbjartsdóttir on behalf of the CBI. In this meeting, charges were announced against the four Aserta traders. Not only were they accused of illegal currency trading. Their office had been raided and the authorities would issue a freezing order on their accounts in both Iceland and Sweden.

---

[17] Reykjanes District Court verdict no. S-180/2013.

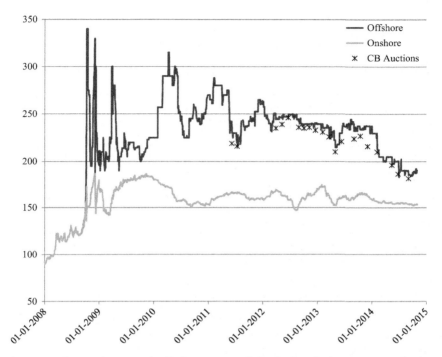

Fig. 7.2 The onshore and off-shore rate of the Icelandic krona towards the euro and rates in currency auctions of the CBI (Source: Reuters and the Central Bank of Iceland)

The meeting was also used to issue a public denunciation against the four, who were condemned for weakening the ISK to the detriment of Icelandic households. They also warned others to realize the consequences of breaching the capital controls, both for themselves personally and the society at large. Promptly after the press conference, the four were arrested and interrogated.[18]

The four traders maintained that they acted in good faith, and with no intent of breaking the law. Furthermore, they insisted that they had asked Guðbjartsdóttir, while she was still a lawyer for Straumur-Burðarás, about the legality of their trading. At that time, they maintained, she had

---

[18] Ægisson, Hörður. (2012, May 24). Hátt reitt til höggs en eftirtekjurnar gætu orðið rýrar. (Serious allegations but the results could be scarce.). *Morgunblaðið*. http://www.mbl.is/greinasafn/grein/1423113/

declared that since their company, Aserta, was a foreign party trading with other foreign parties, it was not in breach of the law.[19]

But after this gaudy public display, there were no further investigations for a year. A lower court in Sweden rejected the freezing order just days after the press conference, and later the Icelandic Supreme Court followed suit. When the four Aserta traders finally had their day in court, they were acquitted of all charges by a ruling in December 2014. As it turned out, in the heat of the crisis in 2008 the CBI had issued a regulation concerning the capital controls in such a haste that the minister of economic affairs had never signed it and thus it had never effectively been passed into law.[20]

Nevertheless, the public condemnation and arrest sent a powerful signal to the Icelandic financial community. The balance shifted from the offshore market to the onshore markets, and the spread between the two would start to widen again.

Authorities next tried to clamp down on the domestic black market. By the capital control legislation, every Icelandic citizen was able to get up to ISK 500,000 (€3300) in foreign currency by presenting an airline ticket at a bank branch. The law also stated that people should return the foreign currency they had not spent when they returned home. There was, of course, a tendency for people travelling abroad to buy the maximum and not return the remainder.

Moreover, the controls also posed a challenge to those involved in underground activities. They could not really take their business through the formal banking system, and they would need to buy an awful lot of plane tickets to get the FX needed for their operations. Thus, the controls raised the price of illegal drugs in Iceland. As a result, the importation of cannabis all but ceased, and locals resorted to growing their own. Then, there were those that saw illegal currency trading using physical bank notes as just a new line of business. The CBI seems to have treated these leakages seriously enough to curtail the limit by roughly a third, to about ISK 350,000 (€2300) in November 2010. This raised the transaction costs of FX trading in the local black market.[21]

---

[19] Reykjanes District Court verdict no. S-180/2013.

[20] Reykjanes District Court verdict no. S-180/2013. (2014, December 18). https://domstolar.is/default.aspx?pageid=347c3bb1-8926-11e5-80c6-005056bc6a40&id=448c87e1-4930-4a90-8dc4-e15d4260ea7e

[21] The Central Bank of Iceland. (2010, November 1). *Rules on Foreign Exchange.* (Press release no. 29/2010). http://www.cb.is/publications/news/news/2010/11/01/Rules-on-Foreign-Exchange/

The next challenge would be the division between capital and current account transactions. The controls only applied to the capital account, and thus current account transactions were permitted. That included not only imports and exports of goods and services, but also payments to factors of productions – such as interest payments and bond coupons, which initially included bond principal and indexation payments as well. This distorted the government bond market. Demand for high-coupon bonds increased as they allowed for higher amounts to be channeled through the onshore currency market.

The biggest bang for the buck was obtained in a short term, index-linked annuity called HFF14; this was a bond series issued by the Housing Financing Fund and set to mature in 2014. An investor that bought the bond in 2010 would annually receive a quarter of its investment in coupon payments, which could be converted to hard currency on the onshore market. In 2011, offshore ISK holders bought up almost the entire stock of the series; its price skyrocketed and the yield went as low as minus 7 % in early 2012. Never before had bond yields gone negative in the Icelandic bond market, where real rates were usually in the range of 3.5–7 %. At the suggestion of the CBI, the exemption for principal and indexation payments was removed on March 13, 2012.[22]

The CBI would next turn its attention to the export companies. According to the capital controls, all export companies had the duty to return their foreign currency earnings to a local bank. But the law could by circumvented by fiddling with transfer pricing within a multinational company, e.g. having a foreign subsidiary buy fish from Iceland at a suppressed price, and reselling it at market price abroad. On March 27, 2012, the special prosecutor's office raided the offices of the largest fishing company – Samherji – on the basis of a complaint from the CBI that the company had been breaching the capital controls through intra-firm exchange between the home office and foreign subsidiaries.[23] By some 'coincidence', the television stations happened to arrive at Samherji's office just before the

---

[22] Act no. 17/2012, March 13, 2012.
[23] Central Bank of Iceland. (2012, March 27). *Gjaldeyriseftirlit Seðlabanka Íslands framkvæmir húsleitir. (The Central Bank's Capital Control Surveillance Unit conducts raids.)* (Press release no. 13/2012).

police came, so the raid was broadcast live on national TV. However, the investigations of the Special Prosecutor would drag on for 2-3 years without yielding sufficient evidence and was belatedly suspended in September 2015.[24]

Nonetheless, these coercive measures were to a large extent successful in establishing the onshore market as a real trading place. The inherent evil of capital controls, however, manifests itself in these examples of questionable judicial decisions and human rights infringements. They make healthy, free-market activity illegal, and can apply to basic conversions, such as one's salary or home equity into another currency. Actions taken against these allegedly illegal currency trades, however, were not entirely new. They mimicked the extensive post-collapse investigations and legal harassment directed at big players at the old banks (see Chap. 4).

The CBI used its new leverage to clear away the carry trade overhang from the Icelandic financial system. It legalized the offshore trading, in a certain manner, by administrating currency auctions from 2011 to 2015 (see Chap. 5). The bank also provided exemptions that allowed pension funds to transfer sums of money out of the controls in 2015. But, otherwise, no outbound capital transfers from Icelandic residents were allowed, and are still not allowed as of this writing.

7.3   The Capital Controls as a Bargaining Tool

The adoption of capital controls does not necessarily involve blocking capital transactions. Instead, they often just politicize them, since capital transfers are subject either to a politically determined exemption process, or are concluded by the state itself. Inbound capital controls tend to result in political intervention that declares how the capital is utilized within the country. The attendant long-term risk is that investments are evaluated in the political arena rather than on the free market, which generally leads to capital misallocation. This was indeed the case in Iceland with the capital controls in place from 1931 to 1994.

---

[24] Central Bank of Iceland. (2015, September 6). *Til upplýsingar vegna frétta af niðurfellingu máls embættis sérstaks saksóknara gegn Samherja. (Information regarding news of the suspension of the Special Prosecutor's case against Samherji.)*

Outbound capital controls, on the other hand, give bargaining power to the authorities against those stuck behind the controls, and impose conditions on them. Taxation in conjunction with capital controls can also be seen as a way to exert this control. It can either delay or impose haircuts on outbound capital; the most notable example is Malaysia in 1999–2001. The primary objective of exit taxes is to convert the rules and regulations in the foreign exchange market into direct taxation. Exit taxes are therefore merely another form of capital controls.[25]

In general, market-based measures are considered to be a more efficient way for the authorities to achieve their objectives than administrative measures. Using the market as a tool for intervention changes all sorts of costly complications – such as waiting periods, exemptions, and a variety of opaque processes – into taxes that generate benefits for both the state and market participants. The state generates revenues and eliminates the problem of deciding which parties should receive exemptions and which should not. Market agents benefit from the predictability and non-discrimination, and can take decisions immediately instead of waiting and wondering whether requests and applications for exemptions will be approved or not.

As regards the foreign exchange market, the conversion of direct capital controls into exit taxes can greatly facilitate the liberalization process, as the taxes can be reduced incrementally without causing upheaval. Authoritarian methods are by nature *either-or* measures, whose implications are rarely foreseeable. Actually, it is possible to ease capital controls by granting increased numbers of exemptions, relaxing rules, and so forth, but this is often an extremely jagged methodology. On the other hand, converting

---

[25] It is important not to confuse an exit tax with foreign exchange market transaction charges. The latter are usually associated with Nobel laureate James Tobin (1918–2002), and called Tobin taxes. Tobin taxes are intended to prevent short-term arbitrage in the foreign exchange market; i.e., to prevent speculators from making large-scale round-trip trades in the market, thereby creating instability. Such taxes have long been under discussion and have been admired by many observers since Tobin first introduced his idea in 1972, in connection with the end of the Bretton Woods system. But they have never been implemented, as introducing Tobin taxes would probably be impossible unless all of the countries in the world should commit to taxing foreign exchange transactions. For further information, see: Tobin, J. (1978). A proposal for international monetary reform. *Eastern Economic Journal*, 4(3), pp. 153–159.

Eichengreen, B., Tobin, J., & Wyplosz, C. (1995). Two cases for sand in the wheels of international finance. *The Economic Journal*, 105 (Jan.), pp. 162–172.

controls to taxes can mark the beginning of an extremely credible liberalization process, as can be seen in the case of Malaysia. Indeed, the CBI's March 2011 plan for the lifting of controls included levying an exit tax that was to be reduced in steps, similar to the Malaysian exit tax.[26]

Malaysia's controls were initially imposed on September 1, 1998, in tandem with a declaration that they would be in place for only 12 months. The Malaysian authorities' methodology for taxation during liberalization was broadly as follows:[27]

(a) On February 15, 1999, it was announced that liberalization had begun and the controls would be converted to an exit tax. The tax was set at 30 %, and would be imposed on both principal and capital gains on offshore assets.
(b) The exit tax declined with investors' increased willingness to wait. After 12 months, the tax on principal was abolished, and the tax on capital gains fell to 10 %
(c) On February 1, 2001, the exit tax was abolished entirely and movement of capital was unrestricted.

The objective of the Malaysian exit tax was therefore to slow the pace of potential capital outflows concurrent with liberalization, and thus reward investors for their patience. It also prevented new players – short-term speculators – from being dragged into the fray and upsetting the liberalization process by causing a stampede in the foreign exchange market. The tax was therefore intended not really as a revenue source for the treasury but as a means of affecting investors' behavior.

All of this worked out in Malaysia, although there is divided opinion on how important the exit tax itself was in the process. The Malaysian authorities were determined from the outset that the capital controls would not remain in place for long, and they presented liberalization strategies three to four

---

[26] Central Bank of Iceland. (2011, March 25). Áætlun um losun gjaldeyrishafta. (A plan for lifting capital controls.) Report to the minister of economics and business.
[27] This discussion is based on the following sources:

Abdelal, R., & Alfaro, L. (2003). Capital and control: lessons from Malaysia. *Challenge*, 46(4), 36–53. Doraisami, A. (2004). From crisis to recovery: the motivations for and effects of Malaysian capital controls. *Journal of International Development*, 16(2), 241–254.

months after imposing them. The exit tax was only one element of a very broad economic program designed to restore international confidence. Most observers agree, however, that levying the tax, with clear and well-defined rules on the relationship between time and taxation, was of critical importance for the credibility of the strategy as a whole.[28]

There are, however, important differences between Iceland and Malaysia. First, the offshore assets in Malaysia were relatively small in scope. The controls were not imposed until nearly a year after the currency crisis began and the domestic currency, the ringgit, had collapsed. During that period, a large amount of relatively transferable foreign capital had exited the country at a very low exchange rate. When the exit tax was subsequently imposed, offshore ringgit assets held by foreigners amounted to about $7 billion, whereas the country's foreign exchange reserves totaled about $30 billion. Moreover, the exit tax in Malaysia was also imposed to reward patient investors and keep capital in the country during the liberalization process, rather than sterilizing offshore assets or generating revenues for the treasury. The authorities in Malaysia considered it very important that offshore ringgit should be converted to long-term foreign investment.

In contrast, Iceland had huge overhang compared to GDP, low foreign reserves, and it wanted to eliminate the offshore ISK holdings from the once-booming carry trade altogether. Thus, the CBI used the controls to divide the FX market in two. On one side, there was an official, onshore market for transfers within the current account; on the other, an offshore auction market for capital account transfers. With this separation, foreign trade could run its course without an interruption while the CBI cleared out the carry trade positions at a discount in its administered auctions. With almost no other currency reserves – except those obtained as loans from the IMF – the CBI could not serve as a counterparty in the auctions. Instead, it had to allow "patient" inbound capital to buy these carry trade positions at a reduced price (see Chap. 5).

---

[28] Foong, K. K. (2008). Managing capital flows: the case of Malaysia (No. 93). ADB Institute Discussion Papers.

Kawai, M., & Takagi, S. (2003). "Rethinking capital controls: the Malaysian experience". Macroeconomics Working Papers, 473. Kochhar, K. (ed.). (1999). Malaysia, selected issues (No. 98–114). International Monetary Fund.

Initially, it seems the old banks' estates had been exempted from the capital controls because it was not anticipated that they would have extensive ISK assets to pay out. After all, the banks were split into foreign and domestic parts in 2008 (see Chap. 3). However, as the recovery progressed, it was discovered that the estates still held ISK assets to the tune of €5–6 billion, or about 50 % of GDP. In March 2012, the Icelandic parliament withdrew the exemption from the controls; this move locked the estates away from the creditors.[29] The legislation was drafted by the CBI after its legal and economic analysis on the capital controls in late 2011 and early 2012. The amendment prevented foreign currency transfers out of Iceland, and substantially improved the Icelandic authorities' bargaining position towards the hedge funds. Creditors managed to push through a further amendment, opposed by the CBI, which granted them rights to payouts of foreign currency reserves already held by the CBI or by foreign financial institutions at the time of the aforementioned legislation.[30] But winding-up proceedings could not be concluded without CBI permission. Thus a new bargaining game was put into motion.

Now, the old banks' estates had significant holdings of ISK assets. Locking these assets was in itself a threat – but not an overwhelming one for the hedge funds. For the estates of Glitnir and Kaupthing, domestic assets were only 37 % and 27 %, respectively, of the total asset base. The hedge funds probably would have accepted matters if these assets became ISK offshore holdings, or were even invested long-term in the Icelandic economy. The funds themselves tried to find foreign buyers of some of these assets – like their stakes in the new banks – but that would not have solved the balance of payments problem.[31] However, the estates had

---

[29] Act no. 17/2012, March 13, 2012.

[30] Ægisson, Hörður. (2012, October 27). Seðlabankinn studdi ekki breytingar. (The Central Bank did not support changes.) *Morgunblaðið.*

[31] There are three reasons for this. One, a foreign buyer could flip the asset, buy it at a low price and sell quickly for a higher price, hence adding to the balance of payments problem. Second, the new banks were overcapitalized, so a new buyer could have stripped the new bank and paid out extraordinary dividends or used other means to get cash out of the asset, which then could be converted into FX. Third, the ISK exposure could be hedged as capital controls were liberalized. Such a hedge would affect the FX market.

about €9 billion in foreign assets, of which €6 billion was in deposits and liquid assets: this was the main prize hedge funds were eager to seize.

However, by withdrawing the exemption the estates had enjoyed, the CBI was empowered to prevent all payouts to creditors, whether in FX or ISK. That greatly enhanced the bargaining power of the Icelandic authorities. No FX payments would be allowed from the estates unless the creditors came to an agreement on how the deal with the transfer problem caused by the failed estates.

This reality dawned on the winding-up boards of Kaupthing and Glitnir in late 2012, as they prepared to ask for an exemption from capital controls to wrap up their respective composition agreements (see Chap. 6). The sudden shift in the Central Bank's attitude made it clear that the creditors would have to wait for an unspecified period for further payments.[32] In response, the creditors' advisory team created a so-called "ISK working group" in 2013. The objective was to find a mutually feasible solution for bypassing the capital controls, without exerting too much negative influence on Iceland's balance of payments.[33]

The creditors became increasingly frustrated with the lack of communication from the authorities. Led by the advisory firm Talbot Hughes McKillop, and seeking to persuade said authorities, the ISK working group went so far as to publish its own analysis of Iceland's net international investment position and current account.[34] It should come as no surprise that they perceived the Central Bank's outlook as far too pessimistic; they also made this position clear when meeting with the bank's representatives to discuss their results.

Next to no progress was made in the following two years. Authorities waited for the creditors to come up with 'reasonable' solutions that didn't threaten economic stability. The creditors complained that they received no guidelines and found any attempts at dialogue to be futile. Both Prime Minister Sigmundur Davíð Gunnlaugsson and Finance Minister Bjarni

---

[32] Glitnir. (2012, November 9). *Announcement from the Winding Up Board of Glitnir hf.*
Kaupthing. (2012, November 13). *Further update on targeted launch of composition.*

[33] Júlíusson, Þórður Snær (2013, February 23). Kröfuhafar stofna krónuhóp. (Creditors form an ISK group.) *Fréttablaðið.*

[34] Ægisson, Hörður (2013, August 22). Fái ekki arð í 20 ár. (No dividends for 20 years). *Morgunblaðið.*

Benediktsson reiterated on numerous occasions that it was not up to the authorities to negotiate private debt with the creditors.[35] 2013 passed without any solution in sight, while the hedge funds' opportunity cost was growing every day. Additionally, the parliament had passed an amendment to the law of a specific tax on financial institutions, which required the estates to start paying a tax amounting to 0.376 % of accepted claims annually.[36]

The hedge funds and other creditors faced the reality of having to come up with solutions that included giving up a large portion of their Icelandic assets in order to attain access to their foreign assets. In 2014, advisors Barry Russell and Matt Hinds voiced their discontent to Reuters. Russell insisted that there was 'no justification' for the government to drastically cut the value of claims.[37] Hinds bemoaned the lack of feedback to their proposals, which he claimed could be helpful in the efforts of lifting capital controls. He also implied that the government's actions towards creditors could end up excluding Iceland from international financial markets.

There was another pressing issue in the background, which concerned the old Landsbanki. The estate had requested an exemption from capital controls to pay out a large part of its €2 billion in foreign assets to priority claim holders.[38] Unlike Kaupthing and Glitnir, the winding-up board of LBI had a strong bargaining position. It held foreign currency bonds worth more than €2 billion, which had been issued by the new Landsbanki at the reconstruction of the banks. Már Guðmundsson – the governor of the CBI – had stated earlier that it was vital for the country's economic stability to extend the bonds. Otherwise, annual payments of €500 million in foreign currency would have to be made for the next four years, with devastating effects on the current account. It is not unreasonable to presume that some hedge funds strategically

---

[35] Segir slitastjórnir þurfa að vera raunsæjar. (Says the winding-up boards have to be realistic.) (2014, January 23). *Viðskiptablaðið*.

[36] Act no. 155/2010 on special taxes on financial institutions.

[37] Spink, Chris (2014, January 14). Iceland cold-shouldered as crisis countries rebound. *Reuters*.

[38] Ægisson, Hörður (2014, February 5). 300 milljarða reiðufé fast í höftum. (300 billion in cash stuck behind controls.) *Morgunblaðið*.

decided to purchase claims on the old Landsbanki, with the main purpose of using the foreign bonds as leverage for escaping capital controls.

As was discussed in the previous chapter, the so-called 'liquidation route' was prominent in public debate. Some government consultants openly advocated for it as a solution to the transfer problem accompanying distributions from the estates. That many of these advocate-consultants were alumni of the InDefence movement was further confirmation that the liquidation route was the scenario the government was most likely to follow.

The liquidation route required Icelandic authorities to make full use of the capital controls, and to in fact appropriate the foreign currency holdings of the estates. In a legal sense, the estates were Icelandic and their foreign currency holdings subject to the same handling as currency holdings of all other Icelandic entities. This meant the estates would have to turn in all of their foreign currency holdings to the CBI at the official onshore exchange rate, and pay their creditors in ISK. This was to happen as soon as the estates were declared insolvent. The creditors were then supposed to exchange the ISK for foreign currency by participating in auctions, along with owners of offshore ISK.

Creditors at first described this approach as the 'nuclear option'; that is, it was a deterrent and not a *real* option. But they came to fear that Prime Minister Gunnlaugsson and his circle of advisors might just be crazy enough to push the button. It is not entirely clear whether this approach was a genuine government policy, given the legal risk it involved. It was most likely a bargaining strategy to press the hedge funds to accept a more moderate approach. After all, firewalling one's own currency area with capital controls so as to determine the valuation of your own printed money was one thing. Going outside that ring of defense, appropriating foreign assets abroad, and bringing them back to the fortress is quite another (see Chap. 6).

7.4 The Carrot and Stick Approach

The situation had now turned into a staring contest. The creditors knew they would have to accept some haircuts to be granted exit – but how large? Lee Buchheit at Cleary Gottlieb, a well-known expert on sovereign debt management and a household name in Iceland after his involvement in the Icesave dispute, was contracted by the government in July 2014 to work with the task force on capital control liberalization. Earlier that year he had co-edited a book on sovereign debt management: its first two chapters were titled 'Sticks' and 'Carrots'.[39] The task force started to devise a new carrot and stick approach to break the impasse – and thus a new form of taxation surfaced: the *stability levy*.

Originally, in 2011, the CBI had considered using a Malaysian-style approach with an exit tax to abolish the controls, but the bank eventually opted for the currency auctions discussed in Chap. 5.[40] Following the Supreme Court's burial of the liquidation route in early November of 2014, other alternatives had been eliminated and the work would now have a single focus. A short while later, on November 18, the front page of *Morgunblaðið* reported plans to levy a 35 % exit tax on capital movements. Such a tax would eventually apply to all the estates' assets, both domestic and foreign, when distributed to foreign creditors, as the transfer of assets between a domestic and a foreign party is a capital movement.[41]

According to a newsflash from Debtwire, lawyers representing creditors of Glitnir appeared for the first time at a regular status hearing for Glitnir in a New York bankruptcy court in March 2015, following the news on taxation.[42] In 2008, all three estates had filed for Chapter 15 protection in the USA, as the old banks had issued Yankee bonds.[43] A lawyer from Akin Gump allegedly vented his frustration at the lack of dialogue, and reiterated that the creditors of Glitnir, Kaupthing, and Landsbanki would never accept a plan including a 35 % exit tax. He is said to have pointed out that the estates had vast foreign assets, including $1.1 billion of US Treasury notes, whose distribution to creditors would not have any adverse effects on Iceland's balance of payments. According to Debtwire the appearance

---

[39] Lastra, Rosa and Buchheit, Lee (Eds.). (2014). *Sovereign Debt Management.* Oxford: Oxford University Press.

[40] Central Bank of Iceland. (2011, March 25). Áætlun um losun gjaldeyrishafta. (A plan for lifting capital controls.) Report to the minister of economics and business.

[41] Greiði gjald fyrir forgang (Pay a Fee for Priority) (2014, November 18). *Morgunblaðið,* p. 1.

[42] Younker, Kyle. (2015, March 10). Glitnir, Kaupthing, Landsbanki bondholders vent qualms as Icelandic bank saga plods on. *Debtwire.*

[43] The bonds were issued under Rule 144A of the Securities Act.

did not go so well as Judge Stuart M. Bernstein simply stated that "this doesn't sound like anything that this court can or would do anything about."[44]

The main drawback of an exit tax is that it can encourage holdouts, since there is an option to wait for the tax rate to go down with the passage of time. After a change in the task force in January 2015, the option to taxing capital movements emerged: taxing the assets of the estates directly. In a plenary speech to the Progressive Party congress on April 10, 2015, Prime Minister Gunnlaugsson referred to the tax as a stability levy (which will be discussed in more detail on Chap. 8). Introduced in June 2015, this was the 'stick': a flat 39 % tax on all of the estates' assets.

The introduction of the stability tax on the estates was a radical measure. The line between taxation and nationalization can be questioned when an asset tax of 39 %, directed at just a handful of entities, is imposed. The tax was intended maybe as just a stick – in threat only – and a carrot was introduced at the same time: exemptions from capital controls gained by meeting the stability conditions.

But the authorities had to be prepared to use the stick if the carrot turned out to be unappealing. The term stability tax, or stability levy, has been used for many different types of taxes imposed in different countries. In 2011, South Korean authorities imposed a tax they referred to as a macro prudential stability levy, for the purpose of stemming the flows of short-term capital to and from the country.[45] The tax was levied on all foreign borrowings by financial institutions, apart from deposits. It was set at 0.2 % of borrowings for periods shorter than a year, and reduced in stages, as the term of the loan grew longer.[46] The tax was paid in US dollars, and its revenues were not intended for government expenditures. Instead they were deposited into a special financial stability fund, which provides foreign liquidity facilities to distressed financial institutions. This

---

[44] Younker, Kyle. (2015, March 10). Glitnir, Kaupthing, Landsbanki bondholders vent qualms as Icelandic bank saga plods on. *Debtwire*.

[45] Macro-Prudential Stability Levy. (2010, December 20). Joint press release from the Financial Services Commission and Financial Supervisory Service. South Korea.

[46] Bruno, Valentina and Shin, Huyn Song. (2014). Assessing Macroprudential Policies: Case of South Korea. *Scandinavian Journal of Economics*, 116(1), 128–157.

South Korean stability levy was therefore a variation on a bank tax, which only extends to the banks' foreign borrowings.

In the second half of 2013, Australian authorities announced their intention to impose a stability levy from 2016 onwards. The levy consists of a 0.05 % tax on bank deposits under AUD 250,000. Revenues from the tax will revert to a special financial stability fund, the purpose of which is to defray potential treasury expenditures in the event of a banking collapse. In Australia, deposits enjoy priority over other claims against banks, but there is no formal deposit insurance scheme in operation in the country. Since October 2008, the state has guaranteed the reimbursement of deposits up to a specified maximum, which was originally set at AUD 1 million but then reduced to AUD 250,000 in 2012. No fee has been charged for this guarantee, however.[47]

Because this proposed tax is levied solely on bank deposits up to a specified amount, and the revenues it generates revert to a special fund, it is in many ways comparable to the contributions paid by the Icelandic banks to the Depositors' and Investors' Guarantee Fund (DIGF), which currently total in the range of 0.225–0.45 % of insured deposits, depending on the risk profile of the bank.

Both the South Korean macro prudential stability levy and the Australian stability levy are examples of some sort of bank tax; neither has much in common with the Icelandic stability tax. A stability levy proposed in response to the banking crisis in Cyprus in 2013 has more similarities. That tax was proposed before capital controls were imposed in Cyprus in late March 2013, as a response to the weak position of the banking system and the imminent capital flight. The proposition was announced on Saturday March 16.[48] It was to be a flat 6.75 % tax on all deposits, domestic and foreign, under €100,000, and 9.9 % on deposits in excess of that threshold. It was projected to generate €5.8 billion in revenues the national treasury could then apply to the rescue of the banking system.

[47] Turner, Grant. (2011, December). Depositor Protection in Australia. *Reserve Bank of Australia Bulletin*.

[48] Eurogroup. (2013, March 16). *Eurogroup Statement on Cyprus*.

When the bill of legislation on the levy was presented before the national parliament on Tuesday, March 19, it was also intended that balances under €20,000 would be exempt from the tax. However, the bill was rejected by the Cypriot parliament that day, and the tax was never levied.[49] A week later, Cyprus imposed capital controls, (see Sect. 7.2). In the end, depositors had to absorb losses, and at the end of July, 47.5 % of all deposits exceeding €100,000 in the Bank of Cyprus were converted to share capital in the bank.

The closest equivalent to the Icelandic stability tax, however, can be found in a tax usually referred to as a *capital levy*. A capital levy is an asset tax that is imposed one time in order to pay down government debt. Many countries have imposed such a tax, very often for the purpose of paying down war-related debt, but with differing degrees of success. There are a few successful examples, such as Italy and Czechoslovakia after World War I, and Japan after World War II.[50] Capital levies apply to the principal value of assets, not to income or gains on them. It is a one-time levy imposed under extraordinary circumstances, typically when government debt has risen sharply. The Icelandic stability levy shares these characteristics, but differs from general capital levies in that it is directed primarily at the financial institutions' estates or creditors. The justification for this targeted application is the extraordinary circumstances that increase the chances that distributions to creditors will upset the foreign exchange market and cause severe economic instability.

Some similarities can also be seen between the Icelandic stability levy and so-called expatriation taxes, which are taxes levied by some countries when legal entities change their domicile to another country, or individuals relinquish their citizenship. Such a tax is levied irrespective of whether the change of domicile calls for foreign exchange transactions or not. It can be part of the enforcement of capital controls, as a way of stopping capital outflows, such as the *exit charge* levied in South Africa during the apartheid regime. Such a tax can also be intended to generate revenues for the national treasury from a selected group of persons or firms. The best-

---

[49] Campbell, Andrew, and Paula Moffat. (2013). *Protecting Bank Depositors after Cyprus*.

[50] Barry Eichengreen. (1989, September). The Capital Levy in Theory and Practice. *NBER Working Paper Series*, no. 3096,

known example of this is the so-called *Reich flight tax,* levied primarily against Jews and Jewish firms in Nazi Germany. In these two instances, a flat-rate tax was levied on amounts exceeding a predetermined asset or income threshold and expatriated from the country.

Imposed in the wake of the 1960 Sharpeville Massacre, the South African exit charge was an attempt to impede capital flight. The charge was an element in very broad-based capital controls, and was therefore an element in the nation's enforcement of the apartheid regime. The exit charge was reduced in increments and abolished in 2010. Even now, however, there are cases awaiting judgment by the Supreme Court, in which it is maintained that the tax was unconstitutional.[51]

The so-called Reich flight tax was levied in 1931, when the Weimar Republic was still intact, and it also was meant to stem capital flight. It amounted to 25 % on assets above a given threshold belonging to those who intended to move out of the country. In 1934, after the Nazis took power, it was changed to a means of appropriating assets from Jews fleeing the country, and it generated enormous revenues for the government.[52]

Nowadays, expatriation taxes are generally a form of capital gains tax, a means for countries to ensure their citizens pay tax on their unrealized capital gains before departure. Most often, tax offices of the countries concerned accomplish this by appraising the market value of the assets to be expatriated, and then imposing capital gains tax on the unrealized gains in accordance with the appraised value. This practice is followed, for instance, in the United States, Spain, and Canada.[53]

In the United States, an expatriation tax is levied on those who relinquish their US citizenship and meet one of the following conditions: owning net assets in excess of $2 million; if their average income over the past five years exceeds $139,000; or if they have not filled out IRS Form

---

[51] For further information, see: Rabkin, Franny. (2015, March 4). Exist charges on taking money out of SA 'not a tax'. *Business Day.* http://www.bdlive.co.za/business/2015/03/04/exit-charges-on-taking-money-out-of-sa-not-a-tax

[52] See also pp. 153–155 in. Feldman, Gerald D. & Seibel, Wolfgang. (2004, December). *Networks of Nazi Persecution: Bureaucracy, Business and the Organization of the Holocaus*t.

[53] For further discussion of the Canadian departure tax, see Emigration from Canada: Tax Implications. (2014, November). *Manulife.* https://repsourcepublic.manulife.com/wps/wcm/connect/5cb1c800433c4450b901ff319e0f5575/ins_tepg_taxtopicemigrtn.pdf?MOD=AJPERES

8854 declaring that they have complied with federal tax law over the past five years. Pension assets are included with total assets. The tax is the equivalent of a 15 % capital gains tax based on the market value of all assets owned by citizens seeking an exit.[54]

7.5   The Stability Contributions

Almost two and a half years after the winding-up boards first requested exemptions from capital controls in tandem with the composition agreements, the wheels started spinning quite fast. By spring 2015, representatives of the Icelandic authorities had started meeting frequently with creditors to discuss their upcoming plans for the lifting of capital controls, and requested feedback.[55]

On June 8, Benediktsson and Gunnlaugsson announced plans that gave winding-up boards two options. They could reach composition agreements with creditors meeting certain stability conditions, or be subjected to a 39 % stability tax on all of their assets.[56] The winding-up boards were given until the year's end to finish a composition agreement and fulfill the stability conditions.[57] The conditions set by the Central Bank were as follows[58]:

- To adopt measures that sufficiently reduced the negative impact of distributing the proceeds of the sale of assets in Icelandic krona;

---

[54] For further information, see the website of the Internal Revenue Service: http://www.irs.gov/Individuals/International-Taxpayers/Expatriation-Tax

[55] Ægisson, Hörður (2015, April 17). Fundað með vogunarsjóðum í London. (Meetings with hedge funds in London). *DV.*

[56] Financial Supervisory Authority (2015, June 8). *Aðgerðaáætlun til losunar fjármagnshafta. (Action plan for lifting capital controls.)*

[57] Act no. 60/2015 on Stability Levy. http://www.althingi.is/altext/144/s/1400.html

[58] Central Bank of Iceland. (2015, June 8). *Announcement concerning capital account liberalization measures.* (Press release No. 13/2015). http://www.cb.is/library/Skraarsafn---EN/Capital-control-liberalisation/Press%20release%20no%2013%202015%20Announcement%20concerning%20capital%20account%20liberalisation%20measures.pdf

- To convert other foreign-denominated domestic assets owned by the failed banks into long-term financing, to the degree required.
- Where applicable, to ensure the repayment of the foreign-denominated loan facilities granted by the authorities to the new banks following the financial market collapse.

By fulfilling these conditions through stability contributions, loan repayments, and debt reconstructions, the estates would get their composition agreements confirmed before a specific date. Thus the stability tax would not be applicable, and the estates would have means to finally transfer funds to creditors. In the following months, creditors unanimously accepted the stability conditions, and the Central Bank granted exemption from capital controls to facilitate the composition agreements.[59]

The stability conditions allowed the estates to tailor their approach and ensure that their composition would not risk economic and financial stability, without resorting to a lump-sum cash settlement via the stability tax. The first condition implies that the estates had to surrender assets that otherwise would negatively impact the balance of payments and cause currency depreciation. This was done with direct asset transfers where possible, but cash sweeps applied to assets that could not be transferred. The second condition applies to long-term financing for the banking system and access to international financial markets on standard terms and conditions. It was intended to secure the financial stability that had been a prerequisite in previous liberalization plans set out by the IMF. The estates of Glitnir and Kaupthing had foreign currency deposits with the new banks that were used to invest in EMTNs issued by the new banks. LBI already held the Landsbanki bond, which could not be considered as market standard; hence the second condition forced LBI to grant Landsbanki an option to convert the bond into EMTN notes at the market rate. The third condition forced the estates to refinance the state and CBI funding of the new banks from 2009 with foreign assets and boost the CBI reserve.

---

[59] Central Bank of Iceland. (2015, October 28). *Seðlabanki Íslands hefur lokið mati sínu á fyrirliggjandi drögum að nauðasamningum. (The Central Bank has concluded its assessment of composition agreement drafts.)*

On November 20, Glitnir's creditors agreed to a composition agreement.[60] Three days later, LBI's composition proposal was approved[61]; Kaupthing's proposal was approved the day after.[62] The compositions were confirmed by the district court of Reykjavik in December.[63] Subsequently, the Central Bank formally granted exceptions from capital controls to Glitnir, Kaupthing and LBI.[64] The winding-up boards were now able to make payments to the creditors and were replaced with holding companies. Creditors received shares and bonds in accordance with their claims, whose value is related to the value of the holding company's remaining assets.[65] To obtain this solution, the creditors had to agree to give Icelandic authorities immunity from lawsuits regarding the implementation of capital controls and stability conditions.[66]

All in all, eight Icelandic estates fell under the conditions of the stability tax act, and all of them chose the option of meeting the stability conditions. One, ALMC, had already concluded composition but came to an agreement with the Central Bank to fulfill conditions to receive an exemption from the Foreign Exchange Act. The estates of the old commercial banks, Glitnir, Kaupthing and LBI, accounted for over 90 % of the size of the problem, therefore their actions would be of prime importance.

In the plan outlaid by Icelandic authorities, the total size of the threat to Iceland's balance of payments and financial stability was estimated at €5.4

---

[60] Glitnir. (2015, November 20). *Results of the Voting at the OCM on 20 November 2015.*

[61] LBI hf. (2015, November 23). *Outcome of voting on the Composition Proposal of LBI hf.*

[62] Kaupthing. (2015, November 24). *Composition Voting Meeting 24 November 2015 – Composition Proposal approved.*

[63] Glitnir (2015, December 5). *Glitnir's Proposed Composition*; LBI hf. (2015, December 18). *Composition confirmed by the District Court*; Kaupthing (2015, December 15). *Composition confirmed by the District Court.*

[64] Glitnir (2015, December 16). *Exemption granted by the Central Bank of Iceland*; Kaupthing (2016, January 15). *Kaupthing Composition – Exemption granted by the Central Bank of Iceland*; LBI hf. (2016, January 11). *Exemption from Capital Controls – final settlement of priority claims.*

[65] Glitnir. (2016, January 8). *Completion of the Composition – Issue of New Notes and New Ordinary Shares*; LBI hf. (2016, March 23.) *Status and fulfilment of the Composition Agreement*; LBI hf. (2016, March 23.) *Status and fulfilment of the Composition Agreement.*

[66] Ægisson, Hörður (2015, September 29). Kröfuhafar geta ekki farið í mál við íslensk stjórnvöld. (Creditors cannot sue Icelandic authorities.) *DV.*

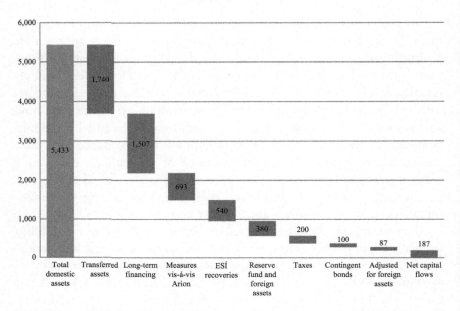

Fig. 7.3 Total size of the stability contributions of the three largest banks. *Amounts in million euros* (Source: Report from the Icelandic Ministry of Finance. 28.10.2015)

billion (816 billion ISK).[67] The stability conditions dealt with this problem in many ways, not only by direct contributions but also with different kinds of debt and equity modifications.

In Fig. 7.3 the left-hand column represents the €5.4 billion problem: it represents all domestic assets, both in ISK and foreign currency, which the estates held. All the other columns show mitigating actions taken to meet the stability conditions. The largest one was the direct contribution of assets, a total of €1.74 billion, from the estates to the government. The biggest factor there was the transfer of Glitnir's stake in Íslandsbanki to the Icelandic government, which alone was estimated at €1.23 billion.

The second largest mitigating action was the modification of the banks' loan structure, which amounted to €1.5 billion. The lion's share, €1

[67] Ministry of Finance. (2015). *Capital Account Liberalization.* http://www.ministryoffinance.is/media/frettatengt2015/Capital-Account-Liberalisation.pdf

billion, was due to an agreement made in 2014 concerning the refinancing of Landsbankinn's bond issue to the LBI estate, but the deal fulfilled most of the stability conditions set on the winding up of LBI. The other two estates agreed to convert their short time foreign currency deposits in the banks into standard international, long-term bond funding. In addition to the deposits, these bond issues covered amounts set aside to reimburse the Treasury and the CBI, and complete terms for the subordinated loans made by the government at the establishment of the new banks.

The third largest action was the special agreement between the government and Kaupthing concerning the sale of Arion Bank, amounting to €693 million. The fourth represents the Central Bank's recoveries, €540 million, through its Holding Company (ESÍ). A total of €380 million in reserves and foreign assets was to be held by the estates, but these funds are supposed to cover a variety of unresolved obligations. If those costs are not realized, the amounts will be transferred to the Treasury. Taxes paid by the estates for the year 2015 totaled €200 million. Risk from disputes over the legitimacy of certain taxes levied on the banks was eliminated with cash sweep provisions. Other smaller contributions were contingent bonds and adjustments for foreign assets.

The net capital outflow due to the winding up of the estates was estimated at €187 million, meaning that it had a net negative effect equal to that amount on the foreign reserves at the Central Bank.[68,69]

Actions taken by the estates to fulfill the stability conditions can be divided into three categories: (1) direct contributions, (2) indirect contributions, and (3) other mitigating actions. Direct contributions consist of a voluntary transfer of assets from the estates to the state or the CBI that are a direct consequence of the composition agreement. Indirect contributions are proceeds from the estates to the state or the CBI that would have been delivered at some point, irrespective of the composition agreement.

---

[68] Central Bank of Iceland. (2015, October 27). *Settlement of the failed financial institutions on the basis of stability conditions: Impact on balance of payments and financial stability.* http://sedlabanki.is/library/Skraarsafn/Gjaldeyrismal/AssessmentOfPreliminaryCompositionProposals.pdf

[69] Ministry of Finance. (2015, June 8). *Capital Account Liberalization.* http://www.ministryoffinance.is/media/frettatengt2015/Capital-Account-Liberalisation.pdf

Table 7.1 Total contributions and other mitigating actions taken by the three estates. Amounts in million euros

	Kaupthing	Glitnir	LBI	Total	% of GDP
Direct contributions					
Measures vis-á-vis Arion	693			693	4.7
Transferred assets	120	1,480	133	1,733	11.8
Cash sweep provisions	40	47	20	107	0.7
Total direct contributions	853	1,527	153	2,533	17.2
Indirect contributions					
ESÍ recoveries	267	180	93	540	3.7
Taxes	80	73	53	207	1.4
Repayments	360	133	0	493	3.4
Total indirect contributions	707	387	147	1,240	8.4
Other mitigating actions					
Long-term financing	280	233	993	1,507	10.2
Adjusted for foreign assets	7	80	0	87	0.6
Reserve fund	193	147	40	380	2.6
Total other mitigating actions	480	460	1,033	1,973	13.4
Total mitigating actions	**2,040**	**2,373**	**1,333**	**5,747**	**39.1**
As a percentage of GDP (2015)	13.9 %	16.1 %	9.1 %	39.1 %	

Source: Central Bank of Iceland (2015, October 27). *Settlement of the failed financial institutions on the basis of stability conditions*

Other mitigating actions are those that do not involve a transfer of assets to the state or the CBI, but which mitigated the effects of the composition agreements on the Icelandic economy. The breakdown of the contributions is shown in Table 7.1 along with each amount as a percentage of Iceland's 2015 GDP.

Direct contributions from the three estates combined amounted to €2.53 billion ISK, or 17.2 % of Iceland's 2015 GDP. The largest two assets in that category were Glitnir's share in Íslandsbanki and Kaupthing's bond issue to the government regarding its share in Arion bank; these totaled €2.16 billion. Other assets included shares in Icelandic companies, cash, bonds, and assets bound by cash sweep provisions.

The indirect contributions, totaling €1.24 billion, consisted of three different contributions. First were recoveries of the claims held by the Central Bank's Holding Company (ESÍ) on the estates, amounting to €540 million combined. ESÍ will recover these funds over the next few years, but the amount was independent of the agreements governing the winding up of the estates. Second, the estates of Glitnir and Kaupthing purchased bonds held by the Treasury for a total of €493 million in foreign currency. Kaupthing purchased Arion Bank's bond from the Central Bank for €360 million, and Glitnir purchased a subordinated Íslandsbanki bond from the Treasury for €133 million. Third, there is the €207 million in taxes paid by the estates for the year 2015, which clearly would have been delivered to the government regardless of the conditions and the contributions.[70]

Both the direct and indirect contributions have already ended up or will end up with the government, which means that the treasury will receive assets amounting to €3.773 billion, or the equivalent of 25.6 % of the country's 2015 GDP.

Other mitigating actions included the extension of debt of the new banks to the estates, reserves held by the estates, and the adjustment for the foreign assets the estates delivered to the treasury. The total amount was €2 billion, but €1.5 billion of that amount was due to the lengthening of liabilities of the new banks. Reserve funds held by the estates to meet its domestic obligations in the coming years amounted to €380 million. However, if those costs are not realized at a certain time, the funds will be delivered to the treasury.

The scale of contributions from the three largest banks was far greater than that of the five smaller estates. These other estates were ALMC (former Straumur-Burðarás), BYR, EA Investments (former MP Bank), SPB (former Icebank) and SPRON. In a report issued by the Central Bank, the total assets of these estates was estimated at €1.15 billion, of which there was €713 million in foreign assets and €147 million in domestic assets in foreign currency. The combined domestic ISK assets of the estates therefore amounted to €280 million, but the total contributions from them amounted to €47 million. In addition, the Central Bank's Holding Company (ESÍ) will recover an equivalent amount to €120 million in foreign currency from the estates, making the combined direct and indirect contributions €167 million.

---

[70] Central Bank of Iceland (2015, October 27). *Settlement of the failed financial institutions on the basis of stability conditions.*

Table 7.2 Direct, indirect and total contributions from all estates

	Smaller estates	Larger estates	Total	% of GDP
Direct contributions	47	2,533	2,580	17.5
Indirect contributions	120	1,240	1,360	9.2
Total contributions	167	3,773	3,940	26.8
% of GDP	1.1 %	25.7 %	26.8 %	

Source: Central Bank, 2015

Four of the smaller estates received an allowance to convert a total of €87 million in ISK assets to foreign currency through the Central Bank. It is unknown what will happen to the remainder of the estates' ISK assets, amounting to €147 million, but they might be used to pay domestic creditors, or held as reserves for future obligations. Total direct and indirect contributions of all eight estates are shown in Table 7.2.

Contributions from all eight estates, which would have fallen under the stability tax, total €4 billion, or the equivalent of 26.8 % of Iceland's 2015 GDP.

The balance of the CBI bond, along with a vast amount of deposits in the banking system, represents the increase in money supply during the years before the financial crash. In its 2016 budget, the government outlaid a plan to pay the remaining 90 billion ISK principal of the bond by the end of the year with the proceeds from the stability contributions.[71] It is not certain how the treasury will allocate the rest of the funds received from the estates, but that will ultimately determine the effects on the money supply, as will be discussed in Chap. 8.

As with any financial carrot-and-stick approach, there had to be clear differences between the stability conditions and the 39 % stability tax that accounted for the legal uncertainty of the tax. The largest estates had different proportions of domestic assets, which were the main problem, so the tax percentage had to be above the highest proportion of domestic assets among the estates. As a consequence, the legal risk, together with time value of money, was assigned a hefty price tag, which influenced the

---

[71] Government Debt Management. (2016, March). *Markaðsupplýsingar. (Market information)*. 17(3). http://www.lanamal.is/GetAsset.ashx?id=8484

comparison between stability contributions on one hand and the stability tax on the other.

This elimination of legal uncertainty is the reason many prominent figures saw the stability contributions as a more desirable conclusion than a stability tax. However, the alleged 'discount' handed to creditors created quite the controversy,[72] considering that a stability tax would have handed the government approximately €4.5 billion (680 billion ISK) instead of €2.5 billion (379 billion ISK). It is important to keep in mind though that the objective was not to raise funds for the state but to solve the transfer problem.

In the weeks after the June 8, 2015, meeting, where the liberalization plan was introduced, Moody's, Fitch, and S&P upgraded Iceland by one notch. The proposals were thought to be credible and a careful process, which was expected to reduce external vulnerabilities and protect economic and financial stability.[73]

7.6   The Textbook Case?

It is very likely that future textbooks will portray the Icelandic capital controls from 2008 as a success – and perhaps an example for others. This success was not due just to macroeconomic benefits; it also reflects how the controls empowered the Icelandic government to impose haircuts on the owners of offshore ISK assets. The numbers are certainly impressive – the Icelandic Treasury was handed assets worth about 27 % of total GDP after a settlement with the creditors of the old banks, as tallied above. That will go a long way towards solving the transfer problem that has paralyzed the Icelandic currency area for eight years at the time of writing. Unprecedented circumstances were met with unconventional measures. IMF

---

[72] InDefence. Umsögn og ábendingar um frumvarp til laga um stöðugleikaskatt, 786. mál og frumvarp til laga um fjármálafyrirtæki (nauðasamningar), 787. mál.

[73] Moody's Investor Service. (2009, June 29). *Rating Action: Moody's upgrades Iceland's sovereign ratings to Baa2; outlook stable.* Standard & Poor's Rating Services. (2015, July 17). *Iceland Ratings Raised to 'BBB/A-2' On Proposals Toward Lifting Capital Controls; Outlook Stable.* FitchRatings. (2015, July 24). *Fitch Upgrades Iceland to 'BBB+'; Outlook Stable.*

testimony, improved credit ratings from the rating agencies and the recovery at large all testify to the success of the plan. Thus it is not unlikely that these measures will become widely accepted and applied elsewhere if needed.

Glitnir ended up handing its 95 % share in Íslandsbanki to Icelandic authorities, and its total contribution was estimated at €1.5 billion (229 billion ISK). Kaupthing's contribution was €0.85 billion (127 billion ISK), and Landsbanki's contribution was €0.15 billion (23 billion ISK).[74] The different contributions of the estates reflect the difference in their asset compositions. Glitnir had the highest ratio of ISK-denominated assets in its portfolio, and hence had to make the largest contribution in order for the distribution to creditors to be capital account neutral.

A nice side effect of the resolution is that it generated windfall revenues for the treasury in the amount of €2.6 billion, or 17.5 % of GDP, in 2015. State and CBI recoveries from the estates through claims and repayment of loans made to the new banks add on another €1.4 billion, or 9.2 % of GDP. Total government revenues therefore amount to €4 billion, or 26.8 % of GDP.

Nevertheless, a strong case can be made that the controls have brought short-term economic gain at a long-term cost.

The controls have deterred investment in Iceland, but that is not the main problem. They have also almost completely prevented investment going out, since they have locked corporations inside their tiny domestic market. Economic growth and productivity in Scandinavia, and elsewhere in the developed world, has been driven by multinationals playing some kind of market niche in the international arena, where capital transactions are of vital importance. Iceland had been able to get ahead with several niche-playing multinationals during the brief period of financial freedom, most notably in the biotech, healthcare and food processing sectors. Most players in these sectors survived the crisis, although some of them have left the country, either because ownership changed hands or the controls proved intolerable. However, the next generation of upcoming

---

[74] Central Bank of Iceland (2015, October 27). *Uppgjör fallinna fjármálafyrirtækja á grundvelli stöðugleikaskilyrða: áhrif á greiðslujöfnuð og fjármálastöðugleika Samkvæmt fyrirliggjandi drögum að nauðasamningum Glitnis hf., Kaupþings hf. og LBI hf.*

multinationals is likely to leave the country during infancy, so that they can grow in a world where capital transactions are free and secure.

The question of capital controls really concerns Iceland's commitment to enjoying the benefits delivered by globalization, especially in terms of productivity that help its industries keep pace with developments abroad. A closed corporate ecosystem can only work for small nations if they have resources that give them a competitive position in export sectors, despite general inefficiencies and a lack of self-confidence in business and industry.

Though Sweden's 1992 market defense was costly – policy rates were briefly raised to 500 % to support the currency – it nevertheless re-invigorated the Swedish krona in the longer term. The extent of that strength is reflected by the nation's decision to opt out of the euro. Post-crisis Sweden moreover is on a route to ever-greater international integration; it is now a leading global player in many fields.

It is clear that Iceland has been taking the opposite route. Partly, this is because in some circles, the financial crisis is still viewed as the inevitable result of reckless international integration. But the effect of capital controls on the future is evident. The controls influence how the currency is trusted and used as a store of value. They are also at heart a serious infringement on the property rights of all holders of Icelandic assets – domestic or foreign alike – and this too will have deep and long-lasting effects. It may well be that the days of the ISK as a freely convertible currency are in fact numbered; it may never really function without the life support of some kind of capital controls.

8

Dealing with Monetary Pollution

8.1 What Happens If You Quadruple the Money Supply in Four Years?

On Friday, April 10, 2015, Sigmundur Davíð Gunnlaugsson, prime minister and chairman of the Progressive Party, gave an opening speech at his party's convention that stunned the nation.[1] Gunnlaugsson had turned 40 just a month before. He had a ministerial, almost religious delivery and a deep, thundering voice that rendered him an air of seniority. The speech quickly formed into a passionate attack on the "vulture" hedge funds controlling the estates of the three fallen banks.

In his speech Gunnlaugsson pointed out that the estates had between them about $20 billion worth of assets, and of course the New York-based hedge funds would go to great lengths to secure them. There was a

---

[1] Gunnlaugsson, Sigmundur Davíð. (2015, April 10). Yfirlitsræða forsætisráðherra og formanns Framsóknarflokksins á 33. flokksþingi framsóknarmanna. (Summary speech given by the prime minister and chairman of the Progressive party at the 33. Progressive Party congress.) http://www.framsokn.is/wp-content/uploads/Yfirlitsræða-Sigmundar-Davíðs-Gunnlaugssonar-á-33.-flokksþingi-Framsóknarflokksins-2015.pdf

Á. Jónsson, H. Sigurgeirsson, *The Icelandic Financial Crisis*, DOI 10.1057/978-1-137-39455-2_8

thriving international industry specializing in industrial espionage, and it was ready to serve the funds. He maintained that most, if not all Icelandic law firms, and all the PR agencies, were on the dole of the hedge funds or related parties. All in all, he said, the creditors had spent about 18 billion ISK to push their interests in Iceland in the past years, and now they quietly guided all public discussion of the collapsed banks' estates. The funds' insidious presence had shaken national trust; no one could be sure who was on the take anymore.[2]

Moreover, the creditors had prepared "secret reports" about developments in Icelandic politics and financial affairs, which nonetheless fed into public discourse. They had also been profiling politicians, journalists and others that had or might express an opinion on how the estates' transfer problem might be resolved. They had even been "doing psychoanalysis on people to determine the best way to deal with them."[3]

Gunnlaugsson then quoted one of the "secret documents" prepared by the hedge funds: "The Progressive Party stands firm on Icelandic interests."[4]

"You can always give it to these fellows that they are clear on the main facts," he exclaimed. Had not the nation learned its lesson from the Icesave debate? The prime minister would never waver from his firm defense of the Icelandic public's interest. Of course, the best solution was the one he had proposed all along: the government should simply have bought claims when they were trading at a huge discount in late 2008 and 2009. But, since this had not been done, Iceland would just have to make the best of things.

With that preface, he announced a new tax – the stability levy – that would deliver "hundreds of billions ISK" to the government and make it possible to lift the capital controls without endangering economic stability.[5]

Gunnlaugsson had built his political career on the Icesave debate (see Chap. 5). Having scored a victory in that affair, he turned his attention to

---

[2] *Ibid.*, p. 9.
[3] *Ibid.*, p. 9.
[4] *Ibid.*, p. 9.
[5] *Ibid.*, p. 11

the vulture funds of the estates of the fallen banks. In spring of 2013, he secured a huge electoral win for his party – and the prime minister's chair for himself – by promising household debt relief via taxes on the estates. Not only should the old banks pay for the damage they caused – restitution could be had from the vulture funds themselves. They had money to spare and had bought the claims at a huge discount, which in Gunnlaugsson's estimation should have profited the Icelandic state instead.

Throughout the campaign season, Progressive candidates had bandied about metaphors involving shotguns and vultures.[6] Once in office, Gunnlaugsson invented a new phrase, 'friends of the creditors', to paste on his opponents and their contrary views. The 'vulture' trope made frequent appearances in his speeches.

Thus Gunnlaugsson's rhetoric on April 10 was nothing new, although his stridency would make for an interesting read. What was revolutionary was his proposal: the stability levy.

The following Monday, April 13, the Central Bank of Iceland (CBI) governor, Már Guðmundsson, faced a battery of questions from MPs at a meeting of the Parliamentary Committee on Economic Affairs and Trade. What did he know about this proposal made before the weekend? Was the Progressive Party just fulfilling a campaign promise by taxing the estates? How would the Icelandic authorities be able to justify such discriminate taxation directed at just one type of agency?

"Actually, to some extent," Guðmundsson said, "these ISK positions that are locked in here are like pollution on our balance sheet – the country's balance sheet – and so a stability tax, when it is introduced, could be viewed as a sort of pollution tax."[7] In other words, the stability levy was sort of a reverse quantitative easing (QE) to reduce money in circulation. The money appropriated with the levy was going to be burned and not used to finance state spending.

---

[6] Frosti Sigurjónsson, an MP candidate for the Progressive Party, for example said in a radio interview on the show Vikulokin on April 6, 2013: "It could also be compared to that the vulture is in the woods, we have a shotgun, do we trust us to go get it or do we trust someone else."

[7] Meeting of the Parliamentary Committee of Economic Affairs and Trade. (2015, April 13). From minute 31:52 to 32:13. http://www.althingi.is/altext/upptokur/nefndafundur/?faerslunr=36

This created a contradiction with Gunnlaugsson's proposal. Later that Monday, in an interview with daily *Morgunblaðið*, the prime minster retracted his statement that income from the tax would be considered governmental revenue.[8]

The three estates – of Landsbanki, Kaupthing, and Glitnir – had between them about €15 billion total assets. Of these total assets, about 41 %, or €6 billion, were domestic, which amounted to 45 % of Iceland's gross domestic product (GDP).[9] Thus, a substantial stability levy on the total assets of the estates would virtually eliminate the domestic assets owned by the estates, which were "polluting" Iceland's balance sheet.

As an economic concept, pollution is an example of an externality, where one party's actions have an economic impact on other, unrelated parties. The general rule regarding pollution taxes is that the polluter pays, thereby internalizing the externalities resulting from his behavior. In the context of the currency market, pollution refers to the estates' domestic assets, which could have a strong negative impact on living standards in the country when general creditors tried to convert them to foreign currency: thus the development the oft-mentioned transfer problem (see Chap. 5).

However, "pollution" applies to a much wider context in monetary economics if one believes there is a fixed relationship between money and prices, as stipulated by the quantity equation.[10] By that assumption, a 100 % increase in money supply would lead to 100 % increase in prices, and the value of the outstanding money balances would be reduced by 50 %. In this simple context, new money in the system has a negative external effect on all pre-existing holders – just like new equity in corporate issues reduces the value held by other shareholders. But how would that apply specifically to the estates of the fallen banks?

---

[8] Sævarsson, Sigurður Bogi & Guðjónsson, Viðar. (2015, April 13). Sumarþing ekki útilokað. (Summer assembly not ruled out.) *Morgunblaðið*.

[9] The domestic asset position varied between the three estates; Glitnir had €2.3 billion worth about 36 % of total assets. For Kaupthing and Landsbanki the numbers were €1.5 billion or 28 % of total assets and €2.2 billion or 73 % of total assets respectively. Figures from annual accounts of the estates of Glitnir and Kaupthing and from quarterly financial information of Landsbanki.

[10] The quantity equation is PY=MV. Where P is price, Y is GDP, M is the stock of nominal money and V is velocity.

And as a matter of fact, the estates had domestic assets to the tune of 900 billion ISK (€6 billion), or about 40–50 % of Iceland's GDP, which were mostly sitting as liabilities on the balance sheets of the new banks. They were mostly either deposits or equity stakes. The new banks had been given a huge write-off advantage at their founding when assets – especially corporate loans – were transferred to them from the old banks. Thus, when the economic recovery began in Iceland in 2011, these assets could be re-valued. Furthermore, as discussed in Chap. 4, due to both greater concentration in the deposit market and ample liquidity kept on hand at the new banks – the interest rates offered on demand deposits declined, which boosted both interest margins and profits at the new banks.

The profits reaped from both revaluation of assets and wider interest rate margins would remain within the new banks. For two of them – Arion Bank and Islandsbanki – the owners were in fact default estates that could not enter composition and pay out to creditors. Instead, the profit would accumulate on the balance sheet as retained earnings or, if paid out as dividends, on deposit from the old banks. Landsbanki was owned by the government, but its ability to pay dividends to its owner was limited until a final settlement was reached concerning the Icesave payments. Therefore, equity ratios of the three banks at the end of 2015 were 24.2 % for Arion Bank, 30.1 % for Islandsbanki and 30.4 % for Landsbanki – numbers modern banks rarely see.

The creditors did not see the domestic assets of the estates as such a problem, and they did not believe they had to be converted into FX in the Icelandic currency market. They made the argument that the excess equity was really the result of the widespread use of currency-linked lending financed with wholesale funding from abroad. Thus, in the pre-collapse days of the old banks, outstanding domestic loans were in excess of the domestic deposit base. Even after steep write-offs, the new banks had considerably more assets than deposits, and had to issue bonds to the old banks to cover the difference.[11] The bonds were later converted into equity when the estates bought Arion Bank and Islandsbanki on

---

[11] Ministry of Finance. (2011, March). *Skýrsla fjármálaráðherra um endurreisn viðskiptabankanna. (Minister of finance report on the restoration of the commercial banks).*

behalf of creditors in 2009 (see Chap. 6). In Landsbanki's case, the government kept control and the bond issued to the old bank was never retracted. Thus, it is possible to look at the equity of the new banks – which formed the main bulk of the estates' domestic assets – as the remains of the original foreign wholesale funding used to fund the Icelandic corporate sector. This is a variation on the classical restructuring approach, in which creditors turn bonds into equity, and thus assume the risk and benefits from a possible downside or upside.

Therefore, the creditors maintained, turning some of that excess equity back into long-term bonds, which subsequently would be sold abroad, should only have small and long-term effects on the balance of payments. After all, the old banks had been, to a large extent, wholesale-funded. The equity left in the banks – the controlling stakes – could just as well be sold abroad. Any remaining ISK that might threaten the balance of payments would be deposited into the CBI for an unlimited amount of time, or until leeway for their distribution to creditors was achieved. Thus, neither the balance of payment nor the currency market would have to be affected by the distribution from the estates.

The Icelandic authorities maintained that this was just postponing the problem. They also worried that if the creditors gained direct control of the new banks, they could siphon money out of the country as dividend payments, which are categorized as current account transaction and therefore not subject to capital controls.

But did this argument justify the imposition of the 39 % stability levy on the estates?

In January 2015, the authors were contracted by the winding-up board of Glitnir as independent advisors to define the conditions under which distributions from the estate might proceed – as they would enter composition – without infringing on the set goals regarding non-socialization of losses. They answered this question in May 2015 with a report titled *An Outline of a Resolution*.[12] In the report, the authors argued that the money supply in the Icelandic financial system was just too high to be sustainable in the longer term. In fact, the current high levels were only sustained by

---

[12] Jónsson, Ásgeir & Sigurgeirsson, Hersir. (2015, May). *Drög að uppgjöri. (A draft of a resolution)*. Reykjavík: Auðfræðasetur. http://audfraedi.is/utgefin-rit/frett/2015/05/06/Drog-ad-uppgjori/

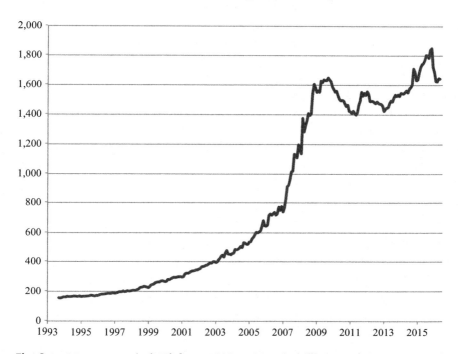

Fig. 8.1 Money supply (M3) from 1993 to 2016 in billion ISK (Source: Central Bank of Iceland)

the capital controls that prevented the excess liquidity from flowing out of the country and causing a depreciation of the currency and a new inflationary outburst. On the other hand, should the controls be kept in place, this excess liquidity would slowly trickle into the Icelandic economy and asset markets and lead to overheating, which in turn would have a negative effect on – and ultimately weaken – the ISK. The merits of this argument can be inferred from the fact that the Icelandic money supply – measured as M3 – quadrupled during the financial boom from 2004 to 2008 (see Fig. 8.1).

Classical money theory offers two explanations of this fourfold increase. The first doubling, which happened between 2003 and 2006, was the result of halving the reserve requirement on deposits in 2003, from 4 % to 2 %. This was a harmonizing measure, launched to make Icelandic banks competitive in the field of lending. In the European Economic Area, the requirement was also 2 %. According to standard textbooks in monetary economics, halving the reserve requirements should double the money multiplier and hence the money supply, especially if the change is implemented at an early stage of a credit cycle. This is indeed what happened in the next two or three years after 2003, as will be discussed in Sect. 8.2.

The next doubling occurred when the bubble was about to burst in the winter of 2007–2008 due to the QE policies implemented by the CBI. By that time, banks around the world were beset with liquidity problems. Central banks responded by printing money and circulating it through collateralized lending to banks, long referred to as repurchase (repo) transactions. However, collateralized lending transactions with commercial banks should be recoverable. The central bank can then return the collateral and demand the return of its money. If the collateral becomes worthless, however, the loan leg is severed and the recoverability disappears. Consequently, the central bank is left with a claim against the estate, while the money is still in the financial system.

This is what happened in Iceland at the default of the three commercial banks, which had secured liquidity from the CBI by placing each other's bonds as collateral. Furthermore, the CBI sustained a loan loss that eroded its capital. Since the owner of the bank is the treasury, and the treasury is funded by the taxpayer, such a loss inevitably ends up on the treasury's balance sheet and ultimately becomes a tax burden on the public. The public will also bear the cost of these loans through increased inflation and currency depreciation.

Thus, we run up against the principle of non-socialization of losses of private banks. To readjust the money supply, a treasury will have to tax the general public and use the revenue to fund the recapitalization of the CBI. This is precisely what would have happened if Greece had been allowed to default; all the repo loans made on the value of Greek treasury bonds would have turned into baseless money printing, which would have been borne collectively by European Union (EU) countries. Thus, the European Central Bank's (ECB's) lending on the value of government bonds issued by some of the member states can be seen as a collectivization of losses.

In the authors' opinion, it was this baseless money that had to be eliminated from the Icelandic financial system before the capital controls could be lifted. Most of this excess liquidity was within the estate of the old banks. Quite naturally, the estates' objective was to convert their assets to liquid funds that they could then distribute to creditors. And of course, the distribution of ISK posed severe problems for the Icelandic foreign exchange market. Nevertheless, it would have been rather reckless to transfer ownership of this excess money from the foreign creditors to some domestic agent, such as the government. That agent would subsequently use the money to buy goods and services, as would be the case if the stability levy were used to finance new public spending. Such a scenario would place these funds back in circulation and stimulate demand. Doing so would scuttle the plan to remove controls, which would have to follow settlement of the estates, since monetary expansion always puts pressure on the ISK exchange rate. This money would therefore have to be returned to the CBI one way or another.

In the end, the stability levy was not applied since the estates were given the option to "voluntarily" contribute their domestic assets to the Icelandic treasury (see Chap. 7). The collected stability contributions amounted to less than the proposed levy: €2.5 billion instead of estimated €4.5 billion stability tax revenues. But since the contributions were voluntary, there was no legal risk involved. It is very likely that creditors would have mounted a legal challenge, thereby sparking an interesting economic debate concerning capital levies as a reversal of QE (i.e. central bank loan losses in a monetary context), and the very definition of "money" in large and small currency areas.

The voluntary stability contributions will also serve as a reverse QE, though on a smaller scale than the proposed stability tax. The treasury has already used some of these funds to pay up the outstanding bond issued to the CBI to cover the losses from its repo lending, mentioned above. The CBI, on the other hand, has regarded these transfers of funds to the state as a sterilization of its FX purchases which, in cumulative terms, amount to 500 billion ISK or €3.5 billion since 2014. These purchases have been possible due to the phenomenal growth of the tourist industry in the past three to four years, which has delivered a trade surplus in the range of 8–10 % of GDP. At the same time, capital outflows from Iceland are limited by the capital controls, and thus the current account inflows dominate the currency market with appreciation effects on the ISK. In fact, the CBI has been buying around 60–70 % of the total turnover in the currency (interbank) market for the past quarters. Normally, when a central bank purchases foreign currency with money hot from its printing press, it is injecting liquidity into the financial system. Thus it is possible to think of the FX purchases coupled with the stability payments as an asset swap of sorts; for the first time in Iceland's post-war history, the CBI has significant unleveraged foreign reserves.

8.2   Doubling the Money Multiplier

The Icelandic króna was created in 1875, after Denmark and Sweden had formed a currency union in 1873 and fixed their currencies at par to each other. Norway joined two years later. The common currency unit was the *krona* (*crown*), and the Nordic currencies were pegged to gold, with each krona worth 0.4 grams of gold. Iceland would enter this monetary union under the auspices of Danish rule, which extended back to the fourteenth century. The Scandinavian Monetary Union lasted until the outbreak of World War I. Although none of the Scandinavian nations took active part in the fighting, the demand pressures that followed it led to different inflation paths in the respective countries, which resulted in an irreversible currency misalignment.

Geopolitics also led to a divorce between the Icelandic and Danish krona. Bismarck had officially united Germany in 1871, and by the turn of the twentieth century the nation state had emerged as a naval power. Great Britain began to see Iceland as a strategic focal point in the North Atlantic, just as US naval operations would during the Cold War. These geopolitical currents removed Iceland from continental European influence, and made it into a game piece of sorts in the UK— Anglo-Saxon alliance. When World War I broke out in 1914, the British effectively took control of Iceland and directed its exports towards both nations. In fact, all Icelandic ships were required to stop in a British port before continuing on to Denmark, and the goods meant for Danish export trade were restricted, or even forbidden, for fear that they would subsequently move on to Germany, as they had for centuries.[13] The unilateral movements humiliated the Danish authorities repeatedly (the British insisted on reading all mail and correspondence that went from the government in Copenhagen to its northern outpost in Reykjavík!). Iceland, its appetite whetted by its new, powerful trading partnerships, demanded sovereignty in 1918, and received it.[14] At last, the Icelandic króna was an independent currency, although the island officially remained in allegiance with the Danish throne.

So began the experiment with the ISK. With a current population of about 330,000, Iceland keeps the world's smallest currency: no other nation with a population below 2 million has an independent currency in the sense that it conducts its own monetary policy. The first currency crisis hit the country in 1920, only two years after sovereignty. By 1990, through a series of monetary expansions, devaluations and inflationary outbursts, the ISK had lost about 98 % of its 1918 parity with the Danish krona.[15] The first 80 years of this currency experiment, therefore, yielded rather dismal results.

The CBI did not emerge as a distinct institution until 1961, more than 40 years into Iceland's sovereignty and the ISK's status as an independent currency. Central banking functions in the new state were handled first by a Danish commercial bank, Islandsbanki, which issued money insured by gold, as most central banks did at the time. In 1926, the rights to issue money were transferred to another retail bank, the state-owned Landsbanki. Both these banks had made too much use of the printing press. They were essentially retail banks vulnerable to the temptation of freshly minted money, which contributed to instability in the balance of payment at the time.

---

[13] Thorsteinsson, Thorsteinn. (1928). *Island under og efter verdenskrigen. En økonomisk oversigt.* (*Iceland during and after the World War. An economic overview*). Copenhagen: G. E. C. Gads Forlag.

[14] One generation later a new war severed the last tie to Denmark. British troops had occupied Iceland from 1940 to 1942, when US troops relieved them. In 1944, with the war turning in the Allies' favor, Iceland unilaterally resigned from its allegiance with still-occupied Denmark, and declared herself a republic.

[15] See the discussion in Chapter 1 of: Ásgeir Jónsson, Sigurður Jóhannesson, Valdimar Ármann, Brice Benaben & Stefaniu Perucci. (2012). *Nauðsyn eða val? Verðtrygging, vextir og verðbólga á Íslandi. (Necessity or choice? Indexation, interests and inflation in Iceland)*. Reykjavík: Icelandic Financial Services Association.

However, a new and separate central bank faced a number of its own challenges. First, political party representatives dominated the bank's supervisory board and made interest rate decisions. The board seldom, if ever, saw the need to raise interest rates, no matter how inflation behaved; the result of this, along with other factors, was a significantly negative turn in real deposit rates. The bank's governor, Jóhannes Nordal, somewhat compensated for this restriction on the bank's policy instruments by applying reserve requirements in order to remove money from circulation. This meant that the banks had to submit 20–30 % of their deposits to the CBI.[16] By applying reserve requirements, the CBI could control lending in the banking system and keep the balance of payments in equilibrium.

This approach worked only during a limited time period, between 1961 and 1971. Thereafter, the CBI was forced to lend out again the funds it had set aside from the banks. Among other things, the CBI had to finance the treasury and provide 'foundation sectors' with production credit at low interest rates. This rendered the reserve requirements meaningless, and turned them into what some bankers and economists sarcastically referred to as 'flow requirements': the CBI took money out of circulation and then redistributed it to the economy on political premises.[17] This effectively changed the reserve requirement from a stability-enhancing tool to an expansionary one. It also created a channel through which the government could put large amounts of money into circulation. Doubtlessly, it played a very large role in the runaway inflation of the 1970s and 1980s.[18]

However, inflation would mostly subside after economic reforms in 1990s (it did remain higher than in other nations, or about 4–5 %

---

[16] Guðnason, Eiríkur. (1989). Bindiskylda. (Reserve requirement). Fjármálatíðindi, pp. 15–26. http://www.sedlabanki.is/library/Skraarsafn/Fjármálatíðindi/Gömul-

[17] For a further discussion of the application of reserve requirements see: Guðnason, Eiríkur. (1989). Bindiskylda. (Reserve requirement). Fjármálatíðindi, pp. 15–26. http://www.sedlabanki.is/library/Skraarsafn/Fjármálatíðindi/Gömul-Fjármálatíðindi/Fjármálatíðindi%201989%20jan%20-%20apr.pdf

[18] Ásgeir Jónsson, Sigurður Jóhannesson, Valdimar Ármann, Brice Benaben & Stefaniu Perucci. (2012). Nauðsyn eða val? Verðtrygging, vextir og verðbólga á Íslandi. (Necessity or choice? Indexation, interests and inflation in Iceland). Reykjavík: Icelandic Financial Services Association.

on average on annual basis). By 2003, however, a great deal had changed. Interest rates were liberalized in 1984–1985, and in 1998 the interbank market was modernized. After these measures, the CBI could apply open market operations to determine the policy rate, and thereby control the economy.

This was the setting on February 28, 2003, when the CBI announced that Icelandic depository institutions' reserve requirements would be lowered in two stages during the year, from 4 % to 2 % of deposits. The official reason for the reduction was to create "an operating environment comparable to that in most European countries"[19] (where 2 % reserves were standard). In the CBI Monetary Bulletin, published earlier that February, the effects of this measure were summed up in a single sentence: "The planned reduction in required reserves will also imply some relaxation of the monetary stance."[20] That proved to be a huge understatement.

The permanent reduction of reserve requirements in February 2003 was doubtless viewed by many as the last farewell wave to old times, when management of the price of money – interest rates – took over from management of the money supply. But the timing was exceptionally unfortunate. The main reason for this is that the supply of money in circulation is composed largely of banking system deposits. It is not only that lower reserve requirements would free up a modest sum of money (in this case about 20 billion ISK) for new lending; according to classical economic theory, the money multiplier should double, which in turn should double the stock of broad money (M3). This is indeed what happened in the three years following the halving of the reserve requirement, as can be seen in Fig. 8.2. Measured as the ratio of M3 over the monetary base (M0), the money multiplier doubled from 10 to 20 before giving in again during the financial crisis.

---

[19] The change was made in two increments. In the former, on 28 February 2003, the reserve requirement ratio was reduced to 3 %, and in the latter, on 2 December 2003, it was reduced to 2 %. For further information, see the Central Bank press release of 28 February 2003.

[20] See p. 2. of: Central Bank of Iceland (2003, February). *Peningamál 2003/1. (Monetary Bulletin 2003/1).*

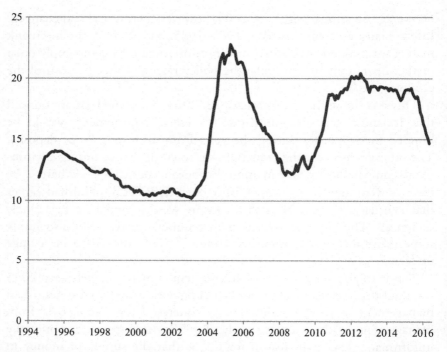

Fig. 8.2 The money multiplier in Iceland measured as the ratio of M3 over M0 from 1994 to 2016, monthly numbers filtered as a 12-month moving average (Source: Central Bank of Iceland)

The banks got more than increased ISK for lending; the new funding also came on favorable terms. The reason is simple: the funding costs of deposit institutions are largely a fixed derivative from the branch network, payment systems, and so forth. Yet the interest on demand deposits is low. Therefore, if the stock of banking system liquidity grows because of systemic changes, such as the multiplier effect of lower reserve requirements, the average cost of deposit institutions' funding declines because new capital flows in at very low marginal cost, boosting profit margins or leading to lower loan rates.[21]

---

[21] This is a standard feature of any textbook model of retail banking; see e.g., Freixas, Xavier and Rochet, Jean-Charles. (2008). *Microeconomics of Banking*. MIT Press.

In the authors' opinion, this measure was one of the key enabling factors behind the Icelandic banks' ability to increase their lending in ISK from 2004 onwards and compete with the government-owned Housing Financing Fund (HFF) in the mortgage market (see Chap. 4). Kaupthing, in particular, took advantage of these conditions.

8.3   The Love Letters

At 2 p.m. on April 25, 2008, Jean-Claude Trichet, the governor of the ECB, called the CBI "upset." He said that the Icelandic banks had €4 billion outstanding with collateral that was "abnormal, artificial."[22] By convention, central banks accept A-rated securities as collateral in their repo lending. All the three banks had credit ratings from international agencies, and all of them could issue bonds meeting the ECB's collateral requirements. They were prohibited from using their own bonds as collateral, but they could circumvent that restriction by just plain swapping and pledging each other's bonds to obtain liquidity from the ECB's vaults. They did this through their subsidiaries in Luxembourg after the international funding had closed at the onset of the financial crisis in the fall of 2007. Moreover, these freshly issued bonds often bore an interest premium well below their CDS spreads in the international financial markets. Through these channels, they could obtain the much-needed euros for their funding.

However, the ECB would not have it. Ultimately it was agreed that the Icelandic banks would only be permitted to submit unsecured bank bonds for 40 % of their total collateral with the ECB. The banks then began to consider covered bonds and other asset-backed bonds for use in transactions with the ECB, but that is another story.[23]

The banks would, on the other hand, continue to swap bonds to obtain freshly printed ISK from the CBI. To this end, they would often use smaller financial institutions – such as Icebank, VBS, or Saga Capital – as

---

[22] Special Investigation Commission. (2010). *Report of the Special Investigation Commission.* Volume 2, p. 47.

[23] See the report by the Parliamentary Special Investigation Commission: Background to and causes of the collapse of Iceland's banks in 2008 and related events, Chapter 7, pp. 45–48.

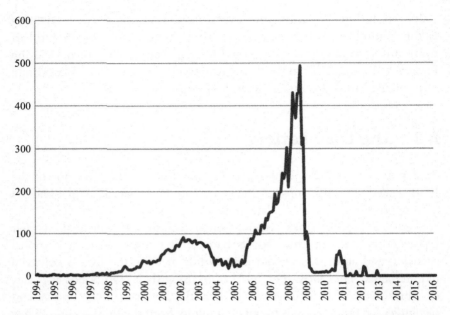

Fig. 8.3 Outstanding Repo loans at the CBI from 1994 to 2016 in billion ISK (Source: Central Bank of Iceland)

intermediaries in their collateralised lending activities. They did this by issuing bonds and delivering them to the small firms, which then posted them as collateral in repo transactions with the CBI. This can be seen, for instance, in Icebank – an institution with about ISK 10 billion in equity. Icebank had an ISK 200 billion loan from the CBI, backed by bank bonds, at the time of the crash. In October 2008, the gross position of CBI repo lending was about €3.3 billion (500 billion ISK), of which €2.3 billion (345 billion ISK) was secured by the banks' unsecured bonds, which now usually are referred to as 'love letters' (Fig. 8.3).[24]

The Parliamentary Special Investigation Commission issued a report on the prelude to and causes of the 2008 banking collapse. It describes the

---

[24] The name can be attributed to then-current Central Bank Governor Davíð Oddsson. See the report by the Parliamentary Special Investigation Commission: Background to and causes of the collapse of Iceland's banks in 2008 and related events, Chapter 19, p. 282.

CBI's lending against love letters as collateral as follows: "The Central Bank's willingness to accept the banks' bonds and bills as collateral entailed a transfer of money printing authority to the banking system."[25] This is correct in and of itself. But the same judgment can doubtless be passed on most Western central banks, which during the current financial crisis have printed money to fund banking institutions at unprecedented levels. This is the equivalent of handing them the keys to the mint, but it also means that central bankers have been working overtime, printing money at the banks' request and easing requirements concerning the quality of collateral, lengthening loan agreements, and so forth. The ECB, for instance, provides European banks with long-term collateralized funding through its so-called long-term refinancing operation (LTRO) program, in which it lends for up to three years.[26] This has prevented large banking institutions from becoming insolvent, which would automatically have resulted in loan losses for the central bank.

However, when lending out to commercial banks, a central bank is in the same capacity as any other lender, and it has to take the loss from the default. That is what happened in Iceland in 2008 when the three banks failed and the collateral they had placed to CBI – their own bonds – became claims on a default estate. In fact, the CBI lending counted as wholesale lending, and thus the prioritization of deposits stipulated by the emergency legislation would actually lower the value of its claims, as was the case for all other general creditors.

The principal amount of the CBI's collateralized loans backed by love letters totalled ISK 345 billion (€2.5 billion). The depreciation requirement deriving from these loans was estimated at ISK 250 billion; therefore, their value was assessed at ISK 95 billion, in light of recoveries from the failed banks' estates. But the CBI entered a write-off of only ISK 75 billion on the loans, and at year-end 2008 it sold them to the treasury for ISK 270 billion. This numbers game was meant to prevent the CBI's equity from turning negative. Immediately after the purchase, the treasury

<hr>

[25] See the report by the Parliamentary Special Investigation Commission: Background to and causes of the collapse of Iceland's banks in 2008 and related events, Chapter 4, p. 166.
[26] See the summary of the ECB's collateralized lending on the bank's website: https://www.ecb.europa.eu/mopo/implement/omo/html/index.en.html

wrote the claims down by ISK 175 billion, which represented the difference between purchase price and assessed value.[27]

The Icelandic treasury paid for the purchase of the CBI's collateralized loans by issuing a bond in the amount of ISK 270 billion (€1.8 billion). The bond was indexed, bore 2.5 % interest, and matured on January 1, 2014.[28] Before the maturity date came, it was extended by exactly one year, and the terms were amended. The indexation clause was removed, and the interest rate was determined based on the rate on credit institutions' current accounts with the CBI. In the fiscal budget proposal for 2014, it was assumed that the bond's maturity would be stretched to 20 years at no interest, but this was amended during parliamentary handling. But at year-end 2014, the bond was extended again, this time for 29 years, although now it was to be paid down in equal annual installments over that period.

In February 2010, the claims due to the collateralized loans were sold back to the CBI and based on the balance at year-end 2009. They were assessed at ISK 93 billion. At the same time, the treasury sold the CBI other collateralized loan claims that it had acquired in the wake of the crisis, for ISK 41 billion. The sales proceeds therefore totalled ISK 134 billion; this amount was used to pay down the CBI bond. As of year-end 2009, the accrued indexation on the bond totalled ISK 23 billion, so that after the sale, the bond principal-plus-indexation totalled ISK 159 billion.[29]

---

[27] The statistical information on which this discussion is based has been taken from the Central Bank of Iceland's Annual Reports from 2012 to 2014; the June 2012 report by the Icelandic National Audit Office on government facilities for financial institutions in the wake of the financial collapse; the Minister of Finance and Economic Affairs' response to Elsa Lára Arnardóttir on the government's interest expense on loans to rescue the financial system (144th legislative session, Parliamentary Document 646 – Case no. 362); and Government Debt Management's Market Information report from January 2015.

[28] Icelandic State Audit. (2012, June). *Report to the Icelandic Parliament. The Governments Facilitation to Financial Companies and Institutions in the Wake of the Banking Crisis. p. 22.*

[29] Since then, five payments have been made on the principal of the bond: ISK 7.4 billion in 2012, 4.8 billion in 2013, 26 billion in 2014, 50 billion in 2015 and 25 billion in early 2016. The payment in 2015 took place with the reduction of Central Bank capital by the same amount and the payment in 2016 was made with proceeds from the stability contributions. After the payment in 2016 the outstanding balance of the bond was ISK 65 billion. (Central Bank of Iceland, Annual Reports 2012–2015).

Now, what is the monetary meaning of a central bank suffering a loss when supplying liquidity to commercial banks? First, one has to look at the meaning of repo lending in general.

A central bank's lending activity is extremely important for retail banks, which fund themselves with deposits that are by and large available for withdrawal at any time. They also lend that money out as long-term loans. This is done with the certainty that withdrawals and deposits to accounts largely cancel each other out, so that the stock of liquidity in deposit accounts remains relatively constant. The fact is that conventional payments made between parties merely transfer funds from one account to another, and do not remove them from the banking system. Deposit institutions thereby insure individuals' liquidity positions in a manner similar to insurance companies covering customers from accident losses. The people can put their money in safe storage while still having unrestricted access to it at any time.

However, the paradox behind liquidity insurance is that the bank has promised its customers that their deposits will always be available for withdrawal, even though they have actually been tied up in long-term assets that cannot be sold, except perhaps at substantial discounts. As a result, retail banks are always vulnerable to a run on deposits if they lose their customers' trust. The first-come-first-serve rule applies to bank withdrawals, and no one wants to come late to a bank run. Therefore, theoretically, if enough depositors demand their money at the same time, even sound banks with solid asset portfolios could fail.

Walter Bagehot's *Lombard Street* (published 1873) is still relevant to discussions of how central banks should conduct themselves as lenders of last resort.[30] Both a banker and an editor of *The Economist*, Bagehot was one of the most influential intellectuals of the Victorian period. *Lombard Street* contains "Bagehot's dictum," which describes how central banks should perform their role as lenders of last resort:

---

[30] Now, however, it is generally conceded that the last-resort lending theory attributed to Bagehot was first introduced in 1797, by Francis Baring, in a book entitled *Observations on the Establishment of the Bank of England*.

Lend freely to temporary illiquid but nonetheless solvent banks at a penalty rate and on good collateral.

Bagehot's dictum is therefore twofold:

(a) Central banks should always lend without restriction to commercial banks in liquidity difficulties, so long as the banks are operable and can offer sound collateral.
(b) The loans should only be temporary and should be granted at a premium on market rates so as to ensure that banks only approach the central bank as a last resort.

Readers should note, however, that the central bank upon which Bagehot based his theory – the Bank of England – was privately owned in his day. At that time, no deposit insurance or any other government guarantee had been given to banking institutions. In the twentieth century, profound changes occurred in central bank operations. Repo transactions with commercial banks became commonplace. The interest rates on these transactions came to be used as policy instruments to achieve various macroeconomic objectives (concerning employment, GDP growth, and inflation), as is widely seen today.[31] However, the actual last-resort loans to distressed banks developed into loans granted without sound collateral, below market rates, and often in collaboration with government authorities. This shift is due to a variety of factors, but the intertwining of government and banking operations certainly helps to explain direct government deposit guarantees and indirect state guarantees of systemically important banks deemed too-big-to-fail.[32] That infamous designation concerns printing and taxation authority in connection with rescue operations for banks.

Thus the task of the lender of last resort was to print money in response to banks' liquidity problems only after all other options had been exhausted. And this money printing was supposed to be a temporary

---

[31] O'Brien, Denis, (2003), The Lender-of-Last-Resort Concept in Britain, History of Political Economy, 35, issue 1, pp. 1–19

[32] Bullard, James, (2009), The Fed as lender of last resort, The Regional Economist, issue Jan.

and recoverable measure, where money was lent to the banks against sound collateral. It is also the case that with collateralized lending, the central bank is not increasing the net asset position of the financial system but merely changing the banks' asset composition. Actually, it can be said that central banks function as a sort of maturity transformer for commercial banks' balance sheets – that is, they give banks the option of shortening maturities on the asset side by placing long-term assets with the central bank as collateral and receiving money in return. Then, when things improve and the commercial banks have regained access to other funding, they are supposed to return the money to the central bank and recover their collateral.[33]

A central bank's equity is not directly comparable to the equity of conventional companies or other banks. Technically, it is not necessary that it be positive: a central bank can actually operate for an unlimited period of time with negative equity. A central bank's liabilities are primarily banknotes and reserves, which never fall due, and it can pay any other domestic liabilities by increasing reserves. But in order to maintain the credibility of the currency it issues, a central bank's equity does need to stay positive to maintain confidence that the value of the currency will not be eroded by excessive or empty increases in the money supply.

The loan losses suffered by the CBI at the default of the three banks reflected the baseless money printing – the so-called helicopter drop – entailed in collateralized loans backed by love letters. When the bond has been paid off, and the CBI has recovered the portion of the collateralized loans released when distributions from the failed banks' estates are made, this money printing, theoretically, is largely reversed. Therefore, it is clear that the money the treasury received upon the settlement of the estates, whether through taxation or other direct or indirect methods, should be used first to pay off the CBI bond, thereby reducing the money supply. However, one could also question the meaning of baseless money printing.

---

[33] Grossman, Richard and Rockoff, Hugh, (2015), Fighting the Last War: economists on the lender of last resort, Departmental Working Papers, Rutgers University, Department of Economics.

8.4   Helicopter Drops and the Bernanke Doctrine

Modern money is called fiat money. The government authority has decreed it to be a standard of value and controls its supply, but does not guarantee its value in other respects. Sometimes it is perceived as being intrinsically valueless, since it has no collateral to back it up. This situation gives governments a certain incentive to print money to finance state expenditures. Such money printing is what Milton Friedman called, in 1969, a "helicopter drop," since it is the equivalent of a central bank governor flying over the country and dropping money down to the people. To employ another metaphor, the drop is a white elephant because, although people have more banknotes in hand, output would remain the same. The only thing that would happen would be that prices would rise with the addition of more money to buy the same volume of goods and valuables.[34]

There are countless examples of governments catalyzing runaway inflation by having money printed in order to finance budgetary deficits, thereby proving Friedman's thesis. One of the best-known examples is probably 1920s Germany. The government tried desperately to print money to pay war reparations (see Chap. 5). But effects of the helicopter drop take time to pass through to the price level. The first demonstrable effect is that the public is delighted with its newfound wealth, and feels richer than before with more banknotes in hand. For this reason, unexpected money printing can boost a country's morale for a short time and stimulate the economy by bolstering demand before the higher prices kick

---

[34] Friedman first introduced the 'helicopter drop' in his 1969 book, *The Optimum Quantity of Money*. The following appears on page 4: "Let us suppose, then, that one day a helicopter flies over our hypothetical long-stationary community and drops additional money from the sky equal to the amount already in circulation. . . . The money will, of course, be hastily collected by members of the community. . . . If everyone simply decided to hold on to the extra cash, nothing more would happen. . . . But people do not behave in that way. . . . It is easy to see what the final position will be. People's attempts to spend more than they receive will be frustrated, but in the process these attempts will bid up the nominal value of goods and services. The additional pieces of paper do not alter the basic conditions of the community. They make no additional productive capacity available. . . . Hence, the final equilibrium will be a nominal income [that has doubled] . . . with precisely the same flow of real goods and services as before."

in. It is therefore no surprise that, throughout history, governments often have been duped into printing money to finance campaign promises, or to stimulate the economy just before elections take place. This is just one reason it is considered necessary to prohibit politicians from having access to the printers, unless under strict supervision.

There have generally been two ways to prevent the abuse of money printing. The first was the use precious metals in trade or as a value guarantee. When currencies are minted in precious metals, a nation could simulate a helicopter drop by diluting minted coins with less expensive metals. A direct guarantee of value via tangible assets, such as gold, is known as the gold standard, which was prevalent internationally from the mid-nineteenth century until the onset of the Great Depression.

Such direct guarantees of value have now been largely discontinued for reasons that extend beyond the scope of this book. Currency boards and even unilateral adoption of another currency can be viewed as variations on this theme, but that, too, is another story.

The second way to prevent abuse of money printing is to separate treasury finances from the central bank. Early on, this policy was pursued so sedulously that central bank operations were entrusted to private entities, as was the case with the Bank of England until 1946.[35] The same was true of Iceland's Islandsbanki from its establishment in 1904 until 1927, when money-printing authority was transferred to Landsbanki. In the latter half of the twentieth century, the general practice was to ensure the central bank's operational independence vis-à-vis elected officials, therefore eliminating the incentive to print money in connection with elections. In Iceland, this separation was not achieved until 1993. Until that time, the finance minister had been authorized to issue cheques on the state government's current account with the CBI, and could therefore print money to cover government

---

[35] See for example discussion in Goodfriend, Marvin, (2012), The Elusive Promise of Independent Central Banking, No 12-E-09, IMES Discussion Paper Series, Institute for Monetary and Economic Studies, Bank of Japan. Grossman, Richard and Rockoff, Hugh, (2015), Fighting the Last War: economists on the lender of last resort, Departmental Working Papers, Rutgers University, Department of Economics.

expenditures. This financial separation of the CBI and the central government is doubtless one of the main reasons inflation fell in the 1990s.[36]

As mentioned above, Friedman posits that helicopter drops should have a highly predictable impact on both the price level and the exchange rate of the currency concerned against other currencies. In this he agrees with the classical view of the effects of money printing (see the discussion in Sect. 8.1). But helicopter drops usually deliver other complexities.

Economists' current views of money printing derive mostly from John Maynard Keynes's *The General Theory of Employment, Interest and Money*, published in 1936 in the depths of the Great Depression. Keynes emphasized the role of money in financial markets rather than in goods markets, which had been the main point of reference in classical economics. Money was a separate financial asset with a special role to play. The need for money was created by demand for liquidity, and for this reason money constituted a given share of people's asset portfolios. If a central bank printed money in excess of this demand for liquidity – such as with a helicopter drop – people would try to shift this new money over to other asset classes. In this way, money printing would raise asset prices when people bought other financial assets, including bonds. But as bond prices rise, yields fall. This means that the central bank can lower the nominal interest rate via money printing. This is what Keynes called the liquidity effect: how money printing lowers interest rates. And this is how you could work against economic contraction and deflation – that is, raise asset prices and lower long-term interest rates – with helicopter drops of money.

This Keynesian view of monetary economics was restated in a now-famous speech given by Ben Bernanke – then newly appointed to Board of Governors at the Fed – on November 21, 2002, at the US National Economists Club. In this speech, Bernanke sketched out what the US Federal Reserve Bank could do to prevent deflation in the unlikely event that the Fed's policy rate fell to zero. The 9/11 terrorist attacks had

---

[36] See the discussion in Chapter 1 of: Ásgeir Jónsson, Sigurður Jóhannesson, Valdimar Ármann, Brice Benaben & Stefaniu Perucci. (2012). *Nauðsyn eða val? Verðtrygging, vextir og verðbólga á Íslandi. (Necessity or choice? Indexation, interests and inflation in Iceland)*. Reykjavík: Icelandic Financial Services Association.

exacerbated fears of economic downturn that began with the dot-com bubble bursting; when Bernanke spoke, some anticipated a severe crisis at hand. Bernanke maintained that as long as a country used fiat money, it would always be possible to prevent deflation by making helicopter drops and allowing the central bank to finance new government expenditures or tax cuts.[37]

American pundits dubbed Bernanke "Helicopter Ben," but the ridicule has long since faded. Now the speech is considered foundational to the "Bernanke doctrine," which outlines how money printing can lower long-term interest rates and raise asset prices, thereby catalyzing an economic recovery. Bernanke gained the chairmanship in February 2006 and took his own theories into action during next financial crisis, which struck little more than a year later.

8.5   The Different Meaning of Money in Small Currency Areas

Sir John Maynard Keynes placed a very strong emphasis on money demand in his magnum opus, *The General Theory of Employment, Interest and Money*. By his analysis, demand for liquidity was determined by three factors: (A) the demand for transactions – i.e., financial transactions must take place if goods or assets are to be bought and sold; (B) precautionary demand, as liquid assets are secure assets and always available for use if needed; and (C) speculative demand, as the main advantage of money as an asset class is that there is no need to fear a fall in value owing to market activity, unlike stocks and bonds, which can rise or fall in price. There are two basic predictions that can be made from this theory.

---

[37] Bernanke's statement in the speech was as follows, verbatim: "A broad-based tax cut, for example, accommodated by a program of open-market purchases to alleviate any tendency for interest rates to increase, would almost certainly be an effective stimulant to consumption and hence to prices. Even if households decided not to increase consumption but instead re-balanced their portfolios by using their extra cash to acquire real and financial assets, the resulting increase in asset values would lower the cost of capital and improve the balance sheet positions of potential borrowers. A money-financed tax cut is essentially equivalent to Milton Friedman's famous 'helicopter drop' of money." See: http://www.federalreserve.gov/boarddocs/Speeches/2002/20021121/

First, with stable liquidity preferences, demand for money should be proportionate to the stock of other assets. People like to keep a certain fraction of their wealth in liquid funds. Thus, the increase in wealth would lead an automatic demand increase for money.

Second, greater pessimism and/or greater uncertainty will lead to an increased money demand, which among other things ensures that money printing during times of hardship does not have the inflationary effect predicted by classical economics.[38]

These two predictions generally held true in Iceland, and they help explain how the money stock could quadruple without leading to hyper-inflation. Between 2003 and 2007, share prices on the Iceland Stock Exchange rose exponentially, and shareholders accrued enormous wealth out of virtually nothing, as always happens during financial bubbles. The bank stocks, which dominated the Icelandic stock market, the ICEX, are a good example. From 2003 to mid-year 2007, Glitnir's stock increased six-to sevenfold in value, Kaupthing's stock by a factor of 10 and Landsbanki's stock by a factor of 11. At the peak, in July 2007, the market value of listed shares on the exchange was about ISK 3000 billion (€20 billion), nearly twice Iceland's GDP at the time. All that increase in wealth undoubtedly increased the demand for liquid balances.

However, by August 2007, the situation reversed completely as the stock market was subject to a drastic selloff. By the end of 2007, the market value of ICEX shares had fallen by half, to around ISK 1500 billion (€10 billion). The dive in stock price and a barrage of bad news from abroad led to a steep rise in liquidity demand – in other words, people sought a higher ratio of their total wealth in secure liquid funds. Thus investors would flee to safety by selling risky assets (like stocks) and deposit the proceeds in deposit accounts with the banks. The spike in the commercial banks' liquidity demand influenced the CBI's decision to ease the collateral requirements for loan facilities in January 2008. As discussed in Chap. 3, the banks used these liquidity facilities from the CBI

---

[38] Increased demand for liquidity surfaces as a reduction in velocity (V) in the classical money equation $MV=PY$, which means that the liquidity position of the economy increases and an increase in M does not emerge as an increase in P. Then Keynes assumed also that interest was the "reward for parting with liquidity" and that lowering interest rates would cause a decline in velocity, as it would be less costly for people to own liquid assets.

to grant loans to various holding companies, which then purchased the banks' shares so as to absorb the massive selling pressure that had developed. And with the love letter transactions and the banks' loans to holding companies (backed by their own shares), an escape route appeared, through which stock gains could be converted into deposits or exported off the island. The substantial supply of money in circulation can therefore be viewed as the remains of the financial bubble that have been converted into government-guaranteed deposits. This situation, plus the residue from the carry trade – the ISK 650 billion offshore overhang – subsequently necessitated the introduction of the capital controls.

As the crisis subsided in Iceland, the demand for liquidity among Icelandic investors tapered off as well. Because foreign investment was prohibited, the only way skittish investors could dispose of their money was to buy domestic assets. Initially, this led to a sharp rise in bond prices and a drop in long-term interest rates, followed by a rise in share prices and then a rise in real estate prices from 2011 onwards.

Therefore, it can be said that the Bernanke doctrine concerning QE measures worked in Iceland under the aegis of the capital controls, and the huge supply of money in circulation led to economic recovery concurrent with falling long-term interest rates and rising asset prices. On the other hand, if the currency market had been open, huge capital outflows would have led to exchange rate depreciation and inflation: the basic classical prediction of excessive money printing.

Nevertheless, at the time of the crash, de novo entities with a massive demand for liquidity appeared in the Icelandic financial market: the failed banks' estates. Naturally, the estates' objective was to convert their assets to liquid funds that they would then distribute to creditors. Thereafter, the domestic assets of the estates and their subsidiaries – the new banks – were sold to domestic investors for liquid assets that sat in the new banks as deposits and excess capital. This is actually nothing more than a shift of the money stock to the estates, not money creation. One can think of the estates as sponges that sopped up the excess liquidity from the Icelandic financial markets in the anticipation that it would be subsequently distributed to creditors.

As stated above, Friedman believed that helicopter drops would increase inflation, as more and more money would be chasing after the same volume of goods and assets. Implied in this analysis is the idea that the exchange rate of the currency concerned would fall in the wake of the drop, which would increase its supply above and beyond that of other currencies.

But this is not entirely the case for large currency areas, and particularly not for reserve currencies such as the US dollar, the pound sterling, the euro, and the Swiss franc. These currencies have value the world over. When money is printed in reserve currencies, it seeks out assets both within the currency area concerned and around the rest of the world. As a result, it is difficult to dilute reserve currencies, even when large amounts are printed, as other countries are glad to accept them in exchange for both goods and assets, and they automatically create their own demand among other countries as a store of value.

The fact is that large currency areas can print money more or less unhesitatingly, without concern that it will create a balance of payments problem. The exchange rate effects exist, however. The application of the Bernanke doctrine in the USA led, for instance, to a depreciation of the US dollar during the first years of the crisis, and the ECB's plans in the same vein have likewise led to a depreciation of the euro in the recent term. These two currency areas were delighted with the depreciation, as it enhanced the competitive position of their exporters and stimulated the economy. But depreciation is not the same thing as a currency crisis.

What is new about the financial crisis of 2008 is that it has affected the largest and most powerful currency areas of the world, which have for long been considered free from such problems. Exactly the same developments had taken place in smaller and weaker currency areas, exhibited by the Nordic banking crisis of 1991–1993, the Tequila crisis in Latin America in 1994, and the Asian crisis of 1997–1998. In each case, a flight of capital and imbalances in the balance of payments led to a currency and banking crisis. The underlying causes of course were an asset bubble, imprudent lending, and excessive domestic demand. The disease is the same, but the symptoms vary by the currency area.

The long-term effects of money printing are also uncertain, as the quantitative easing that has been pursued has few historical precedents. The obvious example is Japan's financial crisis in 1990–1992, which followed an asset bubble and banking expansion. The Japanese yen is a reserve currency and therefore the government could print money to keep the financial system afloat and avoid the pain of rapid economic integration. But the result has been dismal, to say the least. The period 1991–2000 is known as Japan's lost decade; in recent assessments, the malaise has been extended to 2010 and thus represents two lost decades. During all that time, the Japanese economy has been stagnant.[39]

Iceland does not enjoy reserve currency privileges. The ISK has value only in Iceland, and printing money in excess of the domestic need must result in depreciation when the newly printed domestic currency finds its way into the foreign exchange market. In a small currency area, the exchange rate effects of a helicopter drop will always be extremely strong; domestic investors will always want to hold a significant amount of foreign assets in their portfolios. The large-scale money printing of 2004–2008, and the nearly fourfold increase in the money stock over these four years, was bound to lead to massive outflows through the foreign exchange market, ultimately giving rise to the need for the capital controls. This is the money 'pollutant' mentioned in the beginning of this chapter.

8.6   Deposit Funding as a Currency Risk

Helicopter drops aside, the money supply has a dual nature that leads to some confusion and misunderstanding. We can view the money supply both as people's liquid assets, as is done above, and as deposits on the liabilities side of banking institutions' balance sheets. Generally, people store their liquid assets as deposits with banks; the dual nature of the supply is more theoretical. Economists usually look at it in terms of liquid assets, while financial and banking personnel tend to see it in terms of bank liabilities.

---

[39] Lupu, Radu and Calin, Adrian Cantemir, (2014), To QE or Not to QE? The Japanese Experience, *Hyperion Economic Journal*, 2, issue 2, pp. 3–10.

The accepted wisdom among bankers has long been that equity and deposits are the best funding sources available to them. This is true, but only up to a certain point. By their very nature, deposits are extremely short-term funds, as they are always available for withdrawal either on demand or at very short notice. Heavy reliance on deposits for funding always creates the risk of a bank run. Therefore, substantial deposit-based funding can be extremely risky for banks that are vulnerable to loss of credibility, whether such problems stem from the bank itself, the financial system of which it is a part, or the currency area where it operates. Whatever the cause, as soon as credibility is compromised, deposits will begin to flow out of the bank and jeopardize its operations. It is partly for this reason that the authorities in most economies have adopted deposit insurance, which paves the way for central banks to offer liquidity facilities to banks. When deposits are said to represent stable funding, it is apparently assumed that they are government-guaranteed and the central bank can function as a lender of last resort.

Banks are little more than a collection of customers' accounts. The transactions of the customers appear as transfers between accounts within the bank or as netted transfers with other banks. Therefore, foreign exchange markets are by nature interbank markets, in the sense that the transactions always take place between banking institutions. It is no wonder, then, that in small, open economies with independent currencies, balance of payments problems appear simultaneously in the foreign exchange market and the capital market. The reason is simple: When there are net outflows, money flows from accounts with domestic financial institutions through the foreign exchange market to foreign financial institutions. Currency depreciation is a certainty when the newly printed money finds its way to the foreign exchange market in search of an exit route. If a country is part of a larger currency area, there is no need to fear a currency crisis. But the balance of payments still retains its significance: a deficit – whether in the form of a current account deficit or capital flight – causes liquidity to drain out of the financial system instead of a currency depreciation. It is therefore clear that substantial deposit funding poses a risk to the balance of payments, especially in smaller economies.

Somewhat paradoxically, the currency market can provide protection against financial flight for banks in small open economies. The capital

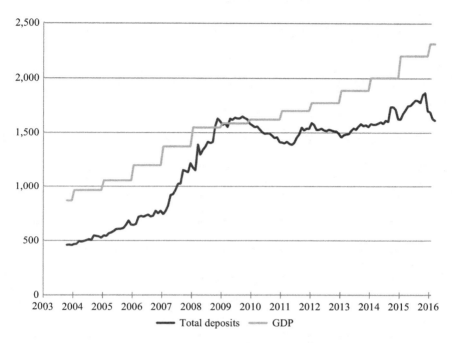

Fig. 8.4 Total deposits and GDP in Iceland from 2003 to 2016, nominal values in billions of ISK (Source: Central Bank of Iceland)

outflows lead to currency depreciation, which automatically imposes haircuts on those wanting to flee with their money. Usually, the currency market will close or just crash into abysmal pricing before the banks run out of domestic liquidity. Therefore, it is possible to look at the banking system as a threat to the currency market in small open economies.

The conditions require watchful consideration in Iceland. Based on the assets side of their balance sheets, some 40 % of the old banks' funding came from deposits and equity. With the new banks, the figure rose to around 80–90 %. As can be seen from Fig. 8.4, the enlarged deposit base was in fact created during the monetary expansion from 2003 to 2008; money is, by definition, deposits.

As the situation is now, the banks' strong capital position provides some level of credibility for the security of deposits. The new banks' capital ratio is in the 26–30 % range, which is astronomical in an international context. It is very difficult to achieve acceptable returns on such a large amount of capital. Actually, the banks are overcapitalized; therefore, this capital will be taken out in the form of dividends. Therefore, it is difficult to view all of this capital as a lasting source of equity funding; most of it is only temporary, and will be so until the banks change hands.[40]

Of course, the same risk applies to countries within the same currency area. The euro crisis provides instructive examples. Within the euro area, money can be transferred from one corner to the other at a constant value, and thus the financial systems of individual countries can practically be emptied out. Countries on the periphery – especially the economically weaker PIIGS countries (Portugal, Italy, Ireland, Greece, and Spain) – have had steep deficits in their balance of payments because capital has fled from those countries to the security of the center, in Germany. The ECB has responded to this capital flight with massive lending to banking institutions, and by buying government bonds issued by countries facing refinancing problems. Through this intervention in the capital market, the ECB has tried to keep the balance of payments in the affected countries in equilibrium so as to prevent the outflows from dragging them down into a banking crisis and economic recession.

Of course, central banks representing large, globally traded currencies are in a much better position to respond to a balance of payments problem. They can simply print money as liquidity support for financial institutions and plug the holes in the balance of payments without strongly affecting the foreign exchange market. The smaller ones are very poorly equipped to support their banking systems, where liquidity facilities are conducive to increasing outflows from the balance of payments and placing the domestic currency in even greater difficulties. The foreign exchange reserves could be totally depleted very quickly in a currency or defensive banking manoeuvre. Furthermore, such interventions

---

[40] As of year-end 2014, Íslandsbanki could pay out ISK 67 billion, Arion Bank ISK 45 billion, and Landsbankinn ISK 80 billion without reducing their capital ratios to below 20 %. The banks all paid dividends in 2015: Íslandsbanki ISK 9 billion, Arion Bank ISK13 billion, and Landsbankinn ISK 24 billion.

are often seen as signs of weakness, and as such can exacerbate capital flight or serve as a beacon for speculators.

There are other ways to look at the money supply. By the quantity equation, the ratio of the money supply to GDP is the inverse of velocity (1/V), which is a well-known measure of financial depth and how developed a financial system is.[41] As can be seen from Fig. 8.4, the quadrupling of the money supply took the ratio of M3 to GDP from about 40–50 % to about 110 %, from which level it has slowly declined in the years that have passed since the crisis.

Perhaps it should come as no surprise if the above ratio is elevated permanently in the twenty-first century, given the rapid advances in the Icelandic financial system. On the other hand, it can be argued that such a huge increase over a relatively short time horizon, coinciding with a banking expansion, only indicates the remnants of an asset bubble. Sooner or later, the remnant will pass into the real economy, with the usual consequences.

As Fig. 8.5 shows, Iceland's money supply was usually around 40 % of GDP during the twentieth century. Two periods stand out, however. The first is World War II. During the war, the German blockade restricted the scope of consumption goods imports. But foreign deposits kept accumulating in the UK when domestic ships sold fish in the ports of Hull and Grimsby. Thus, the blockade led to a forced increase in money demand, as there were no goods to purchase, and people just kept their money on bank accounts while waiting for the war to end. Furthermore, the island was occupied by tens of thousands of British and American troops, who, at the insistence of the Icelandic authorities, were paid in ISK. These two factors combined to increase the money supply to 80–90 % of GDP, but only during the war years. As soon as the war was over and external trade opened up again, the accumulated money supply was fodder for economic expansion and inflation, which then led to an alarming current account deficit and renewed capital controls. Subsequently, the real value of the money supply burned down to the previous level of about 40 % of GDP in a relatively short timespan.

---

[41] See, for example, Levine, R. (1997). Financial Development and Economic Growth: Views and Agenda. *Journal of Economic Literature*, XXXV, 688–726.

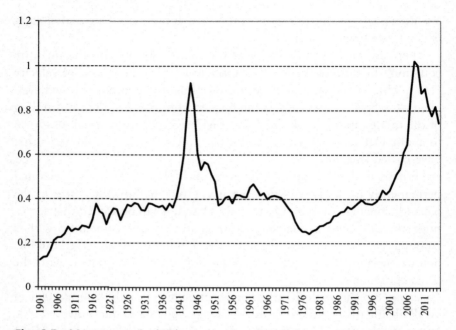

Fig. 8.5 Money supply (M3) as a ratio of GDP from 1900 to the present (Source: Central Bank of Iceland)

All of this creates three kinds of worries. First, the banks simply contain too much liquidity, which presents constant danger to the currency market should a run begin. Second, given the elevated equity ratios and high level of liquidity, the banks have an enormous capability to create money via their own lending and the money multiplier. Thus the stability contributions should be viewed not just as a reverse QE, but also a way to slim down the banking system and its ability to create liquidity.

In discussions of the transfer problem, emphasis is often placed on foreign ownership. It is correct that non-residents' short-term positions create risk in the foreign exchange market, as they generally try to go back home en masse with their money if any turbulence arises. However, domestic investors can flee the country just as quickly if the mood strikes them. In the case of short-term capital, the distinction between foreign and domestic ownership, or between foreign and domestic currency composition, is not of decisive significance. What does matter is how much short-term funding exists in the financial system, which could start to move if concerns arise.

In the authors' estimation, given how dependent the new Icelandic banks are on short-term deposit funding, the liabilities side of their balance sheets could be sensitive to capital account liberalization and unrestricted foreign exchange transactions. It is difficult to endorse a complete lift of capital controls unless such restructuring of the liabilities side of the banks' balance sheets has taken place, and the risk of sudden outflows from the balance of payments has been contained. The matter also concerns the credibility of the Icelandic currency area, Icelandic deposit insurance, and the ISK as a store of value, since limited confidence will cause steady capital flight from the country. Clearly, the introduction of capital controls in the autumn of 2008 greatly eroded confidence in the ISK in and of itself. Anyone who owns capital in Iceland, residents and non-residents alike, must still fear being locked in. Rebuilding that confidence is a delicate process, and it can only be accomplished through the application of responsible economic policy over a long period of time.

8.7 The Stability Conditions

In *An Outline of a Resolution*, the authors defined five stability conditions to which distributions from the estates would have to comply in order to prevent the socialization of losses stemming from the transfer problem. They are as follows:

1. It must be possible to accommodate distributions from the insolvent estates within the capital account, and they may not affect capital flows into and out of the country. Thus, foreign trade will not be affected by the settlement of the estates

2. Disposition of the estates' domestic assets may not be allowed to create a risk to the balance of payments after creditors have received payment, i.e. with liquid assets seeking to exit the country or threatening financial stability in some manner. In other words, the extensive ISK holdings of the estates had to be withdrawn from the economy and

accrued by one means or another to the Central Bank (e.g. repayment of the treasury's debts), and thus removed from circulation.

3. Distributions must take place out of the general FX market, so that this market will not be disrupted, e.g. by speculation. Thus, cat-and-mouse games on the FX market would be avoided, as when the creditors decide to transfer them out of the country. It is also worth considering how the arrangements for payment, their timing and other details can be prevented from upsetting the market and prompting speculation.

4. Action must be taken to prevent holdouts before distributions are made. Under present conditions, holdouts could await an opportunity to exit following eventual capital account liberalization. There is no legal framework to prevent holdouts after a deal has been cut with the majority of creditors; they can subsequently appear and demand full satisfaction of their claims.

5. The process must not create legal risk to the treasury. Claims against the banks' estates cannot become claims against the Icelandic nation. There is no chance of financial rebirth for a nation following insolvency or composition with creditors. Countries can refuse to pay their debts, but they do not become bankrupt in the same manner as private parties. The claims exist for as long as the nation in question does. Nation states can also attempt to negotiate with their creditors, but in actuality compositions are scarcely possible.

These conditions could be met either through composition with the estates or through taxation. A composition approved by the required majority of creditors and ratified by an Icelandic court automatically satisfies conditions 4 and 5. Such a composition applies to all creditors and would not result in any subsequent court actions against the treasury.

Satisfying conditions 1–3, however, depends on how prepared general creditors are to dispose of their domestic assets in accordance with such an agreement. The key aspect of such an agreement is probably how ownership of the new banks is provided for, that is, whether the estates will be given the opportunity of realizing their value in foreign currency with a corresponding reduction to the transfer problem.

Taxation can satisfy conditions 1–3 but leaves conditions 4 and 5 in doubt, as such taxation would always be in a legal grey area. In order for taxation to be effected without possible damages, it would have to be aimed precisely at resolving the transfer problem and at no alternative objectives.

As discussed in Chap. 7, the capital controls provided the government with a bargaining position to deal with the creditors of the estates and fix the transfer problem. The hedge funds with primary stakes in the estates had long since seen the writing on the wall and offered the Icelandic authorities – formally and informally – some concession on their ISK holdings. The final outcome at least went a very long towards satisfying all of the five conditions mentioned above.

It is an open question whether the Icelandic government intended to follow through when it announced its plan to impose the stability levy, or whether it was simply a threat. Either way, it is very likely that Prime Minister Gunnlaugsson's steadfast attitude helped creditors to take the announcement seriously.

It is significant to note that after the Panama Papers surfaced in March 2016, it was claimed that Gunnlaugsson's wife was allegedly among the banks' creditors.[42] It was reported that she was involved in an offshore venture called Wintris Inc., which was registered in the British Virgin Islands. Wintris had large claims to all of the old banks' estates, which Gunnlaugsson maintained were acquired at book value before collapse. It appears that the couple had been joint owners of the company, but Gunnlaugsson sold his stake to his wife for $1 on December 31, 2009, just before new legislation took effect.[43] That legislation would have required him to disclose his company at the parliament register of interest. He resigned as prime minster on April 5, after angry protests broke out before the parliament.[44]

---

[42] „Panama Papers: Iceland PM Sigmundur Gunnlaugsson Steps Down" (2016, April) *BBC* News. http://www.bbc.co.uk/news/world-europe-35966412

[43] „Panama Papers: Iceland PM Sigmundur Gunnlaugsson Steps Down" (2016, April) *BBC* News. http://www.bbc.co.uk/news/world-europe-35966412

[44] *Ibid.*

9

A Full Recovery: Fiscal Cost of the Crisis

9.1   To Cut the Link Between the Sovereign and Banks

At 11:19 p.m. on Monday, October 6, 2008, the Icelandic authorities attempted to cut the link between the banks and the sovereign by passing the Emergency Act into law.[1] This was an application of *force majeure* rights as a means to amend laws affecting Iceland's financial institutions.

On September 15, in the fallout from the Lehman bankruptcy, Iceland's perception of its banks had flipped from too-big-to-fail to being too-big-to-save. To save the republic from bankruptcy the only available option was to let the banks fail, or succumb to a bank run. A tall order in any case, it was complicated by a simultaneous blanket guarantee given to all deposits in the banks, regardless of size or holder. At that time, deposits of domestic branches of the banks were around 110 % of Iceland's gross domestic product (GDP) and foreign deposits added

---

[1] Act no. 125/2008 on the authority for treasury disbursements due to special circumstances in financial markets etc.

© The Author(s) 2016
Á. Jónsson, H. Sigurgeirsson, *The Icelandic Financial Crisis*,
DOI 10.1057/978-1-137-39455-2_9

289

another 125 % of the GDP.[2] Furthermore, the authorities also had to establish and capitalize a new banking system. That new banking system would be smaller – with assets around 170 % of GDP – than the old system, which had grown to ten times GDP before the crisis erupted, with assets close to €100 billion. Nevertheless, the fiscal cost was enormous. Furthermore, the three failed banks did not represent the totality of the Icelandic financial system. In 2008, there were 21 savings funds operating in the country with combined assets of about €5 billion and more than half of all outstanding mortgages were issued by the state-owned and guaranteed Housing Financing Fund (HFF). All these institutions would be caught up in the waves generated by the sinking banks, and most would need recapitalization. It was the same for the Central Bank (CBI) itself, which had lent considerable amounts into the financial system against unsecured bank bond issues that had defaulted.

The Icelandic authorities had one big advantage working in their favor: the banks were to a large extent wholesale-funded. The three banks had issued in total around $46 billion in bonds, and the deposit-to-loan ratios of Glitnir, Kaupthing, and Landsbanki were only 28 %, 44 %, and 63 %, respectively. The wholesale funding consisted mostly of senior unsecured bond issues that – by European law – were *pari passu* to deposits, which effectively gave them an implicit government guarantee. The emergency legislation struck this guarantee down by giving deposits priority over other claims to the assets of the failed banks. This effectively amounted to a €10 billion transfer from the bondholders to depositors.

The action opened up a new chapter in European banking history. For the first time in decades the holders of senior unsecured bonds were made to bear the cost of bank insolvencies. The deposit priority allowed the Icelandic authorities to fully cover domestic deposits by transferring them to new banks, along with enough assets to cover them. Covering foreign deposits proved to be a much greater challenge, especially with regard to the Icesave online accounts offered by Landsbanki in the UK and Netherlands. As discussed in Chap. 5, the British and Dutch authorities demanded an Icelandic state guarantee to the maximum of €20,887 for each account

---

[2] Ministry of Finance. (2011, March). *Skýrsla fjármálaráðherra um endurreisn viðskiptabankanna. (Minister of finance report on the restoration of the commercial banks).*

(which totaled about €4 billion or 40–60 % of GDP depending on the value of the ISK). These demands were twice rejected in national referendums, but it was not until January 28, 2013 that a ruling by the EFTA Court cleared Iceland of all claims – leaving the British and Dutch governments with only "first priority claim" on the Landsbanki estate. As it turned out, asset recovery was more than sufficient to pay all priority claims, including the Icesave claim. Landsbanki paid its last priority claim installment on January 11, 2016, thereby closing the claim.

The recapitalization of the banking system required an initial capital contribution of €2.3 billion (see Chap. 3). After negotiations in 2009, the estates of the old banks provided €1 billion of the needed capital. The remaining €1.3 billion came from state coffers in the form of new treasury bond issues that were placed into the new banks. Glitnir and Kaupthing became majority shareholders in the new banks, with a €400 million capital contribution each, leaving the government with a 5 % share in Íslandsbanki and a 13 % in Arion Bank. The Landsbanki estate got a 19 % share in the new Landsbankinn for a capital contribution of €200 million. In addition, the emergency legislation was later used to transfer deposits from about nine savings banks to the three retail banks – leaving only five small rural funds in operation. The buffer between assets and deposits created by both wholesale funding and better than expected asset recovery made it possible in most cases to fully guarantee deposits of all these savings banks without cost to the treasury. There was only one major exception, Keflavík Savings Bank, where a €140 million shortfall between assets and deposits had to be paid directly out of the state purse. The HFF had at the end of 2008 about €4.25 billion in outstanding bonds that were non-callable and government guaranteed. The HFF suffered considerable losses in the wake of the financial crisis (see Sect. 9.4) and has received a roughly €330 million capital injection from the government.

However, recapitalizing the retail and saving banks, as well as the HFF, was not enough to establish a new banking system. The CBI had loaned considerable amounts to the failed banks, taking their own unsecured bonds as collateral, as was discussed in Chap. 8. Once the banks went into bankruptcy these bonds became delinquent (see Chap. 4). Thus, about €1.8 billion in new debt had to be issued the recapitalize the CBI.

Another loose end was the result in a key exception to the Icelandic authorities' intention to cut fiscal links to the banks at the height of the crisis. Having loaned Kaupthing €500 million on the same day the Emergency Act passed, the government had made a futile attempt to save what might have been the last bank standing. The loan was collateralized with the bank's shares in the Danish subsidiary FIH, a wholesale-funded commercial bank. When Kaupthing followed Glitnir and Landsbanki into receivership, FIH became the responsibility of the CBI, which made several attempts to sell it. As elsewhere in Europe, conditions in the Danish wholesale market were difficult in the wake of the financial crisis; FIH became dependent on liquidity support from the Danish Central Bank (DCB). In 2010, FIH was sold at a considerable loss to the CBI.

Fiscal costs in the wake of a crash inevitably result in increased central government debt. Iceland's increased by a staggering 72 % of the GDP between 2007 and 2012 (jumping from 41 % to 113 % of GDP in those years, see Fig. 9.1). The comparison with other well-known crises defines the terrible cost of Iceland's survival. Among other casualties of the 2008

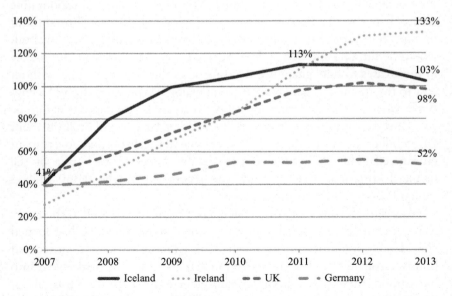

Fig. 9.1 Total central government debt in selected countries, as a percentage of GDP in 2007–2013 (Source: World Bank: World Development Indicators)

upheaval, only Ireland experienced a greater increase in central government debt in the same period (82 % of GDP).

The fiscal cost of a financial crisis can be broadly divided into two categories:

(a) Direct costs relating to equity injections, debt assumed by the state and asset guarantees, as well as (emergency) liquidity support for financial institutions.
(b) Indirect costs, arising from lower tax revenues and higher government spending generated by a crisis-induced recession and loss of output, also including increased interest costs resulting from higher debt levels (and contingent liabilities), and other examples.

Here we will only attempt to estimate the direct fiscal costs of the banking collapse for the Icelandic treasury. The indirect costs are difficult to measure. The GDP of Iceland grew about 30 % between 2003 and 2008 in cumulative terms, but that extraordinary growth was followed by a 10 % contraction from 2009 to 2010. It is very clear that the economy was growing above trend during the years of the boom, which yielded fiscal revenue well in excess of what could be sustained over the long term. Treasury revenues derive in very large part from indirect taxes and turnover-linked fees that rise in line with domestic demand. In the years before the crisis, the treasury received sizeable tax revenues on both the banks' profits and their employees' wages. The booming construction industry, which hired a large number of foreign nationals to work, also contributed robust domestic tax revenues. There had also been very limited fiscal discipline in the years prior to the crash. There is no doubt that the national budget for the 2007 parliamentary election greatly undermined the treasury's foundations, as it provided for tax cuts concurrent with sizeable increases in expenditures. As the collapse in the autumn of 2008 drew nearer, the Icelandic treasury had little debt, but its financial foundations were nonetheless weak. It could in no way cover expenditures unless the financial bubble could be maintained. Thus, the fiscal adjustment, which was carried out under an auspice of the International Monetary Fund (IMF) program, was inevitable, and could not be blamed solely on the banking collapse.

Increased central government debt is one of the most common measures of crisis severity. It measures the gross fiscal cost, and is simple and easily comprehensible. But as with most other simple measures it has limitations. To get a better measure of the *net* fiscal cost of the crisis, an in-depth analysis of the costs incurred and the assets acquired is in order.

In 2012, the IMF estimated both the gross debt incurred during the crash and its aftermath in 2008–2011, and the net cost to the treasury, accounting for the value of assets acquired against that debt.[3] The IMF analysis found that direct costs amounted to 43.2 % of GDP; the net fiscal cost, adjusted for appropriated assets, totaled 19.2 % of GDP.[4]

Since the IMF rolled out its estimates, the government has taken several measures to recover the cost. For example, it has levied special taxes on both the new banks and the estates of the fallen banks. Furthermore, measures taken to counter the transfer problem associated with large foreign holdings of domestic assets have also yielded considerable funds to state coffers (as explained in Chaps. 5 and 7). This includes stability contributions from estates as well as currency auctions held to eliminate the offshore holdings of ISK, residues from the once lively carry trade.

In a 2009 paper published by the European Commission on the Swedish banking crisis of 1991–1993,[5] Lars Jonung compared the net fiscal costs from 38 systemic banking crises between 1970 and 2007.[6] Jonung defined the net fiscal cost as government outlays during the crisis minus recovery values during the five years after the crisis ended. Net fiscal costs ranged from almost none (0 % of GDP) for Brazil, Ukraine, and Sweden in 1988–1991 to over 50 % of GDP for Indonesia in 1997 and Argentina in 1980.

By Jonung's definition, the Icelandic banking crisis lasted from 2008 into 2013. However, in our analysis the recovery period encompasses a full seven years, from 2008 until end-of-year 2015. We follow the example set

---

[3] International Monetary Fund. (2012. April). *Iceland: Ex Post Evaluation of Exceptional Access Under the 2008 Stand-by Arrangement.*

[4] *Ibid.*, p. 4.

[5] Jonung, L. (2009). *The Swedish model for resolving the banking crisis of 1991–93. Seven reasons why it was successful* (No. 360). Directorate General Economic and Monetary Affairs (DG ECFIN), European Commission.

[6] *Ibid.*, Figure 2.

by the IMF and allocate the fiscal cost and recovery to specific factors. In addition to the six factors considered by the IMF (see Table 9.1), we consider four factors that IMF did not consider: The CBI's loan to Kaupthing in early October 2008; special taxes on the estates of the fallen banks; the stability contributions of the estates at year-end 2015; and CBI currency transactions behind capital controls. In addition, we are now in a position to take into account to some extent the treasury's recovery from the estates. At the time of the IMF report, none of these factors had been identified as affecting the fiscal cost of the crisis, and the treasury's recovery from the estates was an estimate from 2009.

Although we follow the IMF's example in allocating the cost to major factors, our results are not directly comparable theirs. The IMF estimated the increase in central government debt caused by each factor and the value of assets acquired by the state in connection with that increase in debt. The asset valuation was an estimate at the time of acquisition. Our approach, however, aims at estimating the cash flow to and from the treasury and the CBI that can be related to each factor. For example, the IMF estimates the gross fiscal cost of recapitalizing the CBI to be €1.8 billion, which amounts to the bond that the treasury issued to the CBI. In contrast, we consider the total outflow of cash from the central bank because of lending against inadequate collateral; this totaled €2.3 billion. The CBI later recovered a part of these loans, which we count as cash flow at recovery.

The main result of the analysis is that in aggregate, nominal terms, the treasury has recovered all outlaid costs from the crash and its aftermath (2008

Table 9.1 International Monetary Fund estimate of the fiscal cost of the crisis in 2008–2011, as a percentage of GDP

	Net fiscal cost	Gross fiscal cost
Recapitalization of the Central Bank	6.8	18.3
Treasury securities lending	6.2	6.2
Recapitalization of the commercial banks	2.3	14.8
Recapitalization of the Housing Financing Fund	2.1	2.1
Savings banks	0	0
Paid State Guarantee Fund guarantees	1.8	1.8
Total	**19.2**	**43.2**

Source: Adapted from International Monetary Fund (2012)

through 2015); additionally, it made a net gain of €1.9 billion.[7] When measured as a percentage of GDP each year, the net result is a full recovery and a gain of 2.6 % of GDP, which amounts to €380 million when measured against the 2015 GDP. The difference between the nominal gain and the net gain as a percentage of GDP stems from the fact that the cost to the treasury was mostly realized early in the period, when GDP was low, whereas the gains have come from recoveries, taxes and stability contributions in the later part, when the GDP was higher. In 2008, the GDP of Iceland was roughly €10 billion, whereas in 2015 it was just shy of €15 billion.

9.2   Central Bank Collateralized Loans and Treasury Securities Lending

The vast majority of the fiscal cost of the crisis can be sourced to the recapitalization of the CBI. The IMF estimated the cost at 6.8 % of GDP in terms of net cost, and 18.3 % in gross terms. This recapitalization was necessary because of the enormous losses sustained by the CBI on the so-called "love letter" transactions (see Chap. 8). The second highest net fiscal cost, according to the IMF, stemmed from treasury securities lending (6.2 % of GDP). These two factors are closely related and are therefore considered together here.

The term "love letters" has been used for unsecured bonds that were issued by the three Icelandic commercial banks and posted as collateral for loans from the CBI prior to October 2008. The term was first used publicly by the CBI governor and former prime minister, Davíð Oddsson, in a TV interview on October 7, 2008. He was describing the collateral Glitnir offered the CBI when applying for a €600 million emergency loan during the last weekend of September. Before the crisis, the CBI accepted as collateral bonds with a credit rating of A or higher, if a few other minor requirements were fulfilled. As the three Icelandic commercial banks all had a credit rating of A or higher from international credit rating agencies

---

[7] As elsewhere in this book, amounts in ISK are converted to euros at the fixed exchange rate of 150 kr. per euro and not at the prevailing rate at the time of discussed events. In the period 2008–2015 the official exchange rate fluctuated in the range 90–187 kr. per euro with average 157 kr. per euro.

(and even Aaa from Moody's for a short period in 2007[8]), the CBI accepted their unsecured bonds as collateral for loans. The commercial banks issued bonds, which they either swapped with each other or sold to other commercial or investment banks. In turn, they posted the bonds as collateral for loans at the Central Bank.

By this procedure, the money printing powers of the Central Bank were effectively handed over to the commercial banks, and the banks actually had access to unlimited amounts of Central Bank reserves. On October 6, 2008, the balance of Central Bank loans with bank bonds as collateral stood at €2.3 billion (345 billion ISK).

Starting in 2001, the Icelandic treasury provided primary dealers in treasury bonds access to borrowing the bonds against collateral to facilitate market making in the bonds.[9] Initially, only treasury bonds were accepted as collateral, but later the requirements expanded to match those the CBI set for its collateralized loans. This included love letters, that is, unsecured bonds of the commercial banks. In 2008, all the three commercial banks were primary dealers in treasury securities, along with Icebank and other three small, domestic investment banks, for a total of seven.[10] Each primary dealer could borrow up to €200 million of securities for a total limit of €1.4 billion.[11] By October 6, 2008, primary dealers had borrowed treasury bonds, collateralized with unsecured bank bonds, for almost half the limit or €650 million.[12]

The total amount of claims on banks by the CBI and the treasury, collateralized with love letters, was thus just shy of €3 billion at the time of the crash: almost 30 % of GDP. This was the gross fiscal cost of the love letters.

---

[8] Moody's upgraded Glitnir, Kaupthing and Landsbanki to Aaa on February 26, 2007 and downgraded them to Aa3 in April 2007.

[9] Government Debt Management. (2001, November 23). Government Debt Management Prospect 2002. http://news.icex.is/newsservice/MMIcexNSWeb.dll/newspage?language=EN&primarylanguagecode=EN&newsnumber=13446

[10] Government Debt Management. (2008, May 23). Signing of agreements regarding issuance and market making in government securities. http://www.lanamal.is/en/investors/primary-dealers-for-government-securities/primary-dealers-agreement/nanar/937/signing-of-agreements-regarding-issuance-and-market-making-in-government-securities-

[11] Government Debt Management. (2008, May 13). Tariffs for securities lending and their limits. http://www.lanamal.is/assets/nyrlanasysla/gjaldskramai_08.pdf

[12] The Icelandic State Audit. (2012, June). Report to the Icelandic Parliament. The Governments Facilitation to Financial Companies and Institutions in the Wake of the Banking Crisis. http://www.rikisendurskodun.is/fileadmin/media/skyrslur/fyrirgreidsla_vid_fjarmalafyrirtaeki2.pdf

The CBI claims were transferred to the treasury at the end of 2008, after they had been written down by €500 million at the CBI. At the end of 2009, the claims were transferred again, after being written down by another €1.2 billion, along with the claims arising from treasury securities lending to a special asset management company, ESÍ, which had been founded by the CBI.

The purpose of the asset management company ESÍ was to administer these assets and either hold them to maturity or sell them when market conditions were favorable. The CBI love letter claims were valued at €600 million, but the value of claims arising from treasury securities lending is not clear. Several other assets of the CBI were also transferred to the holding company, including the FIH loan (see Sect. 9.6) and loans collateralized with covered bonds. The total assets of the holding company were valued at €3.3 billion ISK in the opening balance sheet, which amounted to 42 % of CBI's total balance sheet at the time.

Even though the love letters turned out to be considerably less valuable collateral than the CBI must have anticipated, secured claims still yield more recovery than unsecured; the part of the claim that is not satisfied by the collateral is an unsecured claim against the borrower. Thus the CBI holding company received both the collateral for the claims, which were claims against the estates of the old banks, and unsecured claims against their estates, or against estates of the smaller commercial and investment banks that had been intermediaries in the love letter transactions.

For example, Icebank, the most prominent intermediary in the love letter transactions, had outstanding loans of around €1.07 billion from the CBI and the treasury. The CBI (or rather its subsidiary ESÍ) lodged claims in the amount of €1.3 billion, including penalty interest. When the CBI seized the collateral it was valued at €200 million, so it had a remaining unsecured claim against Icebank of €1.1 billion. The collateral (bank bonds issued by the three banks) was at nominal value €1.07 billion and the ultimate recovery from the bonds was €250 million. The final recovery for general claims against Icebank after composition at year-end 2015 turned out to be 18 % so the CBI got an additional €200 million recovery, giving a €450 million recovery in total, or 42.5 % of the claim amount.[13]

---

[13] See Supreme Court verdict no. 130/2016, May 4, 2016.

Table 9.2 Fiscal cost of the Central Bank loans and treasury securities lending collateralized with 'love letters' in million euros and as a percentage of GDP

	2008	2015	Total
Central Bank love letter loans	−2300	978	−1323
Treasury securities lending	−649	276	−373
Total	**−2949**	**1253**	**−1695**
% of GDP	−28.7 %	8.5 %	−20.2 %

Assuming the same recovery for the remainder of the love letter loans produces a total recovery of €1.25 billion. A more exact estimate of the recovery requires knowledge of the composition of both the collateral and the borrowers, information that has not been made public.

The net fiscal cost of the Central Bank loans and treasury securities lending collateralized with love letters was thus just shy of €1.7 billion in nominal terms, amounting to 20.2 % of GDP (Table 9.2).

Given the large stake the CBI had in the love letters, it should not be surprising that the Financial Services Authority (FSA) considered transferring unsecured bank bonds held as collateral at the CBI to the new banks along with deposits, thereby making them a de facto priority claim. The FSA's first decision on the allocation of the assets and liabilities of Landsbankinn actually contained such a clause, but that decision was revoked shortly after publication. If the bonds had been transferred, the CBI would have had full recovery of its claims, at the expense of other general creditors.

9.3   Recapitalization of the Commercial Banks

To prevent the failure of the banks from imperiling the domestic financial system, the treasury founded new banks to take over the domestic operations of the three failed giants. The emergency legislation facilitated this action. Domestic assets and deposits of the old banks were transferred to the new entities, along with domestic deposits, via a Purchase and Assumption (P&A) transaction. The value of the transferred assets exceeded the assumed deposits; the new banks were to pay the difference by issuing bonds to the failed banks, and the treasury provided the initial required capital, which was estimated at €2.6 billion, or 25 % of GDP. To reduce the risk to both the treasury and the new banks, as well as reduce the gross fiscal cost of the operation, negotiations were opened with the resolution committees of the old banks concerning the estates contributing a part of the capital.

The result was that the treasury contributed around €1.3 billion, or 12.5 % of GDP, of which €0.9 billion were in share capital and €0.4 billion in the form of subordinated loans.[14] Like other national treasuries, the Icelandic treasury did not have to pay for the capital contribution in cash; instead, it could issue a treasury bond to the banks. And so it contributed initial capital with the issue of a new bond series, RIKH 18 1009, which was issued expressly for this purpose.[15]

In return for this capital contribution, the state acquired the new Landsbankinn almost in full,[16] as well as a 13 % stake in Arion Bank and a 5 % stake in Íslandsbanki. Subordinated loans were granted to Íslandsbanki and Arion Bank in ISK (also in the form of the RIKH 18 bond), but the loans were to be repaid in euros. In this way, the treasury acquired interest-bearing claims in the amount of €138 million against Íslandsbanki, and €163 million against Arion Bank.

The contract for Kaupthing's purchase of the treasury's stake in Arion Bank required Arion to pay a dividend in the amount of ISK 6.5 billion on March 1, 2011, due to accrued interest on the initial capital contribution.[17] The dividend was not paid in cash, however, but by issuing two separate subordinated bonds, in the amount of $20 million and £19.9 million.[18]

---

[14] Ministry of Finance. (March, 2011). Report by the minister of finance on the restoration of the commercial banks.

[15] The RIKH 18 1009 bond was issued in September 2009 but bore interest from 9 October 2008. The bond bore interest equivalent to the rates on deposit institutions' accounts with the Central Bank of Iceland. Interest is paid four times a year. The bond matures on October 9, 2018, at which time the principal will be paid in one lump sum. The first interest payment, made on October 9, 2009, included interest for the full year from October 9, 2008.

[16] The state's holding in Landsbankinn is 98.2 %. LBI, the old Landsbanki Íslands, originally owned an 18.67 % stake in Landsbankinn, but the state acquired most of that holding when the contingent Landsbankinn-LBI bond was issued.

[17] Ministry of Finance. (March, 2011). Report by the minister of finance on the restoration of the commercial banks.

[18] The addition to the subordinated loan due to dividend payments was in US dollars and pounds sterling – USD 20 million and GBP 19.9 million – which was the equivalent of ISK 6.5 billion on 1 March 2011.

The treasury has not paid any capital contribution in cash since the new banks were established. The only definable cash contributions were a €15 million initial capital contribution in 2008, and interest payments on the RIKH 18 bond, which totaled €566 million from the time of establishment through year-end 2015.

In return, the treasury has received dividend income on its holdings, interest income on the subordinated loans, and principal payments of the subordinated loans. The banks' total dividend payments during the period 2008–2015 amounted to €647 million, and the treasury's share of those payments totals €419 million. After deducting the ISK 6.5 billion paid by Arion Bank in 2011 (which was not paid in cash but added to the treasury's subordinated loan to the bank), the treasury's dividend income from the banks totals just under €375 million. The interest payments of Íslandsbanki and Arion Bank on the subordinated loans total about €100 million, and in 2015, Arion repaid about two-thirds of its subordinated loan, or €133 million, for a total payment of €233 million to the treasury.

In all, the treasury's income from its capital contributions totals €609 million, and its interest expense and initial cash contribution totals €582 million. Over the 2008–2015 period, the treasury has thus had a net financial income of €27 million from the new banks.

As of year-end 2015, the treasury still owed the entire €1.3 billion principal on the RIKH 18 bond in connection with the capital contribution, but that debt is offset by its equity stakes in the three banks and subordinated loans granted to two of them. The repayment value of the subordinated loans, as of year-end 2015, totaled €200 million.[19] The estates of the failed banks bought the loans from the treasury in early 2016 as part of the stability contributions, so the treasury has recouped that part of the initial capital.

The value of the state's equity stakes in the three banks, however, is subject to some uncertainty. The ultimate value will not be determined until the holdings are sold. The book value of the banks' equity does provide some indication of the value of their share capital. Assuming that the value of the share capital is equal to the book value of equity (i.e. price-to-book), the

---

[19] Annual accounts of Arion Bank hf. and Íslandsbanki hf. for the year 2015.

state's holdings were valued at just short of €2 billion at the end of 2015.[20] The net value of the stakes and the state's subordinated claims against the three banks, net of the repayment value of the RIKH 18 bond, was therefore about €0.9 billion at the end of 2015.

The treasury's cost and returns from the recapitalization of the banks is presented in Table 9.3. The cost and return are shown both in million euros and as a percentage of each year's GDP. On each line in the table, the annual revenues and expenditures of the treasury, due to particular parts of the reconstruction of the banks, are presented, as well as the value of the relevant part at the end of 2015.

The first line, *Dividend income/Share capital*, shows the treasury's dividend income from its holdings in the banks and the value of those holdings at year-end 2015. The second line, *Interest income/Subordinated loans*, contains the treasury's annual interest and principal income on the subordinated loans to Arion Bank and Íslandsbanki, and the value of the subordinated loans at the end of 2015. On the third line is the treasury's annual interest expense on the RIKH 18 bond, which was used to contribute capital to the banks, plus its repayment value as of year-end 2015. This line also shows the initial capital contribution from the treasury, which was made in cash at the end of 2008. The fourth line gives the sum of the first three lines and shows the treasury's net payments (−) or revenues (+) stemming from the foundation of the new banks:

The accounting return of the treasury's re-establishment of the banking system, defined as the period-end sum of revenues less expenditures, and assets net of liabilities, thus totaled €919 million – at each year's nominal value. The accounting return does not, however, adjust for the time value of money. The treasury's contributions to the banks were, for the most part, made in the first half of the period, but the income it received from the banks came in the second half. Therefore, the accounting return does not necessarily give the most accurate indication of the cost or benefit of the treasury's participation in the recapitalization of the banks.

Charting returns as a percentage of GDP for each year accounts for the time value of money. This is the equivalent of calculating the present

---

[20] Annual accounts of Arion Bank hf., Íslandsbanki hf., and Landsbankinn hf. for the year 2015.

Table 9.3 Treasury returns on the re-establishment of the commercial banks, in million euros (accounting return) and as a percentage of GDP for each year

Year	Revenues (+) / Expenditures (−)								Value Year end 2015	Total 2008–2015
	2008	2009	2010	2011	2012	2013	2014	2015		
Dividend income/ share capital						67	140	169	1959	2335
Interest income/ subordinated loans			15	19	18	16	15	150	199	433
Interest expense/ RIKH 18	−16	−190	−88	−44	−55	−64	−64	−61	−1267	−1848
Net (millions)	−16	−190	−73	−24	−37	18	91	258	892	919
Net % of GDP	−0.2 %	−1.8 %	−0.7 %	−0.2 %	−0.3 %	0.1 %	0.7 %	1.8 %	6.1 %	5.5 %

Sources: Commercial banks' annual accounts for 2008–2015, Minister of Finance report on the re-establishment of the commercial banks, RIKH 18 1009 prospectus, and authors' calculations

Table 9.4 The treasury's returns on the re-establishment of the banking system, in million euros and as a percentage of GDP, assuming that the treasury's holdings in the three commercial banks is sold at 60 %, 80 %, 100 %, or 120 % of book value at the end of 2015

Value of the banks as % of equity	60 %	80 %	100 %	120 %
Return in million euros	135	527	919	1311
Return as % of GDP	0.2 %	2.8 %	5.5 %	8.2 %

Source: Authors' calculations

value of the payments and end-of-period value, discounting with interest rates equal to GDP growth for each year. As a percentage of each year's GDP, the return is positive by 5.5 % of GDP.

The most uncertainty in this analysis regarding the treasury's return surrounds the value of its equity stakes in the banks as of year-end 2015. If it is assumed that the value of the banks is equivalent to 80 % of their book value, the book value of the returns declines to €527 million, or 2.8 % of GDP (see Table 9.4.). Even if the banks sell at price-to-book 60 %, the treasury's return will be positive, both in accounting terms and as a percentage of GDP.

9.4 Recapitalization of the HFF and the Savings Banks

In its assessment, the IMF includes the treasury's cost in recapitalizing the Housing Financing Fund (HFF), which totaled €213 million, or 2.1 % of GDP in 2010. Though this expense appeared in 2010, it is not appropriate, in the authors' opinion, to classify it as a consequence of the collapse. According to the report by the Parliamentary Special Investigation Commission on the Housing Financing Fund, the problems and losses sustained by the HFF in recent years are in most part due to the recapitalization of the Fund in 2004, when it swapped its funding from pre-payable Housing Bonds for non-prepayable HFF Bonds.[21] From that time on, prepayments

---

[21] Stefánsson, Sigurður Hallur, Kirstín Þ. Flygenring, & Jón Þorvaldur Heiðarsson. (2013). *Parliamentary Special Investigation Commission Report on the Housing Financing Fund, etc.*

of the HFF's loans have eaten up its interest rate spread, which has diminished steadily, year by year, with no change in sight. It should therefore have been clear that the treasury would have had to contribute additional capital to the Fund, almost irrespective of how economic developments turned out.

From 2010 onwards, the treasury has contributed additional €117 million to the HFF. With the 2010 contribution, the total is about €330 million, and it is likely that some further contributions might be needed in coming years. The HFF's problems therefore stem primarily from mistakes made in its recapitalization in 2004, and not directly from the failure of the three commercial banks.

When the parliament passed the emergency legislation, it was clear that the ongoing events could adversely affect the country's network of savings banks. In the years before the crash, the savings banks were the fourth wheel of the commercial banking structure. They had maintained a robust market share of 15 % in deposits and lending, although that had fallen to 5–10 % as the commercial banks expanded rapidly in the years before the 2008 crisis. The emergency legislation authorized the minister of finance, on behalf of the treasury, to contribute additional capital to each savings bank, up to 20 % of the book value of its equity, if the bank's board of directors requested it. At the end of 2008, the Minister of finance set rules outlining the preconditions for such a contribution.[22] Among other things, it was stipulated that, after the treasury had contributed capital, the savings bank's capital ratio must be at least 12 %. A large number of savings banks applied for capital contributions from the treasury, but none of them could fulfill this requirement. For that reason, the treasury never contributed capital to any savings banks on the basis of this authorization.

However, the treasury acquired a portion of the guarantee capital of several savings banks when Icebank, the bank of the savings banks, failed. After the acquisition, the treasury contributed further guarantee capital for their financial restructuring. The treasury's total contribution to the savings banks amounted to €13 million in 2010. Based on the savings

---

[22] Rules on Capital Contributions to Savings Banks pursuant to Article 2 of the Act on Authority for Treasury Disbursements due to Unusual Financial Market Circumstances, etc., 18 December 2008.

banks' capital position at the end of 2015, the state's portion of their guarantee capital amounts to just €5 million. The salient factor in the €8 million erosion in the treasury's contribution was the failure of Westman Islands Savings Fund at the beginning of 2015.

On April 22, 2010, the FSA took over the second largest savings bank, Byr, after the bank had been granted a year's grace period to meet capital ratio requirements. The FSA used the same method – negotiated P&A – as it did for the failed commercial banks in October 2008; it transferred Byr's deposits and a portion of its assets to a newly established company, Byr hf. The treasury contributed €6 million in initial share capital, and thereby acquired an 11.6 % stake, and the old Byr Savings Bank acquired a stake of 88.4 %, due to the value of the transferred assets in excess of deposits. Byr hf. was then sold to Íslandsbanki hf. for €44 million at the end of 2011, and the treasury received €5 million of the sales price. The direct cost to the treasury for its involvement with Byr Savings Bank therefore totaled €1 million.[23]

The FSA also took over Keflavík Savings Bank on April 22, 2010. Using the same method, it transferred the savings bank's deposits and a portion of its equity to SpKef Savings Bank, a newly established savings bank owned by the state, to which the treasury had contributed €6 million in guarantee capital. The new savings bank never gained sustainable operability, and this journey ended with the merger of SpKef and Landsbankinn, for which the treasury paid Landsbankinn €134 million.[24] The treasury's total contribution for the Keflavík Savings Bank was therefore €140 million, and no assets or payments were received in return.

The net financial cost to the treasury as a result of the restoration of the savings banks is summarized in Table 9.5. The total expense was €149 million, or 1.3 % of GDP, the bulk of this amount stemming from one savings bank, the Keflavík Savings Bank.

---

[23] Hrannar Már S. Hafberg, Tinna Finnbogadóttir, and Bjarni Frímann Karlsson. The Background and Causes of the Difficulties and Fall of the Savings Banks. Parliamentary Special Investigation Commission, 2014.

[24] Landsbankinn hf., annual accounts for 2012, Explanatory Note no. 5.

Table 9.5 Net financial cost to the treasury due to the collapse and re-establishment of the savings banks in million euros and as a percentage of GDP

Year	2010	2011	2012	2015	Total
Byr Savings Bank	−6	5			−1
Keflavík Savings Bank	−6		−134		−140
Smaller savings banks	−13			5	−8
Net (million euros)	**−25**	**5**	**−134**	**5**	**−149**
Net % of GDP	−0.2 %	0.0 %	−1.1 %	0.0 %	−1.3 %

Sources: Landsbankinn annual accounts for 2012, savings banks' annual accounts for 2015, Parliamentary Special Investigation Commission report on the background and causes of the difficulties and fall of the savings banks, and the authors' calculations

9.5   The CBI Loan to Kaupthing and State Guarantees

The €500 million, four-day Kaupthing loan was granted just hours before Prime Minister Haarde gave his 'God bless Iceland' statement. Collateralization came from shares in Kaupthing's Danish subsidiary bank, FIH. The proceeds of the loan were used to meet various margin calls facing Kaupthing at the time, and of course the attempt was nullified two days later when Kaupthing went down.

When the loan was granted, FIH's book value of equity amounted to €1.3 billion. So the Central Bank was convinced that even if Kaupthing failed, the loan could be recovered by selling FIH. Indeed, a formal sales process began on October 19, less than two weeks after the mother bank's demise. The CBI commissioned JP Morgan to administer the sales process,[25] and the investment bank contacted several investors, including Nordic and international banks, to solicit offers. Only one was received, however, and it was not considered acceptable.

FIH remained up for sale, however, and a new group of investors showed interest in mid- 2009. After lengthy negotiations the bank was sold on

---

[25] The CBI never acquired FIH, it remained in Kaupthing's ownership, but the CBI was its beneficial owner in the sense that any proceeds from its sale would go to the CBI. One of the reasons that FIH remained in Kaupthing's ownership was that some of its loans had covenants regarding change of control.

Table 9.6 Central Bank returns on the October 6, 2008, loan to Kaupthing Bank hf., secured by shares in FIH Bank. The loss on the loan totaled 2.6 % of GDP during the years 2008–2010

Year	2008	2010	Total
Amount in FX	€500 million	DKK 1.9 billion	
Equivalent in million euros	−500	255	−245
% of GDP	−5.0 %	2.4 %	−2.6 %

Sources: Central Bank of Iceland, Sale of Danish bank FIH 19 September 2010, and Statistics Iceland

September 19, 2010, to the investor group consisting of two Danish pension funds, a Swedish insurance company, and a Danish investor. The selling price was 5 billion DKK, equivalent to €670 million, so it looked as if the Central Bank would recover the loan in full, with interest. However, only 1.9 billion DKK was paid up front, and a seller's loan was granted for the remaining 3.1 billion DKK.[26] A portion of the seller's loan was to be repaid on 1 January 2015, and another on 1 January 2016. The amount of the payments depended on the value of specified assets owned by FIH as of year-end 2014 and 2015.

All that is known about the status of the seller's loan is that there was no payment in 2016, and that repayment will not exceed DKK 100 million. It is reasonable to assume that no further payments on the loan will be forthcoming.

Table 9.6 shows the Central Bank's payment flows on the loan and the loss sustained on it by the CBI – and therefore the treasury – in an amount equivalent to €245 million, or 2.6 % of GDP.

At the time of the crash, the state still had outstanding guarantees on some of the banks' debt. The debt originates either from the time the banks were in public ownership or from mergers of public funds with private banks.

When Landsbanki was privatized in 2002, all its outstanding debt was guaranteed by the state, and at the time of the crash some of this debt had not yet matured. In addition, Landsbanki acquired the publicly owned Agricultural Loan Fund in 2005 and assumed most of its debt, which

---

[26] Central Bank of Iceland. (2010, September 19). *Sale of Danish bank FIH.*

remained guaranteed by the state. Some payments from the pension fund of Landsbanki also had state guarantees originating from the time Landsbanki was public. The total debt of Landsbanki, guaranteed by the state at year-end 2010, was €150 million. The State Guarantee Fund assumed this debt and filed a claim against Landsbanki.

In total, the State Guarantee Fund assumed state guaranteed bank debt of €210 million in 2009 and 2010. In return, it filed claims against the estates in the amount of €144 million. Estimated recoveries from the claims against the estates is just €20 million, so the net cost of the state guarantees is €190 million, or 1.8 % of GDP.

9.6   Special Taxes and Stability Contributions of the Estates

Ever since the new banks were established, Icelandic authorities have used their power to levy taxes to recover some of the cost of the collapse. They have broadened the tax base in the banking system and have subjected the financial institutions to most of the taxes known in the Western world. Since 2010, the government has levied a special tax on financial institutions – called the bank tax in everyday speech — on credit institutions' total liabilities; a financial activities tax on taxable wages and fees/commissions; and a special financial activities tax, an additional income tax on profits in excess of a billion ISK. Financial institutions in winding-up proceedings were explicitly exempt from the bank tax during the period 2010–2012, but that exemption was revoked in 2013, when the tax was raised substantially and the tax-free threshold set at ISK 50 billion. The purpose of the increased bank tax was to fund the government household debt relief program, as discussed in Chap. 5.[27]

The new taxes generated significant revenues for the treasury, both from the new banks and, from 2010 to 2015, from the failed banks' insolvent estates. For the purposes of our analysis, only direct revenues from special

---

[27] Act no. 164/2010.

Table 9.7 Special tax payments by the estates of Glitnir, Kaupthing, and LBI, in 2012–2015 in million euros

Year	2013	2014	2015	Total
Special financial activities tax	53	7	7	66
Bank tax	172	163	193	529
Special taxes, total	225	170	200	595
% of GDP	1.8 %	1.3 %	1.4 %	4.4 %

Sources: Glitnir and Kaupthing annual accounts for 2012–2015; LBI quarterly financial information for 2012–2014. LBI's financial activities tax is estimated based on paid wages, and the LBI bank tax for 2014 is estimated based on approved claims

taxes levied on the estates are considered recovery of bailout cost. Conventional taxes and special taxes on new banks are not considered.

This may not be an obvious categorization, since taxes on the new banks – and the financial system at large – have been raised considerably to shift a heavy burden of crash recovery onto the financial sector. In general, though, taxes are meant to raise revenues for the general operations of the state; if taxes levied on the new banks were considered cost recovery, it might be difficult to draw the line between cost recovery and general tax revenues.

Table 9.7 shows special tax payments by the three estates over the period 2012–2015. The estates have not paid general income tax because of the substantial transferable tax loss created at the time of the collapse. The special financial activities tax, however, is also an income tax. It amounts to 6 % of the profit for each year, but unlike the conventional income tax, it does not take account of transferable losses or joint taxation with parent or subsidiary companies. The estates have therefore paid this tax in full.

The treasury did not begin to receive direct tax revenues from the failed banks' estates until 2012, when it levied the financial activities tax. Special tax revenues from the estates increased substantially in 2013 and 2014, when the estates' exemption from the bank tax ended in conjunction with a sharp increase in that tax's rate. Between 2013 and 2015, special tax revenues from the estates totaled €595 million, or 4.4 % of GDP.

The final measure undertaken by the government was the introduction of a special stability tax, announced in June 2015. The tax base was the total assets of estates of commercial and savings banks in winding-up proceedings, and the rate was set at 39 %. In 2015, the total assets of the estates were around €15 billion, so a 39 % tax on their assets would have amounted to €6 billion, which roughly equaled the estates domestic assets. However, the estates could be granted certain deductions from the tax by implementing measures that reduced the threat to stability. Indeed, the tax was not primarily a vehicle for revenue. The authorities wanted to drain the estates' domestic assets that otherwise posed a threat to stability when paid out to foreign creditors.

Given the authorities' intent, it allowed the estates to avoid the tax by reaching a composition agreement with their creditors before year-end 2015. The CBI set certain conditions on the composition agreements, mainly in the form of broad proscriptions against any threat to the stability of the Icelandic financial system and economy.

The estates undertook several measures to fulfill the stability conditions. A substantial part of these measures were voluntary, direct contributions of financial assets to the state. The total value of the contributions from the three big estates is estimated to be €2.53 billion (see Sect. 7.5). Additional contributions from smaller estates are valued at around €50 million, for a total of €2.58 billion or 17.5 % of GDP.[28]

9.7   Fiscal Gains from the Capital Controls

Capital controls were necessary in the aftermath of the crisis. While there can be no doubt that they have had indirect costs for the economy, they also enabled the state and the CBI to realize profit through several actions, and indeed generate a new stability in which the controls might even be lifted.

The first action of this nature taken by the CBI was the so-called Avens-deal. Avens B.V. was a Dutch holding company founded by the old Landsbanki for the purpose of acquiring funding from the Central Bank of Luxembourg (BCL). Avens had holdings in bonds issued by the

---

[28] Central Bank of Iceland. (2015, October 27). *Uppgjör fallinna fjármálafyrirtækja á grundvelli stöðugleikaskilyrða: áhrif á greiðslujöfnuð og fjármálastöðugleika. (Settlement of the failed financial institutions on the basis of stability conditions: Impact on balance of payments and financial stability.)* http:// sedlabanki.is/library/Skraarsafn/Gjaldeyrismal/AssessmentOfPreliminaryCompositionProposals.pdf

HFF, which carried a state guarantee. Landsbanki posted covered bonds issued by Avens as collateral for a liquidity facility in euros from the BCL. In May 2010, the CBI bought the bonds for €437 million, paying €402 million of the total with a 15-year treasury bond and the rest in cash.[29] Later that month, the CBI sold the underlying treasury and HFF bonds to 26 domestic pension funds for €549 million,[30] making a profit of €112 million as well as securing 15-year funding of €402 million. The deal was also acceptable to the pension funds, which bought the bonds at a 25 % discount off their market price, although that discount came at the price of paying for the bonds in hard currency.

Another action that has helped to obviate capital controls is resolving the overhang, i.e. offshore ISK. At year-end 2008, the overhang was estimated at €4.3 billion. With a series of currency auctions held by the CBI from 2011 to 2015, as well as transactions that circumvented the capital controls, the overhang had shrunk to around €2 billion at year-end 2015.[31] The CBI usually took a small spread in these auctions, but the net gains were not significant.

A final CBI-sponsored auction, announced in June 2015, was part of the plan for lifting controls; offshore króna owners would have opportunity to exchange them for euros. To prevent holdouts, any offshore króna not dispatched by the auction would be stuck in locked, interest-free deposit accounts. The auction was set at June 16, 2016.[32] Offshore króna holders were offered an exchange rate in the range of 190–210 kr. per euro, depending on auction participation. The overhang was estimated at €2.1bn (320 billion ISK), and if the auction participation was more than €1.2 billion the exchange rate would be 190 kr. per euro. The rate would

[29] Central Bank of Iceland. (2010, May 19). *Central Bank of Iceland, Banque centrale du Luxembourg and the liquidator of Landsbanki Luxembourg S.A. sign an agreement in Luxembourg.* (Press release no. 11/2010).

[30] Central Bank of Iceland. (2010, May 31). *Pension funds purchase Treasury's HFF bonds to strengthen FX reserves.* (Press release no. 13/2010).

[31] Minister of Finance. (2016, May 20). Frumvarp til laga um meðferð krónueigna sem háðar eru sérstökum takmörkunum. (A bill on the treatment of ISK assets that are subject to special restrictions.) (Þskj. 1314 – 777. mál, 145. löggjafarþing.)

[32] Central Bank of Iceland. (2016, May 25). *Central Bank of Iceland foreign currency auction 16 June 2016.* http://www.cb.is/publications/news/news/2016/05/25/Central-Bank-of-Iceland-foreign-currency-auction-16-June-2016-/

rise to 210 kr. per euro if participation was less than €330 million (50 billion ISK). At the time of this writing the auction had yet to be held, but the CBI's gain, with high participation, might approach a gain of up to €600 million.

9.8   A Net Gain

A summary assessment of the net cost and gain to the treasury that can be directly attributed to the collapse and subsequent recovery is presented in nominal amounts in Table 9.8, and as a percentage of GDP in Table 9.9.

From late 2008 through 2015 the treasury therefore received a net gain from the crash and its aftermath of just over €1.9 billion in nominal terms. Most of the cost to the treasury came between 2008 and 2012, but the gains clustered in the latter years, from 2013 to 2015, and in fact the bulk of them arrived in 2015/2016. In terms of percentage of GDP, the crash resulted in a net 2.6 % gain to the treasury. This puts Iceland's net fiscal cost of its financial crisis at the low end of the post-1970 crises analyzed by Jonung.[33] It should be noted, though, that Iceland's recovery period is here defined as seven years, instead of the five-year period Jonung considered.

In summary, the largest cost according to our estimate was due to the Central Bank's love letters – just over €1.3 billion, or 15.7 % of GDP – and the second largest to the treasury securities lending: €373 million, or 4.4 % of GDP. Combined, the cost of the love letter transactions to the treasury was thus just shy of €1.7 billion, or 20.2 % of GDP. The greatest cost recovery for the treasury was through the stability contributions – almost €2.6 billion, or 17.5 % of GDP – and the second greatest derived from the recapitalization of the commercial banks: €913 million, or 5.5 % of GDP. Special taxes on the estates were also a large part of the cost recovery, providing tax revenues of €595 million, or 4.4 % of GDP.

With the gains from the recapitalization of the commercial banks, taxes on the estates, and the stability contributions from the estates, the treasury

---

[33] Jonung, L. (2009). *The Swedish model for resolving the banking crisis of 1991–93. Seven reasons why it was successful* (No. 360). Directorate General Economic and Monetary Affairs (DG ECFIN), European Commission.

Table 9.8 Estimate of the net cost (−) and gain (+) to the treasury from the crash in million euros in the period 2008–2015

	2008	2009	2010	2011	2012	2013	2014	2015	Year end 2015	Total 2008–2015
Central Bank love letters	−2,300								978	−1323
Treasury securities lending	−649								276	−373
Recapitalization of the commercial banks	−16	−190	−73	−24	−37	18	91	258	892	919
Savings banks			−25	5	−134				5	−149
Paid State Guarantee Fund guarantees		−23	−187						21	−189
Central Bank loan to Kaupthing (FIH)	−518		261							−257
Special taxes on the estates						225	170	7	193	595
Stability contributions of the estates									2,573	2,573
Central Bank currency transactions			112							112
Total	−3,482	−214	88	−19	−171	243	261	265	4,939	1,909

Source: The authors' assessment

Table 9.9 Estimate of the net cost (−) and gain (+) to the treasury from the crisis as a percentage of GDP in the period 2008–2015

	2008	2009	2010	2011	2012	2013	2014	2015	Year end 2015	Total 2008–2015
Central Bank love letters	−22.4 %								6.6 %	−15.7 %
Treasury securities lending	−6.3 %								1.9 %	−4.4 %
Recapitalization of the commercial banks	−0.2 %	−1.8 %	−0.7 %	−0.2 %	−0.3 %	0.1 %	0.7 %	1.8 %	6.1 %	5.5 %
Savings banks			−0.2%	0.0%	−1.1%		0.0%			−1.3 %
Paid State Guarantee Fund guarantees		−0.2 %	−1.7 %						0.1 %	−1.8 %
Central Bank loan to Kaupthing (FIH)	−5.0 %		2.4 %							−2.6 %
Special taxes on the estates						1.8 %	1.3 %	0.0 %	1.3 %	4.4 %
Stability contributions of the estates									17.5 %	17.5 %
Central Bank currency transactions			1.0 %							1.0 %
Total	−33.9 %	−2.0 %	0.8 %	−0.2 %	−1.4 %	1.9 %	2.0 %	1.8 %	33.6 %	2.6 %

Source: The authors' assessment

has thus managed to recoup most of the costs incurred as a result of the CBI's losses; the lost securities loans; the state guarantee on the banks' debts; the CBI's loan to Kaupthing; and the restoration of the savings bank system.

All direct costs falling on the treasury originated with actions taken before the crash or efforts to rescue the banking system. With the Emergency Act and subsequent measures, the authorities decided not to rescue the banks and not to socialize the debts or losses of private companies. The only significant exceptions to this fundamental policy were the CBI's loan to Kaupthing, which cost about 2.6 % of GDP, and the measures taken in connection with Keflavik Savings Bank, which cost about 1.1 % of GDP. In other respects, the old banks' shareholders and creditors ultimately bore the losses of the collapse, and even paid most of the cost incurred by the treasury. Developments after the crisis and during the final restructuring of the banks appear to have generated returns for the treasury that amount to 5.5 % of GDP, and the ultimatum to creditors in June 2015 gave windfall gains of 17.5 % of GDP.

The assessment depends to some extent on the success of the commercial banks' sale; thus, the estimate may need to be adjusted in the event of a sale. Based on the current situation, however, it appears that the emergency legislation in large part achieved its objective. Taxpayers have not shouldered the cost of the collapse and recovery. Instead, the banks' general creditors were tasked with the heavy lifting through three key tactical moves: classifying deposits as priority claims, taxing creditors' assets in Iceland, and enforcing the creditors' participation in the transfer problem's solution through special stability contributions.

Bibliography

Abdelal, R., & Alfaro, L. (2003). Capital and control: Lessons from Malaysia. *Challenge, 46*(4), 36–53.

Alistair Darling interview: Britain was two hours away from total social collapse – Former Chancellor on the crisis that erupted FIVE years ago this week. (2013, September 7). *This is Money.* http://www.thisismoney.co.uk/money/news/article-2415003/ALISTAIR-DARLING-INTERVIEW-Britain-hours-away-total-social-collapse--Former-Chancellor-crisis-erupted-FIVE-years-ago-week.html#ixzz4351QimLm

Allir hrægammar heimsins safnast saman í Reykjavík. (All the vultures of the world congregating on Reykjavik). (2008, October 15). *Viðskiptablaðið.* http://vb.is/frettir/allir-hrgammar-heimsins-safnast-saman-i-reykjavik/12451/

Alþingi. (1992, July 1). *Act no. 21/1991 on Bankruptcy etc.* http://www.althingi.is/lagas/145a/1991021.html

Alþingi. (2001, May 26). *Act no. 38/2001 on interest and indexation.* http://www.althingi.is/altext/stjt/2001.038.html

Alþingi. (2003–2004). *Bill on the amendment of the Act on radio no. 53/2000 and the Act on competition no. 8/1993.* http://www.althingi.is/altext/130/s/1525.html

Alþingi. (2008a, December 11). *Act no. 135/2008 on a special prosecutor's office.* http://www.althingi.is/lagas/136a/2008135.html

Alþingi. (2008b, October 7). *Act no. 125/2008 on the authority for treasury disbursements due to special circumstances in financial markets etc. (The Emergency Act).* http://www.althingi.is/lagas/145a/2008125.html

Alþingi (2009). *Frumvarp til laga um stofnun hlutafélags til að stuðla að endurskipulagningu þjóðhagslegra mikilvægra atvinnufyrirtækja. (Bill on the establishment of a limited liability company to promote the restructuring of nationally important companies.)* (Parliamentary document no. 1, case no. 1, 137th congress, 2009.) http://www.althingi.is/altext/137/s/0001.html

Alþingi. (2009, September 2). *Act no. 96/2009 (Icesave I).* http://www.althingi.is/altext/stjt/2009.096.html

Alþingi. (2010a, December 22). *Act no. 151/2010 on the amendment of act no. 38/2001.* http://www.althingi.is/altext/stjt/2010.151.html

Alþingi. (2010b, December 28). *Act no. 164/2010 on government spending.* http://www.althingi.is/altext/139/s/0657.html

Alþingi. (2010c, December 30). *Act no. 155/2010 on special taxes on financial institutions.* http://www.althingi.is/lagas/nuna/2010155.html

Alþingi. (2010d, January 6). *Act no. 1/2010 on the amendment of act no. 96/2009 (Icesave II).* http://www.althingi.is/altext/138/s/0626.html

Alþingi. (2011, February 22). *Act no. 13/2011 (Icesave III).* http://www.althingi.is/altext/stjt/2011.013.html

Alþingi. (2012, March 13). *Act no. 17/2012 on the amendment of the Foreign Exchange Act, no. 87/1992.* http://www.althingi.is/altext/stjt/2012.017.html

Alþingi (2012, March 13). Foreign currency matters (tightened rules on capital transfers). Act No. 17, of 13 March 2012. (Parliamentary document 966, case 608, 140. legislative session.) http://www.althingi.is/altext/stjt/2012.017.html

Alþingi (2014, April 8). *Svar forsætisráðherra við fyrirspurn frá Össuri Skarphéðinssyni um afnám gjaldeyrishafta. (The Prime Minister's answer to Össur Skarphéðinsson's inquiry on the lifting of capital controls.)* (Parliamentary document no. 934, case no. 385, 143. legislative session 2013–2014.) http://www.althingi.is/altext/143/s/0934.html

Alþingi. (2015, July 17). *Act no. 60/2015 on Stability Levy.* http://www.althingi.is/lagas/145a/2015060.html

Anzuini, A., & Fornari, F. (2012). Macroeconomic determinants of carry trade activity. *Review of International Economics, 20*(3), 468–488.

Arion Bank. (2015a, January 13). *Mun snjóhengjan minnka í febrúar? (Will the overhang decrease in February?)* https://www.arionbanki.is/markadir/greiningardeild/greiningardeild-allar-frettir/2015/01/13/Mun-snjohengjan-minnka-i-februar/

Arion Bank. (2015b, March 11). *Snjóhengjan minnkar um 12 milljarða. (The overhang decreases by 12 billion.)* https://www.arionbanki.is/markadir/greiningar-   deild/greiningardeild-allar-frettir/2015/02/11/Snjohengjan-minnkar-um-12-milljarda/

Ashby, B. (2006, March 24). Icelandic banks. Typical investor Q&A, and our response. *European Credit Research.* JPMorgan.

Baldursson, F. M., & Portes, R. (2013, September). Gambling for resurrection in Iceland: The rise and fall of the banks. *Available at SSRN 2361098.*

Basel Committee on Banking Supervision. (2004, April). *Bank failures in mature economies.* Working paper no. 13. http://www.bis.org/publ/bcbs_wp13.pdf

Baugur Group hf. (2002a, August 29). *Tilkynning vegna húsleitar. (Announcement regarding a dawn raid.)* OMX The Nordic Exchange. http://news.icex.is/newsservice/MMIcexNSWeb.dll/newspage?primarylanguagecode=IS&newsnumber=18286

Baugur Group hf. (2002b, December 20). *Baugur-ID kaupir 2,95% hlut í Somerfield PLC í Bretlandi. (Baugur-ID buys a 2.95% stake in Somerfield plc.)* OMX The Nordic Exchange.

Baugur Group hf. (2002c, November 7). *Baugur takes 4.54% stake in House of Fraser plc.* OMX The Nordic Exchange.

Baugur Group hf. (2002d, October 16). *Taveta Offer for Arcadia.* OMX The Nordic   Exchange.   http://news.icex.is/newsservice/MMIcexNSWeb.dll/newspage?primarylanguagecode=EN&newsnumber=18842

Baugur Group hf. (2002e, October 24). *Acquisition of a strategic stake in The Big Food Group plc.* OMX The Nordic Exchange.

Baugur Group hf. (2002f, September 5). *Possible offer for Arcadia.* OMX The Nordic   Exchange.   http://news.icex.is/newsservice/MMIcexNSWeb.dll/newspage?primarylanguagecode=EN&newsnumber=18400

Baugur Group hf. (2002g, September 6). *Stjórn Arcadia samþykkir væntanlegt yfirtökutilboð Philips Greens. (Arcadia's board of directors accepts Philip Green's forthcoming takeover bid.)* OMX The Nordic Exchange. http://news.icex.is/newsservice/MMIcexNSWeb.dll/newspage?primarylanguagecode=IS&newsnumber=18412

Bergström, C., Englund, P., & Thorell, P. (2002). Securum och vägen ut ur bankkrisen, (Securum and the road out of the banking crisis). Stockholm: *SNS.*

Bergsveinsson, J. A. (2009a, June 25). Bankastjórarnir eru alltaf sekir. (The banks' CEOs are always guilty). *Fréttablaðið.*

Bergsveinsson, J. A. (2009b, March 17). Ein leið af mörgum valin í endurreisn. (One proposal of many chosen for restoration.) *Markaðurinn.* http://www.visir.is/ExternalData/pdf/mark/M090318.pdf

Björgólfsson, T. (2014). *Billions to bust and back: How I made, lost and rebuilt a fortune, and what I learned on the way*. London: Profile Books Ltd.

Björgvinsson, S. T. (1994, January 4). Endurmat á framtíð sem fortíð. (A reassessment of the future and the past). *Alþýðublaðið*.

Bleier, M. E. (2008, August). *From 'bad' bank to 'good'*. ReedSmith (Client Alert 08–143). https://www.reedsmith.com/files/Publication/15cda61b-edcc-47dd-a186-cba9a4012fed/Presentation/PublicationAttachment/2e8568c2-06f1-4c05-9641-d2a0a15991ec/bull08143_200809034643.pdf

Braithwaite, T. (2008a, October 15). Green faces battle with TPG for Baugur's assets. *Financial Times*. http://www.ft.com/intl/cms/s/0/5e0c23f6-9a52-11dd-bfe2-000077b07658.html#axzz46wtmyqAJ

Braithwaite, T. (2008b, October 31). Chastened Baugur hopes to navigate debt crisis. *Financial Times*.

Brenna, G., Poppensieker, T., & Schneider, S. (2009, December). *Understanding the bad bank*. McKinsey & Company.

British and Dutch stance on Icesave hardening. (2009, September 28). *IceNews*. http://www.icenews.is/index.php/2009/09/28/british-and-dutch-stance-on-icesave-hardening/

Brogger, T. (2008, October 3). Iceland says to announce rescue plan 'very soon'. *Bloomberg*.

Bruno, V., & Shin, H. S. (2014). Assessing macroprudential policies: Case of South Korea. *Scandinavian Journal of Economics, 116*(1), 128–157.

Bullard, J. (2009). The Fed as lender of last resort. *The Regional Economist*, January issue.

Burton, K., Bit, K., & Valdimarsson, O. R. (2013, November 14). Paulson to Taconic Frozen in Iceland bet five years After. *Bloomberg*.

Campbell, A., & Moffat, P. (2013). *Protecting bank depositors after Cyprus*. Nottingham Trent University.

Central Bank of Iceland. (2003, February). *Peningamál 2003/1. (Monetary Bulletin 2003/1)*.

Central Bank of Iceland. (2004, May 16). *The Central Bank of Iceland concludes swap facility arrangements*. http://www.cb.is/publications/news/news/2008/05/16/The-Central-Bank-of-Iceland-concludes-swap-facility-arrangements/

Central Bank of Iceland. (2008a, May 8). *Fjármálastöðugleiki. (Financial Stability)*.

Central Bank of Iceland. (2008b, November 28). *New foreign exchange regulation*. (Press release No. 44/2008). http://www.cb.is/publications-news-and-speeches/news-and-speeches/news/2008/11/28/New-foreign-exchange-regulation-/

Central Bank of Iceland. (2008c, October 9). *Currency swap agreements and attempts to reinforce the foreign exchange reserves*. http://www.cb.is/

publications/news/news/2008/10/10/Currency-swap-agreements-and-attempts-to-reinforce-the-foreign-exchange-reserves-/

Central Bank of Iceland. (2009a, October 26). *Fjármálastöðugleiki (Financial Stability).* http://www.cb.is/library/Skraarsafn---EN/Financial-Stability-Report/2009/2009%20enska.pdf

Central Bank of Iceland. (2009b, October 31). *First stage of capital account liberalisation.* (Press release No. 33/2009). http://www.cb.is/publications/news/news/2009/10/31/First-stage-of-capital-account-liberalisation-/

Central Bank of Iceland. (2010a, January 5). *The Sovereign ratings company standard & poor's has placed Iceland's ratings on CreditWatch with negative implications.* http://www.cb.is/publications/news/news/2010/01/05/The-Sovereign-Ratings-Company-Standard---Poors-has-placed-Icelands-ratings/

Central Bank of Iceland. (2010b, May 19). *Central Bank of Iceland, Banque centrale du Luxembourg and the liquidator of Landsbanki Luxembourg S.A. sign an agreement in Luxembourg.* (Press release no. 11/2010).

Central Bank of Iceland. (2010c, May 31). *Pension funds purchase Treasury's HFF bonds to strengthen FX reserves.* (Press release no. 13/2010).

Central Bank of Iceland. (2010d, September 19). *FIH to be sold to a consortium of ATP, PFA, Folksam and CPDyvig.* (Press release No. 26/2010). http://www.cb.is/publications/news/news/2010/09/19/FIH-to-be-sold-to-a-consortium-of-ATP--PFA--Folksam-and-CPDyvig-/

Central Bank of Iceland. (2010e, November 1). *Rules on foreign exchange.* (Press release no. 29/2010). http://www.cb.is/publications/news/news/2010/11/01/Rules-on-Foreign-Exchange/

Central Bank of Iceland. (2010f, September 19). *Sale of Danish bank FIH.* http://www.cb.is/publications/news/news/2010/09/19/FIH-to-be-sold-to-a-consortium-of-ATP--PFA--Folksam-and-CPDyvig-/

Central Bank of Iceland. (2011, March 25). *Áætlun um losun gjaldeyrishafta. (A plan for lifting capital controls.)* http://www.cb.is/lisalib/getfile.aspx?itemid=8673

Central Bank of Iceland. (2012a, March 27). *Gjaldeyriseftirlit Seðlabanka Íslands framkvæmir húsleitir. (The Central Bank's capital control surveillance unit conducts raids.)* (Press release no. 13/2012).

Central Bank of Iceland. (2012b, September). *Valkostir Íslands í gjaldmiðils- og gengismálum. (Iceland's options regarding currency and foreign exchange.)* (The Central Bank's special publication no. 7). http://www.cb.is/publications/news/news/2012/09/24/Translation-of-Special-Publication-no.-7/

Central Bank of Iceland. (2013a, March 30). *Annual Report 2012.* http://cb.is/library/Skraarsafn---EN/Annual-Report/Annual%20Report%202012.pdf

Central Bank of Iceland. (2013b, September 30). *Svar til slitastjórnar Glitnis. (Reply to Glitnir's winding-up board)*. http://www.cb.is/publications/news/news/2013/09/30/A-reply-to-the-winding-up-committee-of-Glitnir-hf/

Central Bank of Iceland. (2014, March 28). *Annual report 2013*. http://cb.is/library/Skraarsafn---EN/Annual-Report/AR_Heildarskjal%20N%C3%BDtt.pdf

Central Bank of Iceland. (2015a, June 8). *Announcement concerning capital account liberalization measures*. (Press release No. 13/2015). http://www.cb.is/publications/news/news/2015/06/09/Announcement-concerning-capital-account-liberalisation-measures/

Central Bank of Iceland. (2015b, March 27). *Annual report 2014*. http://cb.is/library/Skraarsafn---EN/Annual-Report/Annual%20Report%202014_01%2004%2015%20(2).pdf

Central Bank of Iceland. (2015c, March 6). *Undanþágulistum og reglum Seðlabanka Íslands um gjaldeyrismál breytt. (Exemption lists and the Central Bank's rules on foreign exchange changed)*. (Press release no. 7/2015). http://www.cb.is/publications/news/news/2015/03/06/Amendments-to-Central-Bank-of-Iceland-Rules-on-Foreign-Exchange-and-exemption-lists/

Central Bank of Iceland. (2015d, October 27). *Uppgjör fallinna fjármálafyrirtækja á grundvelli stöðugleikaskilyrða: áhrif á greiðslujöfnuð og fjármálastöðugleika. (Settlement of the failed financial institutions on the basis of stability conditions: Impact on balance of payments and financial stability.)*http://sedlabanki.is/library/Skraarsafn/Gjaldeyrismal/AssessmentOfPreliminaryCompositionProposals.pdf

Central Bank of Iceland. (2015e, October 28). *Seðlabanki Íslands hefur lokið mati sínu á fyrirliggjandi drögum að nauðasamningum. (The Central Bank has concluded its assessment of composition agreement drafts.)* http://www.cb.is/publications/news/news/2015/10/28/Central-Bank-concludes-assessment-of-preliminary-composition-proposals/

Central Bank of Iceland. (2015f, September 6). *Til upplýsingar vegna frétta af niðurfellingu máls embættis sérstaks saksóknara gegn Samherja. (Information regarding news of the suspension of the Special Prosecutor's case against Samherji.)*

Central Bank of Iceland. (2016a, March 17). *Annual Report 2015*. http://cb.is/library/Skraarsafn---EN/Annual-Report/Annual%20Report%202015_18.03.16.pdf

Central Bank of Iceland. (2016b, May 25). *Central Bank of Iceland foreign currency auction 16 June 2016*. http://www.cb.is/publications/news/news/2016/05/25/Central-Bank-of-Iceland-foreign-currency-auction-16-June-2016-/

Central Bank of Iceland. (2016c, June 4). *Rules on special reserve requirements for new foreign currency inflows*. (Rules no. 490/2016.) http://www.cb.is/library/Skraarsafn---EN/Rules/Rules%20no.%20490%202016.pdf

Central Bank of Iceland. (n.d.). *Terms of auction for the purchase of foreign currency by the Central Bank of Iceland according to the investment programme.* Transaction date: 10 February 2015.

Central Bank of Iceland. (n.d.). *Terms of auction for the purchase of foreign currency by the Central Bank of Iceland in exchange for Treasury securities.* Transaction date: 10 February 2015.

Committee on the restoration of the financial system. (2009, February 5). *Starfsáætlun Nr. 1. (Work schedule No. 1).* https://www.forsaetisraduneyti.is/media/Skyrslur/starfsaaetlun1.pdf

Consultation group on preparedness for possible difficulties in financial markets. (2006, February 17). Viðbúnaður stjórnvalda vegna hugsanlegra erfiðleika á fjármálamarkaði. (A contingency plan for possible difficulties in financial markets). https://www.forsaetisraduneyti.is/media/frettir/Skilabref,_greinargerd_og_samkomulag.doc

CreditFixings. (2008a). *Glitnir Banki hf. CDS Auction Results, Thursday 4th November 2008.* http://www.creditfixings.com/information/affiliations/fixings/auctions/2008/glitni-res.shtml

CreditFixings. (2008b). *Kaupthing banki hf. CDS Auction Results, Thursday 6th November 2008.* http://www.creditfixings.com/information/affiliations/fixings/auctions/2008/kaupth-res.shtml

CreditFixings. (2008c). *Landsbanki Íslands hf. CDS Auction Results, Thursday 4th November 2008.* http://www.creditfixings.com/information/affiliations/fixings/auctions/2008/landsb-res.shtml

Daniel, R. H. (2004). An alternative approach to government managed companies: The Mellon approach. In M. Pomerleano & W. Shaw (Eds.), *Corporate restructuring: Lessons from experience.* Washington DC: The World Bank.

Daníelsson, J. (2008, November 12). The first casualty of the crisis: Iceland. *VOX CEPR's Policy Portal.* http://www.voxeu.org/article/how-bad-could-crisis-get-lessons-iceland

Daníelsson, J., & Jónsson, Á. (2005). Countercyclical capital and currency dependence. *Financial Markets, Institutions & Instruments, 14*(5), 329–348.

Danske Bank. (2006, March 21). *Iceland: Geyser crisis.* http://www.mbl.is/media/98/398.pdf

Darling, A. (2013, February 4). A crisis needs a firewall not a ringfence. *Financial Times.* http://www.ft.com/intl/cms/s/0/3d164732-6ec7-11e2-9ded-00144feab49a.html#axzz4311ZfvHa

Davey, J. (2008, October 11). Philip Green in talks to take on Baugur debt. *Reuters.* http://uk.reuters.com/article/uk-financial-iceland-green-idUKTRE49A0GO20081011

Dawson, T. C. (2002, June 13). *Stiglitz, the IMF and Globalization.* A speech to the MIT Club of Washington. https://www.imf.org/external/np/speeches/2002/061302.htm

Department of Justice. (2008a, December 12). *Special prosecutor is open for application.* https://www.innanrikisraduneyti.is/media/frettir/Auglysing_serstakur_saksoknari.pdf

Department of Justice. (2008b, December 30). *Deadline for the position of special prosecutor extended to January 12.* https://www.innanrikisraduneyti.is/frettir/frettatilkynningar/nr/6593

Diamond, D. W., & Dybvig, P. H. (1983). Bank runs, deposit insurance, and liquidity. *Journal of Political Economy, 91*(3), 401–419.

Does this BBC man have too much power? Reporter blamed for helping trigger shares fall. (2008, October 8). *Mail Online.* http://www.dailymail.co.uk/news/article-1072549/BBC-reporter-Robert-Peston-blamed-helping-trigger-shares-fall.html#ixzz434xWkFkk

Doraisami, A. (2004). From crisis to recovery: The motivations for and effects of Malaysian capital controls. *Journal of International Development, 16*(2), 241–254.

DueDil. (n.d.). *Burlington loan management limited.* Retrieved on May 1 from https://www.duedil.com/company/IE470093/burlington-loan-management-limited

Eagleson, W. R. (1990). How good is a bad bank? *The Real Estate Finance Journal, 6*(1), 71–75.

EFTA Court. (2013, January 28). *Judgment of the court in Case E-16/11 – EFTA Surveillance Authority v Iceland.* http://www.eftacourt.int/index.php/cases/case_e_16_11_efta_surveillance_authority_v_the_republic_of_iceland

Eichengreen, B. (1989, September). The capital Levy in theory and practice. *NBER working paper series,* no. 3096.

Eichengreen, B., Tobin, J., & Wyplosz, C. (1995). Two cases for sand in the wheels of international finance. *The Economic Journal, 105*(Jan.), 162–172.

Einarsson, K. T., & Björnsson, B. J. (2006, December 22). Davíð gangrýnir ákvörðun Straums. (Davíð criticizes Straumur's decision). *Morgunblaðið.* http://www.mbl.is/vidskipti/frettir/2006/12/22/david_gagnrynir_akvordun_straums/

Emigration from Canada: Tax Implications. (2014, November). *Manulife.* https://repsourcepublic.manulife.com/wps/wcm/connect/5cb1c800433c4450b901ff319e0f5575/ins_tepg_taxtopicemigrtn.pdf?MOD=AJPERES

Ernst & Young. (2015a, November 5). *Kaupthing Singer & Friedlander Limited (in Administration) Joint Administrators' Progress Report to creditors for the six month period from 8 April to 7 October 2015.*

Ernst & Young. (2015b, September 6). *Heritable Bank Plc. (in Administration) Administrators' nineteenth progress report to creditors.*

Eurogroup. (2013, March 16). *Eurogroup statement on Cyprus.*

European Monitoring Centre on Change. (2012, May 21). *Banque Havilland, Luxembourg.* http://www.eurofound.europa.eu/observatories/erm/restructuring-in-smes/banque-havilland-luxembourg

Extra help for Icesave customers. (2008, October 8). *BBC News.* http://news.bbc.co.uk/2/hi/business/7658417.stm

Eyjólfsson, Þ. (2014, January 27). Af gjaldeyrisútboðum Seðlabankans. (On the Central Bank's currency auctions). *Morgunblaðið.* http://www.sedlabanki.is/utgefid-efni/frettir-og-tilkynningar/frettasafn/frett/2014/01/28/Af-gjaldeyrisutbodum-Sedlabankans/

Fá starfsmenn Landsbankans greidd laun? (Will Landsbankinn staff be paid salary?). (2008, October 9). *Vísir.* http://www.visir.is/fa-starfsmenn-landsbankans-greidd-laun-/article/2008146114965

Fadnes, O. M. (2009, January 16). Sparebankenes røverkjøp. (Sparebanken's bargain). *Dagens Næringsliv.* http://www.dn.no/nyheter/2009/01/16/sparebankenes-roverkjop

Feldman, G. D., & Seibel, W. (2004, December). *Networks of Nazi Persecution: Bureaucracy, Business and the Organization of the Holocaust.*

Financial crisis: Full statement by Iceland's prime minister Geir Haarde. (2008, October 6). *The Telegraph.* http://www.telegraph.co.uk/news/worldnews/europe/iceland/3147806/Financial-crisis-Full-statement-by-Icelands-prime-minister-Geir-Haarde.html

Financial Supervisory Authority. (2007, February). *Reikningsskil í erlendri mynt. (Accounting in foreign currency).* http://www.fme.is/media/utgefid-efni/08_03_2007_Reikningsskil-i-erlendri-mynt_Skyrsla-FME-um-uppgjor-i-erlendri-mynt.pdf

Financial Supervisory Authority. (2008a, September). *Heildarniðurstöður ársreikninga fjármálafyrirtækja og verðbréfa- og fjárfestingarsjóða fyrir árið 2007. (Summary of annual financial statements of financial companies and mutual and investment funds for the year 2007.)* http://www.fme.is/media/utgefid-efni/2007_Efnahags--og-rekstrarreikningar-banka-og-sparisjoda,-verdbrefafyrirtaekja-og-verdbrefamidlana,-rekstrarfelaga-verdbrefasjoda,-asamt-ymsum-kennitolum-og-odrum-upplysingum-31_12_2007.pdf

Financial Supervisory Authority. (2008b, October 12). *Ákvörðun Fjármálaeftirlitsins um breytingu á ákvörðun Fjármálaeftirlitsins þann 9. október 2008 um ráðstöfun eigna og skulda Landsbanka Íslands hf. til Nýja Landsbanka Íslands hf. (The FSA's decision on the amendment of the FSA's decision from October 9 2008 on the allocation of assets and liabilities of Landsbanki Íslands hf. to New Landsbanki Íslands hf.)* (Reference no. 200810037). http://www.fme.is/media/akvardanir/12.-oktober-2008.pdf

Financial Supervisory Authority. (2008c, October 21). *Ákvörðun Fjármálaeftirlitsins um ráðstöfun eigna og skulda Kaupþings banka hf. til Nýja Kaupþings banka hf. (The FSA's decision on the allocation of the assets and liabilities of Kaupthing bank hf. to New Kaupthing bank hf.)* (Reference no. 200810055). http://www.fme.is/media/akvardanir/22.-oktober-2008.pdf

Financial Supervisory Authority. (2009, March 21). *Ákvörðun Fjármálaeftirlitsins um ráðstöfun eigna og skulda Sparisjóðs Reykjavíkur og nágrennis. (The FSA's decision on the allocation of the assets and liabilities of SRPON.)* (Reference no. 2009030080). http://www.fme.is/media/akvardanir/21.-mars-2009.pdf

Financial Supervisory Authority. (2012, November 21). *Gagnsæistilkynning vegna athugunar á starfsháttum Dróma hf. (Transparency notification regarding examination of working practices of Drómi hf.).* http://www.fme.is/media/gagnsaei/Gagnsaeistilkynning---Dromi-21.11.pdf

Financial Supervisory Authority. (2015, June 8). *Aðgerðaáætlun til losunar fjármagnshafta. (Action plan for lifting capital controls.)*

Financial Supervisory Authority. (2016, June). *Fjármálafyrirtæki o.fl. Heildarniðurstöður ársreikninga 2015. (Financial companies etc. Summary of annual financial statements 2015.)* http://www.fme.is/media/utgefid-efni/Arsreikningabok-2015---lanamarkadur.pdf

Fitch Ratings. (2010, January 5). *Fitch downgrades Iceland to 'BB+'/'BBB+'; outlook negative.* http://sedlabanki.is/lisalib/getfile.aspx?itemid=7555

Fitch Ratings. (2015, July 24). *Fitch Upgrades Iceland to 'BBB+'; Outlook Stable.*

Fletcher, R., & Mason, R. (2008, October 12). Sir Philip Green poised for Baugur bail-out. *The Telegraph online.* http://www.telegraph.co.uk/finance/newsbysector/retailandconsumer/3185137/Sir-Philip-Green-poised-for-Baugur-bail-out.html

Foong, K. K. (2008). Managing capital flows: the case of Malaysia (No. 93). ADB Institute Discussion papers.

Forbes. (2016). *The World's Billionaires.* http://www.forbes.com/billionaires/list/

Gibberd, M., & Hill, A. (2013, August 20). The return of ornamentation. *The Telegraph.* http://www.telegraph.co.uk/luxury/property-and-architecture/7279/the-return-of-ornamentation.html

Glasner, D. (ed.). (1997). *Business cycles and depressions: An encyclopedia.* New York: Garland Reference Library of Social Science.

Glitnir. (2008). *Condensed consolidated interim financial statements. 30 June 2008.*

Glitnir. (2009, December 8). *List of claims.*

Glitnir. (2012, November 9). *Announcement from the winding up board of Glitnir hf.*

Glitnir. (2013a, November 16). *Analysis of trading activity in Glitnir hf. claims.*

Glitnir. (2013b, November 18). *Announcement from the winding up board of Glitnir Hf.* http://www.glitnirbank.com/press-room/548-announcment-from-the-winding-up-board-18-nov2013.html

Glitnir. (2015a, December 16). *Exemption granted by the Central Bank of Iceland.*

Glitnir. (2015b, December 5). *Glitnir's proposed composition.*

Glitnir. (2015c, November 20). *Results of the voting at the OCM on 20 November 2015.*

Glitnir. (2015d, November). *Composition agreement.*

Glitnir. (2016, January 8). *Completion of the composition – Issue of new notes and new ordinary shares.*

Goodfriend, M. (2012). *The elusive promise of independent central banking,* No 12-E-09, IMES discussion paper series, Institute for Monetary and Economic Studies, Bank of Japan.

Gordon Brown mocked over 'save the world' slip-up in Commons. (2008, December 10). *The Telegraph Online.* http://www.telegraph.co.uk/news/politics/3701712/Gordon-Brown-mocked-over-save-the-world-slip-up-in-Commons.html

Government Debt Management. (2001, November 23). Government debt management prospect 2002. http://news.icex.is/newsservice/MMIcexNSWeb.dll/newspage?language=EN&primarylanguagecode=EN&newsnumber=13446

Government Debt Management. (2008a, May 13). Tariffs for securities lending and their limits. http://www.lanamal.is/assets/nyrlanasysla/gjaldskramai_08.pdf

Government Debt Management. (2008b, May 23). Signing of agreements regarding issuance and market making in government securities. http://www.lanamal.is/en/investors/primary-dealers-for-government-securities/primary-dealers-agreement/nanar/937/signing-of-agreements-regarding-issuance-and-market-making-in-government-securities

Government Debt Management. (2016, March). *Markaðsupplýsingar. (Market information).* 17(3). http://www.lanamal.is/GetAsset.ashx?id=8484

Grant Street National Bank (in liquidation) reports results. (1995, January 30). *PR Newswire.*

Green vildi kaupa skuldir Baugs með 95% afslætti. (Green wanted to buy Baugur's debt at a 95% discount.) (2008, October 14). *Morgunblaðið.*

Greiði gjald fyrir forgang. (Pay a Fee for Priority.) (2014, November 18). *Morgunblaðið.*

Grossman, R., & Rockoff, H. (2015). Fighting the last war: Economists on the lender of last resort. *Departmental working papers.* Rutgers University, Department of Economics.

Gunnlaugsson, S. D. (2015, April 10). Yfirlitsræða forsætisráðherra og formanns Framsóknarflokksins á 33. flokksþingi framsóknarmanna. (Summary speech given by the prime minister and chairman of the Progressive party at the 33. Progressive Party congress.) http://www.framsokn.is/wp-content/uploads/Yfirlitsræða-Sigmundar-Davíðs-Gunnlaugssonar-á-33.-flokksþingi-Framsóknarflokksins-2015.pdf

Guðbjartsson, S. (2008, October 8). Bankafólk í kreppu. (Bank staff in a crisis). *Morgunblaðið*

Guðnason, E. (1989). Bindiskylda. (Reserve requirement). *Fjármálatíðindi*, pp. 15–26. http://www.sedlabanki.is/library/Skraarsafn/Fjármálatíðindi/Gömul-Fjármálatíðindi/Fjármálatíðindi%201989%20jan%20-%20apr.pdf

Hafberg, H. M., Finnbogadóttir, T., & Karlsson, B. F. (2014, April 10). *Special investigation commission report on the background and causes of the difficulties and fall of the savings banks.* Parliamentary Special Investigation Commission.

Hay, G. (2008, October 27). Frozen assets. *Breaking Views.* http://www.breakingviews.com/considered-view/icelands-creditors-looking-at-40bn-hit

Heikensten, L. (1998, July 15). Financial crisis – Experiences from Sweden. *Seminar organized by the Swedish Embassy in Korea.* http://www.riksbank.se/sv/Press-och-publicerat/Tal/1998/Financial-Crisis----Experiences-from-Sweden/

Her Majesty's Government. (2013, May). *Scotland analysis: Financial services and banking.* https://www.gov.uk/government/uploads/system/uploads/attachment_data/file/200491/scotland_analysis_financial_services_and_banking_200513.pdf

Her Majesty's Treasury. (2008a, October 17). *The Landsbanki Freezing Order 2008.* (Financial Sanctions Notice). http://www.mbl.is/media/24/1024.pdf

Her Majesty's Treasury. (2008b, October 8). *The Landsbanki Freezing Order 2008.* (Statutory Instruments 2008 No. 2668). http://www.legislation.gov.uk/uksi/2008/2668/pdfs/uksi_20082668_en.pdf

Hermannsson, G. S., & Pálmason, R. (2011, November 16). Umdeildir eigendur að bönkunum. (Controversial bank owners.) *Morgunblaðið.*

Honkaphohja, S. (2009). The 1990s financial crises in Nordic countries. *Bank of Finland Research discussion papers.* 5. http://www.riksbank.se/Upload/Dokument_riksbank/Kat_foa/2009/6_8nov/Honkapohja.pdf

Hosking, P. (2006, July 8). How do I pick my stocks? I hear voices. *The Times.* http://www.thetimes.co.uk/tto/business/columnists/article2621796.ece

Ibison, D. (2008, November 11). Iceland's rescue package flounders. *Financial Times*. http://www.ft.com/cms/s/0/ed069984-b022-11dd-a795-0000779fd18c.html

Iceland close to reaching compensation deal for UK Icesave customers. (2008, November 14). *The Telegraph online version*. http://www.telegraph.co.uk/news/worldnews/europe/iceland/3460807/Iceland-close-to-reaching-compensation-deal-for-UK-Icesave-customers.html

Iceland leader vetoes bank repayments bill. (2010, January 5). *BBC News*. http://news.bbc.co.uk/2/hi/business/8441312.stm

Iceland turns to European Commission for funds. (2008, November 10). *Reuters*. http://www.reuters.com/article/eu-iceland-idUSBRU00697220081110

Icelandic State Audit. (2012, June). *Report to the Icelandic Parliament. The Governments facilitation to financial companies and institutions in the wake of the banking crisis*. http://www.rikisendurskodun.is/fileadmin/media/skyrslur/fyrirgreidsla_vid_fjarmalafyrirtaeki2.pdf

InDefence. (2015, June 17). *Umsögn og ábendingar um frumvarp til laga um stöðugleikaskatt, 786. mál og frumvarp til laga um fjármálafyrirtæki (nauðasamningar), 787. mál*. http://www.althingi.is/altext/erindi/144/144-2306.pdf

Independence Party. (2011, November 20). *Drög að stjórnmálaályktun 40. landsfundar Sjálfstæðisflokksins. (Draft political resolution of the 40th national convention of the Independence Party.)* http://www.xd.is/media/xd/landsfundur-2011/Stjornmalaalyktun-loka.pdf

International Monetary Fund. (2005, October). *Iceland: Selected issues*. (IMF Country Report No. 05/366).

International Monetary Fund. (2008a, November 15). *Iceland: Letter of intent and technical memorandum of understanding*. https://www.imf.org/external/np/loi/2008/isl/111508.pdf

International Monetary Fund. (2008b, November 19). *IMF executive board approves US$2.1 billion stand-by arrangement for Iceland*. (Press Release No.08/296) https://www.imf.org/external/np/sec/pr/2008/pr08296.htm

International Monetary Fund. (2008c, October 24). *IMF announces staff level agreement with Iceland on US$2.1 billion loan*. (Press Release No. 08/256). https://www.imf.org/external/np/sec/pr/2008/pr08256.htm

International Monetary Fund. (2010, October). *Iceland: 2010 article IV consultation and third review under stand-by arrangement and request for modification of performance criteria*. IMF Country Report No. 10/305. https://www.imf.org/external/pubs/ft/scr/2010/cr10305.pdf

International Monetary Fund. (2011a, August). *Iceland: Sixth review under the stand-by arrangement and proposal for post-program monitoring.* IMF Country Report No. 11/263. https://www.imf.org/external/pubs/ft/scr/2011/cr11263.pdf

International Monetary Fund. (2011b, October 27). *Iceland's recovery – Lessons and challenges.* http://www.imf.org/external/np/seminars/eng/2011/isl/index.htm

International Monetary Fund. (2012a, November 14). *The liberalization and management of capital flows: An institutional view.* Washington, D.C.: International Monetary Fund.

International Monetary Fund. (2012b. April). *Iceland: Ex post evaluation of exceptional access under the 2008 stand-by arrangement.* Washington, D.C.: International Monetary Fund

Jännäri, K. (2009, March 30). *Report on banking regulation and supervision in Iceland: Past, present and future.*

Jónsson, Á. (2009a). *Why Iceland?: How one of the world's smallest countries became the meltdown's biggest casualty.* Columbus: McGraw Hill Professional.

Jónsson, J. G. (2009b, April 24). Endurreisn án eftirskjálfta. (Restoration without aftershocks). *Morgunblaðið.*

Jónsson, G. F. (2011, May 30). Í þumalskrúfu vogunarsjóða. (In hedge funds' thumbscrew). *Morgunblaðið.*

Jónsson, Á., & Sigurgeirsson, H. (2015, May). *Drög að uppgjöri. (A draft of a resolution).* Reykjavík: Auðfræðasetur. http://audfraedi.is/utgefin-rit/frett/2015/05/06/Drog-ad-uppgjori/

Jónsson, Á., Jóhannesson, S., Ármann, V., Benaben, B., & Perucci, S. (2012). *Nauðsyn eða val? Verðtrygging, vextir og verðbólga á Íslandi. (Necessity or choice? Indexation, interests and inflation in Iceland).* Reykjavík: Icelandic Financial Services Association.

Jonung, L. (2009). *The Swedish model for resolving the banking crisis of 1991–93. Seven reasons why it was successful* (No. 360). Directorate General Economic and Monetary Affairs (DG ECFIN), European Commission.

Júlíusson, Þ. S. (2009, January 21). Seldur á brot af raunvirði. (Sold for a fraction of real value). *Morgunblaðið.*

Júlíusson, Þ. S. (2013, February 23). Kröfuhafar stofna krónuhóp. (Creditors form an ISK group.) *Fréttablaðið.*

Júlíusson, Þ. S. (2014, December 4). Sjóður eins ríkasta manns heims búinn að selja allar kröfur á Glitni. (The fund of one of the richest men in the world has sold all its claims on Glitnir). *Kjarninn.*

Júlíusson, Þ. S. (2015, January 12). Paulson enn tengdur inn í kröfuhafahóp Glitnis. (Paulson still connected to Glitnir's creditor group.) *Kjarninn*.

Kaminsky, G. L., & Reinhart, C. M. (1999). The twin crises: The causes of banking and balance of payments problems. *American Economic Review, 89* (3), 473–500.

Kaupthing. (2008, November 24). *Kaupthing Bank hf. granted a moratorium.* http://www.kaupthing.com/home/announcements/all-announcements/2008/ 11/24/Kaupthing-Bank-hf.-granted-a-moratorium/

Kaupthing. (2009, February 10). *Kaupthing Bank has secured sufficient funds to pay back the large majority of German Kaupthing EDGE deposits.* (Press release). http://www.kaupthing.com/home/announcements/all-announcements/ 2009/02/10/Kaupthing-Bank-has-secured-sufficient-funds-to-pay-back-the-large-majority-of-German-Kaupthing-EDGE-deposits/

Kaupthing. (2010, November 22). *Kaupthing formally enters winding-up procedure.* http://www.kaupthing.com/home/announcements/all-announcements/ 2010/11/22/Kaupthing-formally-enters-winding-up-procedure/

Kaupthing. (2012, November 13). *Further update on targeted launch of composition.*

Kaupthing. (2014, May 19). *Announcement from Kaupthing's Winding-up Committee.* http://www.kaupthing.com/home/announcements/all-announcements/ 2014/05/19/Announcement-from-Kaupthings-Winding-up-Committee

Kaupthing. (2015a, December 15). *Composition confirmed by the district court.*

Kaupthing. (2015b, November 24). *Composition voting meeting 24 November 2015 – Composition proposal approved.*

Kaupthing. (2016a). *Financial statements for the year ended 31 December 2015.*

Kaupthing. (2016b, February 3). *Announcement regarding distribution of composition entitlements*

Kaupthing. (2016c, January 15). *Kaupthing composition – Exemption granted by the Central Bank of Iceland.*

Kawai, M., & Takagi, S. (2003). *Rethinking capital controls: The Malaysian experience.* Macroeconomics working papers, p. 473.

Kleinman, M., & Mason, R. (2008, October 11). Iceland crisis lures Topshop boss Sir Philip Green to Baugur deal. *The Telegraph.*

Klingebiel, D. (2000, February). *The use of asset management companies in the resolution of banking crisis: Cross-country experiences.* World Bank, Financial Sector Strategy and Policy Group.

Kochhar, K. (ed.) (1999). Malaysia, selected issues (No. 98–114). *International Monetary Fund.*

Krugman, P. (2008a, October 12). Gordon does good. *The New York Times Opinion Pages.* http://www.nytimes.com/2008/10/13/opinion/13krugman.html?_r=0

Krugman, P. (2008b, September 30). The $850 billion bailout. *The New York Times Opinion Pages.* http://krugman.blogs.nytimes.com/2008/09/30/the-850-billion-bailout/

Krugman, P. (2010a, June 30). The Icelandic Post-crisis miracle. *The New York Times.* http://krugman.blogs.nytimes.com/2010/06/30/the-icelandic-post-crisis-miracle/?scp=1&sq=+Iceland%

Krugman, P. (2010b, November 24). Lands of Ice and Ire. *The New York Times.* http://krugman.blogs.nytimes.com/2010/11/24/lands-of-ice-and-ire/?_r=0

Krugman, P. (2010c, November 25). Eating the Irish. *The New York Times.*

Landsbankinn: Einkabankasvið og Verðbréfasvið lögð af. (Landsbankinn: Private banking and Investment banking discontinued.). (2008, October 9). Viðskiptablaðið. http://www.vb.is/frettir/landsbankinn-einkabankasvi-og-verbrefasvi-log-af/12692/

Laryea, T. (2010, January 26). Approaches to corporate debt restructuring in the wake of financial crises. *IMF Staff Position Note,* SPN/10/02. *International Monetary Fund.* https://www.imf.org/external/pubs/ft/spn/2010/spn1002.pdf

Lastra, R., & Buchheit, L. (Eds.). (2014). *Sovereign debt management.* Oxford: Oxford University Press.

LBI hf. (2009a, February 6). *BG Holding ehf placed into administration.* http://lbi.is/home/news/news-item/2009/02/06/BG-Holding-ehf-placed-into-administration/

LBI hf. (2009b). *List of claims.*

LBI hf. (2011, March 2). *LBI financial information 2010.* https://lbi.is/library/Opin-gogn/skyrslan/Q4%20Financial%20Information%20-%20open%20side.pdf

LBI hf. (2015a, December 18). *Composition confirmed by the district court.*

LBI hf. (2015b, November 23). *Outcome of voting on the composition proposal of LBI hf.*

LBI hf. (2015c, November). *Composition agreement.*

LBI hf. (2016a, January 11). *Exemption from capital controls – Final settlement of priority claims.*

LBI hf. (2016b, March 23.) *Status and fulfilment of the composition agreement.*

Lehman Brothers collapse, five years on: 'We had almost no control'. (2013, September 13). *The Guardian Online.* http://www.theguardian.com/business/2013/sep/13/lehman-brothers-collapse-five-years-later-shiver-spine

Levine, R. (1997). Financial development and economic growth: Views and agenda. *Journal of Economic Literature, XXXV,* 688–726.

Lewis, M. (2009, April). Wall Street on the Tundra. *Vanity Fair.* http://www.vanityfair.com/culture/2009/04/iceland200904

Liikanen, E. (2012, October). High-level expert group on reforming the structure of the EU banking sector, Final report.

Lupu, R., & Calin, A. C. (2014). To QE or not to QE? The Japanese experience. *Hyperion Economic Journal, 2*(2), 3–10.

MacFarquhar, N. (2008, October 11). A U.N. Charm offensive topped off by dessert. *The New York Times.* http://www.nytimes.com/2008/10/12/world/12nations.html

Macro-Prudential Stability Levy. (2010, December 20). *Joint press release from the Financial Services Commission and Financial Supervisory Service.* South Korea.

Matthíasson, V. M. (2008, November 12). *Álitsgerð. (Legal opinion).* http://www.visir.is/assets/pdf/XZ672616.PDF

Matthíasson, Þ. (2013, July). The Icelandic response to the collapse of the financial sector in October 2008. *Institute of Economic Studies Working paper series,* (W13), 01.

Maxwell, C. (2009, February 11). *Landsbanki Freezing Order 2008.* https://www.forsaetisraduneyti.is/media/island/frettir/42.pdf

McCrum, D. (2011, July 26). Soros to close Quantum fund to outsiders. *Financial Times.*

Meeting of the Parliamentary Committee of Economic Affairs and Trade. (2015, April 13). *From 31:52 to 32:13.* http://www.althingi.is/altext/upptokur/nefndafundur/?faerslunr=36

Meijer, R. (2008, December 11). Operatie Icesave: 20.000 spaarders moeten formulier nog opsturen! *De Telegraf.* http://www.telegraaf.nl/overgeld/rubriek/sparen/article2771885.ece

Merrill Lynch. (2008, March 12). *Eschatological. Time to go long.*

Mies van der Rohe Prize. (2013). *Harpa – Reykjavik concert hall and conference centre.* http://www.miesarch.com/work/535

Mills, J. (1867). *Article read before the Manchester Statistical Society, December 11, 1867, on credit cycles and the origin of commercial panics.* Transactions of the Manchester Statistical Society, session 1867–68.

Ministry of Finance. (2011a, August 25). *Skýrsla fjármálaráðherra um mat á áhrifum af beitingu Breta á lögum um varnir gegn hryðjuverkum, glæpum og um öryggi fyrir íslensk fyrirtæki, samkvæmt beiðni. (Report of the minister of finance on the impact of the application of the British Anti-terrorism, Crime and Security Act on Icelandic companies, as requested)*. https://www.fjarmalaraduneyti.is/media/utgafa/Skyrsla_fmrh_ahrif_hvl.pdf

Ministry of Finance. (2011b, March). *Skýrsla fjármálaráðherra um endurreisn viðskiptabankanna. (Minister of finance report on the restoration of the commercial banks)*.

Ministry of Finance. (2014a, July 9). Agreement with advisors to work on removal of capital controls. https://www.ministryoffinance.is/news/2014

Ministry of Finance. (2014b, March 26). *Debt Relief Will Reach 100,000 Households*. https://eng.fjarmalaraduneyti.is/news/nr/17835

Ministry of Finance. (2015a, June 8). *Capital account liberalization*. http://www.ministryoffinance.is/media/frettatengt2015/Capital-Account-Liberalisation.pdf

Minister of Finance. (2015b, March 18). *Framgangur áætlunar um losun fjármagnshafta. (The progress of the program of capital account liberalization)*. https://www.fjarmalaraduneyti.is/media/frettatengt2015/Framgangur-aaetlunar-um-losun-fjarmagnshafta-18.3.2015.pdf

Minister of Finance. (2016a, May 20). *Frumvarp til laga um meðferð krónueigna sem háðar eru sérstökum takmörkunum. (A bill on the treatment of ISK assets that are subject to special restrictions.)* (Þskj. 1314 – 777. mál, 145. löggjafarþing.)

Minister of Finance. (2016b, May 31). Svar fjármála- og efnahagsráðherra við fyrirspurn frá Haraldi Einarssyni um byggingarkostnað Hörpu. (The Minister of Finance's answer to Haraldur Einarsson's inquiry on the cost of construction of Harpa.) http://www.althingi.is/altext/145/s/1388.html

Ministry of Foreign Affairs. (2009, August 8). *Skýrsla um framboð Íslands og kosningabaráttu til sætis í öryggisráði Sameinuðu þjóðanna 2009-2010. (Report on Iceland's candidacy and campaign for a seat in the United Nations Security Council 2009-2010.)* https://www.utanrikisraduneyti.is/media/PDF/Lokaskyrsla_um_oryggisradsframbodid_2008.PDF

Moody, J. (2009, March 18). Vanity Fair's Fishy Tales From Iceland. *New York Magazine.* http://nymag.com/daily/intelligencer/2009/03/reality_check_vanity_fairs_fis.html#

Moody's Investors Service (2002, October 20). *Rating action: Moody's upgrades foreign currency ratings of Australia, New Zealand and Iceland to Aaa*

Moody's Investors Service. (2008, September 30). *Rating action: Moody's downgrades Glitnir to Baa2/Prime-2/D from A2/Prime-1/C-.*

Moody's Investor Service. (2009, June 29). *Rating Action: Moody's upgrades Iceland's sovereign ratings to Baa2; outlook stable.*

Moody's Investors Service, Global Credit Research. (2007, March). *Incorporation of joint-default analysis into Moody's bank ratings: A refined methodology.* (Report number 102639).

Mortished, C. (2008, April 3). Iceland puts the freeze on krona speculators as economy boils over. *The Times.* http://www.thetimes.co.uk/tto/business/eco nomics/article2147241.ece

National Audit Office. (2010, December 15). *Maintaining the financial stability of UK banks: Update on the support schemes.* (Report by the comptroller and auditor general, HC 676, Session 2010-2011). https://www.nao.org.uk/wp-content/uploads/2010/12/1011676.pdf

O'Brien, D. (2003). The lender-of-last-resort concept in Britain. *History of Political Economy, 35*(1), 1–19.

Official Journal of the Grand Duchy of Luxembourg: Recueil des Societes et Associations. (2011, September 3).

Outcry Grows Over Transfer of U.K. Funds by Lehman. (2008, September 22). *Wall Street Journal online version.* http://www.wsj.com/articles/ SB122204286442761375

Parliamentary Committee on Foreign Affairs. (2008, December 5). *Nefndarálit um tillögu til þingsályktunar um samninga varðandi ábyrgð ríkissjóðs á innstæðutryggingum vegna innstæðna í útibúum íslenskra viðskiptabanka á Evrópska efnahagssvæðinu. (Committee report on a parliamentary resolution on contracts for government guarantees of deposit insurance for deposits in branches of Icelandic commercial banks in the European Economic Area.).*

Paulson, H. (2010). *On the brink: Inside the race to stop the collapse of the global financial system.* New York: Business Plus.

Peston's Picks: Banks ask chancellor for capital. (2008, October 7). *BBC website.* http://www.bbc.co.uk/blogs/thereporters/robertpeston/2008/10/banks_ask_ chancellor_for_capit.html

Pétursson, M. (2009, December 21). Einn heilbrigður banki á Íslandi. (One sound bank in Iceland). *Fréttablaðið.*

Pétursson, R. (2013, October 5). Talsýn um nauðasamning. (An illusion regarding composition.) *Morgunblaðið.*

Plantin, G., & Shin, H. S. (2011). Carry trades, monetary policy and speculative dynamics.

PM: Iceland cannot wait much longer for IMF payout. (2009, September 29). *IceNews* http://www.icenews.is/index.php/2009/09/29/pm-iceland-cannot-wait-much-longer-for-imf-payout/

Power, H. (2008, April 18). John Paulson becomes $3.7bn hedge fund king betting against sub-prime. *Telegraph.*

Prime Minister's Committee on International Financial Operations. (2006, October). *Alþjóðleg fjármálastarfsemi á Íslandi. (International Financial Operations in Iceland).* https://www.forsaetisraduneyti.is/media/frettir/Skyrsla.pdf

Prime Minister's Office. (2007, May 24). *Policy statement 2007: Policy declaration of the government of the Independence Party and the Social Democratic Alliance 2007.* https://eng.forsaetisraduneyti.is/news-and-articles/nr/2646

Prime Minister's Office. (2008a, November 16). *Agreed guidelines reached on deposit guarantees.* (Press release.) https://eng.forsaetisraduneyti.is/news-and-articles/nr/3229

Prime Minister's Office. (2008b, November 16). *Agreed guidelines reached on deposit guarantees.* https://eng.forsaetisraduneyti.is/news-and-articles/nr/3229

Prime Minister's Office. (2008c, October 6). *Yfirlýsing ríkisstjórnarinnar. (Declaration by the government).* https://www.forsaetisraduneyti.is/frettir/nr/3032

Prime Minister's Office. (2011, August 26). *Iceland completes IMF Programme.* https://eng.forsaetisraduneyti.is/news-and-articles/nr/6864

Rabkin, F. (2015, March 4). Exist charges on taking money out of SA 'not a tax'. *Business Day.* http://www.bdlive.co.za/business/2015/03/04/exit-charges-on-taking-money-out-of-sa-not-a-tax.

Rafnsdóttir, G. L., Snorradóttir, Á., & Sigursteinsdóttir, H. (2014). Vinnufyrirkomulag og líðan í kjölfar kreppu. Yfirlitsgrein. (Work environment and well-being in the wake of a crisis. A summary article.) *Íslenska þjóðfé lagið,* 5(2), 39–55. http://thjodfelagid.is/index.php/Th/article/view/68

Ratification of composition agreements for Glitnir. (2015, November 25). *Lögbirtingablaðið (Icelandic Legal Gazette).*

Ratification of composition agreements for Kaupthing. (2015, November 27). *Lögbirtingablaðið (Icelandic Legal Gazette).*

Ratification of composition agreements for Landsbanki. (2015, November 30). *Lögbirtingablaðið (Icelandic Legal Gazette).*

RBS investigation: Chapter 4: the bail-out. (2011, December 11). *The Telegraph.* http://www.telegraph.co.uk/finance/newsbysector/banksandfinance/8947559/RBS-investigation-Chapter-4-the-bail-out.html

Redburn, T. (1992, September 17). But don't rush out to buy Kronor: Sweden's 500 % gamble. *The New York Times.* http://www.nytimes.com/1992/09/17/news/17iht-perc.html

Reykjanes District Court. (2014, December 18). Verdict no. S-180/2013. https://www.domstolar.is/default.aspx?pageid=347c3bb1-8926-11e5-80c6-005056bc6a40&id=448c87e1-4930-4a90-8dc4-e15d4260ea7e

Reykjavík Mayor. (2013, February 5). Tillaga að fjármögnun Hörpu. (A proposal for Harpa's financing.) (Letter no. R13010037). http://reykjavik.is/sites/default/files/Frettir_skjol/tillaga_greinargerd_harpa.pdf

Ritschl, A. (2012). The German transfer problem, 1920–33: A sovereign-debt perspective. *European Review of History: Revue europeenne d'histoire, 19*(6), 943–964.

Saga ends with Icesave redemption – Ruling vindicates Iceland's policy over rest of Europe's. (2013, January 29). *Financial Times.* http://www.ft.com/cms/s/0/78b96684-6a21-11e2-a80c-00144feab49a.html

Segir slitastjórnir þurfa að vera raunsæjar. (Says the winding-up boards have to be realistic.) (2014, January 23). *Viðskiptablaðið.*

Shakespeare, W. (1623). *The tragedy of Macbeth.* Act 5, Scene 5.

Sherlock, R., Malnick, E., & Newell, C. (2016, May 26). Donald trump signed off deal designed to deprive US of tens of millions of dollars in tax. *The Telegraph.* http://www.telegraph.co.uk/news/2016/05/25/exclusive-donald-trump-signed-off-deal-designed-to-deprive-us-of/

Shockwaves that took Europe by surprise. (2008, October 4). *The Financial Times.*

Sigfússon, K. (2011, November 10). Ég er kúgaður millistéttarauli! (I am an oppressed middle class fool!). *Visir.is.* http://www.visir.is/eg-er-kugadur-millistettarauli!/article/2011711109981

Sigurjónsson, F. (2012, July 26). Losun hafta: Þrotabú bankanna greiði alfarið í ISK. (Removal of controls: The banks' estates make payments exclusive in ISK). *Morgunblaðið.* http://www.mbl.is/vidskipti/pistlar/frostisig/1250825/.

Snorradóttir, Á. (2009). Líðan, heilsa og vinnuumhverfi starfsfólks í bönkum og sparisjóðum. (Well-being, health and work environment in commercial and savings banks.) Reykjavík: Rannsókna- og heilbrigðisdeild Vinnueftirlits ríkisins. http://dev.ssf.is/wp-content/uploads/2013/02/L%C3%AD%C3%B0an-heilsa-vinnuumhv-lokask%C3%BDrsla09_1362860619.pdf

Special Investigation Commission. (2010). *Report of the Special Investigation Commission.*

Spink, C. (2014, January 14). Iceland cold-shouldered as crisis countries rebound. *Reuters.*

Standard & Poor's Rating Services. (2015, July 17). *Iceland ratings raised to 'BBB/A-2' on proposals toward lifting capital controls; Outlook stable.* Statistics Iceland. www.hagstofa.is

Stefánsson, S. H., Flygenring, K. Þ., & Heiðarsson, J. Þ. (2013, July 2). *Parliamentary Special Investigation Commission report on the housing financing fund, etc.* Parliamentary Special Investigation Commission.

Supreme Court of Iceland. (2010a, June 16). *Verdict no. 153/2010.* http://www.haestirettur.is/domar?nr=6714

Supreme Court of Iceland. (2010b, June 16). *Verdict no. 92/2010.* http://www.haestirettur.is/domar?nr=6715

Supreme Court of Iceland. (2010c, September 16). *Verdict no. 471/2010.* http://www.haestirettur.is/domar?nr=6843

Supreme Court of Iceland. (2012a, February 15). *Verdict no. 600/2011.* http://www.haestirettur.is/domar?nr=7876

Supreme Court of Iceland. (2012b, May 10). *Verdict no. 518/2011.* http://www.haestirettur.is/domar?nr=8065

Supreme Court of Iceland. (2012c, October 18). *Verdict no. 406/2011.* http://www.haestirettur.is/domar?nr=8362

Supreme Court of Iceland. (2012d, October 25). *Verdict no. 176/2012.* http://www.haestirettur.is/domar?nr=8373

Supreme Court of Iceland. (2016, May 4). *Verdict no. 130/2016.* http://www.haestirettur.is/domar?nr=11226

Sævarsson, S. B., & Guðjónsson, V. (2015, April 13). Sumarþing ekki útilokað. (Summer assembly not ruled out.) *Morgunblaðið.*

The Darling-Mathiesen Conversation before Britain Used the Anti-Terrorism Legislation against Iceland. (2008, October 23). *Iceland Review.* http://icelandreview.com/news/2008/10/23/darling-mathiesen-conversation-britain-used-anti-terrorism-legislation-against

The District Court of Amsterdam. (2008a, October 13). *Decision in the district court of Amsterdam. Private Law Sector. Petition number HA-RK 08.668.* https://www.forsaetisraduneyti.is/media/island/frettir/13.pdf

The District Court of Amsterdam. (2008b, October 14). *Rectification of this court's decision of 13 October 2008 on the petition with number HA-RK 08.668.* https://www.forsaetisraduneyti.is/media/island/frettir/13.pdf

The riddle of Gordon Brown. (2008, October 16). *The Economist Online.* http://www.economist.com/node/12427804

The White House. (2003, March 27). Who are the current coalition members? http://georgewbush-whitehouse.archives.gov/infocus/iraq/news/20030327-10.html

Thomas, R. (2008, March 31). *Resolving Iceland's banking "crisis".* London: Merrill Lynch.

Thorsteinsson, T. (1928). *Island under og efter verdenskrigen. En økonomisk oversigt. (Iceland during and after the World War. An economic overview).* Copenhagen: G. E. C. Gads Forlag.

Thorsteinsson, V. (2016). Iceland's revolution. *The Jacobin magazine, 20.* https://www.jacobinmag.com/2016/03/iceland-banking-finance-icesave-left-greens/

Tillaga til þingsályktunar um endurreisn íslensku bankanna. (Proposal for a parliamentary resolution on the restoration of the Icelandic commercial banks). (2009). Þskj. 275 – 157. mál. 137. löggjafarþing. http://www. althingi.is/altext/137/s/0275.html

Tobin, J. (1978). A proposal for international monetary reform. *Eastern Economic Journal, 4*(3), 153–159.

Transcript challenges UK position on Iceland. (2008, October 23). *Financial Times online.* http://www.ft.com/intl/cms/s/0/42c0e23c-a153-11dd-82fd-000077b07658.html#axzz43RRr58yd

Treasury officials head to Iceland to resolve banking crisis. (2008, October 10). *The Guardian Online.* http://www.theguardian.com/business/2008/oct/10/banking-creditcrunch

Truempler, K. (2013). On the carry trade in small open economies.

Turner, G. (2011, December). Depositor protection in Australia. *Reserve Bank of Australia Bulletin.*

UK 'disappointment' as Iceland rejects repayment deal. (2011, April 10). *BBC News.* http://www.bbc.co.uk/news/world-europe-13022524

UK to sue Iceland over any lost bank savings. (2008, October 16). *The Guardian.* http://www.theguardian.com/world/2008/oct/08/iceland.banking

United States Census Bureau. *American FactFinder.* http://factfinder.census.gov/faces/tableservices/jsf/pages/productview.xhtml?src=bkmk

Vanity Fair, & Carter, G. (2010). *The great hangover: 21 tales of the new recession from the pages of Vanity Fair.* New York: Harper Collins.

Við sitjum bara hérna og bíðum, segir starfsmaður Landsbankans. ("We just sit here and wait," says Landsbankinn employee). (2008, October 9). *Viðskiptablaðið.* http://www.vb.is/frettir/vi-sitjum-bara-herna-og-bium-segir-starfsmaur-land/12677/

Willmer, S. (2015, September 25). Former Baupost managing director Fidalgo said to plan Hedge fund. *Bloomberg.*

Wirz, M. (2016, May 27). Iceland puts freeze on foreign investors. *The Wall Street Journal.*

Wood, Z. (2008, October 12). From hero to size zero: The Baugur crisis. *The Guardian online.* http://www.theguardian.com/business/2008/oct/12/iceland-baugur-philip-green

Wood, Z., & Mathiason, N. (2008, October 12). Philip Green steps in to save Baugur. *The Guardian online.* http://www.theguardian.com/business/2008/oct/12/philip-green-baugur

Yandle, B. (2013, February 11). *Rahm's rule of crisis management: A footnote to the theory of regulation.* The Foundation for Economic Education. http://fee.org/articles/rahms-rule-of-crisis-management-a-footnote-to-the-theory-of-regulation/#axzz2KizozPJ4

Younker, K. (2015, March 10). Glitnir, Kaupthing, Landsbanki bondholders vent qualms as Icelandic bank saga plods on. *Debtwire*.

Þjóðnýting óhugnanleg. ("Nationalization horrifying"). (2008, September 30). *Fréttablaðið*, front page. http://timarit.is/view_page_init.jsp?issId=278421

Þorsteinsson, L. A., & Valdimarsson, P. (2011a, June 25). *Complaint to the Commission of the European Union.*

Þorsteinsson, L. A., & Valdimarsson, P. (2011b, September 25). *Complaint No. CHAP(2011) 2011 to the Commission of the European Union.*

Ægisson, H. (2012a, May 24). Hátt reitt til höggs en eftirtekjurnar gætu orðið rýrar. (Serious allegations but the results could be scarce.). *Morgunblaðið*. http://www.mbl.is/greinasafn/grein/1423113/

Ægisson, H. (2012b, October 27). Seðlabankinn studdi ekki breytingar. (The Central Bank did not support changes.) *Morgunblaðið*.

Ægisson, H. (2013a, August 22). Fái ekki arð í 20 ár. (No dividends for 20 years). *Morgunblaðið*.

Ægisson, H. (2013b, December 12). „Herra Ísland" ræður ferðinni. ("Mister Iceland" calls the shots.) *Morgunblaðið*.

Ægisson, H. (2013c, December 13). Hagsmunaverðir og ráðgjafar kröfuhafa. (Creditors' lobbyists and advisors). *Morgunblaðið*.

Ægisson, H. (2014, February 5). 300 milljarða reiðufé fast í höftum. (300 billion in cash stuck behind controls.) *Morgunblaðið*.

Ægisson, H. (2015a, April 17). Fundað með vogunarsjóðum í London. (Meetings with hedge funds in London). *DV*.

Ægisson, H. (2015b, February 20). Óttast símhleranir erlendra kröfuhafa. (Fear wire tapping by foreign creditors.) *DV*.

Ægisson, H. (2015c, September 29). Kröfuhafar geta ekki farið í mál við íslensk stjórnvöld. (Creditors can not sue Icelandic authorities.) *DV*.

Index

Note: Page numbers with "n" denote notes.

© The Author(s) 2016
Á. Jónsson, H. Sigurgeirsson, *The Icelandic Financial Crisis*,
DOI 10.1057/978-1-137-39455-2

U
University of Iceland, 37, 37n2
Útrás, 68, 69

V
Vátryggingafélag Íslands (VIS), 72
VBS, 265
vulture capitalists, 173
vulture funds, 170, 189, 206, 252, 253

W
Washington Mutual Bank (WaMu),
    48–53
winding-up board(s), 113n18, 181,
    184, 189, 195, 196, 207, 231,
    232, 239, 241, 256

Y
Yankee bonds, 234